THE IEA PREPRIMARY PROJECT
PHASE 1

FAMILIES SPEAK:

EARLY CHILDHOOD CARE AND EDUCATION IN 11 COUNTRIES

EDITED BY
Patricia P. Olmsted
David P. Weikart
High/Scope Educational Research Foundation

WITH NATIONAL RESEARCH COORDINATORS
Joaquim Bairrão, Arlette Delhaxhe,
Helena Hoas, Mikko Ojala,
Olayemi Onibokun, Sylvia Opper,
Jesús Palacios, Nittaya Passornsiri,
Lucio Pusci, Hans-Günther Rossbach,
Shi Hui Zhong

WITH COMMENTARIES BY
Çiğdem Kağitçibaşi
Boğaziçi University, Istanbul, Turkey
Lilian G. Katz
University of Illinois, Urbana
Robert Myers
*The Consultative Group on Early Childhood Care
and Development, United Nations*
Sylvia Opper
University of Hong Kong

THE HIGH/SCOPE® PRESS
A division of
High/Scope Educational Research Foundation
Ypsilanti, Michigan

Published by
High/Scope® Press
A division of the

High/Scope Educational Research Foundation
600 North River Street
Ypsilanti, Michigan 48198-2898
(313)485-2000, FAX(313)485-0704

A hardcover edition of this book will be published in March 1995 under the title *IEA Preprimary Study: Early Childhood Care and Education in 11 Countries*, by Pergamon Press, Ltd., Oxford, England (ISBN 0 08 041 3948).

Marge Senninger, High/Scope Press Editor

Library of Congress Cataloging-in-Publication Data

Families speak : early childhood care and education in 11 countries / edited by
   Patricia P. Olmsted, David P. Weikart, with national research coordinators
   Joaquim Bairrão ... [et al.] : with commentaries by Çiğdem Kağitçibaşi ... [et
   al.].
         p.   cm.
      At head of title: The IEA Preprimary Project—Phase 1.
      "High/Scope Educational Research Foundation."
      Includes bibliographical references.
      ISBN 0-929816-89-7
      1. Early childhood education—Cross-cultural studies. 2. Child care
   services — Cross-cultural studies. I. Olmsted, Patricia P. II. Weikart, David P.
   III. IEA Preprimary Study. IV. High/Scope Educational Research Foundation.
   LB1139.23.F36 1994
   372.21—dc20
                                                                94-26948
                                                                CIP

ISBN 0-929816-89-7

Printed in the United States of America

FAMILIES SPEAK

Related Materials
Available From High/Scope Press

How Nations Serve Young Children:
Profiles of Child Care and Education in 14 Countries

The *High/Scope International Videotape Series —*
Sights and Sounds of Children
in Belgium • China • Finland • Greece • Hong Kong • Indonesia • Italy
Nigeria • Poland • Romania • Slovenia • South Korea • Spain
Thailand • United States

Available from

High/Scope® Press
A division of the
High/Scope Educational Research Foundation
600 N. River St., Ypsilanti, MI 48198-2898
(313) 485-2000 FAX (313) 485-0704

The High/Scope Educational Research Foundation has also prepared an
IEA Preprimary Project Phase 1 data archive. Please contact the editors of
this book for information about obtaining a copy of the data archive, which
contains the 11-nation data set and documentation.

Contents

TABLES   xiii

FIGURES   xvii

ACKNOWLEDGMENTS   xix

PREFACE   xxi

A WORD ABOUT IEA   xxiii

I.   **THE IEA PREPRIMARY PROJECT: OBTAINING KNOWLEDGE TO IMPROVE THE QUALITY OF CHILDREN'S EARLY EXPERIENCES,** *Marcel Crahay*   3

    Characteristics of the Field —The Difficulties of Designing an International Comparison   5

        Ideological Dissension   5

        Implicit Rather Than Explicit Educational Aims   6

        Institutional Diversity   7

        Variations in Sponsoring Agencies   9

        A Variety of Social Demands   9

    A Two-Level Study   10

    Phase 1 of the Preprimary Project: A Household Survey of Families   14

        Theoretical Framework   14

        The Basic Study Method   15

    References   17

II.   **PHASE 1 PARTICIPANTS —BRIEF PROFILES,** *Marge Melin Senninger*   19

    Belgium (Fr.) — A Long-standing Nursery School Tradition   19

        A Description of the Widespread Nursery School System   20

        Services That Supplement the Nursery Schools   21

    China (PRC) — Timely Scientific Research   22

        The Beginnings of Modern-Day Early Childhood Services   22

        Early Years of Expansion Begin   23

    Finland — Toward a System for Child and Family Total Growth   24

        A Landmark — The 1973 Day Care Law   25

        A System Still Under Development   26

    Germany (FRG) — Quantitative and Qualitative Expansion   27

        Kindergarten Becomes a Stage of the Educational System   28

        The Coverage That Kindergartens Provide   29

    Hong Kong — Need for an Overall Policy   30

The Beginnings of Rapid Preprimary Growth   *30*
Increasing Government Involvement in Preprimary Services   *31*
Reconciling a Dual System   *31*
Italy — Politico-Pedagogical Debate   *32*
The Early 1900s — A "Fertile Moment" for Nursery Schooling   *33*
Government — "Still Singularly Absent From the Scene"   *34*
A Midcentury Awakening of Government Interest in Preschools   *34*
The Two Preschool Systems Today   *35*
More Recently — Research Concerns   *36*
Nigeria — A Need for Data   *36*
Portugal — A Positive Evolutionary Process   *39*
The Past 20 Years — Kindergarten Development   *40*
How Kindergarten Sponsorship Works   *41*
Spain — A New Period of Democracy   *43*
The Goal: School Places for All 4- and 5-Year-Olds   *44*
For Children Under Age 4 — Less Provision   *45*
Thailand — Coordinating Efforts on All Fronts   *48*
Constitutional Government — A Commitment to Preprimary
Programs   *48*
Problems Involved in a Multisponsored System   *50*
The United States — A Decentralized System   *51*
How Two Strands Have Developed   *51*
The Strands Begin to Merge — Government Steps In   *53*
The Last Two Decades — A "Family-Centered Approach"   *53*
The Variety of Care/Education Arrangements   *54*
References   *56*

III.   METHODOLOGY OF THE PHASE 1 STUDY, *Patricia P.
Olmsted with Joaquim Bairrão, Arlette Delhaxhe, Helena Hoas,
Mikko Ojala, Olayemi Onibokun, Sylvia Opper, Jesús Palacios,
Nittaya Passornsiri, Lucio Pusci, Hans-Günther Rossbach, Shi Hui
Zhong*   *58*

General Sampling Information   *59*
The International Sampling Referee   *59*
The Target Population   *59*
Sample Selection   *59*
General Data Collection Information   *62*
The Parent/Guardian Interview   *62*
Procedures for Data Collection   *65*
Preparation of Data for Analysis   *66*

Methodology in Specific Nations   67
    Sampling and Data Collection in Belgium (Fr.)   *67*
    Sampling and Data Collection in China (PRC)   *69*
    Sampling and Data Collection in Finland   *73*
    Sampling and Data Collection in Germany (FRG)   *74*
    Sampling and Data Collection in Hong Kong   *76*
    Sampling and Data Collection in Italy   *77*
    Sampling and Data Collection in Nigeria   *78*
    Sampling and Data Collection in Portugal   *80*
    Sampling and Data Collection in Spain   *81*
    Sampling and Data Collection in Thailand   *82*
    Sampling and Data Collection in the United States   *84*
References   86

IV.   THE PHASE 1 NATIONAL SAMPLES, *Patricia P. Olmsted*   *88*
Characteristics of Parents   *89*
    Parental Age   *89*
    Parents' Educational Attainment   *89*
    Parental Employment   *92*
    Parental Time Away From Children   *95*
Household and Family Characteristics   *95*
    Two-Parent Households   *95*
    Family Size   *97*
    Home Ownership   *97*
    Number of Rooms in Home   *97*
    Household Amenities   *100*
Child Health Information   *102*
    Health Status   *103*
    Health Examinations and Health Problems   *104*
Comparing National Samples With General Populations   *105*
References   107

V.   STUDY FINDINGS: FAMILIES' WEEKLY USE OF EARLY CHILDHOOD SERVICES, *Olayemi Onibokun, Patricia P. Olmsted   108*
Whether or Not Families Use Early Childhood Services   *109*
Details of Families' Use of Early Childhood Services   *112*
    Types of Settings Used   *112*
    Number of Settings Used Each Week   *115*

Combinations of Settings Used by Families   *115*
Time Children Spend in Extraparental Settings   *118*
Time Children Spend Traveling to First Settings   *120*
Mode of Transportation to First Settings   *122*
Meals or Snacks Provided in the First Setting   *124*
Parental Cost for Various Types of First Settings   *124*
Parents' Satisfaction With Early Childhood Services   *129*
Problems With Early Childhood Services   *132*
Reasons Parents Give for Using Early Childhood Services   *133*
Influences Related to Use of Services   *138*

VI.   **Study Findings: Use of Organized Facilities,** *Mikko
Ojala, Sylvia Opper*   *141*
Organized Facilities — Extent of Use and Nature of Program   *143*
Time Spent in Organized Facilities   *144*
Reasons Parents Give for Using Specific Organized Facilities   *147*
Sponsors of Organized Facilities   *150*
Auxiliary Services in Organized Facilities   *152*
Health Services   *152*
Special Education Services   *153*
Social Services   *155*
Transportation   *155*
A Cross-National Comparison Regarding Auxiliary Services   *156*
Occasional Alternative Arrangements for the Organized Setting   *158*
Contact Between Educators and Parents   *159*
Availability of Educator-Parent Contacts   *162*
Frequency of Educator-Parent Contacts   *164*
Problems With Organized Facilities   *168*
Problems Related to the Setting   *168*
Problems Related to the Program   *168*
Problems Related to the Educator   *171*
Satisfaction With Organized Facilities   *171*
National Summaries   *174*
Belgium (Fr.)   *175*
China (PRC)   *175*
Finland   *176*
Germany (FRG)   *177*
Hong Kong   *178*
Italy   *178*

Nigeria   *179*
Portugal   *180*
Spain   *181*
Thailand   *181*
The United States   *182*

VII.   STUDY FINDINGS: CHILDREN'S DAILY ROUTINES, *Arlette
Delhaxhe, Genevieve Hindryckx, Patricia P. Olmsted, Zhenkui Ma   185*

Methodology   *186*
    The Daily Routine Chart   *186*
    Data Collection Procedures   *188*
    Limitations   *188*
The Daily Routine Data   *189*
    Caregivers   *189*
    Locations   *192*
    Caregiver/Location Combinations   *192*
    Groupings of Caregivers and Locations   *195*
    Patterns of Caregivers and Locations   *208*
The Daily Routine Data in a Weekly Context   *230*
    Belgium (Fr.)   *231*
    China (PRC)   *231*
    Finland   *232*
    Germany (FRG)   *232*
    Hong Kong   *233*
    Nigeria   *233*
    Portugal   *234*
    Spain   *234*
    Thailand   *235*
    The United States   *235*

VIII.   A NATION-BY-NATION LOOK AT THE FINDINGS, *Patricia P.
Olmsted   238*

Belgium (Fr.) — Part-day Services and Full-day Needs   *238*
    The Families Surveyed in Belgium   *239*
    The Findings About Belgium's Preprimary Care/Education   *240*
China (PRC) — Striving for Modernization   *242*
    The Families Surveyed in China   *243*
    The Findings About China's Preprimary Care/Education   *243*

Finland — Aiming at Integrated National Policies   247
    The Families Surveyed in Finland   247
    The Findings About Finland's Preprimary Care/Education   248
Germany (FRG) — Meeting the Needs of a Changing Population and
        a Changing Nation   250
    The Families Surveyed in Germany   251
    The Findings About Germany's Preprimary Care/Education   252
Hong Kong — Adding Quality to Quantity   253
    The Families Surveyed in Hong Kong   254
    The Findings About Hong Kong's Preprimary Care/Education   255
Italy — Two Systems, Regional and Urban-Rural Variations   257
    The Families Surveyed in Italy   258
    The Findings About Italy's Preprimary Care/Education   258
Nigeria — Mostly Home-Based Care   261
    The Families Surveyed in Nigeria   262
    The Findings About Nigeria's Preprimary Care/Education   262
Portugal — Kindergartens and Grandparents   266
    The Families Surveyed in Portugal   266
    The Findings About Portugal's Preprimary Care/Education   267
Spain — From Schoolmasters and "Friendly Women" to Public and
        Private Preprimary Centers   269
    The Families Surveyed in Spain   269
    The Findings About Spain's Preprimary Care/Education   270
Thailand — Working Toward a Goal   272
    The Families Surveyed in Thailand   273
    The Findings About Thailand's Preprimary Care/Education   273
The United States — A Multifaceted System of Preprimary Services   276
    The Families Surveyed in the United States   277
    The Findings About United States Preprimary Care/Education   277
References   282

IX.   QUESTIONS ANSWERED, QUESTIONS RAISED —
      A SUMMARY, *David P. Weikart*   285

The Context of the IEA Preprimary Project   286
What Makes This IEA Project Unique?   288
The Phase 1 Findings   290
    Workforce Participation and Utilization of Care/Education Services   291
    Perseverance of the Trend   291
    The Number of Settings Attended   292

Extent of Time in Extraparental Settings   *292*
Education, A Goal for the Home Setting   *293*
Sponsors of Out-of-Home Child Care and Education   *293*
Auxiliary Services to Children   *294*
Mothers as Principal Caregivers   *294*
Nonfamilial Caregivers or Teachers   *295*
Location of Children's Services   *295*
Final Comments   *296*
References   297

APPENDIX A: SUPPLEMENTARY TABLES   *299*

APPENDIX B: PARENT/GUARDIAN INTERVIEW   *309*

APPENDIX C: IEA PREPRIMARY PROJECT PHASE 1
    NATIONAL RESEARCH CENTERS AND COORDINATORS   *341*

COMMENTARIES   *347*

Perspectives on the IEA Preprimary Project
Çiğdem Kağitçibaşi   349

Commentary on the Results of the Phase 1 IEA Preprimary Study
Lilian G. Katz   359

Commentary on *Families Speak*
Robert Myers   364

Education or Care? A Parent's Dilemma — Education and Care! A
    Parent's Choice
Sylvia Opper   373

TABLES

3.1 Characteristics of national sampling plans *68*

3.2 National data collection procedures *70*

4.1 Mean age (in years) of national sample mothers and fathers *90*

4.2 Years of education completed by national sample mothers and fathers *91*

4.3 Maternal employment for national samples *92*

4.4 Paternal employment for national samples *94*

4.5 Percentage distribution of national sample mothers according to weekly hours away from 4-year-old child *96*

4.6 Percentage distribution of national sample fathers according to weekly hours away from 4-year-old child *98*

4.7 Family and residence characteristics of national samples *99*

4.8 Percentages of national samples having various amenities *101*

4.9 Percentage distribution of national sample 4-year-olds according to health status *103*

4.10 Percentages of national sample 4-year-olds having various health examinations and exhibiting vision/hearing problems *104*

4.11 Types of information used to assess the representativeness of national samples *106*

5.1 Percentage of 4-year-olds in at least one extraparental care/education setting each week *110*

5.2 Percentage distribution of families according to reasons for exclusively caring for their 4-year-olds at home *111*

5.3 Percentage distribution of 4-year-old service-users according to type of first setting *113*

5.4 Percentage distribution of 4-year-old service-users according to number of extraparental settings attended each week *116*

5.5 Percentage distribution of 4-year-old service-users according to type of second setting attended *117*

5.6 Average hours 4-year-old service-users spend each week in individual settings and in all settings combined *119*

5.7 Percentage distribution of 4-year-old service-users according to time spent traveling to their first settings *121*

5.8 Percentage distribution of 4-year-old service-users according to mode of transportation to their first settings *123*

5.9 Percentage distribution of 4-year-old service-users according to types of meals/snacks provided in their first settings *125*

5.10 Average monthly parental cost in U.S. dollars for various types of extraparental care/education *126*

5.11 Percentage distribution of service-using families according to level of satisfaction with first and second settings   *130*

5.12 Percent of families very satisfied with first settings, according to type of setting   *131*

5.13 Percentage distribution of service-using families according to types of problems with first setting   *134*

5.14 Percentage distribution of service-using families according to major reason for using first setting   *136*

5.15 Results of regression analyses of hours of use of early childhood services on various predictor variables   *139*

6.1   Percentage of all children attending organized facilities as the first or second setting   *142*

6.2   Percentage distribution of organized facility users (children) according to type of organized program they attend   *143*

6.3   Average time children spend per week in their organized facilities   *145*

6.4   Percentage distribution of children according to number of weekly hours spent in organized facilities   *146*

6.5   Children's daily hours in organized facilities   *148*

6.6   Percentage distribution of parents according to major reason for choice of a specific organized facility   *149*

6.7   Percentage distribution of children's organized facilities according to types of sponsors   *151*

6.8   Availability and use of health services in children's organized facilities   *153*

6.9   Availability and use of special education services in children's organized facilities   *154*

6.10 Availability and use of social services in children's organized facilities   *156*

6.11 Availability and use of transportation services in children's organized facilities   *157*

6.12 Percentage distribution of service-using parents according to the alternative arrangement made during planned (P) and unplanned (UP) closings of facilities   *160*

6.13 Percentages of organized facility users (parents) engaging in various kinds of educator-parent contacts   *163*

6.14 Frequency of educator-parent contacts   *166*

6.15 Percentages of organized facility users (parents) reporting problems related to setting   *169*

6.16   Percentages of organized facility users (parents) reporting problems related to program   *170*

6.17   Percentages of organized facility users (parents) reporting problems related to educators   *172*

6.18   Percentage distribution of parents according to degree of satisfaction with their child's organized facility   *173*

6.19   Percentage distribution of children according to their degree of enjoyment of their organized setting   *174*

7.1   Number of waking hours that 4-year-old children spend with various caregivers   *190*

7.2   Number of waking hours that 4-year-old children spend in various locations   *193*

7.3   Hours of care of 4-year-old children during waking hours by various caregivers in various locations   *207*

7.4   Hours of caregivers and locations for 4-year-old children in Belgium   *210*

7.5   Hours of caregivers and locations for 4-year-old children in China   *212*

7.6   Hours of caregivers and locations for 4-year-old children in Finland   *214*

7.7   Hours of caregivers and locations for 4-year-old children in Germany   *216*

7.8   Hours of caregivers and locations for 4-year-old children in Hong Kong   *218*

7.9   Hours of caregivers and locations for 4-year-old children in Nigeria   *220*

7.10   Hours of caregivers and locations for 4-year-old children in Portugal   *222*

7.11   Hours of caregivers and locations for 4-year-old children in Spain   *224*

7.12   Hours of caregivers and locations for 4-year-old children in Thailand   *226*

7.13   Hours of caregivers and locations for 4-year-old children in the United States   *228*

8.1   China's urban/rural information for selected family and household characteristics   *245*

8.2   Finland's urban/rural information for selected family and household characteristics   *249*

8.3   Percentages of families in Italian communes using extraparental
      care/education services, by commune location and density   *260*

8.4   Nigeria's urban/rural information for selected family and household
      characteristics   *264*

8.5   Thailand's urban/rural information for selected family and house-
      hold characteristics   *275*

8.6   U.S. care and education for children aged 3–4 in 1987 and in present
      study   *278*

8.7   U.S. early childhood care and education service usage for families
      with various characteristics   *281*

A.1   Percentage distribution of 4-year-old service-users according to type
      of first setting   *301*

A.2   Percentage distribution of urban/rural 4-year-olds according to use
      or nonuse of first settings   *303*

A.3   Median hourly cost and median weekly cost to parents in U.S. dollars
      for services in extraparental care/education settings   *304*

A.4   Mean and standard deviation of variables used for regression analysis
      on hours of use of early childhood services   *306*

A.5   Correlation between the variables used for regression analysis on
      hours of use of early childhood services   *307*

FIGURES

5.1 Most-frequent combinations of extraparental settings used by families in various countries each week *118*

7.1 Number of waking hours that 4-year-old children spend with various caregivers *191*

7.2 Number of waking hours that 4-year-old children spend in various locations *194*

7.3 Percentage of waking hours that 4-year-old children in Belgium experience various caregiver/location combinations *196*

7.4 Percentage of waking hours that 4-year-old children in China experience various caregiver/location combinations *197*

7.5 Percentage of waking hours that 4-year-old children in Finland experience various caregiver/location combinations *198*

7.6 Percentage of waking hours that 4-year-old children in Germany experience various caregiver/location combinations *199*

7.7 Percentage of waking hours that 4-year-old children in Hong Kong experience various caregiver/location combinations *200*

7.8 Percentage of waking hours that 4-year-old children in Nigeria experience various caregiver/location combinations *201*

7.9 Percentage of waking hours that 4-year-old children in Portugal experience various caregiver/location combinations *202*

7.10 Percentage of waking hours that 4-year-old children in Spain experience various caregiver/location combinations *203*

7.11 Percentage of waking hours that 4-year-old children in Thailand experience various caregiver/location combinations *204*

7.12 Percentage of waking hours that 4-year-old children in the United States experience various caregiver/location combinations *205*

7.13 Patterns of time spent with different caregivers between 6:00 a.m. and 10:00 p.m. (Belgium, $N = 424$) *211*

7.14 Patterns of time spent with different caregivers between 6:00 a.m. and 10:00 p.m. (China, $N = 12,835$) *213*

7.15 Patterns of time spent with different caregivers between 6:00 a.m. and 10:00 p.m. (Finland, $N = 576$) *215*

7.16 Patterns of time spent with different caregivers between 6:00 a.m. and 10:00 p.m. (Germany, $N = 509$) *217*

7.17 Patterns of time spent with different caregivers between 6:00 a.m. and 10:00 p.m. (Hong Kong, $N = 947$) *219*

7.18 Patterns of time spent with different caregivers between 6:00 a.m. and 10:00 p.m. (Nigeria, $N = 1,251$) *221*

7.19 Patterns of time spent with different caregivers between 8:00 a.m.
and 12:00 midnight (Portugal, $N=581$)   *223*

7.20 Patterns of time spent with different caregivers between 8:00 a.m.
and 12:00 midnight (Spain, $N=480$)   *225*

7.21 Patterns of time spent with different caregivers between 5:00 a.m.
and 9:00 p.m. (Thailand, $N=2,466$)   *227*

7.22 Patterns of time spent with different caregivers between 6:00 a.m.
and 10:00 p.m. (United States, $N=428$)   *229*

ACKNOWLEDGMENTS

Our gratitude goes to all those who have assisted in making this book a reality. We acknowledge Carnegie Corporation, the Spencer Foundation, the U.S. Department of Health and Human Services, and the U.S. Department of Education for their support of High/Scope's IEA Preprimary Project activities. We also thank High/Scope Press editor Marge Senninger for her invaluable assistance in all phases of manuscript preparation and research associate Mei-Yu Yu for her careful attention to the data. Finally, we acknowledge the word-processing assistance of Kay Long and Diana Knepp.

PREFACE

The first publication of the IEA Preprimary Project, *How Nations Serve Young Children* (Olmsted & Weikart, 1989), used information from *public records* to draw up profiles of early childhood care and education in various nations. This second publication, *Families Speak*, describes each country's early childhood care and education situation based on information gleaned from conducting *household surveys* in those same countries. As the major work of Phase 1 of the IEA Preprimary Project, it thus provides a "reality check" on the profiles of the earlier work. In addition to describing the three-phase Preprimary Project and revealing its major Phase 1 findings, *Families Speak* is able to present for each country a comparison of the information from the household survey with that from public records.

People often wonder how specific countries come to be involved in a study such as the IEA Preprimary Project. (See "A Word About IEA," p. xxiii, for background on the study's sponsoring organization.) Any nation interested in cross-national educational studies may join IEA and then participate in decision making about the study projects to be undertaken by the organization. Once a project proposal has been officially approved by the IEA General Assembly, any member country can then choose whether to participate in the given study. However, since IEA may be conducting several studies simultaneously, member countries generally participate only in those most relevant to their national needs and goals. Thus, the countries participating in Phase 1 of the IEA Preprimary Project do not constitute the entire set of IEA member countries.

A particular strength of this study is that its participating countries provide variety on a number of dimensions, including form of government, population, and stage of development. In general, the participating countries are ones that do not have extremely high infant-mortality rates and thus have been able to move from concerns about child survival to concerns about providing adequate education and care services for their young children.

Another strength of the study is that it was conducted with the significant cooperation and contributions of early childhood researchers around the world. Each participating country set up its own coordinating center for the study, usually within a university or government agency (e.g., an education ministry). This coordinating center, under the direction of a National Research Coordinator, procured necessary financial support; ensured that the survey questions were appropriate for families in that country; and supervised the sampling, data collection, and data processing. At all stages of the Phase 1 study, including the writing of this final report, the National Research Coordinators and their staffs worked closely with the project's International Coordinating Center in the United States, the High/Scope Educational Research Foundation in Ypsilanti, Michigan.

In developing a report such as this, decisions must be made about how to organize the presentation so it conveys both the national and the international aspects of the study. For example, the report could have been composed of a series of chapters each presenting the findings for an individual country (a chapter on Belgium, a chapter on China, and so on). However, because the editors and authors considered it important to be able to view the IEA Preprimary Project findings for any one nation within an international context, they chose to present the national sample characteristics and the major findings of the study (that is, the information in Chapters 4–7) cross-nationally. This provides readers with a sense of the range of the findings for a specific variable across the group of nations participating in the study. However, for the reader primarily interested in the findings for a particular country, the introductory chapters (Chapters 1–3) and Chapter 8 are recommended reading.

Another decision concerned the mode of data presentation. Although figures and graphs sometimes have more "eye appeal" than tables, preparation of clear figures or graphs often requires omitting certain details (such as range and standard deviation). Consequently, in many cases, the editors chose to use tables rather than graphic representations, so their presentation of data could be as complete and useful as possible.

The findings reported in this book have already been used as a basis for Phase 2 of the IEA Preprimary Project, which is an *observational study* of the major types of early childhood care and education settings in participating nations; analysis of Phase 2 data is now under way. Of the 11 nations participating in Phase 1 (the household survey), 9 have continued with Phase 2 (the observational study). Also, 6 additional nations have joined Phase 2: Greece, Indonesia, Ireland, and 3 Eastern European countries – Poland, Romania, and Slovenia.

So far, in connection with the observational study, High/Scope Foundation has produced a series of videotapes of early childhood care and education settings in the Phase 2 countries; a series of monographs dealing with Phase 2 findings is also planned. Thus, this book, together with *How Nations Serve Young Children*, represents only the beginning of what will come from the IEA Preprimary Project.

Patricia P. Olmsted
David P. Weikart
June 1994

A Word About IEA

"IEA" is the acronym of the International Association for the Evaluation of Educational Achievement, a nongovernmental, nonprofit organization of research institutions in more than 60 countries that is well known for its 30 years of comparative international surveys in science, mathematics, written composition, and other academic areas. IEA research projects have been instrumental in demonstrating the feasibility of large-scale cross-national empirical studies and advancing the methodology of comparative education.

IEA views its comparative educational surveys as a necessary first step in both national and international policy-related research. IEA findings have affected educational systems around the world as specific educational problems have been identified and policymakers have made decisions based on these research findings. Some of the international educational issues IEA has chosen to examine include identifying the effects of different practices in grouping or tracking students, investigating the effects of comprehensive secondary schooling, and examining the effects of specific instructional practices.

Additional information regarding IEA can be obtained from the IEA Secretariat, 14 Sweelinckplein, NL 2519 The Hague, the Netherlands.

FAMILIES SPEAK

I

THE IEA PREPRIMARY PROJECT: OBTAINING KNOWLEDGE TO IMPROVE THE QUALITY OF CHILDREN'S EARLY EXPERIENCES

Marcel Crahay, *Professor*
Universities of Liège and Geneva

This book is a report on the first phase of the Preprimary Project being conducted in three phases in 11 to 15 countries under the sponsorship of the International Association for the Evaluation of Educational Achievement (IEA). Spanning the years 1987 to 1997, the project represents the first extension of IEA inquiry into the years before children enter the formal educational system. The impetus for such research consists largely of two trends that emerged and converged during the 1960s and 1970s in most IEA member countries, namely:

1. Increasing acceptance of the proposition that early life experiences make a strong and probably enduring contribution to all subsequent development
2. Increasing incidence of families sharing the care and education of their preschool-aged children with others outside the home — a phenomenon that is variously attributed to social, economic, and demographic changes worldwide.

When considering these two trends together, one must keep in mind the probability that the greater the contribution of early experiences to the total development of an individual and of society, the greater the benefits that can accrue to them from *good-quality* early experiences and, by the same token, the greater the harm that can be done to them (the individual and society) by poor-quality early experiences. Therefore, any investigation, like the IEA Preprimary Project, that can illuminate the nature and effects of various kinds of early childhood experiences on the long-term development of young children is a welcome addition to existing knowledge.

The IEA Preprimary Project was also initiated in the hope that as a cross-cultural and cross-national study, it would be especially valuable in strengthening and deepening understanding of the impact of early experiences on young children's development. The following benefits that LeVine (1970) attributed to cross-cultural study in child psychology could apply equally well to cross-national study of preprimary education:

> [It provides] a research strategy for using measurable variations among human populations (in behavior patterns, environmental conditions, frequencies) to search systematically for the causes of individual behavior and development. From this perspective, cross-cultural study should serve child psychology as social epidemiology serves pathology in medicine, by expanding the range of observable variation (given ethical restraint on experimental intervention by investigators), by discovering the limits of this range for the human species, by identifying extreme or unusual populations in which experimental or quasi-experimental studies (e.g., longitudinal studies) would shed especially crucial light on etiological issues (p. 559).

Bronfenbrenner (1979) has also pointed to the usefulness of cross-national comparisons. In his discussion of the influence of day care experiences on adult aggressiveness, he noted that cross-cultural investigations have revealed, in some countries, a relationship between early day care experience and adult aggression, but in others, no observable relationship. He went on to say that "the tendency of the peer group in a given culture to predispose children, especially boys, toward greater aggressiveness, impulsivity, and egocentrism appears to be associated with an ideology of individualism and social structure that emphasizes segregation by age" and "the somewhat higher aggressiveness observed in children with day care experience . . . may not be a consequence of early upbringing in group settings per se, but rather a reflection of the general role of peer groups as contexts of socialization in some cultures" (p. 180).

In addition to these earlier investigations, several more-recent multinational studies and reports focusing on early childhood services have attested to the growing interest in and importance of cross-cultural preprimary research (e.g., Tobin, Wu, & Davidson, 1989; UNESCO, 1991; Myers, 1992).

Characteristics of the Field — The Difficulties of Designing an International Comparison

Ideological Dissension

As mentioned earlier, it is largely recognized that early life experiences greatly influence human development. The findings of the Consortium for Longitudinal Studies (Lazar & Darlington, 1979), as well as those of the High/Scope Perry Preschool study (Berrueta-Clement, Schweinhart, Barnett, Epstein, & Weikart, 1984; Schweinhart, Barnes, & Weikart, 1993) clearly demonstrate that the effects of early childhood education can extend into adulthood. However, beyond this general agreement concerning the importance of preschool experiences, great dissension exists regarding the kinds of daily experiences that should be provided to foster young children's development.

No doubt all spheres and levels of education are subject to ideological differences. But preprimary education, perhaps because it is a subject very "close to home," is especially blessed with divergence. The controversies surrounding it are fueled by differences in societal values and attitudes concerning the place of women, the functions of the family, the relevance of schooling, the pressure for industrialization, and so forth. Thus, one might even say that deep ideological differences constitute a *central feature* of the subculture of preprimary education.

One main issue that ideological disputes revolve around concerns the relative merits of young children being placed in out-of-home settings versus their being cared for by a mother or a mother-surrogate at home. The available research on relevant variables (such as attachment, loss, and separation anxiety) and the accumulation of reassuring evidence concerning these variables have little influence on the ideological battle between some moralists or politicians who claim that young children's out-of-home care or education threatens family life, and feminist groups who press for group care/education for the young. Faced with the research evidence, opponents of out-of-home care object that there are some important things tests cannot measure.

In the field of elementary education, it is obvious to everybody that assessment of children's competency in reading, writing, and mathematics is relevant. Assessment of some other competencies (for example, fluency in a second language) involves more controversial issues, but there is a large social consensus that the task of elementary teachers is at least to teach reading, writing, and computing. Moreover, this consensus is international and

allows intercountry comparisons (as in IEA studies). In the field of preprimary education, however, there is very little consensus on a minimal
definition of the task that out-of-home teachers/caregivers have to accomplish. According to Katz (1975), "An apparent consequence of the ideological character of early childhood education is the development of encamp-
ments: Piagetians, behaviorists, neo-Freudians, open educators, etc. Each
camp seems to avoid the examination of counterevidence . . ." (p. 269).

IMPLICIT RATHER THAN EXPLICIT EDUCATIONAL AIMS

Amidst the theoretical currents described by Katz (1975), every camp has
more-or-less explicitly stated educational objectives and curriculum.
However, in the wider field of general preschool care and education, it is
often the case that a preprimary setting has no explicit curriculum. In fact,
several countries have some out-of-home child care settings that do not
subscribe to formal educational objectives. And, of course, this is the case
in *all* countries in most family settings. Therefore, how does one rigorously address the issue of the relative merits of in-home versus out-of-home
care? Also, how does one rigorously compare the merits of various categories of out-of-home settings if some categories have no explicit educational aims?

Obviously, the IEA Preprimary Project could not be conceived
according to the approach traditionally used by IEA. In the present state
of the art, it is impossible to look at cross-national variations by treating
educational objectives as self-evident and then testing the achievement of
these objectives in random samples of children. Since preprimary objectives themselves constitute the core of contemporary controversy, to avoid
considering the existing diversity would be to overlook a principal problem in the early childhood field.

In considering this diversity, it may be useful to look at whether children's various socialization settings differ in the extent to which they set
objectives. That is, to begin with, it may be useful to take the position that
preschool educational institutions can be distinguished from family life by
the extent to which their actions are intentional. But this distinction could
be viewed in another way: Some *preprimary institutions* have no rigorously articulated objectives, whereas some *families* are capable of articulating
in detail the intentions behind their practices.

Furthermore, considering preprimary setting diversity, it seems
appropriate to replace the term *objectives* with the term *expectations*. The

latter term is more appropriately applied in the case of the family or some other informal socialization setting. In another sense, *expectations* could describe the hopes one has with respect to some event or institution; it could also refer to the anticipations one develops concerning the behavior of someone or of something one knows of; finally, it could refer to *the demands society places on an institution.*

Institutional Diversity

As indicated by some hints from the international compilation *How Nations Serve Young Children: Profiles of Child Care and Education in 14 Countries* (Olmsted & Weikart, 1989), the liveliness of the ideological disputes, the degree of educational intentionality, and the importance of the consensus around the merits of out-of-home preprimary education vary from country to country, and these differences are reflected in the types and uses of services that are available:

- Some countries have few formal services, and those they have are utilized by very small numbers/proportions of children (e.g., Nigeria).
- Some countries offer a wide range of types of care used in a wide variety of ways (e.g., the United States).
- Some countries offer primarily one type of preschool service that is almost universally used by families (e.g., Belgium, Italy, Hong Kong).
- In most countries, different services are offered for different age groups (e.g. Finland, the Federal Republic of Germany).

At this level again, the landscape of preschool education differs from that of elementary education, and this difference presented difficulties regarding the design of the preprimary study. Earlier IEA studies, which have dealt with elementary and secondary education, have focused their research on educational institutions. However, to focus the Preprimary Project on educational institutions alone would have run the risk of ignoring the socialization settings that are provided by more-informal arrangements, and it was suspected that in some countries, more children were cared for in out-of-home informal settings than in formal settings. **So the question arose, Which category (or categories) of child care settings were to be selected for the preliminary study?** For some countries

(Belgium, Italy, Hong Kong) the choice was easy. As just mentioned, such countries have only one major kind of out-of-home service, which is attended by a high percentage of children. In most of the countries, however, various kinds of services are available. Moreover, the labels used to designate preprimary institutions vary from country to country as well as within countries. Consider, for example, this nonexhaustive list of the current terms used in the early childhood field:

preschool (Australia)	*playgroup* (UK, NZ, Australia, etc.)
preschool program (US)	*under-fives* (UK, etc.)
day care center (US)	*infant class or school* (UK, etc.)
infant care center (US)	*crèche* (several countries)
family day care (US)	*childminders* (Nigeria)
nursery school (UK, US, etc.)	*école maternelle* (France, Belgium)
nursery class (UK)	*école gardienne* (Belgium)
day nursery (UK, etc.)	*garderie* (Canada)
reception/transition class (UK)	*kindergarten* (several countries)

In addition to the multiplicity of terms applied to institutions for young children, a wide array of occupational titles describe the adults who work in them (e.g., *teacher, child care worker, nursery nurse, sister, institutrice, enseignante, puéricultrice, Lehrerin, social pedagog, Erzieherin*). These occupational titles are related, to some extent, to the type of employing institution, and to some extent, to the type of job training and job performance required.

In many countries, the personnel working in preprimary settings have no training or qualifications at all. In some countries, their qualifications range all the way from none at all to advanced graduate training. In addition, some countries and regions report extremely high rates of turnover or burnout — so much so that preservice training appears not to be worthwhile for programs. Some countries have adopted, or are in the process of adopting, tested or new strategies for inservice training and a variety of more-or-less permanent support-systems for personnel, in accord with the findings of a large-scale study of day care in the United States. The *National Day Care Study Final Report* (Ruopp, Travers, Glantz, & Coelen, 1979) indicated that relevant training is related to the quality of day care programs. A more recent study, the High/Scope Training of Trainers Evaluation (Epstein, 1993), has supported and expanded on these findings, providing "strong evidence for the general assertion that inservice training can contribute to program quality and children's development"

(p. xv). Understandably, this training aspect of the field is of great interest to many policymakers and planners.

Variations in Sponsoring Agencies

In most countries, the various types of preprimary institutions alluded to earlier (in the list of current terms) are only partially or tangentially related to other higher level educational institutions. In some countries, preprimary services are the responsibility of the department of social services; in others, the department of health; in still others, the department of public assistance, family welfare agencies, larger church organizations, and so forth. Even within countries or regions, depending on the age of the clientele or the duration of the services provided, different agencies monitor or subsidize preprimary institutions. One dramatic example of such agency variation can be seen in the successful and strident campaign that was launched in the United States, during the 1970s, to keep the nation's Head Start program within the federal Department of Health and Human Services rather than to transfer it to the newly created Department of Education. It is pertinent to this discussion to note that one of the central arguments behind keeping it out of the Department of Education was that Head Start is, by origin and intent, a comprehensive program with nutritional, social, health, and other components, and therefore too broad in scope and function to be turned over to educators.

Partially because of the multiplicity of agencies that fund, license, and monitor settings for young children, there is usually no one agency responsible for collecting basic data concerning what preprimary services are available and who participates in them. Hence, for most countries there is a serious lack of comprehensive data, especially as compared with the more readily available data on such mainstream institutions as elementary and secondary schools.

A Variety of Social Demands

The social demands placed on preprimary education are, as mentioned earlier, a factor to be considered. In the Western world, more and more children are enrolled in preschool institutions; early out-of-home schooling of children is also increasing in the Third World (e.g., UNESCO 1991; Myers, 1992). This phenomenon seems, at first glance, to be associated with such factors as improved infant-survival rates, industrial development, increasing family mobility, and the growing incidence of single-parent and two-parent employment in families with young children. However, some hints from national studies lead one to think that these are not the only factors influencing families' use of out-of-home services for their preschool-aged children. And, indeed, two sets of Phase 1 findings of the IEA Preprimary Project (presented in later chapters) give sense and confirmation to these insights. Phase 1 observations correspond strongly with one preliminary insight of the project concerning the diversity of the social demands placed on child care institutions: It was suspected that in countries where families believe in the educational value of preprimary out-of-home experiences, the demand for good early childhood settings would be strong. In other countries, families would place their children in such settings only when obliged to. In these latter countries, the social demand for high-quality care settings would most likely be weak.

In summary, the domain of interest of this present IEA study — the IEA Preprimary Project — differs in several important ways from what is usually examined in studies undertaken by IEA. Essentially, preprimary services are less homogeneous and monolithic within and between countries than are elementary or secondary education services. In many respects, *variety is the rule* in the field of young children's education. Because of this variety, the problems of defining and comparing elements or components are significant. Because of the variety of agencies responsible for preprimary institutions, there are great gaps in the early childhood field's basic descriptive and utilization data.

A TWO-LEVEL STUDY

In its earliest planning stages (see "History of the Project"), the IEA Preprimary Project was intended to be a single-phase study, focusing on the quality of life of children in those out-of-home environments specially provided for them (e.g., preschools), with an emphasis on assessing how those environments contribute to children's current and subsequent development. This would entail researchers observing children in selected formal preprimary settings along dimensions considered as crucial and meaningful ones and then relating these observations to developmental measures.

HISTORY OF THE PROJECT

The idea of expanding the scope of IEA inquiry to the preprimary years was first broached during the late 1970s by a small group of researchers who sensed the importance of educators' knowing what happened to children prior to their encounter with formal schooling. It was clear from the start that this kind of study would present special challenges – much of the needed information could not be obtained from the education agencies who typically collect IEA data. Yet, finding sufficient interest among the IEA member nations, the IEA General Assembly saw fit to establish a preprimary planning group, which began meeting in 1981 in Belgium. Fourteen representatives from seven member countries made up this initial group: Marcel Crahay (Belgium); Ron Davie (Great Britain); Arlette Delhaxhe (Belgium); Gilbert De Landsheere (Belgium); Lilian Katz (United States); Suzan Montovani (Italy); Annette Marion (France); Jean-Pierre Pourtois (Belgium); Rachel Presser (Canada); Antonio Schizzerotto (Italy); Anne-Marie Thirion (Belgium); Wolfgang Tietze (Federal Republic of Germany); Bill Wall (Great Britain); and David Weikart (United States).

Between 1982 and 1984, the project took further shape. First a draft proposal for the Preprimary Project was approved by the IEA General Assembly, and invitations to participate in the project were extended to all member nations. Next came appointment of a project steering committee (Lilian Katz of the United States, Marcel Crahay of Belgium, Wolfgang Tietze of the Federal Republic of Germany, and Richard Wolf of the United States) and selection of the project's International Coordinating Center (High/Scope Educational Research Foundation, Ypsilanti, Michigan, USA). Thus was the way paved for completion of the final project proposal in early 1984.

Representatives from all interested member nations (17 to start with) met in Singapore in 1984 to discuss the details of participation in the Preprimary Project – establishing national research centers, developing instruments and procedures, and locating within-country funding as well as funding for the international coordination activities. Individual countries then spent the next 2 years actually seeing to these various needs. In 1987, fourteen countries launched Phase 1 by each putting together a "national profile" of early childhood data drawn from existing sources. These profiles, based on existing sources and published in How Nations Serve Young Children: Profiles of Child Care and Education in 14 Countries (Olmsted & Weikart, 1989), were a starting point, to be followed by the major effort of Phase 1, a survey of families. This book completes Phase 1 by presenting the findings from that survey.

As work proceeded, it appeared relevant to broaden the scope of the project and to treat the kind of study planned initially as a specific part of a more ambitious enterprise. The project's resultant general framework can be characterized by five statements:

1. **The general focus of the study is on the total set of early childhood care/education settings typically experienced by the young child ("total" means that even the child's own home is included as a setting in the study).** This choice of focus is based on the reality that many of today's young children experience various settings throughout a typical day or throughout a typical week. Knowing the number and types of settings a child typically experiences each week can provide information about the child's socialization and about the persons who play major roles in this socialization.

2. **The enlarged focus of the study requires selecting one age group as the point of departure for the research. Four-year-olds have been chosen as the target age.** More precisely, the age-range of the children to be studied by the project is 3 years 6 months to 4 years 6 months. In most participating countries, this age-range takes in the child's last full year before entry into a formal school environment; it is also the age-range for which there is the widest variety of early childhood care and education settings.

3. **The study, in each country, of what kinds of provisions are available and how they are used by a representative sample of 4-year-olds has been a necessary first step.** (This step has produced the Phase 1 findings reported in this volume.) Many countries lack precise statistics concerning child care provisions; they do not know enough about the numbers of various kinds of settings, how and by whom the settings are used, their periods of operation, and so forth.

4. **The expansion of the aims of the study is particularly of interest in that it leads to consideration of the relationships that exist between the diverse preprimary settings used by families.** The expression *relationship between settings* refers to

   - The *relative importance of various kinds of settings* in the life of preschool-aged children
   - The *compatibility of the various settings*, that is, how preschool-aged children are able to use multiple settings.

By describing the day-to-day life of a typical 4-year-old in each participating country, study findings will point up the relationships that exist between diverse settings. Rather than considering children as elements included in a particular kind of setting, **the research will identify patterns of children's daily lives.** It may be possible to establish a relationship between such data and the diversity and quantity of provisions that are available for the 4-year-olds in various countries.

5. **The impact of various kinds of socialization settings on children's development will also be considered.** This calls for an in-depth study of the quality of children's experiences in each kind of setting (Phase 2 of the project) and a longitudinal developmental assessment (Phase 3 of the project). The effects of a socialization setting should ideally be evaluated both in terms of the expressed values within the setting and in terms of the expectations ascribed to it by adults in associated settings. For example, the effect of an out-of-home child care setting should be evaluated in terms of the expressed expectations of the caregivers but also in terms of the expressed expectations of families who place their children in that child care setting. Similarly, what happens within a setting should be congruent with the values and expectations of the caregivers and of the families who trust that care setting. Furthermore, one must take into account that caregivers have to cope with contextual parameters that constrain or support their practices. Therefore, the in-depth study of the quality of children's experiences in various settings must include the following:

- A direct assessment of the quality of children's experiences in the settings by observing what the children have the opportunity to do and how they interact with adults and peers

- A long-term evaluation of a wide range of developmental aspects, so we can establish some relationships between children's development and the quality of life in their preprimary settings

- An investigation of the values and expectations of caregivers and of parents, so we can assess whether settings are run by caregivers in a way that is congruent with parents' wishes

- An analysis of the contextual factors that foster or impede the implementation of a high-quality educational environment

In summary, the IEA Preprimary Project has been designed to be conducted in the following three interrelated phases:

- **Phase 1:** This phase consists primarily of a household survey in each participating nation to determine the types of early childhood care and education services used by families and to determine some of the characteristics of the families and of the services they use. It will also provide a picture of the daily-life patterns of 4-year-olds in each country.
- **Phase 2:** A sample of settings identified in Phase 1 will be studied in-depth to ascertain the quality of children's experiences in their various care/education settings. Extensive observational and interview data will be used to examine the interactive and structural characteristics of the major early childhood settings and to explore the impact of programmatic and familial factors on children's developmental status at age 4
- **Phase 3:** This phase consists of a follow-up, at age 7, of the development of the children studied in Phase 2, and examination of their progress since the end of their preprimary experience.

This report focuses on Phase 1 and on what has been learned from it so far. The following section describes the theoretical framework of this phase of the study.

PHASE 1 OF THE PREPRIMARY PROJECT: A HOUSEHOLD SURVEY OF FAMILIES

THEORETICAL FRAMEWORK

The family plays an important role in the child's weekly and daily life. First of all, it constitutes a background that may or may not be rich in stimulation. It also represents an authority regulating the child's life, because, after all, parents are the ones who make decisions about their child's weekly and daily routines. However, there are constraints on parents' decisions. For example, the parents' daily schedules may affect the approach taken to a child's care or education. Their expectations regarding the child's development will also play a role. The child's weekly and daily routine will depend not only on the parents' needs and expectations but also on the opportunities offered by the surrounding community.

To solve its problem, the family will probably take advantage of a variety of available services. For example, in Belgium the timetable of the école maternelle doesn't usually correspond to parental schedules, but the institution offers supplementary caretaking systems: morning, midday, and evening nurseries. Although the nurseries constitute resources that families can use, parents who prefer more-domestic solutions use care by grandparents, neighbors, or acquaintances for the child's transition from the école maternelle to home.

Thus the family can be characterized as an ecosystem that offers the child his immediate life-surroundings but also organizes the rest of the child's life according to the family's interactions with other ecosystems: the father's and mother's employment system; the network of neighbors, friends, and relatives; and the formal care/education services. These interactions, which have not been much investigated until now, can be very complex. Many factors must be taken into account: the availability and cost of care/education services; the need for travel to and from care/education settings; the quality of relationships with neighbors, friends, relatives; the parents' educational philosophy; the parents' distribution of roles (in a two-parent family); and the expectations of society.

The Basic Study Method

In relation to this theoretical framework, Phase 1 consisted of a household survey employing a 50-minute Parent/Guardian Interview to collect information about parents' use of early childhood care and education services. This strategy of collecting information about early childhood services directly from families is unique to the IEA Preprimary Project. Most other studies have gone directly to care providers and teachers for information. By interviewing families, the Preprimary Project encompassed even the most informal child care settings, those that would have been missed by a study interviewing only out-of-home sources. Furthermore, the family-interview strategy was able to document children's attendance at multiple care and education settings, thereby giving an unprecedented picture of the total experience of each child studied.

The Parent/Guardian Interview questions, which were jointly developed by the project directors from the participating countries, were designed to yield the following information:

1. To what extent do today's families use out-of-home services for the care or education of their preschool-aged children? To what extent is care at home by parents the norm?

2. What factors lead parents to seek out-of-home services for their children? Why do some parents remain their children's sole caretakers? How much choice is involved, and do parents turn to out-of-home care/education for adult-centered or child-centered reasons?

3. What within-country and country-to-country variations exist in forms of out-of-home care/education?

4. What various ways are care/education programs sponsored, or supported? What types of support services (e.g., health, transportation) are offered by early childhood programs?

5. For children who do attend out-of-home settings, how much of their day is spent there? Are multiple settings involved, and how much travel between settings is necessary?

6. When parents use out-of-home care/education services, how much contact do they have with those responsible for their child? How satisfied are parents with the services provided, and what problems do they encounter?

7. What persons play important caretaking roles when children are in their own homes? When children are in out-of-home settings?

This wealth of information, never before assembled in precisely this way, in and of itself is already providing baseline data for early childhood policymakers and planners in each of the 11 nations who completed Phase 1 of the Preprimary Project. And, as mentioned earlier, the Phase 1 data allow researchers in each participating country to select a relevant sample of service settings for the Phase 2 study — which examines the quality of children's experiences in their various settings and the age-4 developmental status of those children. Phase 2 data, in turn, will be the basis for the Phase 3 investigation into the relationship between early childhood experiences and later development.

At this writing, Phase 1 data collection and analyses have been completed. Phase 2 data collection and analyses are nearing completion, and a series of monographs and videotapes reporting the findings is in preparation. At the same time, instrument design for Phase 3 is also under way.

The 11 nations/territories whose Phase 1 data are reported here are Belgium (French-speaking [Fr.]), China (People's Republic of China [PRC]), Finland, Germany (Federal Republic of Germany [FRG]), Hong

Kong, Italy, Nigeria, Portugal, Spain, Thailand, and the United States. At the outset of Phase 1 in 1989, each of these nations assembled a "national profile" of early childhood provisions, based on data sources (mostly government sources) available at the time. This constituted a starting point for the family-based study that was to come — the household survey.

The next chapter summarizes the 11 national profiles, to provide a background for the report of findings derived from household survey data. Two subsequent chapters describe first the Phase 1 methodology and then the national samples, giving an idea of the care taken to assure representativeness and of the characteristics of families involved in the survey. Then come findings about the full variety of arrangements families make for their 4-year-olds' care/education — including everything from care at home by parents to care in highly organized facilities. A special look at organized facility settings is the subject of the next chapter; this is followed by a chapter centering on children's daily routines. Two concluding chapters summarize the key findings country-by-country and draw out the implications of the overall findings. They capsulize the information gleaned when families around the world speak about the care and education of their 4-year-old children.

References

Berrueta-Clement, J. R., Schweinhart, L. J., Barnett, W. S., Epstein, A. S., & Weikart, D. P. (1984). *Changed lives: The effects of the Perry Preschool Program on youths through age 19* (Monographs of the High/Scope Educational Research Foundation, 8). Ypsilanti, MI: High/Scope Press.

Bronfenbrenner, U. (1979). *Ecology of Human Development.* Cambridge, MA: Harvard University Press.

Epstein, A. S. (1993). *Training for quality: Improving early childhood programs through systematic inservice training* (Monographs of the High/Scope Educational Research Foundation, 9). Ypsilanti, MI: High/Scope Press.

Katz, L. (1975). Early childhood programs and ideological disputes. *Educational Forum, 34* (3) 267–271.

Lazar, I., & Darlington, R. (1979). *Lasting effects after preschool.* (Summary report). Washington, DC: U.S. Department of Health, Education and Welfare.

LeVine, R. (1970). Cross-cultural study in child development. In P. H. Mussen (Ed.), *Carmichael's Manual of Child Psychology* (Vol. 2, pp. 559–612). New York: Wiley.

Myers, R. (1992). *The twelve who survive.* London: Routledge.

Olmsted, P. P., & Weikart, D. P. (Eds.) (1989). *How nations serve young children: Profiles of child care and education in 14 countries.* Ypsilanti, MI: High/Scope Press.

Ruopp, R., Travers, J., Glantz, F., & Coelen, C. (1979). *Children at the center: Summary findings and their implications* (Final report of the National Day Care Study, Vol. 1). Cambridge, MA: Abt Associates.

Schweinhart, L. J., Barnes, H. V., Weikart, D. P. (1993). *Significant benefits: The High/Scope Perry preschool study through Age 27* (Monographs of the High/Scope Educational Research Foundation, 10). Ypsilanti, MI: High/Scope Press.

Tobin, J. J., Wu, D. Y. H., & Davidson, D. H. (1989). *Preschool in three cultures: Japan, China, and the United States.* New Haven, CT: Yale University Press.

United Nations Educational, Scientific, and Cultural Organization (UNESCO). (1991). *Early childhood care and education: A world survey.* Paris: Author.

II
PHASE 1 PARTICIPANTS —
BRIEF PROFILES

Marge Melin Senninger, *Senior Editor*
High/Scope Educational Research Foundation
Ypsilanti, Michigan

A wide spectrum of 11 IEA member nations undertook Phase 1 of the Preprimary Project. Whether a developed or a developing nation, each of them had its unique reasons for wanting to learn more about domestic and worldwide early childhood provisions and practices. They came to the project with various backgrounds and needs, which they described in "national profiles" of early childhood care and education. In fact, preparation of a national profile by the research team in each participating country was the first major activity of Phase 1. The profiles, which largely had to be based on government statistics available at the time in each country, were published in 1989 in a volume entitled *How Nations Serve Young Children: Profiles of Child Care and Education in 14 Countries* (Olmsted & Weikart, 1989). To provide a context for understanding and interpreting Phase 1 data, this chapter presents thumbnail sketches of the national profiles for the 11 countries involved in Phase 1.

BELGIUM (FR.) — A LONG-STANDING NURSERY SCHOOL TRADITION

Belgium's profile, written by Researcher Arlette Delhaxhe of the Department of Pedagogical Research, University of Liège, traced the nation's early childhood infrastructure back to its origins before Belgium's proclamation of independence in 1830 (1989, pp. 13–37).[1] The network of care for young children at that time had charitable origins and consisted of *salles d'asile* (rooms of shelter) that were primarily concerned with children's health and protection. A century ago, however, educational recommendations were introduced. Hence, modern-day nursery schools (*écoles maternelles*, for 2½ to 6-year-olds) aim at preparing children to succeed in later schooling. Delhaxhe described them as "places where children's socialization and personality development are nurtured."

The Belgian profile described a country where (at the time of writing, in 1989) a majority (66 percent) of mothers of children under age 10 were "economically active," meaning employed full-time, employed part-time, or actively seeking employment. Reflective of this economic picture is Belgium's explicit family policy of maternity leave, child care leave, and subsidization and supervision of day care for children under age 2½. Furthermore, since 1969, children aged 2½ to 6 years have been able to attend nursery schools that are subsidized, regulated, and supervised by the National Ministry of Education.

A DESCRIPTION OF THE WIDESPREAD NURSERY SCHOOL SYSTEM

With the rare exception of a handful of schools that charge for admission, Belgian nursery schools are free. Almost 100 percent of 4-year-olds (the target age of the IEA Phase 1 study) attend them. Rather than being a *consequence* of the extensive maternal employment, however, this high level of nursery school attendance is explained by the educational character of the nursery schools. As long ago as the early 1950s, official recommendations were advising Belgian mothers to entrust their preschool-aged children to educational professionals.

The Ministry of Education is the central administrative body that is responsible for planning the programs and for regulating the establishment and functioning of schools, including nursery schools. Belgium has three educational networks. Of the approximately 2,000 nursery schools in the French-speaking part of Belgium, about half are **local-authority schools**, about a third are **private (mainly Roman Catholic schools)**, and the rest are **French-speaking Community schools**.

To obtain Community funding, schools must adhere to governmental regulations and be subject to supervision. Thus every nursery school, whether local-authority, Roman Catholic, or Community, observes the same equipment norms, salary schedule, student-teacher ratios, timetable, and so on. Nursery school teachers must undergo 3 years of study in a vocational school (the *institut supérieur pédagogique*). They also receive inservice training from supervisors (teachers who have passed a national examination and who have at least 10 years of experience). The French-speaking Community provides funding to cover staff salaries in each network. Community funding also covers all operating costs in the Community schools, but for local-authority schools, as well as private schools, only part of operating costs are supported by the French-speaking Community.

Though each school network has a recommended nursery school curriculum, implementation of that curriculum may vary from teacher to teacher. According to Delhaxhe,

> The relative importance assigned to socioaffective development and to academic learning depends on the point of view of the teacher. Some teachers think that it is important to teach children discipline and academic knowledge; these teachers have a "traditional" understanding of the educational role of the école maternelle. Other, more "progressive" teachers give priority to play, social interaction, and autonomy of the children.

As stated earlier, the nursery schools function as preparation for primary school. They are often annexed to the primary school, and they have the same operating hours as the primary school: 8:30 to 12:00 in the morning, and 1:30 to 3:00 in the afternoon for 5 days a week during the school year (with the exception that schools are closed on Wednesday afternoons). Most but not necessarily all 4-year-olds attend for the full day. As the earlier statistic regarding mothers' economic activity would indicate, many 4-year-olds have need for care and supervision outside of nursery school hours.

Services That Supplement the Nursery Schools

Delhaxhe reported that in the 1980s, many services had been created that take care of children when schools are closed — *halte garderie* (similar to baby-sitting), *ludothèque* (toy-lending service), and sports clubs or artistic clubs. As she put it, "A not-yet-determined number of children . . . are being cared for on the premises of nursery schools outside official curriculum hours." For other children, care by grandparents is the alternative to the extracurricular care services at school.

Unlike the nursery school services, the extracurricular care services on school premises are not the responsibility of the National Ministry of Education. They depend on local organizing authorities, have no regulations governing them, and are provided with only meager government subsidies. Some troublesome issues concerning the extracurricular services are

- The large numbers of children and the noise
- The lack of available activities for children
- The inadequate facilities
- The lack of trained care staff
- The lack of universal availability

Getting a precise idea about how parents cope with their need for care outside the nursery school hours was one of the original motives for Belgium's participation in Phase 1 of the IEA Preprimary Project.

CHINA (PRC) — TIMELY SCIENTIFIC RESEARCH

The Chinese profile, written by Shi Hui Zhong, Professor at the Central Institute of Educational Research, Beijing, delves back further than that of any other nation, citing the existence of an early childhood curriculum in the eleventh century B.C. (1989, pp. 241–254). This curriculum, along with other writings from the seventh and second centuries B.C., indicates the importance that the ancient Chinese attached to training in early childhood, albeit training of the child within the family.

THE BEGINNINGS OF MODERN-DAY EARLY CHILDHOOD SERVICES

The first institutional training for young children surfaced in modern times, in the early twentieth century, when Tao Xing Zhi's *Zouding School Constitution* established a school system prototype that included an early childhood component. This was followed by the gradual development of a number of rural and urban *kindergartens* that "did not cost much and served the common people," namely, the workers and the peasants. In 1923 the first experimental center for early childhood education was set up in Nanjing by Chen He Quin, a noted modern Chinese educator whose work serves to this day as a guide for early childhood educators. He proposed this early education philosophy:

- The kindergarten must fit the actual situation of China.
- Both kindergarten and family should take responsibility for the child's education.
- Kindergartens should first of all pay attention to children's health.
- Kindergartens should develop children's good habits.
- Play and games should be the major teaching approach.
- Teachers should be friends with children.
- Teaching should be primarily in small groups.

In addition to the "common people's" kindergartens, a fairly extensive system of government-sponsored kindergartens arose in China between 1937 and 1949 to serve the children of military personnel and defense workers during the war with Japan. Also in the first half of the twentieth century, along the coastline of China, some kindergartens were established with the help of patriotic overseas Chinese, and these usually adopted American or European curricula and methods of instruction.

Early Years of Expansion Begin

The founding of the People's Republic in 1949 brought on the most extensive and rapid growth of early childhood institutions. Throughout the 1950s a series of government issuances defined, guided, and set requirements for kindergarten (for children aged 3 to 6 years), which was to "foster healthy development in children before primary school" and "lighten mothers' child care burdens so that they could take part in political, productive, cultural, and educational activities." The state called for factories, the army, governmental and academic institutions, neighborhoods, and villages to all run their own kindergartens "according to their needs and resources" and asked local boards of education to help in providing teachers.

Between 1949 and 1985, the number of kindergartens in China grew from approximately 1,300 to approximately 170,000. About three quarters of the 170,000 were rural kindergartens, a fact that reflects not only the agricultural nature of the country but also the increasing attention being paid to the collective care and education of young children in rural areas. Despite this rapid proliferation of institutional care, the kindergartens could accommodate only about a fifth of China's preschool-aged children by 1985.

Chinese kindergartens do try to meet the needs of working parents.

The hours of operation vary, with four general types of kindergarten being offered: daytime service (usually from 7:00 a.m. to 6:00 p.m.); boarding service (the whole week, day and night, except for Sunday); half-day service; and temporary service (covering just a season or certain hours, according to the needs of various kinds of workers).

Issues China faces are the expected ones for a care and education system that has grown so far so fast: Teacher training lags behind the need for qualified teachers, and research lags behind educational practice and policymaking. Participation in the IEA Preprimary Project comes at a time when planning activities for China's early childhood services have just been decentralized, shifting principal program-planning responsibility from the State Education Commission to committees at the provincial level. The 10 Chinese provinces participating in the Preprimary Project look forward to using project data as a basis for their new provincial early childhood education plans.

FINLAND — TOWARD A SYSTEM FOR CHILD AND FAMILY TOTAL GROWTH

The profile of Finland's system of early childhood education was authored by Mikko Ojala, Professor of Early Childhood Education in the Department of Education at the University of Joensuu (1989, pp. 87–118). He described a system with beginnings in the mid-nineteenth century. At that time, Uno Cygnaeus, founder of the Finnish public education system and a strong proponent of Friedrich Froebel's kindergarten ideals, saw to it that Finland's first teacher-training college included a nursery school (for children under age 4) and a kindergarten (for children aged 4 to 10). Like Froebel working in Germany before him, Cygnaeus saw "the pedagogical insufficiency" of existing social welfare institutions for young children and, through the kindergarten, hoped to bring about the *education* of young children before school age through training of mothers and child nurses in educational tasks. (In Germany, this had turned out to be an ideal suited largely to middle-class families.)

Despite Cygnaeus's intentions, Finland's kindergartens, after his death in 1888, changed over to "popular kindergartens" for children of poor families — primarily social welfare institutions. Though kindergartens were at first (from 1887 on) administered by school authorities, after Finland's 1918 Civil War, administration did pass over to social welfare authorities, and the administration of Finland's early childhood services has remained so to this day.

Kindergartens providing care for Finland's 3- to 7-year-olds grew in number from 80 (in the late 1920s) to 150 (in the late 1940s). Post-World War II growth was somewhat more rapid, with the number peaking at 350 by the late 1960s. Though kindergartens could be either private or public, from their inception most were public. However, by fulfilling certain government-set conditions of operation, both kinds were eligible for state aid.

Other care services at the time were *nurseries*, established in the late 1900s, which served primarily children under age 3 but also, in some cases, an "expanded" population of 0- to 7-year-olds. Either public or private, these were not eligible for state aid. Also, in the late 1940s, *dayclubs* arose, serving children 4 to 7 years old, for a few hours a week. In most cases church-sponsored, these institutions also received no state aid. Another, publicly sponsored, less formal type of care also deserves mention: *Playground programs* serving 4- to 10-year-olds 2 to 8 hours daily began in Finland around 1910 and almost rivaled kindergartens in number by the late 1960s.

A LANDMARK — THE 1973 DAY CARE LAW

By the end of the 1960s, the rapid industrialization and urbanization that occurred in Finland after World War II brought about national discussion of families' critical day care needs (by 1970 about three-fifths of women were employed outside the home). The discussion, which involved controversy over the merits of "home care" versus "day care," culminated in a reorganization of early childhood services under the 1973 Children's Day Care Law. This law has required each municipality to provide public or publicly supervised private care services as needed. Enrollment priority is given to children whose parents are employed, ill, in school, or otherwise unable to care for their children. Also, some children with special needs — minorities, returning emigrants, the handicapped, and those in children's homes — receive special consideration.

With enactment of the law, kindergartens became *day care centers*, and a new form of institutionalized care, *family day care*, came into being. Both forms of care can be either public or private, are subject to supervision of social welfare boards, and (except for private family day care) can receive state subsidies. Both forms can serve, in principle, children aged 0–6 (school-entry age is 7). However, in practice, family day care, which is small-group care in the child's or another's home, is preferred for infants and toddlers. In 1983 about one fifth of 4-year-olds were in day care centers, and one sixth were in family day care. Though part-time care is an option, both in centers and in homes the majority of children were in full-time care (generally 8 to 10 hours daily).

Another form of care defined by the 1973 law is supervised play activity. Intended as a complement to center and home care, play activity primarily takes the form of *playclubs* (mostly private) and *playground activities* (public).

A slowdown in its population growth and prospects of population decline have led Finland to institute quite extensive family policy, including maternity allowance, maternity and paternity leave, maternity and child health care, child benefits, housing subsidies, and so on. In line with this is the government involvement — both supervisory and financial — that one finds in early childhood services. In 1983, because of national and municipal government subsidies, Finnish parents paid (on a sliding-scale basis) less than a fifth of the costs of day care for their children. Government direction of day care has traditionally come from the national, provincial, and local levels, under the aegis of social welfare.

A SYSTEM STILL UNDER DEVELOPMENT

The day care system set up by the 1973 law has demanded continuing development. Although enactment of the law nearly tripled the number of available day care places in 10 years, by 1983 the number of mothers employed outside the home had increased such that only three fifths the Finnish children needing care could be served by the day care system. To meet this increasing demand for services, Finland set a goal of creating 7,000 new day care places per year for 1986–90, envisioning that supply will have balanced demand by the mid-1990s.[2] Along with this quantitative improvement, qualitative improvement is also called for. Important "reform" issues are increasing the number of trained personnel, coordinating personnel training and graduate and continuing education, promoting development of curriculum, and conducting basic research (like the IEA study), so reform can be based on "scientific rather than pragmatic ideas."

Though central government involvement has helped to bring about the present Finnish system of early childhood services, most recently, with the new social welfare law enacted in 1984, a trend *away* from central government control has emerged. To "bring day care services closer to their users," in the future, municipalities will have more say in determining the form and content of day care, and they will play a greater role in research and experimentation. Another development — recent central government proposals for more flexibility in parents' work hours — may eventually lead to a decreasing need for family day care and a restructuring of center-based care schedules. A third development — the 1984 inclusion in the Day Care Law of a set of educational goals — may mean that after 100 years, Cygnaeus's ideals of early childhood education are being realized. Ojala's Finnish profile ended with a statement of hope for development of a system that will provide "support for the child's and family's total growth according to their individual needs."

Germany (FRG) — Quantitative and Qualitative Expansion

The authors of Germany's national profile are Wolfgang Tietze, Professor of Education; Hans-Günther Rossbach, Senior Researcher; and Karin Ufermann, Research Assistant — all from the Department of Education, Westfälische Wilhelms-Universität Münster. Their profile (1989, pp. 39–85), goes back to the late 1700s, when with the formation of the bourgeois notion of the family and of the central role of the mother-child relationship, "childhood began to be perceived as a separate state of being. . . needing to be subjected to a deliberate molding." The country's rapid industrialization in the 1800s meant that the earliest institutionalized forms of care and education for young children were support for those who could not live up to bourgeois ideals — the impoverished families in which mothers had to work outside the home. These social welfare origins of Germany's early childhood institutions explain why the churches gained an early foothold in their provision.

The German profile described, in particular, the evolution of Friedrich Froebel's *Kindergarten* — which in the mid-nineteenth century started as a "pedagogical principle" aimed at "providing a new basis for the education of children within the family itself." It eventually became not merely a principle but an *extrafamilial institution* that had an enduring influence both in Germany and elsewhere. Consequently, the term *kindergarten* is now part of many languages, either in its original or in translated form.

KINDERGARTEN BECOMES A STAGE OF THE EDUCATIONAL SYSTEM

As early as 1848 there were calls to make kindergarten an integral element and the basis of a national system of education. However, amidst Germany's ensuing political events of the nineteenth and early twentieth centuries and amidst shifting opinions about the social welfare role versus the educational role of preschool institutions, kindergarten was not actually to achieve this status until 1970. Then, in the process of fundamental reform of the entire education system to better meet the needs of a developed industrial nation, the German Council on Education, in its reform recommendations, coined the term *Elementarbereich* (elementary level) to describe the kindergarten stage of education for 3- to 5-year-olds. The result was a rapid expansion of kindergarten places, so that by 1977 well over half of German 3- to 5-year-olds were enrolled. Though kindergarten was not to be compulsory, the goal was to reach all children by providing an ample supply of places.

This development was followed by controversy about how to link the new basic stage of the educational system — the play-oriented, age-3-to-5 kindergarten — with the primary stage (for ages 6 to 9). Various proposals for introducing children to "school-oriented" learning, most of them involving some special handling of 5-year-olds, were put forth. Behind this pedagogical struggle was a "power struggle," however, as to whether the state should assume responsibility for educating 5-year-olds (thus making age 5 the compulsory-school-attendance age) or whether the traditional organizing bodies of kindergartens, in particular the churches, should continue to hold sway. The latter won out; today most 5-year-olds remain in kindergartens, and only a small portion of them take part in a preparatory phase in primary school.

Perhaps as a result of the social welfare origins of Germany's preschools (their early protection and custody role), the present-day kindergarten, though a stage of the educational system, is administered by the youth welfare offices and is often provided by an independent agency, such as a parish or some type of welfare agency. Only when such authorities fail to provide kindergartens is the public authority required to be the provider (about one third are publicly provided). Kindergartens are parent-, agency-, community-, and state-subsidized; only low-income families are exempt from paying kindergarten fees.

The Coverage That Kindergartens Provide

Statistics from 1986 reveal that about two fifths of 3-year-olds and two thirds of 4-year-olds attend kindergarten. The profile authors estimated that about 1 out of 6 German children enters primary school with no kindergarten experience. Kindergarten programs operate from 8 a.m. to midday, close at midday for 2 hours, and many times offer 2 or 3 hours of afternoon care. Most children who do attend kindergarten receive only a half-day program, with a smaller number returning for care during the afternoon hours. Full-day provisions with special adaptations (e.g., smaller groups and rooms for children to rest in) also exist, but only about 12 percent of kindergarten-aged children are cared for over and beyond midday.

The social context for Germany's early childhood provision is much like that of other industrialized countries: rising educational levels among women, a rising divorce rate, a rising female-employment rate, and decreasing rates of childbirth and three-generation households (meaning that for households where a single parent or both parents work outside the home, the alternative of "grandparent care" for their children is becoming more problematic, and multiple care arrangements are more common). Germany's female-employment rate is not as high as those in some other industrialized countries. Over a third of employed mothers with preschool-aged children work 40 or more hours a week, but all-day places are available for only half of their children.

Thus, after the increase in quality and quantity that occurred in kindergartens in the 1970s, when they became a part of the educational system, Germany is again looking to expand both the quantity and quality of its early childhood provisions in ways that respect the needs of modern families and children. In the same spirit with which the nation has begun to provide social benefits and labor market regulations enabling parents to better care for their children, the federal government has begun to look at early childhood education issues: the child's legal right to a place in kindergarten,[3] the need for all-day places for many children, the need for flexible school schedules to meet families' differing lifestyles, and the need for maintaining high-quality care *and* education in expanded programs. The IEA Preprimary Project fits easily into this scenario.

HONG KONG — NEED FOR AN OVERALL POLICY

Sylvia Opper, Lecturer at the Department of Education of the University of Hong Kong, is the author of the profile of early childhood services in the Territory of Hong Kong (1989, pp. 119–142). At the outset, the profile describes a situation of almost universal preprimary coverage by two kinds of privately offered services — *kindergartens* and *child care centers*. About 90 percent of the 3-, 4-, and 5-year-old children attending are in kindergartens, and 10 percent, in child care centers.

The backdrop for this "almost universal" coverage by private services must be understood: First of all, in Hong Kong, formal education is an important avenue to social and economic mobility, since it has the potential to lead to a much-sought-after university education available to less than 2 percent of the population. What is surprising is that although the majority of Hong Kong's compulsory 6-year primary schools and 6-year secondary schools (3 years of which are compulsory) are government or government-aided, the preschool sector is almost entirely in the hands of private sponsors. Government does play a role in preschool education and care, however, as the profile goes on to tell.

THE BEGINNINGS OF RAPID PREPRIMARY GROWTH

The Hong Kong profile's historical information deals mainly with the post-World War II years. Though the early part of the twentieth century saw the development of some charitable preprimary institutions for abandoned children along with a few kindergarten classes attached to primary schools, the most significant preprimary developments have occurred in fairly recent times. Beginning in 1945, Hong Kong's population surged because of a high birthrate, an influx of refugees from mainland China, and the return of residents who had fled the Japanese occupation. This, along with the problem of many separated or abandoned children, led to almost overwhelming demands for child care services. At the same time, strong competition for entry into a limited elementary school system resulted in more and more kindergartens being set up to prepare children for elementary school entrance examinations.

In response to the postwar demands, and as Hong Kong residents became aware of the benefits of early education and affluent enough to afford it, the number of privately run, profit-making kindergartens grew dramatically. Unfortunately, because of their extremely rapid growth and because of only minimal government involvement, the kindergartens were overcrowded (often set up in residential flats) and understaffed. By 1971, the kindergarten teacher-child ratio was 1 to 35, and with teacher-training programs stretched beyond their limits, only about a fifth of teachers were trained. Government involvement consisted of the setting up, in 1953, of a Kindergarten Section within the Hong Kong Education Department to help with program planning and implementation and to run training courses for teachers.

The early postwar years also brought a sharply increased need both for child care for needy working mothers and for child protection services. A government Social Welfare Office, set up in 1948, began to oversee the growing number of child care institutions being set up by voluntary agencies. The government further involved itself by providing the agencies with premises or land grants, with financial subsidies, and with training courses for caretakers.

Increasing Government Involvement in Preprimary Services

In the later postwar years (from 1975 on), professional bodies and the public began to ask for more government involvement in the preprimary sector. One result was a 1981 white paper that, for the first time, set out government policy on early education and care. The paper dealt with the need for improved teacher training and for a fee-assistance scheme for low-income families, and it contained facility and equipment recommendations as well as suggestions for improving curriculum.

Unfortunately, a serious economic recession during the 1980s caused the postponement of many of the measures suggested in the 1981 white paper. A fee-assistance scheme for low-income parents was instituted, however, within the Social Welfare Department. As of 1989, the white paper's percentage goals for kindergarten teachers' inservice training had been only partially met. Its goals of introducing kindergarten teachers' preservice training and establishing a Joint Training Institute for the kindergarten and child care sectors were deferred. Other kindergarten-upgrade recommendations — for a better teacher-child ratio and unified standards for the two preprimary sectors — were made in 1986 by a group of eminent business persons and educators, the Education Commission. These, too, at the time Sylvia Opper wrote the Hong Kong profile, were awaiting action.[4]

The government's role in the child care sector increased with its adoption in 1975–76 of ordinances and regulations for child care centers. This legislation governs the operation of centers; staff qualifications and training; staff-child ratio; and minimum space, safety, and health standards. Adoption of the legislation was followed by intense training efforts that resulted in the majority of child care workers being trained by 1983.

RECONCILING A DUAL SYSTEM

Despite the nearly universal service provision for preschool-aged children, and despite the somewhat increased government involvement of the 1970s and 1980s, Hong Kong is left with a dual early childhood provision system. One sector (kindergartens) is controlled largely by commercial interests and the other sector (child care) is controlled largely by voluntary agencies. The two sectors are regulated by different government departments, have different teacher-training requirements, and have different curriculums (parents perceive the more formal approach of the kindergarten as "education" and the learning-through-play approach of the child care centers as only "care"). Whereas most child care centers operate full-day programs, kindergartens, which are the parental choice for 90 percent of preschool placements, provide only a half-day program. Thus, employed parents must resort to other informal care arrangements for the remainder of the day — care by household maids, relatives, friends, or neighbors. Overcrowding, unsuitable teacher-pupil ratios, and a large percentage of untrained teaching staff still plague the kindergartens, in particular. Both sectors need improved teacher training, more-extensive curriculum development, and unified standards.

Concluding that "the distinction between kindergartens and child care centers results in anomalies and discrepancies in the delivery of services to young children," the profile of Hong Kong's early childhood services ended with a plea for "an overall policy" on the part of government for the field of early education and care. Data from the IEA Preprimary Project could be valuable in the formulation of such a policy.

ITALY — POLITICO-PEDAGOGICAL DEBATE

The history of preschool provisions in Italy, according to profile author

Filomena Pistillo of the Ministry of Public Instruction (Rome) and the European Center for Education (Frascati), is closely tied to the country's political, social, economic, and structural changes (1989, pp. 151–202). Pistillo's profile described the care and education of young children as a "terrain on which to defend rival interests, . . . a political battleground." The rival interests have been governmental ("the state") and religious ("the Roman Catholic church").

In the early nineteenth century, the first modern Italian preschools were set up based on the model of Abbot Ferrante Aporti's first *asilo di carita* (charitable shelter) for young children. But by mid-century, public interest in the preschools and in education in general began to wane. After the unification of Italy in 1861, a law establishing age 6 as the compulsory school-entry age led to the state's further deemphasis on education *before* that age. This left the care and education of young children up to private interests, primarily the church, which began to emphasize the charitable aspect of its preschools. Following suit, the few existing state-run preschool institutions shifted over to the Ministry of the Interior, which ran all public assistance programs. For the remainder of the century, preschool development, which was now mostly in private hands, progressed slowly and unevenly throughout the country, and the quality of the services offered was "distressing." No longer running the preschools, the Ministry of Education was able to exert only minimal influence.

In the later 1800s, with the founding of the first Froebelian kindergartens in Italy, preschool quality became an issue. A debate ensued between supporters of Aporti's and of Froebel's methods. The fact that Catholics saw Froebel's method as a "foreign and Protestant invention" gave fuel to this debate. Eventually, however, Froebel's methods gained a secure foothold, and a law in 1889 actually annexed the Froebel kindergartens to teachers' colleges, thus facilitating the movement. "Changes were afoot."

The Early 1900s — A "Fertile Moment" for Nursery Schooling

The early part of the twentieth century Filomena Pistillo described as "a particularly fertile moment in Italy for child education in general and nursery schooling [preschools] in particular." Women's part in the country's industrialization led to questions about welfare and women's and children's rights. Educators began to show increased interest in early childhood and preprimary education. Rosa and Carolina Agazzi were developing their educational method at this time, as was Maria Montessori. The debate between Agazzi and Montessori partisans led to Italy's "first instance of serious methodological inquiry and confrontation in the field of preprimary education."

GOVERNMENT — "STILL SINGULARLY ABSENT FROM THE SCENE"

Though public preschools continued to experience near-zero growth throughout the early 1900s, the Roman Catholic church steadily strengthened and extended its preprimary system. The result was that by 1920, a fourth of children aged 3 to 5 were in preschools. The preschools, however, were confined to the better-off parts of the country, and whether using the Aporti, Agazzi, Froebel, or Montessori method, they packed children into overcrowded rooms with teacher-pupil ratios of 1 to 45.

When the Fascist party came to power in the 1920s, it "reformed" education so as to better serve party purposes, but in doing so it "left preprimary education to one side, . . . solving none of its problems and, if anything, accentuating the negative effects of the preceding system." The fascists did, however, change the name of preschools from *asili* (shelters) to *scuole materne* (nursery schools), and they declared the Agazzi method as "*the* method of the Italian preschool system."

A MIDCENTURY AWAKENING OF GOVERNMENT INTEREST IN PRESCHOOLS

After the Liberation in 1943, government inattentiveness to preprimary affairs continued until the Christian Democrats, "with no small help from the church," won Parliamentary control in 1948. Finally, preschool education (the "fief of the church") got the government's attention in the form of a study by the National Committee for School Reform. The study publicized the ills of the preschool system, ranging from inadequate facilities, equipment, curriculum, and teacher qualifications to inadequate geographic distribution. The government, while assuring church officials that it had no intentions of taking over the system, pledged its help in expanding and subsidizing private preschool services.

Toward the mid-1950s, lay political parties began to be concerned about early childhood needs and to denounce the lack of direct government involvement and the "excessive religious control" over preschools. This concern coincided with Italy's "boom years" — its rapid industrial development and the resultant changes in social values and family lifestyles. Against this backdrop, in 1958, for the first time, government guidelines for activities in *non-state* preschools appeared. By 1960, a government Three-Year Plan allocated money not only for expanding the non-state system but also for building a few state-run preschools. And in 1968, Law No. 444 at last officially recognized the government's right to be directly involved in preprimary education. This was quickly followed by the 1969 issuance of government guidelines for activities in *state* nursery schools.

THE TWO PRESCHOOL SYSTEMS TODAY

Today Italy has two preschool systems that between them enroll almost all children 3, 4, and 5 years of age: *state nursery schools* (run directly by a ministry or agency of the national government) and *non-state nursery schools* (run by private organizations or by communal, provincial, or regional government). Though the non-state nursery schools are subject to supervision by the Ministry of Education, the accumulated legislation governing them is so complex that "authorities find it difficult to know just what to enforce." Adding to the complexity is the fact that non-state nursery schools are subsidized by state funds in spite of the economic losses they habitually incur. However, along with the prohibitive magnitude and cost of the task, a constitutional principle of maintaining "economic pluralism and freedom of choice" keeps the national government from taking the non-state system over entirely.

Official 1985–86 statistics showed the two systems enrolling almost equal numbers of children, but with non-state nursery schools slightly ascendant. Rural areas depend mostly on state-run provisions, whereas urban areas have a concentration of non-state nursery schools. Attendance at state schools (which have a combination of communal, regional, and national support) is free of charge; parents must pay fees for their children's attendance at non-state (private) nursery schools. About two thirds of state nursery schools remain open as much as 8–10 hours a day (two half-day sessions) for 10 months of the year. Non-state nursery schools sometimes have longer and more-flexible hours of operation.

More Recently — Research Concerns

A 1982–83 study of 2,000 urban Italian families with preschool-aged children found that at least in the eight cities studied, nursery school supply was "almost" meeting demand. However, nursery school offerings (facilities, equipment, curriculum, auxiliary services) and parents' utilization of those offerings (versus part-time or full-time utilization of care by mother, domestic help, relatives, or friends) vary with geography, type of school management, and family socioeconomic and educational levels.

Since the 1960s, classroom and institutional experimentation — or innovation — in both state and non-state nursery schools has been a growing phenomenon. However, Pistillo's profile indicated that better documentation and analysis of this experimentation is needed if it is to have an effect on the lively "politico-pedagogical debate" that characterizes Italy's preprimary development today, as in the past.

At the outset of Italy's participation in the IEA Preprimary Project, the principal national issues under debate were these: updating of staff training, reform of the 1969 educational activity guidelines, organization of state and non-state nursery schools into a single national system, establishment of autonomous headships and elected management bodies for nursery schools, establishment of a continuity between nursery schools and compulsory schooling, lowering the starting age for compulsory education, improving the quality and quantity of nursery schools in the South and the Islands, resolving the issue of teaching religion in preschools, and adjustment of the nursery school calendar to coincide with the calendar of compulsory school.

Nigeria — A Need for Data

The profile of Nigeria makes one emphatic point — the need for all kinds of national data regarding the early childhood population. Rather than being able to rely on government statistics, the profile's author, Olayemi Onibokun, Senior Research Fellow at the Institute of Education, University of Ibadan, found much of the data for the profile (1989, pp. 219–240) by conducting her own surveys in several of Nigeria's 21 states.

Nigeria, which became fully independent in 1960 and a republic in 1963, has a fairly recent history of child care institutions and an even more recent history of government involvement in them. The first preschools appeared in the 1950s, when Nigerians returning from studying abroad established them for their children. Based for the most part on models of out-of-home care seen in Great Britain, these early preschools were "elitist, serving children of educated parents in major urban centers."

It was not until 1969, which marked the first official statement of school-entry age, that the government spoke out on the role of preschools. The government's emphasis, at that time, on their *primary-school preparatory* role for 3- to 5-year-olds may explain what Onibokun described as "the rigorous academic content of Nigerian preschool programs."

The 1970s were Nigeria's oil-boom era, and this period also saw a boom in the setting up of preschools. As a result, a preprimary section was set up in the Ministry of Education to draw up guidelines for the establishment and supervision of the schools. Since then, the federal government has revised its 1981 *National Policy on Education* and published its 1987 *Guidelines on Preprimary Education*. Besides this, there has been no federal funding and no direct participation of the federal government in preschool education. Responsibility for the control, supervision, and administration of preprimary programs is delegated to the states, who in turn leave preprimary service provision in private/corporate hands.

As mentioned earlier, many of the Nigerian profile's statistics had to be produced by Onibokun's own surveys. For example, she reported that her 1987–88 survey in seven states revealed that over 90 percent of preprimary institutions were run by private individuals, religious bodies, or voluntary organizations, and fewer than 10 percent were government-sponsored (connected to universities, teacher-training colleges, or polytechnics). The private institutions are supported by proprietors' capital and by fees collected from parents. According to Onibokun, "most Nigerian families do not earn the income to support their children in preprimary institutions."

Because each state keeps its own records, it is difficult to determine the total number of preschool institutions nationally. It is also difficult to get information from private proprietors about per-center populations and teacher-pupil ratios. However, Onibokun's seven-state survey was able to roughly gauge the adequacy of preprimary facilities by comparing numbers of preprimary institutions to numbers of primary schools in each state. The best ratio found was 1 preprimary for 8 primary schools; the worst was 1 preprimary for more than 100 primary schools. Not surprisingly, Onibokun found a preponderance of preprimary institutions in urban, rather than rural, areas.

Nursery or *kindergarten* is the name most often given to an institution serving 3- to 5-year-old children in Nigeria, though some children in this age-range are in *day care centers* (which usually provide custodial care for children 0 to 2 years old). In each state, nurseries and kindergartens must be approved by the Ministry of Education, and day care centers, by the Ministry of Health. This requirement seems to be largely ignored, however. Lack of uniform standards regarding curriculum, enrollment policies, and fees, and lack of adequate state supervision are other administrative problems cited by Onibokun.

Typical operating hours for a nursery school are 7:30 a.m. to 2:00 or 3:00 p.m., to coincide with the "working hours of public servants." However, parents are free to drop their children off and pick them up whenever it is convenient. Day care centers often have somewhat longer hours, such as 7:00 a.m. to 6:00 p.m. The calendar for preprimary institutions usually follows that of the public school system, with quarterly holiday periods. Some schools provide boarding facilities.

Onibokun explained that the purpose of preprimary services is to provide "social and educational services in looking after children of working mothers," which accounts for their concentration in towns, where the rate of female employment is very high. But, the profile also stated that "the vast majority of Nigerian women, whether in urban or rural areas, whether educated or illiterate, are economically active to insure their immediate families against financial inadequacy." Mothers working in the informal sector — on the farms, in the markets — often work and care for their children at the same time. It is the educated mothers employed in the formal sector of the economy, outside the home for a fixed period each day, who seek extrafamilial care for their children. Recruiting house-help (maids, or nannies, who are "young school-leavers and dropouts migrating into the cities") or recruiting unemployed relatives for child care has in recent times become less of a possibility for these mothers, because the potential "childminders" are able to find better-paying jobs in service industries.

Thus, Onibokun presented a profile of a country with a relatively youthful population, but with increasing need for extrafamilial child care. Situated mostly where they accommodate formally employed mothers, existing preprimary institutions charge fees, provide rigorous scholastic education, and "are not sited according to children's special social needs." Consequently they fail to provide large numbers of Nigerian children with much-needed stimuli for optimum physical, social, and intellectual development. Onibokun cited the need for government provision of services for economically disadvantaged children, for better state regulation and supervision of preschools in general, and for teacher training more suited to early childhood needs. Underlying all this is the need for data about the preschool population and families' needs. "Until efforts to collect such data are made at the federal level, Nigeria will be without a basis for planning."

Portugal — A Positive Evolutionary Process

The complicated process of searching out available statistical information about Portugal's preprimary services was undertaken by five profile authors: Joaquim Bairrão, Maria Barbosa, Isolina Borges, Orlanda Cruz, and Isabel Macedo-Pinto, all of the Faculty of Psychology and Education, Porto University (1989, pp. 273–302). The process, they explained, was complicated by the fairly recent (1970s and 1980s) proliferation of public kindergartens in Portugal and by two decades of structural modifications in one of the administrative agencies dealing with early childhood needs. As in some other countries, the history of preprimary services in Portugal has produced two parallel systems, with two government ministries sharing responsibility for them.

The Portuguese profile described Portugal as going through the same stages of early childhood service development as other European countries have, but with a "significant delay" in the growth of kindergartens. Private institutions that were asylums for impoverished children first appeared in Portugal in 1834 (and these have persisted until quite recent times). It was not until the centennial of Friedrich Froebel's birthday in 1882, however, that Portugal saw the opening of its first Froebelian kindergarten, in Lisbon. About this time, two noted Portuguese educators, João de Deus and José Augusto Coelho, were also promulgating their ideas about early education. As kindergartens slowly spread, and as a significant movement developed on behalf of preparing children for primary school, the 1880s gave rise to intensive government measures stating objectives of preschool education and specifications for preschool teacher training.

With the establishment of the Portuguese First Republic in the early twentieth century, a new government declared that implementation of kindergartens would be part of their program. More pro-preschool legislation ensued. Yet, because of the difficult economic situation and the political instability, only 12 new kindergartens (7 public and 5 private) were created in the years of the First Republic (1910–1926), and the percentage of children receiving early childhood education never even reached 1 percent.

The succeeding government did no better, and realizing the drain extensive preschool education would be on the public treasury, the new government eventually terminated the Ministry of Education's early childhood role and instead encouraged families and private institutions to address preprimary education. The remaining government-run services for young children, presided over by other ministries and staffed by persons lacking educational expertise, concentrated not on education but on decreasing child mortality. This situation of government deemphasis on preschool education prevailed until the early 1970s, when under the Veiga Simão Reform, preprimary education was reinstated as part of the public educational system.

THE PAST 20 YEARS — KINDERGARTEN DEVELOPMENT

Because the Veigo Simāo plan for reform of the entire educational system acknowledged the importance of professional training, in 1973 the first two public schools for training preschool teachers began operation. (A few other, private training institutions had been operating since the early 1950s.) Implementation of the Veigo Simão reform plan was interrupted by Portugal's April 25 Revolution in 1974. Nevertheless, since that time, there have been significant increases in the numbers of kindergartens (for 3-, 4-, and 5-year-olds) and of training schools for preschool teachers. The profile showed the number of Ministry of Education public kindergartens, for example, increasing twentyfold between 1978 and 1988. During the same time, Ministry of Education private kindergartens increased by about one fifth. The result has been that the ministry's public kindergartens outnumber private ones by more than 6 to 1.

By 1984, about a third of Portuguese children aged 3, 4, and 5 were attending public or private kindergartens, but not all of these kindergartens were the responsibility of the Ministry of Education. A pre-Revolution legacy was that services for young children were dispersed among several ministries besides the Ministry of Education. Therefore coordination of efforts to help young children has been another public policy thrust during the past two decades. As mentioned earlier, the ministries sponsoring early childhood care and education are now just two: the Ministry of Education (ME) and the Ministry of Work and Social Security (MWSS). The ME sponsors just kindergartens; the MWSS sponsors many institutions connected with care and education of children aged 3 months to 6 years, and among these are various kindergartens and joint nursery/kindergartens that serve 3-, 4-, and 5-year-olds (nurseries typically provide child care just for children under age 3).

The ME-sponsored kindergartens include both public and private ones, with the public ones being located mostly in the poorer, rural areas. This is the result of a "compensatory strategy" that the ministry has adopted for creating new kindergartens where the private system has little foothold. Compared with private ME kindergartens, public ME kindergartens tend to have better child-teacher ratios (no more than 25 to 1), and in 1987–88, about a fourth of them (mainly located in rural areas) even had fewer than 15 children. The profile authors, noting that "only 60 percent of Portugal's available kindergarten places are actually occupied," hinted that better adaptation of child care options to the desires and characteristics of local populations might be in order.

The various kindergartens and nursery/kindergartens under the MWSS include ones that are private nonprofit, private for-profit, cooperative, factory-sponsored, and publicly sponsored (by autarchies, or local authorities). The first of these categories — the private nonprofits — is the largest. It includes the *Private Institutions of Social Solidarity* (IPSS), which are a group of private nonprofit publicly cosponsored institutions (such as resident associations, parishes) that constitute a counterpart to the Social Security system.

How Kindergarten Sponsorship Works

The result of having both the ME and MWSS systems of preprimary services is that there are multiple financing arrangements and management structures, as well as different requirements for teacher training. Only the ME public kindergartens require no fees of parents. Kindergartens under the ME follow the "educational model," which means that available space and age are the criteria for enrollment, and programs operate 6 hours per day, Monday through Friday, closing down 45 days for summer holidays and 2 weeks around both Christmas and Easter. Kindergartens under the MWSS follow the "social welfare model," meaning that enrollment depends on various family/child needs and considerations, and programs operate 10 −12 hours per day, Monday through Friday, with usually only 1 month off for summer holidays.

Though the preprimary programs are targeted primarily to meet children's needs, they are also intended to meet the needs of families. Portugal's percentages of employed mothers vary, with the highest percentages occurring in industrialized areas. In 1981, per-district percentages ranged from about 10 to 60 percent, with an overall rate of about 30 percent. This female-employment rate, as well as the social and cultural deprivation of the area and the population of 3- to 6-year-olds, is taken into consideration both by the ME and the MWSS in selecting where to establish kindergartens. In a given area, the ME considers not only the three factors just named but also the degree of school success that children experience in the first level of primary school and the lack of other educational facilities. Since the two ministries have different emphases — one on preparation for primary school and the other on supporting social and economic needs of families — the establishment of any new kindergartens requires considerable coordination.

The profile authors stated that "there are children where there are no kindergartens and there are kindergartens where there are not enough children." For example, in rural areas, where geographical isolation is a problem, a large percentage of public ME kindergartens operate with small numbers of children. This fact points out the need for adapting child care options to the characteristics and needs of local populations, to optimize the benefits of public investment in preschool education. Furthermore, the reverse condition, "children where there are no kindergartens," suggests that some employed mothers resort to informal care arrangements for their 3- to 5-year-olds, such as care by home day care mothers. These caregivers may be licensed by the Regional Center for Social Security or unlicensed ("underground").

Not surprisingly, no single curriculum dominates the multisponsored, noncompulsory Portuguese preschools. The profile described three prevalent models, however: Project Pedagogy (a semistructured program that promotes autonomy, creativity, and socialization); the João de Deus method (which consists of highly structured activities as a preparation for academic learning); and the Modern School Movement (which employs a "workshop" approach with classroom "interest areas" to promote free individual expression, cooperative activity, logical thinking, and initiation of reading and writing).

Portugal's April 25 Revolution (in 1974) not only introduced a new dynamic into Portuguese life in general but also started "a positive evolutionary process" for preprimary care and education. And the evolution continues. Though there is already a trend toward better coordination of efforts of the ME and the MWSS, in the future, Portugal hopes to include all existing education and care options under the sponsorship of the ME. Also, there are promising efforts to expand the rate of preschool coverage (to 80 percent by 1991–92) and at the same time suit the needs of the specific regions of the country. Data obtained from the participation in the IEA Preprimary Project can play a role in this expansion.

Spain — A New Period of Democracy

Spain's profile depicted a country "forging a new social, administrative, and political identity" — a country with stable families, extensive preschool coverage for 4- and 5-year-olds, and statistics that "do not always reflect the reality of the situation" (Palacios, 1989, pp. 303–341). Regarding this insufficiency of present statistics, the profile's author, Jesús Palacios, Professor in the Department of Developmental Psychology, University of Sevilla, had two explanations: (1) Spain's ongoing process of decentralization over the last two decades makes it difficult to present data that refer to the country as a whole, and (2) the fact that some preprimary situations fall outside of government control means that little is known about them.

Throughout Spain's history, preprimary care and education has been initiated by local government ("town halls"), by private individuals or institutions, or by the central government ("the state"). For example, the earliest records of preprimary activity (in the fifteenth through seventeenth centuries) described town halls contracting with schoolmasters or with religious orders to provide education for very young children. Other initiatives at that time were the *escuelas de amigas* (friendly women's schools). The "friendlies," as they were called, were women who accepted pay to look after other women's children, providing them with both care and education. For centuries, then, schoolmasters, religious orders, and friendlies attended to Spain's very young children.

The first state involvement in preprimary education began in the mid-1800s, with the Royal Ordinance of 1836, which required the government to set up preprimary schools in population centers with more than 10,000 inhabitants. This was followed by the Law of Primary Education of 1868, which required preprimary schools to be set up in every town having enough funds. The result was that by the end of the 1880s, Spain had over 800 preprimary schools, almost half of them state-run. During this period of development, different methodologies sprang up: Froebelian kindergartens became popular, and Spain's Andrés Manjón established his Ave María Open-Air Schools.

The beginning of the 1900s brought the New School movement and its concern with active methods. Maria Montessori's approach was one important influence at this time. The Spanish Civil War (1936–39) ended any experimental preprimary education, however, and from then on, "as happened in other aspects of life, the education of preprimary-aged children suffered." A law passed in 1945 finally began to reverse this trend by establishing *maternal schools* (for children up to age 4) and *infant schools* (for children aged 4 and 5). Child welfare, rather than academics, was to be the principal concern of these schools. A later law, in 1970, established the major forms of preprimary education in existence today: *nursery schools* (for 2- and 3-year-olds) and *kindergartens* (for 4- and 5-year-olds). However, because the high birthrates of the 1960s forced the public sector, in the 1970s, to concentrate its resources on children of compulsory school-age, the 1970 law was not followed by much development in state-sponsored nurseries or kindergartens. Meanwhile, the number of privately sponsored preprimary institutions did increase, albeit with little state oversight or regulation.

THE GOAL: SCHOOL PLACES FOR ALL 4- AND 5-YEAR-OLDS

A most significant turning point in Spain's preprimary service provision has been the "new period of democracy" that began in 1975, when after 40 years of dictatorial rule, Spain became a federation of "autonomous communities" (regions). Since 1977, with its 17 autonomous communities all in various stages of assuming responsibilities from the central government, the country has been aiming at providing school places for all 4- and 5-year-olds. As of 1986, this goal had almost been met: Over 90 percent of these children (85 percent of 4-year-olds and 95 percent of 5-year-olds) were in kindergartens. About two thirds of the kindergartens they attended were government-run (by a ministry of the central government or by the autonomous community), and one third were privately owned or church-sponsored.

Most kindergartens — especially the public ones — are staffed by teachers specialized in preprimary education, and most operate for a full day. The public kindergartens linked to the Ministry of Education and Science are free, and those linked to other ministries either are free or charge on a sliding, income-based scale; the private and church-sponsored kindergartens charge parents fees commensurate with the prestige or quality of the institution.

Kindergarten attendance is not compulsory, but the almost universal enrollment in these schools is due not only to the large supply of public kindergartens but also to parents' growing awareness of the preparatory role of preprimary education. There has also been, in some cities and their surrounding areas, a shortage of primary school places, and enrolling their child in kindergarten has been a way that parents can assure the child's acceptance into the affiliated primary school.

FOR CHILDREN UNDER AGE 4 — LESS PROVISION

The situation for children under age 4 is not so clear-cut. The stability of Spanish families (the profile described fewer than 10 percent as single-parent families) and a relatively low percentage of employed mothers (only about a fourth with children under age 6 are employed) may explain why care of under-4s by their mothers at home predominates. According to official 1986 statistics, only about 1 in 20 two-year-olds attended nursery school and only about 1 in 6 three-year-olds did so. The profile's analysis was this: "The typical Spanish family's lifestyle provides a favorable context for the upbringing of small children. This pattern is most frequently broken in large cities and, in such cases, in families with better-educated parents. . . . We cannot say whether this situation is a consequence of the population's high regard for family values and recognition of the importance of childrearing, whether it results from the scarcity of favorable alternatives, or whether it is a result of both factors."

Official statistics also indicated that the nursery schools attended by children under age 4 were primarily privately owned or church-run (only about one sixth are state-run). Of course, the official statistics that are available about rates of nursery school attendance and sponsorship of nursery schools do not take into account the unregistered or unofficial private day care centers attended by some children. There are also no statistics on the children under age 4 who may be cared for in their own homes by relatives or paid caregivers (a situation that occurs primarily in cities and in upper-middle-class families).

In the words of the profile, "The heterogeneous nature of the system [for children under age 4]. . . is its most significant feature." The scarce public provisions include such variety as day care centers set up by the Ministry of Employment for the use of employed mothers, day care centers at places of work set up by business with state assistance, and preprimary educational programs initiated and supported by municipal trustee boards. In some rural areas, traveling preschools or home-based preschools have developed. In addition to institutional forms of care, the private provisions may also include a few cases of children being cared for in small groups in caregivers' homes (perhaps a continuation of the friendly women's schools).

The profile described the private provisions for children under age 4 as exhibiting great variation in terms of quality: "[The provisions] range from custodial care in questionable conditions to educational programs that are very worthwhile. There are not many worthwhile programs, however, and those that do exist are expensive. Thus many parents have trouble finding a young children's educational center that really inspires their confidence and that they can afford." Noting that "setting up a day care center in Spain is easier than setting up a butcher shop or a bar, in terms of satisfying licensing and regulation requirements," the profile attributed the rapid growth of private centers to increasing demand and "the complete lack of regulations concerning their operations."

As mentioned earlier, Spain is in the process of forging a new identity. In addition to the rapid growth of preprimary services in the last 15 years, other changes have been occurring: extensive migration to the cities in the 1960s and, more recently, gradual improvement of the unattractive rural social conditions that caused this migration; a birthrate drop in the early 1980s to below that needed for generation replacement; an emergence of government policies in support of families — especially of families with employed mothers — in the 1980s; and a gradual assumption by the autonomous communities of responsibilities formerly held by the central government.

This last process, because it is unevenly completed as of now, may account for much of the diversity in preprimary provisions throughout Spain. For example, at the time the profile was written, Spain had no official curriculum for children below school age, although the central Ministry of Education and Science did establish official guidelines in 1981. At the same time, some autonomous communities have developed their own specific preschool curricula. According to the profile, what actually happens in classrooms may ultimately depend on the degree of training of the teacher. Those with some level of specialization are likely to develop innovative programs and be interested in pedagogic techniques; those with little or no training depend more on textbooks and methods that encourage passive learning, focusing on acquiring skills more appropriate for older children.

There are also differences among the autonomous communities regarding how well the demands for preprimary services are being met, regarding the predominance of public versus private preschools (the latter have fewer specialized teachers), and regarding preprimary teacher-pupil ratios (which are higher in the private than in the public sector). When one adds to this the lack of regulation of private providers and the lack of statistics about unlicensed providers, it is no wonder that as recounted in the profile, a 1984 report on preprimary education described "a conglomeration of schools over which there is little control."

At the very time that Spain's profile was being written, a public debate on the education system in Spain was in process. The debate concerned a 1987 ministry proposal suggesting a major change in attitudes toward preprimary education. The proposal would view birth to age 6 as the first (noncompulsory) link in the education chain, emphasizing the *educational* as well as the *care* aspect of all preprimary services. It would divide services into those serving two preprimary age groups: children from birth through age 2; and children aged 3, 4, and 5. This would include expanding state-provided education to include all 3-year-olds (only 16 percent were officially included as of 1986). For children under age 3, the ministry proposed offering support for initiatives of nonprofit groups or cooperatives. The ministry would also introduce improvements in the quality of the services being provided and introduce government-sanctioned regulations (with an inspection system) for all preprimary schools regarding building characteristics, hygiene, staff qualifications, and teacher-pupil ratios. The proposal would favor adoption of teaching methods that encourage active learning and parent participation (a notably missing factor in many Spanish preprimary programs). A new law, to be promulgated by 1989, was the anticipated outcome of the ongoing debate over the proposal.

Jesús Palacios, in concluding Spain's profile, expressed hope that the new law would bring about real change. He also pointed out Spain's need for "more longitudinal research. . . to evaluate the long-term effects of different educational approaches and the differences between children who have experienced only home care and those who have experienced a formal preprimary program."

THAILAND — COORDINATING EFFORTS ON ALL FRONTS

In Thailand, preprimary care and education have a history almost as long that of formal education. Both go back to the late-nineteenth-century reign of King Rama V, who founded the first formal school in the Royal Palace and whose consort Princess Sai Savali built the first orphanage in Thailand. According to the Thai profile by Nittaya Passornsiri, Pusadee Kutintara, and Arrome Suwannapal, all faculty at the school of Educational Studies, Sukhothai Thammathirat Open University, Nonthaburi, the National Education Program 1898, devised during King Rama V's reign, "required that preprimary classes and kindergartens be set up to prepare children for primary education" (1989, pp. 343–363).

As a result of these beginnings, by the start of King Rama VI's reign in 1911, a large number of formal schools had been opened all over the country. As Froebel's and Montessori's methods became known, both private and government-run preprimary programs came into existence, the latter being attached to government primary schools. The start-up of the first private kindergarten classes in 1911 at the famous Wattanawittayalai School marked the beginning of the strong role that the private sector has always played in Thailand's preprimary services.

CONSTITUTIONAL GOVERNMENT — A COMMITMENT TO PREPRIMARY PROGRAMS

After Thailand's change to a constitutional monarchy in 1932, the first constitution upheld the government commitment to preprimary programs by calling for the establishment of kindergartens to prepare children for formal schooling. This led to sending educators to Japan to study their early childhood education and, eventually, to the founding of a "model government kindergarten" in Bangkok in 1940. Gradually, other government 2-year kindergartens were set up, but these were confined mostly to Bangkok and other urban areas.

Since that time, preprimary care and education has spread to other parts of Thailand, and numerous kinds of preprimary services have developed. A series of government reports and national development plans in the 1970s and 1980s emphasized the need for coordinating efforts "on all fronts" — for making the care of the young child the joint responsibility of the family, the community, and the government.

Over the years, government plans variously called for (1) placing responsibility for implementing preprimary programs mainly with local districts and the private sector, but with government supervision; (2) the government providing model kindergartens and relevant research; (3) developing preprimary programs of various types appropriate to local conditions, laying a foundation for the next stage of education; (4) establishing "child nutrition centers" that would provide comprehensive early childhood services and at the same time improve the nutritional conditions of rural children; and (5) setting up cost-effective 1-year preprimary classes annexed to primary schools, with the aim of having at least one in each district.

At the time Thailand's profile was written (1989), the *Sixth National Education Development Plan (1987–1991)* had set a goal of expanding preprimary programs to serve at least 37 percent of 3-, 4-, and 5-year-old children. (About the same time, an expansion program called The Rural Kindergarten was launched, assuring that this goal would be met.) The *Sixth Plan* emphasized giving disadvantaged children more opportunity to receive "readiness training." It also addressed improving the quality of preprimary education in the following ways: developing service models appropriate to local conditions, improving methodology in accordance with the psychology of child development, upgrading health and nutrition standards, and improving supervision and evaluation. The *Sixth Plan* stated clearly that different agencies should coordinate and cooperate, so that services could effectively be given to children throughout the country.

"Coordination and cooperation" are indeed the key to Thailand's early childhood care and education future, since types and sponsors of programs have proliferated over time. Presently, preprimary services continue to be both government-run and private, as they have been from early times. Private sponsors include voluntary or nonprofit councils, associations, and foundations; government sponsors include three different kinds of local government and four different central-government ministries: Education, the Interior, Public Health, and University Affairs. Within these ministries, 10 different operating departments are involved.

The types of preprimary programs offered by this multitude of sponsors fall into three major categories:

1. Two-year (or 3-year) formal education in kindergarten for children aged 4 to 6 (age 7 is compulsory school-age).
2. One-year preprimary classes annexed to primary schools for children aged 5 to 6.

3. Nonformal education in centers of various types, such as child development centers, child nutrition centers, day care centers, and child care centers. In these centers, the children's ages can range from birth to 7 years.

In the 1980s, the number of Thai children enrolled in preprimary institutions grew rapidly in comparison with growth of the preschool-aged population. Though the population of children 3 to 6 years old increased by only 3 percent, preprimary enrollment more than tripled between 1979 and 1987. The number of preprimary institutions almost quadrupled in that time. As in many other countries, Thai families' needs for out-of-home care and education programs are increasing as female labor force participation (at 65 percent in 1985) increases and as family structure changes from extended to nuclear.

An analysis of types and sponsors of institutions, by regions, indicates that government-sponsored services are found primarily outside of Bangkok. Preprimary children in Bangkok are served mainly by private kindergartens and private day care centers. Children in areas outside of Bangkok are served mainly by child development centers, child nutrition centers, and preprimary classes annexed to primary schools.

PROBLEMS INVOLVED IN A MULTISPONSORED SYSTEM

Thailand's variety of programs and sponsors presents many-faceted problems. The profile summarized the problems as follows:

1. Having so many different agencies sponsoring programs means that programs sometimes have conflicting objectives, sometimes duplicate services, sometimes provide uneven service-coverage.
2. The quality of services offered varies widely because programs have different funding arrangements, different staff-training arrangements, different guidelines. In some cases, a lack of systematic supervision also affects quality.
3. The training of preprimary personnel needs improvement. Existing college and university preservice training needs to be more practical. Large numbers of untrained child care workers in the rural programs need inservice training. Since, beginning in 1986, the government has been adding 2,000 new preprimary classes a year, more qualified preprimary teachers are needed.

4. Although the government's view of early education has, over the years, changed from an emphasis on formal teaching to an emphasis on promoting the child's total development, this change in emphasis is not always reflected in what actually happens in the classroom. Many caregivers and teachers succumb to parental pressure, or to their own lack of training in preprimary methods, and teach "the three Rs."

5. There is inequality of educational opportunity at the preprimary level, not only because of variations in program quality but also because of the lack of programs or lack of program affordability for so many children. According to the profile, "The government has invested more in children with the best opportunities, with the poor having to pay more than the rich because of the differing degrees of government support for various types of preprimary schools and centers."

Undaunted by these problems, Thailand is clearly in the midst of an ambitious preprimary expansion program. Participation in the IEA Preprimary Project, with the data it produces, may help Thailand with the task of "coordinating efforts on all fronts."

THE UNITED STATES — A DECENTRALIZED SYSTEM

The United States, one of the largest and most populous of the nations taking part in Phase 1 of the IEA Preprimary Project, also has one of the most decentralized systems of early childhood care and education. The factors leading to the development of this kind of a system were described in the profile written by Patricia P. Olmsted, Research Associate at the High/Scope Educational Research Foundation, Ypsilanti, Michigan (1989, pp. 365–400).

HOW TWO STRANDS HAVE DEVELOPED

As in many other countries, preprimary provisions in the U.S. have developed in response to children's care and school-preparation needs. But the

U.S. profile also cited two strong American beliefs that have influenced the course of provision development: The first is a belief that childrearing is the private province of family members (especially the mother), to be carried out, in a pluralistic society, as each family sees fit. The second is a belief that personal fulfillment comes through work (increasingly, in modern society, work for pay, outside the home). The tension created by these two beliefs has heightened over the years as more and more American mothers, for personal or economic reasons, have entered the labor force. The tension manifests itself in the variety of arrangements families make for child care (often informal, family-based arrangements) and in the ongoing controversy over who (family, community, national government) should be responsible for child care.

Having explained this background, the U.S. profile traced the history of "two strands" of early childhood services. The first strand, with roots in a social welfare tradition, concerns the provision of care for young children, particularly for those from poor and troubled families. The second strand, with roots in the German kindergarten movement, concerns the provision of early education.

The care strand began after America's early-nineteenth-century flood of immigration. It took the form of "day nurseries" sponsored by philanthropic agencies in the mid- to late-1800s. These were to protect "day orphans" while their mothers worked. Concentrating mainly on physical care, the nurseries also had a strong concern for children's moral care and proper upbringing.

The beginnings of the second strand, early childhood education, can be traced to the mid-nineteenth-century development of Froebel's kindergarten. Though American *kindergartens*, with their emphasis on learning through play, existed from Froebel's time on, they increased rapidly in the early twentieth century, eventually becoming widely accepted as a 1-year school-preparatory program attached to primary schools. Today, for most American 5-year-olds, a year of kindergarten precedes entry into first grade at age 6.

Meanwhile, after the early-twentieth-century development of Maria Montessori's infant schools (in Italy) and Rachel and Margaret McMillan's nursery schools (in England), the American *nursery school* for 3- and 4-year-olds made its appearance by the 1920s. The educational methods used in most of these nursery schools were based on the ideas of Froebel or Montessori or the McMillans. By the 1930s, significant numbers of upper- and middle-class families were enrolling their young children in part-day, private nursery school programs.

The Strands Begin to Merge — Government Steps In

The care and education strands first merged when the Great Depression of the 1930s gave birth to almost 2,000 government-supported nursery school programs, authorized under the Work Projects Administration (WPA) to provide jobs for unemployed teachers. Located in public schools, these programs, which lasted until WPA funds ran out, provided year-round all-day care with educational components. Another instance of federal involvement in preprimary provision occurred during World War II, when Congress passed the Lanham Act to provide matching funds for states to establish day care centers and nursery schools for families involved in the defense industry. This program was largely dismantled at the end of the war.

The 1960s brought renewed interest in early care and education and a closer meshing of the two strands. Along with the increasing labor force participation of women (necessitating more child care programs for all families, not just for poor or troubled families) there was also an academic "rediscovery" of early childhood education. In particular, several well-known studies of the effectiveness of early childhood education for disadvantaged children were launched. This decade saw the beginning of the federally funded Head Start program to provide early education for children from low-income families.

The Last Two Decades — A "Family-Centered Approach"

Throughout the 1970s, families' needs for early care and education increased as more mothers of young children continued to enter the labor force and as more families saw early education programs as beneficial for their children. However, in this decade a congressional bill that would have established a national child care program for the first time in the United States was vetoed by President Richard Nixon, who opposed "[committing] the moral authority of the national government to the side of communal approaches of childrearing over against the family-centered approach."

The 1980s witnessed three trends in the federal government's role regarding early childhood provisions: *decentralization* (federal funding cutbacks and elimination of matching-fund requirements for states); *pri-*

vatization (open support for a diverse child care market through employer incentives, easing of requirements for private providers, and tax benefits to families); *deregulation* (failure to enact federal guidelines for child care services, thereby leaving regulation up to individual states). The result of these policy trends has been a highly decentralized system of early childhood care and education services, with federal, state, local, and private (for-profit and nonprofit) providers. There is considerable variation among the 50 states as to relative state and federal funding levels, regulations and licensing standards, and populations served. Also, a large variety of forms of child care and education exist, with some states continuing a two-strand system and others blending the care and education strands into one.

Federal funding of services, in keeping with a national policy of non-interference in family affairs, has primarily targeted families with special needs or families at risk because of economic or social circumstances. Funding policies that do exist are intended to promote family choice in the selection of child care and to encourage the development of many forms of services. These policies are a combination of social benefits for specific types of low-income families, tax benefits for families paying income taxes (i.e., with parents employed), direct services for specific children (e.g., Project Head Start for children from low-income families), and tax incentives for employers (to provide care or to provide flexible benefit plans that cover child care).[5]

THE VARIETY OF CARE/EDUCATION ARRANGEMENTS

As already mentioned, U.S. families use numerous types of early childhood care and education arrangements, both formal and informal. The major types are these:

- Care in the child's own home by a relative or nonrelative
- Care in another home by a relative
- Family day care homes (care by a nonrelative, on a regular basis, in the caregiver's home — including everything from informal, shared-caregiving agreements between friends to formal licensed homes)
- Part-day educational programs (large-group, institutionally based, usually with a curriculum and scheduled activities during half-day sessions, 5 days per week)

- Child care centers (large-group care that may be private for-profit, private nonprofit, publicly operated, parent-cooperative, or employer-provided)

The profile's statistics concerning families' use of these various forms of care and education were arrived at by combining information from "a piecemeal effort" of data collecting. The resulting statistics were these: In 1987, slightly more than half of U.S. 3- and 4-year-olds had mothers active in the labor force. Also, about a third of U.S. 3- and 4-year-olds were in institutional education or care programs, but almost half of these children had mothers who were *not* employed. Of employed mothers, almost half chose to entrust their 3- and 4-year-olds to in-home care, relative care, or a family day care home. (The extent to which combinations of the various types of care are used by families and the extent to which parents' care and education choices reflect family income, family values, or availability of services are information to be determined by data from the IEA Preprimary Project.)

Leaving responsibilities up to states has produced not only a great variety of program types but also much state-to-state variation in licensing, staff-training requirements, and program requirements (for staff-child ratios, space, curriculum). For family day care, in particular, there are states that lack home licensing requirements and states that require no experience or education of providers. Staff wages vary, with the highest being paid to teachers in educational programs attached to public schools and the lowest, to workers in day care centers and family day care homes (who also have the lowest educational requirements). These latter two groups — in day care centers and family day care homes — understandably have the highest staff turnover.

Overall, with all this variety, U.S. parents have few assurances regarding the quality of care in many of the settings available to them. Furthermore, in such a decentralized system, many families must bear the responsibility for locating and supporting the services for their own children. As the early childhood care and education system continues to grow, U.S. policymakers need to step back to assess whether the system is meeting the needs of young children and their families, whether it is viable as an employment system for adults, and whether it relates as well as it might to other systems, such as employment and education. Most important, Americans need to assess the impact of the system on the children it is serving.

ENDNOTES

1. In the summary of each country's profile, all direct quotes may be found within the pages indicated for that country's profile.

2. As of this writing, Finland's official statistics for 1988 indicated the existence of 200,000 day care places.

3. As of this writing, the parliament has passed legislation for 1996 guaranteeing the child's right to a place in kindergarten.

4. As of this writing, steps have been taken to improve the teacher-child ratio, but unification of the two sectors still awaits action.

5. Since the writing of the U.S. profile, further federal actions relating to early childhood have included (1) increasing funding to states for the provision of child care for low- and moderate-income families and for the improvement of quality and availability of services and (2) increasing funding for Head Start (which currently serves only a portion of needy children). Stopping short of mandating standards in federally funded programs, the most recent national legislation continues to give individual states most of the responsibility for the design, implementation, and regulation of early childhood programs.

REFERENCES

Bairrão, J., Barbosa, M., Borges, I., Cruz, O., & Macedo-Pinto, I. (1989). Care and education for children under age 6 in Portugal. In P. P. Olmsted & D. P. Weikart (Eds.), *How nations serve young children: Profiles of child care and education in 14 countries* (pp. 273–302). Ypsilanti, MI: High/Scope Press.

Delhaxhe, A. (1989). Early childhood care and education in Belgium. In P. P. Olmsted & D. P. Weikart (Eds.), *How nations serve young children: Profiles of child care and education in 14 countries* (pp. 13–37). Ypsilanti, MI: High/Scope Press.

Ojala, M. (1989). Early childhood training, care, and education in Finland. In P. P. Olmsted & D. P. Weikart (Eds.), *How nations serve young children: Profiles of child care and education in 14 countries* (pp. 87–118). Ypsilanti, MI: High/Scope Press.

Olmsted, P. P. (1989). Early childhood care and education in the United States. In P. P. Olmsted & D. P. Weikart (Eds.), *How nations serve young children:*

Profiles of child care and education in 14 countries (pp. 365–400). Ypsilanti, MI: High/Scope Press.

Olmsted, P. P. & Weikart, D. P. (Eds.). (1989). *How nations serve young children: Profiles of child care and education in 14 countries.* Ypsilanti, MI: High/Scope Press.

Onibokun, O. M. (1989). Early childhood care and education in Nigeria. In P. P. Olmsted & D. P. Weikart (Eds,). *How nations serve young children: Profiles of child care and education in 14 countries* (pp. 219–240). Ypsilanti, MI: High/Scope Press.

Opper, S. (1989). Child care and early education in Hong Kong. In P. P. Olmsted & D. P. Weikart (Eds.), *How nations serve young children: Profiles of child care and education in 14 countries* (pp. 119–142). Ypsilanti, MI: High/Scope Press.

Palacios, J. (1989). Child care and early education in Spain. In P. P. Olmsted & D. P. Weikart (Eds.), *How nations serve young children: Profiles of child care and education in 14 countries* (pp. 303–341). Ypsilanti, MI: High/Scope Press.

Passornsiri, N., Kutintara, P., & Suwannapal, A. (1989). Child care and early education in Thailand. In P. P. Olmsted & D. P. Weikart (Eds.), *How nations serve young children: Profiles of child care and education in 14 countries* (pp. 343–363). Ypsilanti, MI: High/Scope Press.

Pistillo, F. (1989). Preprimary education and care in Italy. In P. P. Olmsted & D. P. Weikart (Eds.), *How nations serve young children: Profiles of child care and education in 14 countries* (pp. 151–202). Ypsilanti, MI: High/Scope Press.

Shi, H. Z. (1989). Young children's care and education in the People's Republic of China. In P. P. Olmsted & D. P. Weikart (Eds.), *How nations serve young children: Profiles of child care and education in 14 countries* (pp. 241–254). Ypsilanti, MI: High/Scope Press.

Tietze, W., Rossbach, H.-G., & Ufermann, K. (1989). Child care and early education in the Federal Republic of Germany. In P. P. Olmsted & D. P. Weikart (Eds.), *How nations serve young children: Profiles of child care and education in 14 countries* (pp. 39–85). Ypsilanti, MI: High/Scope Press.

III
METHODOLOGY OF THE
PHASE 1 STUDY

Patricia P. Olmsted, *Senior Research Associate*
High/Scope Educational Research Foundation
Ypsilanti, Michigan

With **Arlette Delhaxhe,** Belgium; **Shi Hui Zhong,** China; **Mikko Ojala,** Finland; **Hans-Günther Rossbach,** Germany; **Sylvia Opper,** Hong Kong; **Lucio Pusci,** Italy; **Olayemi Onibokun,** Nigeria; **Joaquim Bairrão,** Portugal; **Jesús Palacios,** Spain; **Nittaya Passornsiri,** Thailand; **Helena Hoas,** United States

As described in Chapter 1, the IEA Preprimary Project (IEA/PPP) is a cross-national three-phase study investigating the nature, quality, and effects of the experiences of children prior to formal schooling. The major objectives of Phase 1 of the project were (1) to develop a representative picture of the variety of care and education settings attended by 4-year-old children in each of the participating countries; (2) to examine certain basic features of each country's early childhood settings; (3) to explore, in each country, the relationships between use of early childhood settings and family characteristics; and (4) to describe the daily care patterns for 4-year-old children in each country.

To achieve these four objectives, Phase 1 researchers used household survey techniques to collect data directly from parents (or guardians) about their use or nonuse of extraparental care or education services for their 4-year-old children. This chapter presents general information about the Phase 1 sampling plans and data collection procedures, and it describes and summarizes the specific methodology used by each of the 11 countries taking part in Phase 1.

GENERAL SAMPLING INFORMATION

THE INTERNATIONAL SAMPLING REFEREE

Leslie Kish serves as international sampling referee for the IEA Preprimary Project. Dr. Kish is a professor emeritus at the University of Michigan, where he was a founder of the Institute for Social Research. He is the author of *Survey Sampling* (1965) and *Statistical Design for Research* (1987). In the past he has served as president of the American Statistical Association (1977) and of the International Association of Survey Statisticians (1983–85). In his role as sampling referee for the IEA/PPP, Dr. Kish worked closely with the ICC in supervising the preparation of the project's sampling documents, monitoring the development of national sampling plans, and granting formal approval of each national plan.

THE TARGET POPULATION

The target population for Phase 1 sample selection was defined as children 3½ to 4½ years old (4 years ± 6 months) at the time of Phase 1 data collection (i.e., at the time of the interview with each child's parent/guardian). In each participating country, the target population excluded children living out-of-country or in institutions, as well as children with serious physical or mental handicaps. In most participating countries, the 4 years ± 6 months age-range takes in the child's last full year before entry into a formal school environment; it is also the age-range for which there is the widest variety of early childhood care and education services. However, for funding reasons, IEA/PPP researchers in Hong Kong found it necessary to begin their project operations before determination of this international target age-range. Thus the range used for sample selection in Hong Kong was 4 to 5 years of age.

SAMPLE SELECTION

In general, in each participating nation, researchers hoped to identify a probability sample of children in the target age-range. However, the sampling referee and the ICC faced several challenges in attempting to obtain probability samples while maintaining high sampling standards. Only a few of these challenges are noted here: First, educational researchers having little or no national survey sampling experience or training would be carrying out the sampling operations. Second, since most national research teams had limited resources, national samples would have to be small — generally between 400 and 1,000 children; the challenge would come in spreading these small samples over large populations of households. Finally, since generally only 4 to 10 percent of households contain a 4-year-old child, researchers in some countries would have to screen large numbers of households to find the relatively small proportion with 4-year-old children.

A sampling plan for each country

Generally, in cross-national household survey studies, constructing *similar* sample frames for all participating countries is not attempted, because the procedure would be prohibitively expensive and at the same time counterproductive, in light of the different sources of population information available in various countries. In the IEA/PPP, the International Coordinating Center (ICC) and the sampling referee assisted each National Research Coordinator (NRC) in custom-designing a national sampling plan that would produce a probability sample of children. In doing so they used the most-recent, most-accurate sources of population information that each country had available.

As Dr. Kish noted in the *IEA/PPP Phase 1 Interim Sampling Report* (Weikart, Kish, & Olmsted, 1988), "We want to emphasize that flexibility in sample design in comparative and cooperative studies is permissible; it is also desirable, in order to better utilize the distinct resources and selection frames to be found in the participating countries. It is common to use distinct designs for separate domains, even within single countries" (p. 4). In each country, the sampling referee required a probability sample that was as close to perfect as local conditions would allow. The procedures followed in this study were similar to those followed in other international comparative studies that have allowed for different sample designs but used standardized definitions of variables and populations (e.g., the World Fertility Survey).

The Sampling Questionnaire

To assist NRCs in understanding general sampling issues, locating sources of population information, and developing a proposed sampling plan, the ICC, with the help of Dr. Kish, designed an IEA/PPP Phase 1 Sampling Questionnaire (Olmsted, Kish, & Weikart, 1987). The questionnaire, which used a question-and-answer format with skip patterns to accommodate the variety of situations found in the participating countries, was based on two of the sampling referee's published works (Kish, 1965, 1987). The major sections of the questionnaire covered the following topics: sample size and subpopulations of special interest, existing sets of survey data, population registers, and national census data.

To complete the sample-size section of the Sampling Questionnaire, each NRC obtained national population information, considered subpopulations of special interest (e.g., regional or ethnic subgroups), considered the resources available for Phase 1 of the IEA/PPP, and estimated a proposed sample size. To complete the remaining three sections of the questionnaire (on existing sets of survey data, population registers, national census data), the NRC contacted the national statistical office, research organizations, and other agencies, to determine the existence and availability of various types of information that might be useful for developing the sampling plan or for selecting the sample. Using the information collected in completing the Sampling Questionnaire, the NRC then developed a proposed national sampling plan. After reviewing this proposed plan the ICC and the sampling referee, together with the NRC, determined a proposed sample design and a proposed sample size that would both be feasible and produce sufficient data to meet specified confidence limits for the estimation of population values.

To accompany the Sampling Questionnaire, the ICC developed a supplementary-information document that included (1) definitions of sampling terminology, (2) proposed sampling designs, and (3) special considerations (e.g., types of recently conducted surveys that might provide sample frames useful for the IEA/PPP Phase 1 study). Members of the IEA Technical Advisory Committee reviewed the IEA/PPP Phase 1 Sampling Questionnaire (Document No. IEA/PPP/20) and the supplementary-information document (Document No. IEA/PPP/21), and the IEA General Assembly approved the documents in September 1987.

Weighting the data

Although the aim of each national sampling design was equal probability of selection, departures from equal probability occurred in a few nations for various reasons. However, in each country where this happened, the NRC provided the probabilities of selection for every case, enabling the ICC to assign weights to individual cases and examine weighted versus unweighted findings. After the sampling referee reviewed the unweighted and weighted results for several key variables, he recommended whether weighting should be used in calculating the Phase 1 results. The three major reasons for weighting the data of a few countries were these: (1) selection of fixed-size samples (of children) from unequal-sized units (villages, regions), (2) unequal response rates, and (3) a need to obtain national estimates from provincial estimates.

GENERAL DATA COLLECTION INFORMATION

THE PARENT/GUARDIAN INTERVIEW

Phase 1 employed a 50-minute Parent/Guardian Interview (P/G Interview) to collect information about families' use or nonuse of early childhood care and education services (the P/G Interview, which is Document No. IEA/PPP/31, is in Appendix B). A major portion of the interview concerned the care or education arrangements parents made for their 4-year-olds during a typical week. Interviewers asked parents why they selected certain care or education settings, what problems they encountered in those settings, and how satisfied they were with each setting. Additional information collected concerned what parents paid for care or education arrangements, what distances children had to travel to their various settings, and what means of transportation they used. The P/G Interview also asked questions about the family background, including parental education levels and occupations, living accommodations, and household composition.

Another part of the interview, the daily routine chart, asked parents for a detailed description of a typical 24-hour day in their child's life, including the child's whereabouts and caregiver(s) throughout the day previous to the interview. (Some countries — Belgium, Finland, Germany, and Spain — formatted this part of the interview into a Daily Routine Booklet, which children carried with them for a day or a week to have various caregivers "log into" throughout the day.) This daily routine chart or booklet sought to get at the typical "care patterns" children experienced in each country.

Researchers from each participating country contributed to the development of the P/G Interview by indicating areas of interest or by suggesting specific questions. One objective of involving the NRCs in the development was to design an instrument that would (1) provide sufficient information about the use of early childhood care and education services within each participating country and (2) allow for cross-national comparisons of various types of information. The challenge, then, was to create an instrument that would address issues of national as well as international concern without overburdening every country's interview with questions relevant to only one or a few of the countries. Researchers met this challenge by designating three types of interview items: *international core* items, *international option* items, and *national option* items.

International core items

The international core items were those questions that every country participating in the project included in its P/G Interview. Core items were, by definition, questions of cross-national interest. For a question to be designated an international core item, every participating country had to indicate that the item was nationally relevant. For example, all the participating countries expressed interest in learning more about the range of formal and informal care or education arrangements families make for their 4-year-old children. Therefore, the core items included questions about the types of early childhood care or education services families used; the characteristics of those services (e.g., cost, distance from home, problems encountered); parents' reasons for making their particular arrangement(s) for the care or education of their child; the range of services offered by the child's major extraparental caregiver; and the extent of parental involvement in the child's care setting. In addition, the core items included questions about household composition (e.g., the numbers and ages of the household's adults and children) and about family-background characteristics (e.g., parental education, occupation, income). Also designated as core items were the questions about the child's care pattern, or daily routine (the child's whereabouts and caregivers for a typical 24-hour period). A country could exclude a core item from its version of the P/G Interview only if the item was one that would produce a uniform response across the entire national sample (e.g., if every family in the sample would answer yes to having a source of light in their home, or if every family in the national sample would answer yes to having a private kitchen). Also, if necessary, a country could modify a core item's phrasing to clarify it or make it culturally appropriate. Similarly, where necessary, a country could use alternative methods to obtain some of the information requested in core items, as will be explained later in the discussion of Hong Kong's methodology.

International option items

In addition to the core items, the ICC also developed some questions that many but not all countries considered relevant. These were designated as *international option items*. For example, several international option items asked parents about types of health examinations their child may have had. These questions were excluded by a few countries simply to limit the length of the interview procedure. Each country could determine whether to include a specific international option item, depending on the appropriateness or applicability of the item.

National option items

Several countries, on their own, developed and formatted additional items for their version of the P/G Interview. These were designated as *national option items*. Since each such item was unique to a specific country, this chapter will not include a discussion of the national option items.

Pilot-testing of the international P/G Interview

After the countries had agreed on the questions to include in the international interview instrument and designated each question as an international core item or an international option item, the ICC prepared the final international instrument, based on the countries' decisions. The ICC then conducted two forms of pilot-testing on the international instrument.

First, to determine the stability of responses across time, on two separate occasions 2 weeks apart, ICC staff interviewed 25 families with children between the ages of 3 and 5 years. (This procedure is similar to the test-retest method of measuring reliability.) The 25 families varied with respect to family structure, annual household income, family size, use of early childhood services, and so forth. They were from both rural and urban areas in southeastern Michigan. For each of 10 P/G Interview items for which a respondent's answers would be expected to remain the same over the two-week interval (e.g., questions about annual household income, or about parental years of full-time education), ICC staff calculated the percentage of families whose answers agreed on the two separate occasions. The results were as follows: Of the 10 items, 1 item produced 100 percent agreement, 5 items produced 90–99 percent agreement, and 4 items produced 80–89 percent agreement. Since 80 percent agreement was considered adequate, ICC staff deemed the items to have sufficient stability.

Second, the ICC pilot-tested the daily-routine questioning procedure, to insure that parents' recollections of their 4-year-old child's whereabouts and care providers on the day previous to the interview would be sufficiently accurate to make this an appropriate data-collection procedure. The method used for the pilot test involved an ICC staff member observing 10 four-year-old children for a minimum of 6 hours each during a single day and recording all changes of caregivers, settings, and social context (i.e., the number of other adults and children present) that each child experienced. The following day, an ICC staff member administered the P/G Interview to each child's family and compared the information parents provided in the instrument's daily routine chart with the observations of the previous day. The results indicated that parents' recollections were extremely accurate concerning the caregivers and settings for their children.

Preparation of the national P/G Interview instruments

After developing the national option items that they wanted to add to the international core and option items, project staff in each country prepared their national P/G Interview instruments. National researchers then conducted within-country pilot tests to assess the clarity, cultural appropriateness, and usefulness of the national instrument. To insure that the instrument would be effective across all populations in the sample areas, most countries selected pilot-test families from geographically dispersed areas. Some countries conducted a two- or three-stage pilot test, making revisions in the instrument after each stage. The sample sizes for the these pilot tests ranged from 25 to 200.

Procedures for Data Collection

The data collection period

The time span for data collection was from October 1987 to September 1989; in general, countries collected most of their data between May and November of 1988. The data collection period differed from country to country because of such factors as availability of funds, time constraints governing the use of funds, and holiday and seasonal schedules.

Selection of interviewers

Each country was responsible for selecting its own interviewers. As a result, the criteria for interviewer selection varied according to the specific characteristics that national project staff considered important. Generally the interviewers were university students or graduates, preprimary teachers or caregivers, or persons with prior experience in conducting surveys. In many countries, a person's level of education was the major factor influencing his or her selection as an interviewer, while in a few countries, previous experience with research was the major factor. Several countries also considered familiarity with the care or education settings, with children and families, or with a specific geographical area as an important selection criterion.

Training of interviewers

Since each country developed its own interviewer training methods and materials, the duration and type of training varied from country to country. In almost every country, national project staff conducted the interviewer training sessions. Topics addressed during training included the goals and design of the study; the various sections of the P/G Interview; administration of the P/G Interview (e.g., how to contact families, how to interview, how to handle potential problems); and the role of the interviewer/data collector. Almost all countries developed a training or instruction manual for the interviews, and most used a combination of the following methods along with the manual: examination of the interview instrument, practice interviews, training videotapes, role play, trial runs of the interview with local families, and group discussion. In some countries the training was a two-stage process wherein project staff trained several interviewers, who subsequently returned to local areas and recruited and trained additional interviewers.

Preparation of Data for Analysis

For countries to use in coding their P/G Interview data, the ICC prepared and distributed a coding manual for the international core items and international option items. In addition, ICC staff developed and distributed guidelines for cleaning the data, building data files, and sending the data to the ICC. Using these materials, national project staff coded their interview data, built a complete raw data file, cleaned the data, and transmitted it to the ICC.

When the ICC received a set of data from a country, to verify the correctness of the data, the data manager examined the descriptive statistics for a large number of major variables. If the data manager detected errors in a data set (e.g., missing data or miscoded data), the ICC requested additional information from the NRC and, as necessary, corrected the data set. After checking (and, if necessary, correcting) a data set, the data manager prepared weighted and unweighted printouts for a basic set of 20 variables, for examination by the sampling referee. Three project participants — China (PRC), Hong Kong, and Nigeria — used weighted data for analysis.[1]

METHODOLOGY IN SPECIFIC NATIONS

Table 3.1 summarizes various types of information about the national sampling plans, including the achieved sample sizes, sample designs, primary sampling units, and response rates. Table 3.2 summarizes information about the data collection procedures used by various nations. In addition, brief narrative descriptions of each country's sampling plan and data collection procedures are presented in the remainder of this chapter.

SAMPLING AND DATA COLLECTION IN BELGIUM (FR.)

In French-speaking Belgium the target population included all nonhandicapped children who were between the ages of 3½ and 4½ and living at home. Using two-stage cluster sampling and PPS (probability proportional to size) sampling procedures, researchers first selected 106 PSUs (primary sampling units), which fell into 73 communes (from a total of 279 communes). Then, for each PSU, researchers randomly selected 4 children for the primary sample and 4 children for replacements.

The Belgian sampling frame for the selection of communes consisted of documents from the National Institute of Statistics. The sampling frame for selection of children consisted of commune-level, index card files of inhabitants, which are updated regularly.

Belgium's overall response rate was only 67 percent, with approximately half of nonresponses due to refusals. The achieved sample size was 424. Because of the large number of nonresponses and the differences in nonresponse rates among communes, the sample was not entirely self-weighting. Comparisons between weighted and unweighted statistics for several variables revealed no appreciable differences, and therefore, unweighted results were recommended by the sampling referee (Delhaxhe & Hindryckx, 1989).

The main data collection instrument used in Belgium was the P/G

Table 3.1 Characteristics of national sampling plans

Country/ Territory	Sample Design	Primary Sampling Units	Response Rate %	Refusal Rate %	Achieved Sample Size, N	Weighted Data
Belgium (Fr.)	Two-stage cluster with PPS	73 communes	67	18	424	No
China (PRC)	Multistage stratified cluster with PPS	10 provinces	99	0	12,835	Yes
Finland	Two-stage stratified cluster with PPS	80 units in 68 countries	85	5	576	No
Germany (FRG)[a]	Multistage cluster with PPS	525 electoral districts	67	15	509	No
Hong Kong	Multistage stratified cluster with PPS	65 early childhood facilities	95	0	947	Yes
Italy	Multistage stratified cluster with PPS	50 communes	85	7	1,000	No
Nigeria	Multistage stratified cluster with PPS	56 enumeration areas	95[b]	0	1,295	Yes
Portugal	Two-stage stratified cluster with PPS	76 units in 57 counties	76	3	581	No
Spain	Two-stage cluster with PPS	160 units in 45 provinces	29	35	480	No
Thailand	Multistage stratified cluster with PPS	38 units in 33 provinces	99	0	2,466	No
United States	Judgment sites with PPS within each	11 geographical locations[c]	85	6	432	No

[a]The study was conducted before unification of the Federal Republic (FRG) with the German Democratic Republic.

[b]Estimate is based on similar surveys conducted by the Federal Office of Statistics in Nigeria (agency conducting this survey).

[c]Not true PSUs, but included in table for general information.

Interview. The international option items Belgium added included questions relating to the degree of parental satisfaction with the care and education services their child received and to the child's health status. Researchers pilot-tested the P/G Interview by conducting 90 interviews. The pilot test made possible an analysis of (1) the content of the interview (to determine where adaptations were needed), (2) the English-to-French translation of items, and (3) the clarity of the interviewer's instructions to the respondents.

Belgium's interviewers were students in the field of psychology or of education, persons hired part-time for this job, and "job-workers" (generally, unemployed friends, former students, or relatives of the researchers). All interviewers had a high level of education, and the majority were 20 to 25 years of age. Their training consisted of two 3-hour group sessions conducted by a researcher. During these sessions, interviewers learned the goals and expected uses of the research and examined the P/G Interview in detail, with attention to the sections that the pilot study had revealed to be of particular importance. After each interviewer conducted a trial run with parents of a 4-year-old, the results were discussed in one of the group sessions.

The Belgian interviewers collected Phase 1 data in the French-speaking Community of Belgium between December 1987 and January 1989. They administered the P/G Interview face to face, primarily in the respondents' homes, and recorded all responses in writing. National project staff maintained contact with all interviewers by phone, mail, or in person. Project staff reviewed a sample of the completed questionnaires to assess the quality of the data collected (Hindryckx & Delhaxhe, 1989).

Sampling and Data Collection in China (PRC)

China's target population included all nonhandicapped children who were in the target age-range and living at home. First, national project researchers formed 10 strata from the 30 provinces by combining economic, cultural, and geographic information, and then they selected 1 province (PSU) from each stratum. Using multistage stratified cluster sampling, within each province chosen, the statisticians used PPS sampling procedures to select 10 urban areas (secondary sampling units, or SSUs) and 10 rural areas (SSUs).

In each urban SSU chosen, the sampling frame for selecting children

Table 3.2 National data collection procedures

Country/ Territory	Data Collection Dates	Pilot Test Sample	Data Collectors Characteristics	Training	Data Collection Method
Belgium (Fr.)	Dec. 1987–Jan. 1989	90 families	College students	Two 3-hour sessions, group meetings, practice interviews	Face to face
China (PRC)	Oct. 1987–July 1988	200 families	Early childhood education officers from 10 provinces ($N = 1,000$)	7–9 days, group meetings, practice interviews, examination	Face to face
Finland	Sept. 1988–Sept. 1989	31 families	2nd- and 3rd-year students from 12 colleges ($N = 145$)	8 hours, discussions, role-play techniques	Face to face
Germany (FRG)	May 1988–Oct. 1988	88 families	Employees of survey research institute	Conducted by survey research institute and IEA/PPP staff	Face to face, written (few)
Hong Kong	Oct. 1987–June 1988	50 families	Preschool teachers and child care workers ($N = 220$)	4-hour session, discussions	Face to face, written
Italy	May 1988–Nov. 1988	50 families	Teachers or college graduates ($N = 136$)	3-day course, discussions, role play, practice interviews	Face to face

Table 3.2 National data collection procedures (continued)

Country/ Territory	Data Collection Dates	Pilot Test Sample	Data Collectors		Data Collection Method
			Characteristics	Training	
Nigeria	Oct. 1988–Nov. 1988	40 families	Federal Office of Statistics employees	4-hour workshop, discussions, role-play techniques	Face to face
Portugal	April 1988–June 1988	35 families	College graduates (N = 34)	Two 1-day sessions, discussions, practice interviews	Face to face
Spain	May 1989–June 1989	30 families	Persons with 2 or more years of college	6 to 8 hours, discussions, practice interviews	Face to face
Thailand	March 1989–July 1989	52 families	Health care workers, teachers, and college faculty (N = 118)	3-day seminar, discussions, practice interviews	Face to face
United States	Oct. 1988–Aug. 1989	25 families	Persons with 1 or more years of college	2-day workshop, discussions, role play, practice interviews	Face to face, telephone

was the set of citizen registers that are maintained at police stations and updated regularly. The researchers used computer procedures to randomly select 400 target children from the many citizen registers that covered the urban areas within a given province. For each rural SSU chosen, statisticians selected 68 towns and townships, using PPS sampling procedures. For each town selected, they randomly selected 20 registration books from the complete set of citizen registers and then randomly chose 13 children from these books for the primary sample and 7 additional children for replacements. For each township selected, project staff randomly chose 4 villages and then, using random-walk procedures, selected 13 target children from across these villages. The final proposed sample for China consisted of 12,840 children from 10 provinces, including 4,000 from urban and 8,840 from rural areas.

China's overall response rate was 99 percent, and the final achieved sample size was 12,835. Because the sample was not entirely self-weighting, weights were computed for each case by combining the probabilities of the 10 provinces with the probabilities in two stages of (1) selecting urban areas, towns, and townships and (2) selecting children within them. For national results, the 10 provincial results were weighted by populations of 4-year-olds in the respective strata (Shi, 1989b).

Chinese researchers used the international core P/G Interview to collect Phase 1 data. Because of the magnitude of their data collection project, the researchers chose to take full advantage of the opportunity it afforded to study issues of national interest as well as issues of interest to the IEA/PPP. Thus, China's interview instrument contained many national option items (e.g., questions about parents' attitudes toward the sex of their child and about parents' expectations for their child). Chinese researchers conducted a pilot test of their version of the P/G Interview with 200 families from several geographical areas of the country.

In 1987 project staff set up a national research center in Beijing and nine other provincial research centers to train interviewers and collect data. The NRC and two members of the technical group of the national research center conducted a trial training-session in Beijing, after which training was conducted for data collectors in the remaining nine provinces.

Interviewers were high-level early childhood education officers (at or above the level of the county board of education) or kindergarten head teachers or administrators. Other interviewer qualifications included completion of at least junior middle school, interest in early childhood education and educational research, and a certificate from the national research center stating that one's work met required standards. Before training, researchers videotaped a properly conducted interview and distributed the tapes and accompanying instructions to each of the 10 provinces. Approximately 1,000 interviewers (60 to 120 per province) attended 7 to 9 days of training. Besides the videotapes, training included a highly detailed manual (explaining the P/G Interview, administration procedures, and solutions to potential problems); demonstrations of proper interviewing techniques; practice interviews and tests; an examination; and, in some provinces, field practice after the examination.

China's interviewers collected data between October 1987 and July 1988. They worked in pairs, with one person asking questions while the other recorded the answers. Using this method, the two interviewers were able to check each other's work (Shi, 1989a).

SAMPLING AND DATA COLLECTION IN FINLAND

Finland's target population included all nonhandicapped children who were in the target age-range and living at home, except for those residing on the island of Åland (who constituted less than 1 percent of the age group). Using a complete set of population information for all counties and two-stage stratified cluster sampling, researchers first used PPS procedures to select a sample of 80 PSUs that fell into 68 counties. For each PSU selected, research staff determined a sampling ratio that would produce a national self-weighting, Epsem (equal probability of selection method) sample.

The Finnish sampling frame for the selection of children was a central population register that is maintained and updated every month or so by the National Population Central Register Office in Helsinki. For each PSU, researchers used systematic sampling procedures to select individual children's names from this register. The final proposed sample for Finland consisted of 680 children from 28 urban areas and 40 rural areas, both spread throughout the country.

Finland's initial overall response rate was 68 percent. However, with extra effort a final response rate of 85 percent was attained, and only a third of the nonresponses were refusals. Since the achieved sample ($N =$ 576) was an Epsem sample, and because the nonresponse was low and uniform across PSUs, the sampling referee did not consider it necessary to weight the data (Ojala & Siekkinen, 1989b).

Data collection in Finland employed the P/G Interview, including most of the international option items. In April 1987 four interviewers conducted a pilot study with 31 families from an urban and a rural community in eastern Finland. As a result of the pilot study, researchers determined that it was important to conduct the interview only with the child's mother or female guardian.

Interviewers were 145 student volunteers from 11 kindergarten teacher-training institutes, the University of Joensuu, and a training institute of social pedagogy. Most were in their second or third year of teacher training. All of the interviewers had completed a matriculation examination and were at least 19 years old. Prior to training, national project staff had developed a detailed manual that described the study and had provided general and specific guidelines for the P/G Interview. They had also developed a videotape illustrating the proper approach for arranging and completing an interview. Three members of the national project staff trained the interviewers in two sessions (totaling 8 hours), using the manual and videotape along with role-playing techniques and discussion.

Finnish interviewers collected data from September 1988 to September 1989. National research staff closely monitored the interviewers, who submitted their completed P/G Interviews on a monthly basis. Using the completed interviews, staff contacted 5 percent of the sample families by phone to verify their responses to 10 P/G Interview items and found no problems (Ojala & Siekkinen, 1989a).

SAMPLING AND DATA COLLECTION IN GERMANY (FRG)

The German study was conducted in the "old" states of the Federal Republic of Germany, before unification with the former German Democratic Republic, which occurred in 1990. In Germany, the target population for the IEA study consisted of nonhandicapped children who were between the ages of 3½ and 4½ and living in a household (1) maintained by a German-surnamed householder and (2) containing the child's genetic or "social" mother. Using multistage cluster sampling and PPS procedures, a survey research institute hired by the researchers selected 525 districts from a total of 50,000 electoral districts. After using random-route procedures to develop a master sample containing 110 households from each of the 525 electoral districts chosen, the firm's personnel randomly selected 3,826 households (from all eligible households) for the Preprimary Project Phase 1 sample. Germany's national study actually encompassed children from birth to 6 years of age, and their researchers estimated that for purposes of the cross-national study, this sample size would yield a minimum of 400 households with children in the target age-range of 3½ to 4½ years.

Germany's sampling frame consisted of a household listing developed through random-route procedures. The final proposed sample consisted of 400 children from 525 electoral districts throughout the country. The country's overall response rate was only 67 percent, and its refusal rate was 15 percent. The achieved sample ($N = 509$) was not entirely self-weighting, hence weights were computed for every case. Because comparison between weighted and unweighted statistics for several variables revealed no appreciable differences, unweighted results were recommended (Rossbach, 1989b).

The research team in Germany used the format of the international P/G Instrument as the basis for their national version of the P/G Instrument. Owing to the nature of their fundraising process, German researchers had to begin to develop and pilot-test their P/G Interview before completion of the international version. Also, the German researchers found it necessary to expand the age-range and scope of the project within their country. Thus their final P/G Interview included a few international option items and several national option items, such as questions relating to paternal involvement in child care, the care history of the child, and parental preferences regarding care arrangements. GFM-GETAS, the survey research institute hired by the national research center, conducted a pilot test with 88 families between February and April of 1988. In addition, the national research center conducted a small number of pilot tests.

GFM-GETAS selected interviewers from members of their own staff. All interviewers had previous experience with social surveys and training in general interview procedures. To train the interviewers for this particular study, the national project center and GFM-GETAS developed materials that included both general and detailed descriptions of the various sections of the P/G Interview, explanations of rules and procedures of data collection, and an explanation of how to use the daily routine materials (the booklet mentioned earlier).

GFM-GETAS conducted the data collection between May and October of 1988. Most of the interviews were carried out in person, and responses were recorded immediately. GFM-GETAS, in checking the administration of all interviews completed by approximately 20 percent of the interviewers, found no problems with the data collection. Also, after each interviewer sent completed interview materials back to the survey research center, GFM-GETAS reviewed them for thoroughness and accuracy (Rossbach, 1989a).

SAMPLING AND DATA COLLECTION IN HONG KONG

Hong Kong's target population included all nonhandicapped Cantonese-speaking children between the ages of 4 and 5 who were enrolled in early childhood facilities (96 percent of the age group). Hong Kong researchers first developed 12 strata that reflected geographic location, type of facility, and size of facility, and then, using PPS procedures, they selected early childhood service facilities within each stratum. Within each facility chosen, a single classroom of children was designated for inclusion, and 15 of the classroom's children were randomly selected.

The sampling frame for the selection of facilities was demographic statistics from the Hong Kong government census and affiliated departments, while the sampling frame for the selection of children was classroom registration lists. Hong Kong's final proposed sample consisted of 1,000 children from 65 early childhood facilities in the various areas of Hong Kong. Hong Kong had a response rate of 95 percent and no refusals; their achieved sample size was 947. Since the sample was not entirely self-weighting, weights were computed for every case. Comparisons between weighted and unweighted statistics for several variables revealed many appreciable differences, and therefore weighted results were recommended by the sampling referee (Opper, 1989b).

The Hong Kong research team used the P/G Interview with several international option items and three national option items related to parents' educational aspirations for their child, the child's activities at home, and the family's religious affiliation. The NRC at the University of Hong Kong conducted three separate pilot tests with a total of 50 children and their parents. Researchers first administered the P/G Interview to staff members of the university and collected feedback about the interview questions. The second pilot test demonstrated that some questions were too sensitive or personal and would not be answered honestly in a face-to-face interview. Consequently, researchers divided the P/G Interview into two parts: an interview to be administered face to face and a written questionnaire to be completed by the respondent and returned directly to the NRC.

When the final pilot test used the interview-and-questionnaire format with positive results, the research team adopted this format for the study.

The caregivers of the target children — preschool teachers and child care workers — served as interviewers. Principals and heads of participating preschools selected the interviewers in their respective schools and acted as their supervisors. Training consisted of 15 four-hour sessions, each conducted by the research team and attended by 20 to 25 of the 220 interviewers and their supervisors. The research team made allowance for the fact that as experienced teachers, the interviewers were already familiar with most of the procedures used in conducting interviews with parents. During training, researchers provided an overview of the study and familiarized interviewers with their role as data collectors.

Data collection took place between October 1987 and June 1988. The NRC received the completed interviews in three waves, each of which was checked carefully by researchers for accuracy; if there were any problems, researchers contacted the interviewer to discuss them. The NRC then sent out the next set of interview and questionnaire forms with a letter emphasizing specific points and suggesting ideas for preventing future difficulties. The research team contacted each interviewer at least once during data collection and strongly encouraged interviewers to contact their supervisors or the NRC at any time for assistance (Opper, 1989a).

SAMPLING AND DATA COLLECTION IN ITALY

Italy's target population included all nonhandicapped children who were in the target age-range and living at home. Using multistage stratified cluster sampling, the research team first defined 4 geographic strata (northern, central, and southern Italy, and the islands [Sardinia and Sicily]) and then subdivided each geographic stratum into 4 substrata representing different population densities. From the resulting 16 substrata, researchers used systematic sampling procedures and PPS strategies to select 50 communes. From each commune chosen, they then selected 24 children by using systematic sampling procedures.

The Italian sampling frame for selecting children within each chosen commune consisted of commune-level lists of 4-year-olds. The final proposed sample for Italy consisted of a total of 1,200 children from the 50 communes selected throughout Italy. The achieved sample size was 1,000, with an overall response rate of 85 percent and a refusal rate of 7 percent. Since the sample was not entirely self-weighting, weights were computed to assess the necessity of weighting during data analysis. Because comparisons between weighted and unweighted statistics for several variables revealed no appreciable differences, the sampling referee recommended that unweighted results be reported (Pusci, 1989b).

For data collection, Italy used the P/G Interview with all the international option items. They added two national option items related to the care history of the child and parent-child activities. A pilot test of the interview with 50 Italian households during the winter of 1987–88 revealed that the instrument needed several revisions before being used for actual data collection.

The NRC, who was responsible for training interviewers, asked primary education inspectors and headmasters of schools in each of the 50 sample communes to select three to six competent preprimary teachers who they felt could be trained to conduct interviews. Of the 160 potential interviewers selected in this way, 145 were chosen to undergo a 3-day training course (20 to 35 candidates at a time) at the national project center. Before training, the NRC sent copies of the P/G Interview training manual to each of the course participants. During the 3-day course, participants received copies of the interview instrument, so they could practice and make audiotapes of themselves role-playing interviews. After reviewing the quality of the practice interviews on the audiotapes, the NRC selected 136 course participants to be interviewers.

Italy's NRC organized two periods of data collection between May and November of 1988. In many communes, before data collection, parents and teachers of preprimary school children received information about the purpose of the study, to increase the likelihood of families' agreeing to participate. All interviews were conducted face to face, and all responses were recorded in writing only. Research staff contacted a sample of approximately 100 families by telephone to verify their responses to five or six interview items (Pusci, 1989a).

SAMPLING AND DATA COLLECTION IN NIGERIA

In Nigeria, the target population included nonhandicapped children who were between the ages of 3 and 5 and living at home. Using multistage stratified cluster sampling, Nigerian researchers first used a combination of educational, religious, sociopolitical, linguistic, and geographic information to form the country's 19 states into 5 strata. Then, from each stratum, they selected 1 state by judgment. Working from the master sample developed by the Nigerian Federal Office of Statistics (120 enumeration areas per state), for each of the 5 states chosen, the researchers used PPS procedures to select 56 enumeration areas. Within each enumeration area chosen, they then used systematic sampling procedures to select 12 households for screening. According to estimates, after screening, approximately 5 households in each enumeration area would contain children in Nigeria's target age-range.

The sampling frame for the selection of households was a household listing for each enumeration area. Nigeria's final proposed sample consisted of 1,400 children from the 5 selected states. Data to calculate the response rate were not available, but the response rate for another household survey conducted using similar procedures in these 5 states during the same period of time was approximately 96 percent. The achieved sample size was 1,295. Within each of the 5 states, the urban and rural samples were separately self-weighting. For national results, the 10 sets of results (5 states, urban and rural) were weighted by total census populations in the respective strata (Onibokun, 1989).

The main data collection instrument in Nigeria was the P/G Interview, including all international option items and one national option item relating to the child's developmental status. Pilot-testing took place in September 1987 with a judgment sample of 40 urban and rural households in one state. Results revealed both strengths and weaknesses of the P/G Interview procedure: Strengths included the effectiveness of using interviewers from the Federal Office of Statistics (FOS) to collect data, while weaknesses included problems encountered in eliciting accurate responses to income-related questions.

As just mentioned, the Federal Office of Statistics assisted the NRC with this study. The Nigerian research team consisted of the NRC (at the University of Ibadan), five state research coordinators, and five assistant coordinators (state supervisors from the FOS). The FOS state supervisors selected from their offices a minimum of 10 interviewers per state. Criteria used for interviewer selection were completion of secondary education, familiarity and experience with household survey techniques and procedures, and being a native of the state in which the interview would be conducted.

The NRC held 4-hour workshops to train the state research coordinators. After these coordinators had been introduced to the study, the P/G Interview and training manual, and the interviewing procedures, they each role-played an interview with the NRC and received feedback about the interview. After this training, each coordinator returned to his or her respective state and trained the assistant coordinator (the FOS state supervisor) in proper administration of the P/G Interview. The FOS interviewers also attended three training sessions organized by the research coordinators in their states. (The interviewers had also been trained by the FOS for a previous household study.)

Data collection took place in October and November of 1988. All interviews were conducted face to face, and responses were recorded in writing. The NRC kept in close touch with each of the coordinators and the assistant coordinators. To ensure that problems were handled correctly, assistant coordinators (FOS state supervisors) accompanied interviewers on their field assignments. Also, before an interviewer was paid for his or her work, the coordinators checked each interview form carefully to be sure it had been completed properly (Onibokun, 1991).

SAMPLING AND DATA COLLECTION IN PORTUGAL

In Portugal, the target population included all nonhandicapped native-born children between ages 3½ and 4½ and living at home, except for those who were residents of the autonomous regions of the Azores and Madeira archipelagoes (approximately 1 percent of the age group). Using two-stage stratified cluster sampling, researchers first divided Portugal's 275 counties into 26 strata, using a combination of socioeconomic, demographic, health, and education information. Next, they used systematic sampling procedures and PPS strategies to select 76 PSUs, which fell into 57 counties. From each PSU chosen, the researchers used systematic sampling procedures to select 10 children.

The Portuguese sampling frame for the selection of children consisted of county-level birth-registration records. Through a pilot study, Portuguese researchers found that although birth records were several years old, over 85 percent of children in the target age-range could still be located from information contained in them. The final proposed sample for Portugal consisted of 580 children in 57 counties.

Overall, Portugal's response rate was 76 percent, and its refusal rate was 3 percent. The achieved sample size was 581. The sample was not entirely self-weighting; so weights were computed to assess the necessity of weighting for data analysis. Comparisons between weighted and unweighted statistics for several variables revealed no appreciable differences. Therefore, the sampling referee recommended that unweighted results be used for data analysis (Abreu, Abreu-Lima, Bairrão, Barbosa, & Cruz, 1989).

Researchers in Portugal used the P/G Interview with international option items relating to the child's health status. Pilot-testing of the P/G Interview took place in October 1987. For a pilot test with 35 families (18 in northern Portugal, 17 in southern Portugal), four nonprofessional interviewers used the May 1987 version of the P/G Interview. The pilot-testing resulted in a decision to eliminate some national option items and revise the international option items. Researchers also thought the length of the interview should be decreased (pilot-test interviews ranged from just over ½ hour to just under 2 hours).

Because of concerns about the quality of interviewers, the national project staff based selection primarily on the criterion of having a degree in psychology or another human science. Field-work coordinating centers for training and data collection were set up in Porto and Lisbon (northern and southern Portugal, respectively), and the research team, using a manual that explained the P/G Interview, trained interviewers at these centers in two 1-day sessions. At the first training session, researchers gave each interviewer two interviews to complete; a week later the interviewers attended a second 1-day session to review and receive feedback on the interviews they had completed and to meet individually with the research team. A total of 34 interviewers successfully completed training in Porto and Lisbon.

During data collection, which took place between April and June of 1988, interviewers completed 581 interviews. When researchers contacted 204 respondents by telephone to verify their responses, they found no problems with the data collection (Bairrão, Abreu-Lima, Barbosa, & Cruz, 1989).

Sampling and Data Collection in Spain

In Spain, the target population included all nonhandicapped children who were between the ages of 3½ and 4½ and living at home. Using two-stage cluster sampling, Spanish researchers first used PPS procedures to select 160 PSUs, which fell into 45 provinces. From each PSU, they then selected 3 children, using random selection procedures when listings of 4-year-olds were available and random-route procedures when such listings were not available.

For most PSUs, the sampling frame for the selection of children was a local register. For the few remaining areas, the researchers did not have access to a sampling frame and thus used random-route procedures. Spain's final proposed sample consisted of 480 children from 160 localities throughout the country.

The overall response rate for Spain was 29 percent, and the refusal rate was 35 percent. The country had an achieved sample size of 480. When a family could not easily be contacted, the researchers often substituted another home rather than recontacting the original home several times. The sample was not entirely self-weighting, hence weights were computed to assess the necessity of weighting during data analysis. Since comparisons between weighted and unweighted statistics for several variables revealed no appreciable differences, the sampling referee recommended that unweighted data be used for the analysis (Palacios, 1989).

The research team in Spain used the P/G Interview with a majority of the international option items and a few national option items. Two of the national option items involved expanding the daily routine chart to ask about the previous Sunday and to record not only the child's whereabouts and caregivers but also the child's activities throughout the day. The researchers pilot-tested the interview with approximately 30 families from three geographical regions with various social, economic, and cultural characteristics.

Interviewers were women and men aged 21 to 35 who had a university degree or were in their last 2 years of study for a degree. Preference was given to interviewers affiliated with private firms having expertise in conducting field surveys as well as experience with qualitative and random-route survey procedures. Training lasted an average of 6 to 8 hours and was conducted in one or two sessions by two members of the national project center staff. Topics covered included the background, design, and goals of the study; the P/G Interview and its training manual; and proper interview techniques and procedures. In addition to studying the P/G Interview in detail, interviewers completed and reviewed practice interviews and discussed any problems encountered in the practice.

Spain collected data in May and June of 1989. The research team required all interviewers to maintain telephone contact with the national project center and to send in their completed interviews to be checked. Project staff contacted a sample of families by phone or in person to verify that their interviews had been conducted and to confirm their responses to a selected set of questions (Palacios et al., 1989).

SAMPLING AND DATA COLLECTION IN THAILAND

The target population for Thailand included all nonhandicapped children who were in the target age-range and living at home. Researchers first identified 5 geographic regions (strata) and then divided each region into municipal and nonmunicipal areas. Using multistage stratified cluster sampling and PPS procedures, research staff next selected 38 PSUs (9 municipal, 29 nonmunicipal) in 33 provinces in these 5 strata. They then selected 149 SSUs (blocks/villages) from the 38 PSUs. The information used to construct the 5 strata consisted of 1980 population and housing census data as well as 1987 population projection figures. The final proposed sample consisted of 2,400 children from 9 municipal and 29 nonmunicipal areas in the 5 geographic regions.

The overall response rate was 99 percent, and the achieved sample size was 2,466. Because the sample was not entirely self-weighting, weights were computed for every case. When comparisons between weighted and unweighted statistics for several variables revealed no appreciable differences, the sample referee recommended that unweighted data be used for analysis (Passornsiri, 1989b).

For data collection, the Thai research team used the P/G Interview with all of the international option items. Researchers conducted two pilot studies with the interview, one in 1987 and one in 1988. First, using the May 1987 version of the P/G Interview, the research team interviewed 52 families in four geographic regions (urban and rural) and metropolitan Bangkok to detect any linguistic or cultural problems. Later, using the revised interview instrument, the team interviewed families in two provinces to check families' comprehension of questions and the usability of the administration manual. The time required to administer the interview ranged from 30 minutes to an hour.

Major interviewers were 6 faculty members from Sukhothai Thammathirat Open University (STOU) and 31 health officers from 33 provinces, most of whom had at least a bachelor's degree in nursing or health science. These health officers were invited to attend training at the national project center (STOU) and to act as coordinators for the data collection. Using a P/G Interview training manual, national project staff trained interviewers in a 3-day seminar. Training procedures included an explanation of the project, in-depth study of the interview and manual, presentation of guidelines for data collection, practice interviews with STOU staff and with families in a nearby village, and discussion of problems encountered during interviews. Acting as coordinators, the 31 health officers recruited and trained other provincial health care workers as interviewers. Also, two STOU faculty members trained a health officer in one province and helped with the interviews. In Bangkok, interviewers included the national project staff, STOU faculty, health workers, teachers, and graduate students. The total number of interviewers was 118. Data collection took place between March and July of 1989 (Passornsiri, 1989a).

SAMPLING AND DATA COLLECTION IN THE UNITED STATES

For the United States, the target population included nonhandicapped children between the ages of 3½ and 4½ living at home but was restricted to a set of 11 sites. These 11 sites were selected so that, as a group, they covered all four U.S. census regions, included both urban and rural sites, and included families from all major racial/cultural and socioeconomic groups. For each site, statistical staff used PPS procedures to select 12 area segments. For most area segments, all households with children in the target age-range were included in the sample, but for the few extremely large segments, random households were selected with equal probability. In each area segment that was selected, trained staff used carefully developed household listing and screening procedures to ensure that all families with children in the target age-range were located for inclusion in the study.

The sampling frame for selecting area segments for 10 of the sites was the U.S. Bureau of the Census computer file of the 1980 population and housing data for census blocks and enumeration districts. For the 11th site, the sampling frame was a state register that is updated yearly. The final proposed sample for the United States consisted of 600 children from 11 sites located around the country.

The United States achieved an overall response rate of 85 percent, and its refusal rate was 6 percent. Achieved sample size was 432. Within each of the 11 sites, the research staff selected samples with equal probability that were self-weighting. The weights for the national findings were based on pseudostrata constructed to represent the 11 sites. When weighted and unweighted results for several variables were compared, there were no appreciable differences. Consequently, the sampling referee recommended that unweighted results be reported (Hoas & Olmsted, 1989).

The major data collection instrument in the U.S. was the P/G Interview with all of the international option items and several national option items. National project staff conducted two pilot tests, 2 weeks apart, with the instrument. For the pilot tests, they used both in-person and telephone interviews with 25 families of children between the ages of 3 and 5 in urban and rural areas of southeastern Michigan.

A panel of Head Start directors from 11 sites representing the four U.S. census regions (the Head Start Research Cooperative Panel) was responsible for selecting interviewers and coordinating data collection. The panel selected 41 interviewers (2 to 7 per site) from Head Start staff and parents and from other hired persons; all interviewers were at least 22 years old, and most had some college background. The director and one staff member from each site attended a full 2 days of training at the national project center. Training included following a detailed training manual, role-playing interviews with emphasis on critical areas within the interview (with feedback from project staff), and watching videotapes illustrating professional interviews and ways to handle potential difficulties. Each trainee also conducted a trial interview with a member of the national research center staff. Project staff carefully reviewed the trial interviews and provided feedback to ensure understanding of and familiarity with the interview. On returning to their respective sites, the director and staff member trained additional interviewers with materials and guidelines provided by the national project staff. Approval as an interviewer required successful completion of two audiotaped interviews, as determined by national research center staff.

Data collection extended from October 1988 to August 1989. Interviews were conducted in person or by phone, and responses were recorded in writing and on audiotape (unless the interviewee did not consent to audiotaping). This double recording assisted interviewers and coders in checking the accuracy and thoroughness of written responses. Throughout data collection, Head Start directors closely supervised the interviewers while national project staff monitored their progress by continually reviewing the quality of interviews submitted to them (Hoas, 1990).

* * *

The sampling procedures outlined in this chapter indicate how each of the countries participating in Phase 1 of the IEA Preprimary Project overcame, in its own way, the problems involved in locating a national probability sample. The generally high response rates and low refusal rates reported here attest to the success that Phase 1 countries met in their data collection efforts. Careful sample location and data collection procedures, such as those just described, are important, since both kinds of procedures influence the quality of results from a household survey. The next five chapters present the IEA/PPP Phase 1 findings. First, Chapter 4 characterizes the national samples and discusses how representative they were of their respective general populations.

Endnotes

1. By agreement with the sampling referee, sampling errors were not computed. This departure from preferred statistical procedures (which are often violated) was based on the following reasons: First, though the possible errors of measurement and response may have been more dominant and important in these surveys than the sampling errors, it would not have been feasible to design experiments to measure *all* these types of errors. Second, computing sampling errors for all 11 countries would have been costly and difficult because of each country's distinct and complex sample design. Third, a presentation of the results of sampling error computations would have been inappropriate for the intended audiences of this book. Moreover, it may be that the well-known formulas for standard errors, such as $p \pm t/(pq/n)$, are underestimates of the actual variabilities present in the data.

References

Abreu, J. G., Abreu-Lima, I., Bairrão, J., Barbosa, M., & Cruz, O. (1989). *IEA Preprimary Project Phase 1 sampling report: Portugal.* Porto: University of Porto.

Bairrão, J., Abreu-Lima, I., Barbosa, M., & Cruz, O. (1989). IEA *Preprimary Project Phase 1 data collection report: Portugal.* Porto: University of Porto.

Delhaxhe, A., & Hindryckx, G. (1989). *IEA Preprimary Project Phase 1 sampling report: Belgium.* Liège: University of Liège.

Hindryckx, G., & Delhaxhe, A. (1989). *IEA Preprimary Project Phase 1 data collection report: Belgium.* Liège: University of Liège.

Hoas, H. (1990). *IEA Preprimary Project Phase 1 data collection report: United States.* Ypsilanti, MI: High/Scope Educational Research Foundation.

Hoas, H., & Olmsted, P. P. (1989). *IEA Preprimary Project Phase 1 sampling report: United States.* Ypsilanti, MI: High/Scope Educational Research Foundation.

Kish, L. (1965). *Survey sampling.* New York: Wiley & Sons.

Kish, L. (1987). *Statistical design for research.* New York: Wiley & Sons.

Ojala, M., & Siekkinen, M. (1989a). *IEA Preprimary Project Phase 1 data collection report: Finland.* Joensuu: University of Joensuu.

Ojala, M., & Siekkinen, M. (1989b). *IEA Preprimary Project Phase 1 sampling report: Finland.* Joensuu: University of Joensuu.

Olmsted, P. P., Kish, L., & Weikart, D. P. (1987). *IEA Preprimary Project Phase 1 sampling questionnaire.* Ypsilanti, MI: High/Scope Educational Research Foundation.

Onibokun, O. (1989). *IEA Preprimary Project Phase 1 sampling report: Nigeria.* Ibadan: University of Ibadan.

Onibokun, O. (1991). *IEA Preprimary Project Phase 1 data collection report: Nigeria.* Ibadan: University of Ibadan.

Opper, S. (1989a). *IEA Preprimary Project Phase 1 data collection report: Hong Kong.* Hong Kong: University of Hong Kong.

Opper, S. (1989b). *IEA Preprimary Project Phase 1 sampling report: Hong Kong.* Hong Kong: University of Hong Kong.

Palacios, J. (1989). *IEA Preprimary Project Phase 1 sampling report: Spain.* Seville: University of Seville.

Palacios, J., González, M. M., Hidalgo, V., Moreno, C., Capote, M., & Ruiz, A. (1989). *IEA Preprimary Project Phase 1 data collection report: Spain.* Seville: University of Seville.

Passornsiri, N. (1989a). *IEA Preprimary Project Phase 1 data collection report: Thailand.* Nonthaburi: Sukhothai Thammathirat Open University.

Passornsiri, N. (1989b). *IEA Preprimary Project Phase 1 sampling report: Thailand.* Nonthaburi: Sukhothai Thammathirat Open University.

Pusci, L. (1989a). *IEA Preprimary Project Phase 1 data collection report: Italy.* Frascati: Centro Europeo dell'Educazione.

Pusci, L. (1989b). *IEA Preprimary Project Phase 1 sampling report: Italy.* Frascati: Centro Europeo dell'Educazione.

Rossbach, H.-G. (1989a). *IEA Preprimary Project Phase 1 data collection report: Germany.* Münster: University of Münster.

Rossbach, H.-G. (1989b). *IEA Preprimary Project Phase 1 sampling report: Germany.* Münster: University of Münster.

Shi, H. Z. (1989a). *IEA Preprimary Project Phase 1 data collection report: China.* Beijing: Central Institute of Educational Research.

Shi, H. Z. (1989b). *IEA Preprimary Project Phase 1 sampling report: China.* Beijing: Central Institute of Educational Research.

Weikart, D. P., Kish, L., & Olmsted, P. P. (1988). *IEA Preprimary Project Phase 1 interim sampling report.* Ypsilanti, MI: High/Scope Educational Research Foundation.

IV
THE PHASE 1 NATIONAL SAMPLES

Patricia P. Olmsted, *Senior Research Associate*
High/Scope Educational Research Foundation
Ypsilanti, Michigan

Before considering the Phase 1 study's major findings about families' care and education arrangements for their 4-year-olds, it is useful to know something about the life circumstances of the families and children who took part in the study in each of the 11 countries. Therefore, this chapter describes the major parental, family, household, and child health characteristics for each of the national samples. It also addresses the question of how the national samples compared with the general populations in their respective countries.

The national sample descriptions include data about parents' ages, educational attainment, and employment status; about family size and whether children live in two- or one-parent households; about how much time parents spend away from their 4-year-olds; and about other key household features and amenities. The last category — key household features and amenities — gives some idea of family resources or affluence (e.g., by indicating whether families had telephones, automobiles, few or many rooms to live in). However, attempts to determine amounts and sources of family *income* encountered a variety of problems (e.g., a high percentage of nonresponses, indications of underreporting of amounts), and therefore this chapter does not include information about family income.

In each country, to gather the following data characterizing the national samples, researchers used household survey procedures with the Parent/Guardian Interview instrument, as described in Chapter 3.

Characteristics of Parents

Parental Age

Table 4.1 contains data about the ages of mothers and fathers in the national samples. The data indicate that mothers in the 11 national samples were, on average, between 30.0 and 32.8 years old. The average age of national sample fathers was between 31.9 and 35.5 years. Because the national samples were made up of families having young children, in each country the average ages of sample mothers and fathers were less than the average age in the country's general adult population. Consequently, differences were to be expected when we compared certain key characteristics of sample parents with those of the general adult population in a specific nation. Educational attainment, which follows, is one such age-dependent characteristic.

Parents' Educational Attainment

Table 4.2 presents the years of education completed by national sample mothers and fathers in the 11 countries. Sample parents in Thailand averaged the lowest number of years of education (4.8 years for mothers, 5.4 years for fathers), whereas sample parents in the United States averaged the highest number of years of education (12.8 years for mothers, 13.8 years for fathers). In 8 of the 11 nations, fathers had from 0.5 to 1.5 more years of education than mothers had. In each of the remaining 3 countries (Finland, Italy, and Portugal) the number of years of education completed by sample mothers was nearly the same as the number of years completed by sample fathers.

Researchers in several countries were able to locate information about the average number of years of education completed by adults in the general population. In nearly every one of these countries, national sample parents had slightly higher levels of educational attainment than adults in the general population had. This is not surprising, since national sample parents (on average) tended to be younger than the average adult in their respective general populations, and the trend in many countries in recent decades has been for young people to obtain more education.

Table 4.1 Mean age (in years) of national sample mothers and fathers

Country/ Territory	Mothers		Fathers	
	n	Mean (SD)	n	Mean (SD)
Belgium (Fr.)	407	31.0 (4.5)	398	33.6 (5.4)
China (PRC)[+]	12,402	30.1 (3.9)	11,729	31.9 (4.1)
Finland	561	32.8 (5.0)	525	35.5 (5.7)
Germany (FRG)	497	30.9 (4.6)	453	34.0 (5.3)
Hong Kong[+]	—	—	—	—
Italy	983	31.3 (5.2)	970	35.5 (5.9)
Nigeria[+]	—	—	—	—
Portugal	572	30.0 (5.4)	543	32.9 (6.1)
Spain	473	31.3 (5.1)	457	34.2 (5.5)
Thailand	2,321	30.3 (6.2)	2,087	33.9 (7.2)
United States	418	30.5 (5.7)	298	33.8 (5.9)

Note. The symbol [+] indicates weighted data were used for analysis. A dash indicates that no data were available.

Table 4.2 Years of education completed by national sample
mothers and fathers

Country/ Territory	Mothers		Fathers	
	n	Mean (SD)	n	Mean (SD)
Belgium (Fr.)	421	12.0 (3.7)	403	12.7 (4.0)
China (PRC)[+]	12,363	6.9 (4.0)	12,370	8.1 (3.4)
Finland	568	12.4 (3.1)	527	12.1 (3.4)
Germany (FRG)	500	10.3 (2.4)	451	11.0 (3.1)
Hong Kong[+]	880	9.1 (2.7)	895	9.9 (3.2)
Italy	258	10.3 (4.1)	253	10.5 (4.5)
Nigeria[+]	677	6.2 (5.2)	711	7.5 (5.1)
Portugal	573	5.6 (3.1)	553	5.7 (3.1)
Spain	458	11.4 (4.8)	428	12.0 (5.2)
Thailand	2,249	4.8 (2.7)	2,194	5.4 (3.2)
United States	414	12.8 (3.5)	321	13.8 (3.6)

Note. The symbol [+] indicates that weighted data were used for analysis.

Table 4.3 Maternal employment for national samples

Country/ Territory	N	Percentage Active in Labor Force[a]	Percentage in Each Occupational Category[b]							
			1	2	3	4	5	6	7	8
Belgium (Fr.)	424	57	44	1	23	10	16	0	6	0
China (PRC)[+]	12,835	98	7	2	2	6	0	56	27	0
Finland	576	75	8	1	25	5	42	6	13	0
Germany (FRG)	509	43	22	0	29	12	22	5	9	2
Hong Kong[+]	947	51	24	4	27	10	6	2	27	0
Italy	1,000	46	26	2	25	8	14	0	22	3
Nigeria[+]	1,295	67	29	3	9	23	0	32	1	3
Portugal	581	65	7	0	14	10	24	13	31	1
Spain	480	35	21	1	25	15	28	1	9	0
Thailand	2,466	57	4	0	1	16	4	60	15	0
United States	432	50	22	7	26	5	29	1	10	0

Note. The symbol [+] indicates that weighted data were used for analysis.

[a]Includes mothers working for pay either in the home or outside the home.

[b]1 = professional, technical; 2 = administrative, managerial; 3 = clerical; 4 = sales; 5 = service; 6 = agricultural, forestry, fishery; 7 = production; 8 = no classification, armed forces.

PARENTAL EMPLOYMENT

The International Standard Classification of Occupations (ISCO) was used to code the occupations of mothers and fathers in all participating nations. This classification system was developed by the International Labour Organization and has been used extensively in cross-national studies because it provides a standard list of occupational groups for international use (International Labour Office, 1990).

Tables 4.3 and 4.4 present employment information for national sample mothers and fathers. The information includes, for each nation, the percentage of mothers and of fathers in the labor force and the percentage of mothers and of fathers employed in various occupational categories. As Table 4.3 indicates, 7 of the 11 nations reported 43 to 67 percent of sample mothers working for pay either in the home or outside the home. The highest rates of labor force participation for mothers were in China (98 percent) and Finland (75 percent), whereas the lowest rate was in Spain (35 percent). Researchers in several countries were able to locate general population statistics regarding the proportion of women in the labor force. However, in most cases, the statistics covered all adult women; so, as expected, the sample's proportion of women active in the labor force (the sample consisting only of mothers with at least one 4-year-old child) was generally lower than the corresponding proportion for the entire adult female population. In a few countries where the population statistics were several years old (e.g., from 1980), the sample's proportion of labor-force active women was *larger* than the general population's proportion. This is explained by the fact that in most countries of the world, female participation in the labor force has been on the increase for the last few decades.

When we examine the proportion of sample mothers employed in various occupational categories, we note that in 7 nations, about one fourth were employed in *clerical* positions (category 3), and in 6 nations, about one fourth worked in *professional/technical* jobs (category 1 — as doctors/nurses, accountants, teachers, social workers). In Belgium 44 percent of sample mothers were employed in *professional/technical* positions. Only 3 countries (China, Hong Kong, Portugal) reported more than a fourth of sample mothers employed in *production* jobs (category 7 — as textile workers, laundry workers, produce graders/packers).

As Table 4.4 indicates, in 10 of the 11 nations, over 90 percent of sample fathers were working for pay, with only Nigeria having a percentage lower than this (78 percent). In 3 countries (China, Nigeria, and Thailand) the occupational category with the largest percentage of sample fathers was *agriculture, forestry, fishery* (category 6). In 7 other countries (Finland, Germany, Hong Kong, Italy, Portugal, Spain, and the United States) *production* (category 7) was the predominant occupational category for sample fathers (this category includes such occupations as machine operator, textile worker, truck/bus driver).

Only a few countries had available population statistics concerning the distribution of general population men and women among the various occupational categories. In the few cases where comparisons could be

94 OLMSTED

Table 4.4 Paternal employment for national samples

Country/ Territory	N	Percentage Active in Labor Force[a]	Percentage in Each Occupational Category[b]							
			1	2	3	4	5	6	7	8
Belgium (Fr.)	424	92	32	3	11	5	12	2	32	3
China (PRC)+	12,835	98	7	4	5	4	0	48	31	1
Finland	576	98	13	4	3	11	13	13	41	2
Germany (FRG)	509	98	26	1	12	6	2	4	42	7
Hong Kong+	947	99	17	6	9	15	6	2	45	0
Italy	1,000	91	13	5	16	6	7	5	45	3
Nigeria+	1,295	78	24	8	2	25	6	28	1	6
Portugal	581	98	5	1	9	8	9	11	57	0
Spain	480	94	16	8	15	8	13	6	32	2
Thailand	2,466	95	4	1	1	6	3	54	30	1
United States	432	94	20	22	6	5	11	3	32	1

Note. The symbol + indicates that weighted data were used for analysis.

[a]Includes fathers working for pay either in the home or outside of the home.

[b]1 = professional, technical; 2 = administrative, managerial; 3 = clerical; 4 = sales; 5 = service; 6 = agricultural, forestry, fishery; 7 = production; 8 = no classification, armed forces.

made between sample parents and general population men and women, either there was rough agreement, or expected differences were found, based on the relatively young ages of sample parents. For example, when compared with Hong Kong's general adult population, Hong Kong's sample parents had higher proportions in the *professional/technical* category and lower proportions in the *production* and *service* categories. The Hong Kong project coordinator considered this difference to be consistent with the higher levels of educational attainment found among Hong Kong's sample parents.

Parental Time Away From Children

One factor that relates directly to children's need for nonparental supervision is the amount of time that parents spend away from their children. Thus, researchers gathered data about the number of hours that each national sample parent spent away from their 4-year-old child in a typical week (e.g., for purposes of employment, education, other family duties, social/community activities). Tables 4.5 and 4.6 present this information for national sample mothers and fathers, respectively.

Table 4.5, on the next page, indicates that for the 10 countries reporting data, the average number of hours per week that sample mothers were away from their 4-year-olds varied from 18.5 hours (in Germany) to 52.2 hours (in China). Sample mothers in China, Portugal, and Thailand spent the most time away, with more than half of them being away over 40 hours a week. Sample mothers in Germany and the United States spent the least time away from their 4-year-olds. This is surprising, considering that both are highly industrialized nations, where one would expect high participation of mothers in the labor force and consequent high needs for extra-parental care for young children.

For the 10 countries reporting Table 4.6 data, (on p. 98) the average number of hours per week that national sample fathers spent away from their 4-year-olds ranged from 47.2 hours (in Italy and Finland) to 76.4 hours (in Thailand). As Table 4.6 illustrates, 60 percent of Thailand's sample fathers were typically away more than 60 hours a week. In China, Nigeria, and Portugal, the percentage of sample fathers away this much ranged from 33 to 38 percent. The 3 countries whose sample mothers averaged the most time away from their young children (China, Portugal, and Thailand) also reported sample fathers averaging the most time away.

Household and Family Characteristics

Two-Parent Households

Ten countries reported the percentage of sample families in which the

Table 4.5   Percentage distribution of national sample mothers according to weekly hours away from 4-year-old child

Country/ Territory	N	Mothers Responding n (% of N)	% of n Absent the Following Number of Hours:				Mean Hours Absent (SD)
			1–20	21–40	41–60	>60	
Belgium (Fr.)	424	252 (59)	27	47	23	3	32.2 (15.7)
China (PRC)[+]	12,835	9,255 (72)	6	18	56	20	52.2 (25.4)
Finland	576	457 (79)	21	44	33	2	33.9 (16.8)
Germany (FRG)	509	237 (47)	64	24	11	1	18.5 (16.6)
Hong Kong[+]	—	—	—	—	—	—	—
Italy	1,000	164 (16)	18	63	18	1	30.8 (12.5)
Nigeria[+]	1,295	713 (55)	31	39	23	7	31.0 (21.2)
Portugal	581	386 (66)	18	21	50	11	42.8 (21.2)
Spain	480	230 (48)	30	49	18	3	31.3 (16.9)
Thailand	2,466	1,116 (45)	26	25	23	26	43.7 (31.4)
United States	432	285 (66)	43	36	20	1	26.7 (16.8)

Note. The symbol [+] indicates that weighted data were used for analysis. A dash indicates that no data were available.

parents were married and both present in the household. As shown in Table 4.7, on p. 99, all but 1 of the 10 countries reported a high percentage (86 percent or higher) of *married spouse present* households. The United States sample stands alone with a relatively low percentage (69 percent) of *married spouse present* households. Two of the 10 countries were able to compare their samples with their general populations on this characteristic, and in both cases the national sample and the general population were similar.

FAMILY SIZE

Table 4.7 also presents the average family size for 9 of the 11 national samples. The 9 countries exhibit a fairly small range of family sizes, with the smallest average size (3.9 members) being found in Germany and the largest average size (5.1 members) being found in Thailand. In 7 countries, researchers compared the average family size of the sample with the average family size in the general population. In 4 of these countries the sample's average family size and the population's average family size were similar. In the other 3 countries, the sample had a slightly larger average family size than the population had.

HOME OWNERSHIP

As Table 4.7 indicates, the sample families in Hong Kong and Portugal reported considerably lower rates of home ownership (41 percent and 44 percent, respectively) than did the sample families from other nations. In China, Finland, Spain, and Thailand, 70 percent or more of sample families owned their homes. Only United States researchers were able to compare sample and general population statistics for rates of home ownership, and they found the percentages (53 percent and 56 percent, respectively) to be very similar.

NUMBER OF ROOMS IN HOME

As can be seen in Table 4.7, sample families in Thailand (with 2.1 rooms per household) and China (with 2.6 rooms per household) had the smallest average home sizes. Sample families in Belgium (with 6.4 rooms per

Table 4.6   Percentage distribution of national sample fathers according to weekly hours away from 4-year-old child

Country/ Territory	N	Fathers Responding n (% of N)	% of n Absent the Following Number of Hours:				Mean Hours Absent (SD)
			1–20	21–40	41–60	>60	
Belgium (Fr.)	424	367 (87)	2	27	59	12	48.8 (14.4)
China (PRC)[+]	12,835	10,429 (81)	2	11	51	36	65.1 (34.8)
Finland	576	491 (85)	5	28	56	11	47.2 (17.5)
Germany (FRG)	509	373 (73)	2	13	71	14	51.9 (14.6)
Hong Kong[+]	—	—	—	—	—	—	—
Italy	1,000	235 (24)	3	34	52	11	47.2 (15.6)
Nigeria[+]	1,295	810 (63)	6	17	44	33	53.9 (20.7)
Portugal	581	530 (91)	2	9	51	38	63.8 (28.1)
Spain	480	435 (91)	2	37	42	19	51.1 (20.5)
Thailand	2,466	1,873 (76)	3	11	26	60	76.4 (42.1)
United States	432	310 (72)	5	18	61	16	52.1 (21.5)

Note. The symbol [+] indicates that weighted data were used for analysis. A dash indicates that no data were available.

Table 4.7 Family and residence characteristics of national samples

Country/ Territory	n	% With Married Spouse Present	Average Number of Members in Family (SD)	% Owning Home	Average Number of Rooms in Home (SD)
Belgium (Fr.)	424	95	4.4 (1.2)	65	6.4 (2.4)
China (PRC)[+]	12,835	91	4.0 (1.3)	75	2.6 (1.4)
Finland	576	87	4.4 (1.3)	78	4.5 (1.4)
Germany (FRG)	509	91	3.9 (1.0)	—	4.3 (1.4)
Hong Kong[+]	947	—	—	41	2.9 (1.2)
Italy	1,000	94	4.2 (1.1)	59	4.1 (1.5)
Nigeria[+]	1,295	92	—	67	4.0 (2.3)
Portugal	581	90	4.4 (1.4)	44	3.7 (1.4)
Spain	480	93	4.4 (1.3)	70	4.3 (2.4)
Thailand	2,466	86	5.1 (1.8)	76	2.1 (1.1)
United States	432	69	4.5 (1.4)	53	5.7 (1.9)

Note. The symbol [+] indicates that weighted data were used for analysis. A dash indicates that no data were available.

household) and the United States (with 5.7 rooms per household) had the largest average home sizes.

When statistics about family size and number of rooms in the home are combined, the following picture emerges: Of all the national sample families, Thailand's had the most family members, but they were living in the least number of rooms. Belgium and the United States fell in the middle range of the nations with regard to family size, but they had the largest averages regarding number of rooms to live in. Portugal's average family size was about equal to family size in Belgium and the United States, yet the Portuguese homes had, on average, at least 2 fewer rooms than did Belgian and U.S. homes.

HOUSEHOLD AMENITIES

The presence or absence of certain kinds of living amenities in sample family households was also of interest in this study. Researchers believed that the amenities, listed in Table 4.8, could relate to the amount of time parents had available to devote to their children. Some of them (e.g., forms of private transportation and communication) could also indicate how much access children had to people and events beyond the immediate household.

Indoor running water

Although the interviewers asked families whether their homes had heat, light, or running water, only the data for indoor running water is given in Table 4.8. The other two features, because they were almost universally present where appropriate, (e.g., heat) are not included here.

As Table 4.8 shows, 7 of the 11 countries reported at least 98 percent of sample families having indoor running water. Of the remaining 4 countries, Portugal reported 83 percent with indoor running water, whereas Nigeria, China, and Thailand reported only 42 percent, 35 percent, and 18 percent, respectively. This means that in these 3 of the 11 countries, more than half of families needed to carry water daily from an outdoor source.

Private transportation

In many countries, moving a 4-year-old child beyond his or her immediate surroundings depends on the availability of private transportation. Therefore, interviewers asked families if they owned a working automo-

Table 4.8   Percentages of national samples having various amenities

Country/ Territory	N	Indoor Water[a]	Auto-mobile	Bicycle	Tele-phone	Tele-vision	Clothes Washing Machine	Refrig-erator
Belgium (Fr.)	424	100	93	—	83	97	97	100
China (PRC)[+]	12,835	35	1	74	0	56	29	10
Finland	576	99	95	98	98	—	—	—
Germany (FRG)	509	100	—	—	—	—	—	—
Hong Kong[+]	947	100	17	13	97	98	89	97
Italy	1,000	98	95	70	81	99	98	99
Nigeria[+]	1,295	42	11	13	6	31	3	25
Portugal	581	83	46	39	—	56	53	88
Spain	480	100	—	—	—	—	—	—
Thailand	2,466	18	8	56	2	44	2	21
United States	432	100	87	67	93	99	80	100

Note. The symbol [+] indicates that weighted data were used for analysis. A dash indicates that no data were available.

[a]This question was not asked in Belgium and Germany, but offical information indicates that 100% of families in those countries have indoor running water.

bile, bicycle, or other form of transportation. In 7 of the 9 nations asking this question, at least about half of sample families owned an *automobile* or a *bicycle*. In Hong Kong, public transportation is frequently used by nearly all families, so the low percentages of sample families owning cars or bicycles were not unexpected. In Nigeria, where public transportation is not generally available, very small percentages of sample families owned a car or bicycle, which means that for their children, the world was likely to be limited to the immediate surroundings.

Telephone and television

Table 4.8 shows that the 8 countries reporting data about *telephone* ownership fell into two groups: a group in which nearly all sample families had telephones (5 countries) and a group in which no sample families or relatively few sample families had telephones (China, Nigeria, Thailand).

The sample families in the 8 countries also split into two groups regarding ownership of *television* sets: a group in which at least 97 percent of sample families owned at least one television set (Belgium, Hong Kong, Italy, and the United States) and a group in which a moderate percentage of families (31 to 56 percent) owned one or more television sets (China, Nigeria, Portugal, and Thailand).

Household appliances

The two household appliances included in Table 4.8 are ones that relate to the amount of time families spend in the major tasks of washing family clothes and obtaining and storing food. In 4 of the 8 countries reporting on these appliances, at least 80 percent of sample families had *clothes washing machines*. In 2 of the countries, moderate percentages had washing machines (53 percent in Portugal and 29 percent in China). Two countries, Nigeria and Thailand, reported virtually no families owning a machine for washing clothes.

When examining the percentages of sample families owning a *refrigerator*, we must keep in mind that in some countries, a refrigerator is viewed as essential for food storage, whereas in other countries, common food-preservation methods do not necessitate this appliance. In the 5 industrialized nations reporting on ownership of refrigerators (Belgium, Hong Kong, Italy, Portugal, and the United States) at least 88 percent of sample families owned this appliance. In the remaining 3 nations (China, Nigeria, and Thailand) 10 to 25 percent of sample families owned this appliance.

Child Health Information

Although only indirectly related to the use of early childhood services, national sample data about children's health status, examinations, and problems were also obtained by researchers in 10 of the 11 countries participating in the study. Tables 4.9 and 4.10 summarize this data.

Table 4.9   Percentage distribution of national sample 4-year-olds
according to health status

Country/ Territory	N	Health Status			
		Excellent	Good	Fair	Poor
Belgium (Fr.)	424	40	45	13	2
China (PRC)[+]	12,835	48	45	6	1
Finland	576	58	38	4	0
Germany (FRG)	509	—	—	—	—
Hong Kong[+]	947	17	38	43	2
Italy	1,000	22	62	15	1
Nigeria[+]	1,295	45	48	5	2
Portugal	581	12	57	26	5
Spain	480	41	53	5	1
Thailand	2,466	14	61	22	3
United States	432	71	24	4	1

Note. The symbol [+] indicates that weighted data were used for analysis. A dash
indicates that no data were available.

Health Status

Table 4.9 shows over 90 percent of sample families in 5 countries (China,
Finland, Nigeria, Spain, and the United States) reporting their 4-year-old
children to be in *excellent* or *good health*. In the remaining 5 countries the
corresponding percentages (for *excellent* or *good health*) ranged from 55
percent (for Hong Kong) to 85 percent (for Belgium).

Table 4.10 Percentages of national sample 4-year-olds having various health examinations and exhibiting vision/hearing problems

Country/ Territory	N	% With					
		Medical Exam	Dental Exam	Vision Exam	Vision Problem[a]	Hearing Exam	Hearing Problem[a]
Belgium (Fr.)	424	—	—	—	—	—	—
China (PRC)[+]	12,835	40	—	—	—	—	—
Finland	576	98	95	93	7	91	4
Germany (FRG)	509	—	—	—	—	—	—
Hong Kong[+]	947	—	—	—	—	—	—
Italy	1,000	93	16	21	22	33	47
Nigeria[+]	1,295	53	10	10	—	3	—
Portugal	581	92	10	10	33	13	46
Spain	480	91	—	—	—	—	—
Thailand	2,466	42	9	1	9	1	21
United States	432	94	56	44	6	53	12

Note. The symbol [+] indicates that weighted data were used for analysis. A dash indicates that no data were available.

[a]Percentage is based on the number who had vision (or hearing) checked.

HEALTH EXAMINATIONS AND HEALTH PROBLEMS

As Table 4.10 shows, 8 countries reported data about the percentage of 4-year-olds who had undergone a *medical* examination during the previous year. In 5 of these countries (Finland, Italy, Portugal, Spain, and the United States) over 90 percent of the children had been examined during the previous year. In China, Nigeria, and Thailand the *medical* examination percentages ranged from 40 to 53 percent.

Six nations reported information about children's *dental, vision,* and *hearing* examinations. In Finland over 90 percent of national sample children had undergone all three types of examinations during the past year — much higher percentages than those reported by any of the other 5 countries. Also in Finland, only small percentages of those undergoing vision and hearing check-ups were found to have related problems. In the United States approximately half of national sample parents reported that their children had received each of the three (*dental, vision,* and *hearing*) examinations, and only small percentages of those examined were found to have *vision* or *hearing* problems.

The remaining countries (Italy, Nigeria, Portugal, and Thailand) reported no more than a third of national sample children having received *vision* or *hearing* tests. Three of these countries (Italy, Portugal, and Thailand) reported information about problems, and although only small percentages of children received the check-ups, at least a fifth of those examined were found to have problems in *vision* or *hearing.*

COMPARING NATIONAL SAMPLES WITH GENERAL POPULATIONS

As noted earlier in this chapter, parents in any given national sample represented a relatively young segment of the nation's adult population. Consequently, when researchers compared characteristics of national samples with characteristics of their respective general populations, certain differences were to be expected. For example, during the past few decades, many nations have increased the requirements for the number of years one must remain in school. Therefore, it was not surprising to find that across the nations, the relatively young parents in the national samples generally averaged more years of education than did adults in the general population.

For certain variables, it was difficult to locate corresponding population statistics to compare with the national sample statistics. This was the case for the variable of maternal employment. Whereas the national samples consisted generally of women 25 to 36 years old with at least one 4-

Table 4.11 Types of information used to assess the representativeness of national samples

Country/ Territory	Years of Education		Occupation Types	Mothers in Labor Force	Family Structure	Family Size	Other
	Mothers	Fathers					
Belgium (Fr.)	X	X	X	X	X	X	
China (PRC)	X	X	X			X	
Finland	X	X		X		X	X
Germany (FRG)				X	X	X	X
Hong Kong	X	X	X	X		X	
Italy	X	X		X		X	
Nigeria							
Portugal	X	X	X				
Spain							
Thailand	X	X	X	X		X	X
United States	X	X		X		X	X

year-old child, general population statistics about women's labor force participation are given for adult women of all ages, or for women between specific ages (e.g., ages 25 to 39). There are no general population statistics for the subgroup of women who have children of preschool age. Also, in many countries, population statistics are collected and published only every 5 to 10 years. This sometimes made them outdated and thus inappropriate for a comparison concerning a variable that changes as rapidly as maternal employment does.

Despite all these considerations, it is possible to make some statements about whether national samples were representative of their general populations. Recall that earlier, this chapter presented data for individual characteristics (e.g., parents' educational attainment, mothers' labor force participation), and for such characteristics, the differences found between samples and general populations were expected ones, based on the relative youth of parents in samples and the lack of suitable population statistics for comparison. Table 4.11 shows that 7 of the 11 participating countries were able to compare their national samples with their general populations on at least 4 different characteristics. Another 2 countries were able to make a comparison on 3 characteristics. In each of these 9 countries, since the differences found were generally in the expected direction, the 9 national samples may be deemed representative of their respective general populations.

In Nigeria the last reliable census was conducted in 1963, and another is planned for 1992–93. Because of the lack of up-to-date population information, it is not possible to make an accurate assessment of the representativeness of the Nigerian national sample. Spain was also unable to locate population statistics. That fact, combined with Spain's very high nonresponse and refusal rates reported in an earlier chapter, make it difficult — if not impossible — to assess the quality of the Spanish national sample.

REFERENCES

International Labour Office. (1990). *1989–90 yearbook of labour statistics.* Geneva: Author.

V
Study Findings: Families' Weekly Use of Early Childhood Services

Olayemi Onibokun, *Senior Research Fellow*
Institute of Education
University of Ibadan
Ibadan, Nigeria

Patricia P. Olmsted, *Senior Research Associate*
High/Scope Educational Research Foundation
Ypsilanti, Michigan

A premise of the IEA Preprimary Project is that care or education provided to young children by someone other than their parents — what we refer to as *extraparental,* or *early childhood,* services — takes many forms. The services can be formal or informal; they can take place in a private home (the child's or someone else's) or in an organized facility; they can involve one-on-one, small-group, or large-group settings — and these settings can include various kinds of caregivers or teachers, ranging from helpful friends or relatives to highly trained professionals. This chapter looks at questions such as these regarding the use of early childhood services:

In the various countries taking part in the Phase 1 study of the IEA/PPP, how many families typically turn to extraparental care or education for their 4-year-old children? What types of early childhood services do these families choose? When 4-year-olds do receive services, what does their week typically consist of — how many different settings (including caregivers/teachers) do they encounter, and how much time do they spend in each setting? Besides answering these questions and more, the chapter also presents information about the relationships between various household and family characteristics and family use of early childhood services.

Whether or Not Families Use Early Childhood Services

The study's 11 participating nations reported great variation regarding the use of extraparental care/education services for 4-year-old children. Table 5.1 presents the proportion of children in each country who attend at least one extraparental early childhood setting each week. (For this study, *attendance at a setting* or *use of an early childhood service* is counted if a 4-year-old is in a given extraparental care/education setting at least 2 hours per week.) The table shows that in Hong Kong and Belgium, nearly every 4-year-old attends an extraparental setting. In the rest of the study's industrialized European nations (other than Belgium) only about 70 to 85 percent of families use extraparental services for their 4-year-old children. Sizable, but even lower, are the corresponding percentages for the United States and China. Of all the study's countries, Nigeria and Thailand have the lowest proportions of parents enrolling their children in early childhood settings, 33 percent and 36 percent, respectively.

Before we look into the types of early childhood services families use and the extent of their service use, we will consider the reasons why some families in various nations *do not* use such services. If a family reported not using extraparental care/education services, the interviewer asked why exclusive parent/guardian care was the family's choice. Research staff coded the responses into the following four major categories: (1) *parent/guardian related* reasons, including (a) *social/emotional* reasons (such as wanting to be the primary adult in the child's early years), (b) *educational* reasons (such as wanting to teach the young child), and (c) *other* parent/guardian-related reasons (such as not having considered any other alternative); (2) *child-related* reasons (such as concern for special physical/developmental needs of the child or concern about the child's emotional closeness to the parent/guardian); (3) *facility-related* reasons (such as unavailability of services or lack of specific desired features); and (4) *other* reasons.

For each nation in which at least 10 percent of families reported using exclusively parent/guardian at-home care for their 4-year-olds, Table 5.2 shows the percentage distribution of families according to their reasons for choosing this type of care. The table includes the subcategories for *parent/guardian-related* reasons, since the percentages for these subcategories are relatively large and the patterns of percentages across these subcategories differ from country to country. This discussion is limited to the 7 countries in which the majority of sample families responded to the

Table 5.1 Percentage of 4-year-olds in at least one extraparental care/education setting each week

Country/ Territory	N	Non-Service Users (In Own Home, P/G Care, Only)		Service Users (In at Least 1 Extraparental Setting)		No Information	
		No.	% of N	No.	% of N	No.	% of N
Belgium (Fr.)	424	8	2	416	98	0	0
China (PRC)[+]	12,835	7,124	55	5,468	43	243	2
Finland	576	145	25	431	75	0	0
Germany (FRG)	509	92	18	417	82	0	0
Hong Kong[+]	947	—	—	947	100[a]	0	0
Italy	1,000	148	15	852	85	0	0
Nigeria[+]	1,295	841	65	435	33	19	2
Portugal	581	171	29	410	71	0	0
Spain	480	101	21	379	79	0	0
Thailand	2,466	1,555	63	894	36	17	1
United States	432	168	39	264	61	0	0

Note. The symbol [+] indicates that weighted data were used for analysis. Attendance at a setting, or use of a service, was counted if a 4-year-old was in a given extraparental care/education setting at least 2 hours per week. *P/G* denotes parent/guardian.

[a]Because 95 percent of 4-year-old children in Hong Kong attend *organized facility* settings, the Hong Kong sample was selected from those settings.

Table 5.2 Percentage distribution of families according to reasons for exclusively caring for their 4-year-olds at home

Country/ Territory	N	n Who Use P/G Care Only (% of N)	% of n Citing the Following Type [a] of Reason:						
			Parent/Guardian-Related						
			S/E	Educa-tional	Other	Child-Related	Facility-Related	Other	No Info
Belgium (Fr.)	424	8 (2)	—	—	—	—	—	—	—
China (PRC)[+]	12,835	7,124 (55)	1	47	3	13	32	3	1
Finland	576	145 (25)	11	45	33	2	7	1	1
Germany (FRG)	509	92 (18)	35	0	0	1	8	0	56
Hong Kong[+]	947	0	—	—	—	—	—	—	—
Italy	1,000	148 (15)	30	17	7	22	9	7	7
Nigeria[+]	1,295	841 (65)	8	16	6	3	9	6	52
Portugal	581	171 (29)	13	9	47	5	0	25	1
Spain	480	101 (21)	28	10	18	32	5	0	7
Thailand	2,466	1,555 (63)	29	16	40	6	0	7	2
United States	432	168 (39)	43	10	20	8	10	6	3

Note. The symbol [+] indicates that weighted data were used for analysis. Belgium and Hong Kong have no entries in the table because so few of their parents cared for children at home exclusively.

[a]Types of reasons are identified as follows: *S/E* refers to social/emotional needs of parent. *Educational* refers to parent's desire to teach child at home. *Child-related* refers to physical/developmental needs and personal/emotional needs. *Facility-related* refers to facility either being unavailable or lacking desired characteristics.

question about their reason for choosing parent/guardian at-home care.

In all 7 countries more than 50 percent of sample families gave *parent/guardian-related* reasons for choosing to be the sole providers of care for their 4-year-olds. This suggests that a lack of availability of early childhood care/education services (such as child care centers or family day care homes) is not the major reason parents do not use such services.

Within the *parent/guardian-related* category, *social/emotional* reasons were the most-often cited in each of 3 countries (Italy, Spain, and the United States) *educational* reasons were the most-often cited in 2 countries (China and Finland); and *other* reasons were the most-often cited in the remaining 2 countries (Portugal and Thailand).

Sizable percentages of families in Italy and Spain gave *child-related* reasons for being the sole providers of care/education for their 4-year-olds. China was the only country in which a sizable percentage cited *facility-related* reasons.

DETAILS OF FAMILIES' USE OF EARLY CHILDHOOD SERVICES

TYPES OF SETTINGS USED

To obtain data about what types of extraparental settings 4-year-olds in various countries attend each week, the National Research Coordinators (NRCs) jointly decided to categorize extraparental services as follows: (1) care in the child's *own home* (by a nonparent); (2) care in some *other home*, including informal care by a friend or relative as well as formal (licensed, or regulated) care (i.e., in a family day care home); (3) care in an *organized facility*, including both care-oriented and education-oriented large-group settings. Table 5.3 presents for each country the percentages of service-using 4-year-olds attending these three categories of settings. The percentages refer to the extraparental setting in which the child spends the *most time* each week (which the NRCs jointly decided to call the child's *first setting*).

Considering children's *first settings*, we can say that in 7 countries, including ones in Europe, Asia, and North America, the majority of service-using children are in *organized facilities*. This is true in countries with fairly low rates of extraparental-setting attendance (e.g., in China,

Table 5.3 Percentage distribution of 4-year-old service-users according to type of first setting[a]

Country/ Territory	N	n Who Attend 1 or More Settings (% of N)	% of n Attending the Following Type of First Setting:			
			Own Home (Nonparent)	Other Home	Organized Facility	Other
Belgium (Fr.)	424	416 (98)	1	4	95	0
China (PRC)[+]	12,835	5,468 (43)	12	10	76	2
Finland	576	431 (75)	7	47	46	0
Germany (FRG)	509	417 (82)	18	22	60	0
Hong Kong[+]	947	947 (100)	—	—	100[b]	—
Italy	1,000	852 (85)	3	3	94	0
Nigeria[+]	1,295	435 (33)	66	9	25	0
Portugal	581	410 (71)	23	35	41	1
Spain	480	379 (79)	6	6	87	1
Thailand	2,466	894 (36)	42	25	33	0
United States	432	264 (61)	14	28	58	0

Note. The symbol [+] indicates that weighted data were used for analysis.

[a]The child's *first setting* was defined as the extraparental care/education setting in which he/she typically spent the most time each week.

[b]Because 95 percent of 4-year-old children in Hong Kong attend *organized facility* settings, the Hong Kong sample was selected from those settings.

with 43 percent attendance) as well as in countries with high rates of extraparental-setting attendance (e.g., in Italy and Belgium).

In 2 countries (Finland and Portugal), relatively large proportions of families choose each of two types of extraparental settings: *other home* and *organized facility*. In both Nigeria and Thailand the largest proportion of families use *own home* (nonparent care) settings. However, whereas Nigerian families *principally* use this kind of setting, Thailand also reported quite sizable percentages of families using *organized facility* settings and *other home* settings.

Subcategories of types of settings

Table A.1 in Appendix A, p. 301, presents more-detailed information about the types of care/education settings that serve as children's first settings. For the *own home* and *other home* categories, the table gives the percentage breakdown for *relative* and *nonrelative* care; for the *organized facility* category, it gives percentages for the subcategories of *care, education, unclassified*, and *miscellaneous*.

In 4 of the 8 countries reporting at least 5 percent of children in *own home* care, it is *relatives* who provide all or most of this type of care (in China, Germany, Portugal, and Thailand). In 3 of the 8 countries (Finland, Spain, and the United States) *relatives* and *nonrelatives* alike provide the *own home* care, while in 1 of the 8 countries (Nigeria) *nonrelatives* are the usual *own home* care providers.

In *other home* settings various divisions between *relative* and *nonrelative* care can also be seen. Of the 8 countries where at least 5 percent of children attend *other home* settings, there are 5 (China, Germany, Portugal, Spain, and Thailand) where *relatives* are most often the caregivers. In the 3 remaining countries (Finland, Nigeria, and the United States) *nonrelatives* predominate as caregivers in *other home* settings. In Finland and the United States the *other home* setting is usually a family day care home, while in Nigeria the *other home* setting is more often an informal arrangement among friends.

Examination of the subcategories of *organized facility* across the various countries reveals that *educational* settings are most common in 9 of the 11 countries. In the remaining 2 countries (Portugal and Spain) the subcategory *unclassified* applies to all the organized facilities children attend. In 3 countries (China, Thailand, and the United States) more than 10 percent of 4-year-olds attend organized facilities classified as *care* settings. Finally, in Finland approximately 15 percent of children attend organized facilities classified as *miscellaneous*.

Types of settings used in urban versus rural areas

Researchers examined the use of extraparental care/education services for families living in urban areas and also for families living in rural areas. Table A.2 in Appendix A, p. 303, gives the information for these two groups of families across 8 nations. In 6 of the nations (China, Finland, Nigeria, Spain, Thailand, and the United States) there are notable differences in use patterns. For each of these 6 countries, a chi-square analysis indicated a significant difference between the distribution of urban families and the distribution of rural families among the following categories of settings: (1) *own home, parent care only;* (2) *own home, nonparent care;* (3) *other home;* and (4) *organized facility.* In each of these 6 countries, a higher percentage of rural families than of urban families reported caring for their 4-year-olds themselves (*own home, parent care only*). Also, a higher percentage of urban children than of rural children attend *organized facilities.*

NUMBER OF SETTINGS USED EACH WEEK

In studying children's weekly care patterns, researchers looked at how many different extraparental settings the 4-year-olds of the study's various countries typically experience. Table 5.4 concerns children who are service users (those attending at least one extraparental setting) and distributes them according to how many different settings they typically attend each week. In 8 of the 10 countries with findings reported in Table 5.4, at least two thirds of service-using children typically attend just one setting per week, and virtually no service-using children attend more than two different settings each week. The exceptions to this finding are Belgium and Germany, where the data indicate that sizable percentages of service-using 4-year-olds attend two settings, and fair percentages even attend three or four settings, each week.

COMBINATIONS OF SETTINGS USED BY FAMILIES

Since in many (7) of the nations, at least 20 percent of service-using 4-year-olds attend at least two extraparental settings each week, it is useful to look at the types of settings that families select as *second settings.* (The NRCs jointly decided to define the child's *second setting* as the extraparental setting in which he or she spends the *second-longest time* each week.) Table 5.5 distributes service-using children in 9 nations according to the type of *second setting* they typically attend. Compared with the

Table 5.4 Percentage distribution of 4-year-old service-users according
to number of extraparental settings attended each week

Country/ Territory	N	n Who Attend at Least 1 Setting (% of N)	% of n Attending the Following Number of Settings:			
			1	2	3	4
Belgium (Fr.)	424	416 (98)	31	41	23	5
China (PRC)[+]	12,835	5,468 (43)	84	14	2	0
Finland	576	431 (75)	79	19	2	0
Germany (FRG)	509	417 (82)	48	36	10	6
Hong Kong[+]	947	947[a] (100)	—	—	—	—
Italy	1,000	852 (85)	71	28	1	0
Nigeria[+]	1,295	435 (33)	95	5	0	0
Portugal	581	410 (71)	70	26	4	0
Spain	480	379 (79)	68	29	3	0
Thailand	2,466	894 (36)	88	12	0	0
United States	432	264 (61)	71	27	1	1

Note. The symbol [+] indicates that weighted data were used for analysis.
[a]Information was requested for one setting only.

findings about children's first settings, Table 5.5 findings reveal more variety. In only 3 of the 9 nations is *organized facility* the most common second setting; in 3 nations *other home* is most common, and in 3 nations *own
home (nonparent)* is most common.

Figure 5.1 illustrates the combination of first and second settings that
one is most likely to find in each of the study's participating countries

Table 5.5 Percentage distribution of 4-year-old service-users according to type of second setting[a] attended

Country/Territory	N	n Who Attend at Least 2 Settings (% of N)	% of n in Each of the Following Types of Second Settings:			
			Own Home (Nonparent)	Other Home	Organized Facility	Other
Belgium (Fr.)	424	310 (73)	5	25	70	0
China (PRC)[+]	12,835	706 (6)	53	34	4	9
Finland	576	90 (16)	19	22	59	0
Germany (FRG)	509	218 (43)	37	50	13	0
Hong Kong[+]	947	0[b]	—	—	—	—
Italy	1,000	249 (25)	38	56	6	0
Nigeria[+]	1,295	0[c]	—	—	—	—
Portugal	581	124 (21)	39	48	8	5
Spain	480	122 (25)	46	41	6	7
Thailand	2,466	106 (4)	61	28	11	0
United States	432	77 (18)	27	34	39	0

Note. The symbol [+] indicates that weighted data were used for analysis.

[a]The child's *second setting* was defined as the extraparental setting he/she attended for the second-longest time each week.

[b]Information was requested for one setting only.

[c]Insufficient information was available for inclusion.

Type of First Setting

	Own Home	Other Home	Organized Facility
Own Home	Thailand		China Spain
Other Home			Germany Italy Portugal
Organized Facility		Finland	Belgium United States

(left axis label: Type of Second Setting)

Note. Hong Kong and Nigeria are not included in Figure 5.1. In Hong Kong, information was requested about one setting only. In Nigeria there was insufficient information available about the second setting.

Figure 5.1 Most-frequent combinations of extraparental settings used by families in various countries each week

(except for Hong Kong and Nigeria). The cell in which a country appears represents the type of first setting most frequently used and the type of second setting most frequently used for extraparental care/education in that country. Notice that in the figure, five of the nine cells contain at least one country, which indicates the diversity in combinations of extraparental early childhood settings used by families around the world.

TIME CHILDREN SPEND IN EXTRAPARENTAL SETTINGS

When children participate in one or more extraparental settings each week, how much time do they typically spend there? Table 5.6 presents the average number of hours service-using children spend in their first,

Table 5.6 Average hours 4-year-old service-users spend each week in individual settings and in all settings combined

Country/ Territory	Setting(s)											
	First			Second			Third			Combined		
	No. of Service Users	Mean Hr. Spent	SD	No. of Service Users	Mean Hr. Spent	SD	No. of Service Users	Mean Hr. Spent	SD	No. of Service Users	Mean Hr. Spent[a]	SD
Belgium (Fr.)	416	25.8	6.8	310	8.6	5.1	116	5.2	1.7	416	33.9	11.6
China (PRC)[+]	5,468	52.6	22.5	686	27.2	28.4	—	—	—	5,468	55.5	24.2
Finland	430	31.9	14.2	88	7.4	6.0	—	—	—	430	33.7	15.2
Germany (FRG)	411	19.6	11.4	207	8.0	6.1	61	4.6	3.3	411	24.5	15.1
Hong Kong[+]	947	17.2	7.0	—	—	—	—	—	—	—	—	—
Italy	852	32.6	9.2	248	11.2	7.3	—	—	—	852	35.9	11.4
Nigeria[+]	435	35.1	11.9	—	—	—	—	—	—	—	—	—
Portugal	409	39.7	20.2	124	13.8	9.5	—	—	—	409	44.1	21.5
Spain	379	29.1	11.4	117	17.7	10.9	—	—	—	379	35.0	16.3
Thailand	886	52.9	33.5	106	26.9	24.6	—	—	—	882	55.6	34.9
United States	263	25.0	16.6	75	8.5	6.9	—	—	—	263	27.8	17.7

Note. The symbol [+] indicates that weighted data were used for analysis. For China, Finland, Italy, Portugal, Spain, Thailand, and the United States, dashes indicate that there were too few cases with a third setting. In Hong Kong and Nigeria, information was requested for one setting only. Numbers of service-users may be lower than in Tables 5.4 and 5.5 because of missing information.

[a]Because of varying sample sizes, the sum of the mean hours for individual settings does not equal the mean hours for combined settings.

second, and third settings and in all their extraparental settings combined. The averages for *all settings combined* vary greatly, from 24.5 hours per week in Germany to 55.6 hours per week in Thailand. Besides Thailand, China is the only other nation that reported an average of over 50 hours per week for *all settings combined*. In 5 countries children average 30 to 45 hours per week in *all settings combined*, and in 2 countries (Germany and the United States) they average fewer hours than this.

In several countries, average time spent in *all settings combined* equals or is close to average time spent in the *first setting;* these are nations in which most of the service-using children attend only one extraparental setting. Nine countries reported enough children participating in at least two settings to permit calculation of the average time spent in each setting, the first and the second. As expected (because of the definitions of *first setting* and *second setting*), for each of the 9 countries, the average time spent in the first setting is greater than that spent in the second setting. However, our findings about the two settings do point up this difference: In most of the 9 countries (such as Finland and the United States), children are in their second settings for comparatively few hours per week, but in 3 of the 9 countries (China, Spain, and Thailand) children spend more than a third of their "extraparental hours" in their second settings.

When findings about the time children spend in all extraparental settings are combined with findings about the number of settings they attend, we can make the following observations: (1) Service-using children in China and Thailand spend large amounts of their time in their first settings, and if they attend second settings, they spend only about half as much time there. (2) Service-using children in Belgium, Germany, and the United States typically spend relatively small amounts of their time each week in each of two or more extraparental settings (20 to 26 hours in the first setting and less than 10 hours in the second setting).

Time Children Spend Traveling to First Settings

Because researchers were interested in how convenient families find their children's care/education arrangements, sample families were asked how much time service-using 4-year-olds spent traveling to their first settings (i.e., out-of-home first settings). For the 11 nations taking part in the study, Table 5.7 presents the data that answer this question. A cursory look at the table reveals that in general, most children attending extraparental settings travel for only a few minutes to reach their first settings. In 7 coun-

Table 5.7 Percentage distribution of 4-year-old service-users according to time spent traveling to their first settings

Country/ Territory	N	n Who Travel to First Settings (% of N)	% of n Traveling the Following Number of Minutes:[a]				
			1–5	6–10	11–15	16–30	31+
Belgium (Fr.)	424	406 (96)	64	26	5	5	0
China (PRC)[+]	12,835	4,890 (38)	0	0	73	24	3
Finland	576	396 (69)	57	23	12	7	1
Germany (FRG)	509	321 (63)	50	33	12	4	1
Hong Kong[+]	947	946 (100)	0	0	81	14	5
Italy	1,000	816 (82)	58	26	10	6	0
Nigeria[+]	1,295	135 (10)	35	31	15	18	1
Portugal	581	308 (53)	54	19	11	11	5
Spain	480	353 (74)	52	26	14	7	1
Thailand	2,466	515 (21)	58	20	10	10	2
United States	432	213 (49)	47	27	14	9	3

Note. The symbol [+] indicates that weighted data were used for analysis.

[a]In asking about travel times, China and Hong Kong used only three categories: 15 minutes or less, 16–30 minutes, more than 30 minutes.

tries (Belgium, Finland, Germany, Italy, Portugal, Spain, and Thailand) at least 50 percent of children travel less than 6 minutes. In most of these 7 countries an additional 20 to 30 percent of children travel 6 to 10 minutes. This means that at least 70 percent of children in these 7 countries live within at most 10 minutes of their first settings.

The percentages for the United States are close to those for the 7 countries just mentioned; about three fourths of service-using children in the United States travel for no more than 10 minutes to reach their first settings. In Nigeria, nearly equal percentages of children travel for 1 to 5 minutes (35 percent) and for 6 to 10 minutes (31 percent) to reach first settings. This results in 66 percent traveling for no more than 10 minutes.

Though, across the 11 countries, most children travel no more than 10 to 15 minutes to reach the care/eduction setting where they spend the most time each week, some children must travel for much longer periods of time (more than 30 minutes). Table 5.7 data indicate that in each of 2 countries (Hong Kong and Portugal), 5 percent of families live more than 30 minutes from their children's first settings. In the remaining 9 countries, the percentages for over 30 minutes of travel are lower — all 3 percent or less.

MODE OF TRANSPORTATION TO FIRST SETTINGS

Knowing travel times is useful only if the *mode* of transportation is also taken into account. Table 5.8 presents the data obtained when families were asked about what form of transportation they and/or their children used to get to first settings.

Traveling by *foot* is the most common form of transportation in 8 countries (China, Germany, Hong Kong, Italy, Nigeria, Portugal, Spain, and Thailand). When Table 5.8 data are combined with Table 5.7 data, it is evident that those countries where walking is most common are generally those where most children travel no more than 5 minutes. The findings are less clear for China and Hong Kong, both of whom included a category of "15 minutes or less" in their P/G Interviews.

In Germany similar percentages of parents reported their children traveling by *foot* (46 percent) and by *private auto* (38 percent). In 3 countries (Belgium, Finland, and the United States) majorities of parents reported transporting their children by *private auto*. At least 1 percent of families in each country reported using *public transport* (i.e., municipal bus, streetcar, subway) to reach the first setting, but the percentages for the various countries are low, and no country's percentage exceeds 10 percent. In 5 countries

Table 5.8   Percentage distribution of 4-year-old service-users according to mode of transportation to their first settings

Country/ Territory	N	n Traveling to First Setting (% of N)	% of n Traveling by: Foot	Private Auto	Public Transport	Other[a]
Belgium (Fr.)	424	394 (93)	41	57	1	1
China (PRC)[+]	12,835	4,903 (38)	59	0	3	38
Finland	576	396 (69)	36	55	2	7
Germany (FRG)	509	321 (63)	46	38	3	13
Hong Kong[+]	947	946 (100)	64	3	8	25
Italy	1,000	826 (83)	85	0	7	8
Nigeria[+]	1,295	137 (11)	79	14	7	0
Portugal	581	306 (53)	63	21	7	9
Spain	480	355 (74)	74	18	8	0
Thailand	2,466	525 (21)	55	17	10	18
United States	432	220 (51)	15	74	1	10

Note. The symbol [+] indicates that weighted data were used for analysis.

[a]Other includes such forms of transportation as bicycle, motorcycle, boat, and provider-supplied transportation (i.e., van, school bus).

(Belgium, China, Finland, Germany, and the United States) the *public transport* percentages range from only 1 to 3 percent. In the remaining 6 countries (Hong Kong, Italy, Nigeria, Portugal, Spain, and Thailand) the *public transport* percentages range from 7 to 10 percent.

Families in 9 countries reported their children using *other* forms of transportation to first settings. In 5 countries, this category included at least 10 percent of children. The forms of transportation included in the *other* category varied from nation to nation and included bicycle, motorcycle, boat, and provider-supplied van or school bus.

Meals or Snacks Provided in the First Setting

The auxiliary features of care/education services, such as any nutritional features, were of interest to researchers. Consequently, families were asked what meals or snacks their children received in their first settings. Table 5.9 presents, for 10 nations, the percentages of children for whom various meals/snacks are provided in the first setting. The table includes information about three meals (*morning, midday,* and *evening*) and three snacks (*morning, afternoon,* and *bedtime*).

The findings indicate that in 9 of the 10 countries, at least 25 percent of children are in settings that provide at least two meals/snacks. The type of meal or snack most commonly provided varies from country to country, but it is generally the *morning meal,* the *midday meal,* or the *afternoon snack.* In Belgium, very few children attend a first setting in which meals/snacks are provided, but 17 percent do receive a *morning snack.* (For nearly all 4-year-olds in Belgium, the first setting is a part-day preschool.) In 4 countries (China, Germany, Nigeria, and Thailand) an *evening meal* is provided for more than 20 percent of the 4-year-olds attending first settings.

Parental Cost for Various Types of First Settings

Researchers in each country asked sample parents how much they paid for their child's extraparental care or education. Table 5.10 presents cost data for children's first settings. The table indicates the number of sample families *using* each of three types of settings, the number of these same families *who paid for* their child's attendance at the setting, and the average monthly cost for parents who paid.

Table 5.9 Percentage distribution of 4-year-old service-users according to types of meals/snacks provided in their first settings

Country/ Territory	N	n in Settings With Meal or Snack (% of N)	% of n Receiving the Following Type of Meal or Snack:					
			Mrng. Meal	Mrng. Snack	Midday Meal	Aftn. Snack	Eve. Meal	Bdtm. Snack
Belgium (Fr.)	424	415 (98)	1	17	1	1	1	0
China (PRC)[+]	12,835	3,453 (27)	28	32	77	32	36	0
Finland	576	366 (64)	74	12	98	90	7	3
Germany (FRG)	509	149 (29)	49	54	61	46	22	10
Hong Kong[+]	947	947 (100)	—	—	—	—	—	—
Italy	1,000	675 (68)	5	7	96	25	2	1
Nigeria[+]	1,295	26 (02)	20	32	65	5	27	0
Portugal	581	246 (42)	27	30	83	77	13	0
Spain	480	129 (27)	13	21	77	54	6	0
Thailand	2,466	596 (24)	34	27	86	48	30	3
United States	432	190 (44)	39	53	67	64	6	1

Note. The symbol [+] indicates that weighted data were used for analysis. Dashes indicate that no information was available.

Table 5.10 Average monthly parental cost in U.S. dollars for various types of extraparental care/education

Country/Territory	MHI[a]	Own Home			Other Home			Organized Facility		
		No. Using	No. Paying	Cost/Mo (% of MHI)	No. Using	No. Paying	Cost/Mo (% of MHI)	No. Using	No. Paying	Cost/Mo (% of MHI)
Belgium (Fr.)	—	5	0	—	15	2	$132	396	65	$5
China (PRC)[+]	—	—	—	—	—	—	—	—	—	—
Finland	$2,396	31	20	$230 (10)	201	174	$137 (6)	199	154	$136 (6)
Germany (FRG)	$1,910	73	10	$272 (14)	92	12	$166 (9)	252	242	$35 (2)
Hong Kong[+]	$705	—	—	—	—	—	—	947	947	$27 (4)
Italy	$1,800	27	5	$4 (<1)	25	2	—	800	327	$35[b] (2)
Nigeria[+]	—	287	252	$7	40	33	$8	109	87	$2
Portugal	$347	93	18	$26 (7)	144	54	$26 (7)	168	160	$24 (7)

Table 5.10 Average monthly parental cost in U.S. dollars for various types of extraparental care/education (continued)

Country/ Territory	MHI[a]	Own Home			Other Home			Organized Facility		
		No. Using	No. Paying	Cost/Mo (% of MHI)	No. Using	No. Paying	Cost/Mo (% of MHI)	No. Using	No. Paying	Cost/Mo (% of MHI)
Spain	—	—	—	—	—	—	—	—	—	—
Thailand	$134	370	34	$18 (13)	225	31	$8 (6)	297	280	$2 (1)
United States	$2,166	38	21	$100 (5)	74	54	$120 (6)	152	117	$144 (7)

Note. The symbol [+] indicates that weighted data were used for analysis. Dashes indicate that no information was available.

[a]MHI is the average monthly household income for 1988 (or the closest year available) converted into U.S. dollars. Currency exchange rates for 1988-89 were used for the conversion.

[b]Because of missing data, cost per month for *organized facility* was provided by Italy's National Research Coordinator.

In Belgium only a small proportion of sample parents pay for their children's attendance at any type of setting. However in 4 other countries (Germany, Italy, Portugal, and Thailand) relatively large proportions of families using *organized facilities* pay for their children to attend this type of setting, while much smaller proportions pay for *own home* and *other home* settings. In the remaining nations, most families using any of the three types of settings pay for these services.

Examination of monthly parental costs across the various types of settings within a country reveals some patterns. For example, in Portugal parental costs are almost identical for the three different types of settings, while in other countries (e.g., Finland, Germany, Thailand, and the United States) parents pay quite different amounts, depending on the type of setting. In a few countries, in fact, one type of setting stands out as costing, on average, either much more or much less than the other two types. *Own home* settings in Finland are an example of this.

For some countries, the data present a picture of financial support of one or more types of settings by some agency or organization (such as government or a religious group). For example, in Belgium support of *organized facility* settings is evident, whereas in Finland support of *other home* and *organized facility* settings is clear. (Earlier, Chapter 2 presented some information about public and private support of services in various countries.)

For 6 of the nations in Table 5.10, researchers were able to determine parental cost for services as a percentage of average monthly household income (MHI). Across these 6 countries, they found that the highest percentage (14 percent) of MHI is paid by the relatively small number of parents in Germany who choose *own home* extraparental care; the lowest percentage (less than 1 percent) of MHI is paid by the small number of parents in Italy who choose *own home* extraparental care. Overall, in Germany, Italy, and Thailand most families pay, on average, a very small percentage (only 1 to 2 percent of MHI) for care/education services. In Hong Kong the majority pay an average of 4 percent. In Finland, Portugal, and the United States most families pay an average of 6 to 7 percent of MHI for early childhood services.

Table A.3 in Appendix A, p. 304, presents additional information about the various countries' parental costs for 4-year-old children's attendance at three types of settings. The table shows the median hourly cost and the median weekly cost for each type of setting, and it lists the average number of hours per week that children attend each type of setting. As indicated in the table, in most countries parents reported different average attendance hours for the different types of settings. For example, German children attend *other home* settings an average of 30.0 hours a week and *organized facility* settings an average of 20.5 hours a week. These differences in total attendance-hours affect the calculation of average parental cost per week, as shown in Table A.3. (Of course, they also affect calculation of average cost per month, as shown in Table 5.10.)

Parents' Satisfaction With Early Childhood Services

The household-survey approach of this study gave researchers a unique opportunity to gauge parental satisfaction with existing early childhood services. Table 5.11 presents the levels of parental satisfaction with the first setting and with the second setting attended by their children (data were reported by parents in 10 nations and 8 nations, respectively). With first settings in 9 of the 10 countries, more than 50 percent of parents are *very satisfied*. Only in Hong Kong is the percentage of *very satisfied* parents less than 50 percent. Examining, across the 10 countries, the percentages of parents who gave their children's first settings either level of positive rating (*very satisfied* or *somewhat satisfied*), reveals that positive-rating parents constitute 93 to 100 percent of parents rating first settings.

Inspection of parents' levels of satisfaction with their children's second settings indicates that in every one of the 8 countries with data available for both settings, the percentage of parents reporting *very satisfied* with the second setting is equal to or higher than the percentage reporting *very satisfied* with the first setting. When percentages for the two positive ratings (*very satisfied* and *somewhat satisfied*) are combined, in each of the 8 countries, positive-rating parents make up 95 to 100 percent of those rating second settings.

Researchers also looked at the relationship between level of parental satisfaction with the child's first setting and *mother's years of education*, *father's years of education*, and *type of setting* across the 10 nations reporting parental satisfaction data. In only 3 nations did they find significant relationships between parental level of satisfaction and either parent's years of education. In Italy and Nigeria families in which fathers have more years of education are more satisfied with their children's care/education settings. In Spain the direction of this relationship is reversed: Families in which fathers have fewer years of education are more satisfied with their children's care/education settings.

Table 5.12 presents, for each type of first setting, the percentage of parents using that type who are *very satisfied* with it. For 9 countries,

Table 5.11 Percentage distribution of service-using families according to level of satisfaction with first and second settings

Country/ Territory	n_1 Rating First Setting (n_2 Rating Second Setting)	% of n_1 Rating First Setting as:				% of n_2 Rating Second Setting as:			
		Very Satis.	Some-what Satis.	Not Very Satis.	Not at All Satis.	Very Satis.	Some-what Satis.	Not Very Satis.	Not at All Satis.
Belgium (Fr.)	395 (234)	57	38	4	1	61	34	3	2
China (PRC)[+]	5,570 (693)	52	41	6	1	52	43	4	1
Finland	428 (86)	81	18	1	0	85	14	1	0
Germany (FRG)	—	—	—	—	—	—	—	—	—
Hong Kong[+]	906	14	86	0	0	—	—	—	—
Italy	847 (249)	62	32	5	1	72	25	3	0
Nigeria[+]	449	78	16	5	1	—	—	—	—
Portugal	405 (119)	66	32	2	0	66	32	2	0
Spain	376 (121)	78	19	2	1	85	12	3	0
Thailand	890 (105)	80	19	1	0	85	15	0	0
United States	262 (76)	88	10	2	0	89	11	0	0

Note. The symbol [+] indicates that weighted data were used for analysis. Dashes indicate that no information was available. Missing-data cases were deleted, and percentages were calculated using remaining cases. No country reported over 10 percent missing data for this item.

Table 5.12 Percent of families very satisfied with first settings, according to type of setting

Country/Territory	N	Own Home (Nonparent)		Other Home		Organized Facility		χ^2
		No. Using	% Very Satisfied	No. Using	% Very Satisfied	No. Using	% Very Satisfied	
Belgium (Fr.)	424	—	—[a]	6	83	389	57	0.79
China (PRC)[+]	12,835	656	70	558	75	4,108	46	283.86*
Finland	576	30	87	200	80	198	80	0.81
Germany (FRG)	509	—	—	—	—	—	—	—
Hong Kong[+]	947	—	—	—	—	906	14	—
Italy	1,000	27	67	25	76	795	62	2.41
Nigeria[+]	1,295	285	85	40	78	105	61	157.25*
Portugal	581	93	76	144	73	167	55	17.38*
Spain	480	24	79	21	71	327	78	0.49
Thailand	2,466	368	88	225	84	295	66	47.60*
United States	432	37	92	74	88	151	87	0.58

Note. The symbol [+] indicates that weighted data were used for analysis. Dashes mean no data were available.

[a]Too few cases to be included.   * $p < .01$ (χ^2 analysis)

researchers used chi-square procedures to compare parental satisfaction among the different types of settings. In 4 of the 9 countries (China, Nigeria, Portugal, and Thailand) they found a significant relationship between type of setting and percentage of parents who are *very satisfied*. In each of these 4 countries, the group of parents using *organized facility* settings contains the lowest percentage of *very satisfied* users; the percentages of *very satisfied* users are generally similar for *own home* and *other home* settings. There are similar but nonsignificant relationships between level of satisfaction and type of setting for most of the remaining countries. In general, the lowest percentage of *very satisfied* parents is found in the group of families using *organized facility* settings.

PROBLEMS WITH EARLY CHILDHOOD SERVICES

Researchers wondered whether parents were giving superficial answers to the generally stated satisfaction question and whether their responses to questions about specific problems with settings might reveal a different picture. However, as Table 5.13 shows, across the study's 11 countries, only small percentages of sample parents responded that specific problems applied to their children's first settings. (Examination of the data revealed very few problems related to second settings, therefore those data are not included in Table 5.13.) Across the 11 countries, a total of 143 specific problems were posed (i.e, Belgian researchers asked parents about 9 possible problems; Chinese researchers, about 15 possible problems). Only 43 (30 percent) of these 143 posed problems were cited by at least 1 percent of parents in some nation. Of these 43 problems, 32 (74 percent) were cited by at most 5 percent of parents in any given nation. In summary, across the 11 nations, very few parents were willing or able to cite specific problems with the early childhood settings their children attended.

Examination of Table 5.13 data country by country indicates that although the percentages of Nigerian parents reporting problems were small, parents did report problems in 9 of the 15 possible categories. Chinese parents noted problems in 8 of the 15 categories, with percentages ranging from 3 to 10 percent. In 2 countries, at least 1 percent of parents cited problems in every category posed in their country's questionnaire (Germany posed only 4 categories; Hong Kong, only 8 categories).

When we examine the data by problem categories, we note that at least 2 percent of parents in 6 countries (Belgium, China, Hong Kong,

Italy, Nigeria, and Portugal) cited *facility/equipment* problems. At least 1 percent of parents in each of 5 countries (Belgium, China, Germany, Italy, and Nigeria) noted problems with the *hours of operation* of the setting, and at least 1 percent of parents in each of 5 countries (Belgium, China, Germany, Hong Kong, and Nigeria) responded that they had problems with *other children* in the setting. Finally, *cost* was a problem for 2 percent or more of the parents reporting in each of 5 countries (China, Germany, Hong Kong, Nigeria, and Portugal).

It is interesting to note which specific categories of problems were reported by parents in *very few* countries. For example, in only 1 nation (Portugal) were problems of *safety, sanitation, or nutrition* cited by parents. *Unqualified teacher/caregiver* was noted as a problem by parents in only 3 countries (China, Hong Kong, and Nigeria). Also, *staff turnover* was cited as a problem by parents in only 3 countries (Belgium, China, and Hong Kong). Finally, parents in only 3 countries (China, Hong Kong, and Nigeria) responded that the *location* of their children's care/education settings was a problem.

For each country, researchers examined the relationship between level of parental satisfaction and reporting of problems with the first setting. In every country the proportion of *very satisfied* parents who cited first-setting problems was significantly lower than the proportion of less-satisfied families who cited first-setting problems.

REASONS PARENTS GIVE FOR USING EARLY CHILDHOOD SERVICES

Do parents use early childhood services because they are employed and need child care during their working hours — or because they believe that an extraparental care/education experience is important for one or more aspects (e.g., cognitive or social aspects) of their child's development? Table 5.14 presents, for 9 nations, the major reasons sample parents gave for using care/education services (first settings). If parents gave multiple reasons, they were asked to specify the "most important" reason.

In each of 5 countries (Finland, Nigeria, Portugal, Thailand, and the United States) at least 50 percent of parents indicated that a *parent-related* reason led to their decision to use the first setting. In each of these 5 countries, *employment or job* was the most frequently cited parent-related reason.

In each of 4 countries (Germany, Hong Kong, Italy, and Spain) at least

Table 5.13 Percentage distribution of service-using families according to types of problems with first setting

Country/Territory	N	n Using at Least 1 Setting (% of N)	% of n Reporting the Following Types[a] of Problems:														
			1	2	3	4	5	6	7	8	9	10	11	12	13	14	15
Belgium (Fr.)	424	416 (98)	—	2	NA	3	NA	—	NA	—	NA	5	NA	NA	3	2	—
China (PRC)+	12,835	5,468 (43)	3	3	—	4	—	9	—	—	—	10	—	—	3	3	3
Finland	576	431 (75)	—	—	—	—	—	—	—	—	—	—	—	—	—	—	—
Germany (FRG)	509	417 (82)	NA	10	NA	NA	NA	NA	NA	4	NA	NA	NA	NA	1	NA	4
Hong Kong+	947	947 (100)	7	NA	NA	NA	10	3	NA	20	NA	21	NA	NA	13	6	18
Italy	1,000	852 (85)	—	1	—	1	—	—	—	—	—	2	—	—	—	—	—
Nigeria+	1,295	435 (33)	4	1	1	—	2	1	1	—	—	2	—	—	2	—	3
Portugal	581	410 (71)	—	—	—	2	—	—	1	—	—	2	1	—	—	—	2

Table 5.13 Percentage distribution of service-using families according to types of problems with first setting (continued)

Country/ Territory	N	n Using at Least 1 Setting (% of N)	% of n Reporting the Following Types[a] of Problems:														
			1	2	3	4	5	6	7	8	9	10	11	12	13	14	15
Spain	480	379 (79)	—	—	—	—	—	—	1	—	—	—	—	—	—	—	—
Thailand	2,466	894 (36)	—	—	—	—	—	—	—	—	—	—	—	—	—	—	—
United States	432	264 (61)	—	—	—	—	—	—	—	—	—	—	—	—	—	—	—

Note. The symbol + indicates that weighted data were used for analysis. A dash indicates that no data were available or that the entry is less than 1 percent. *NA* indicates the question was not asked.

[a]1 = location; 2 = hours of operation; 3 = exclusion of sick children; 4 = personal characteristics of teacher/caregiver; 5 = unreliability of teacher/caregiver; 6 = unqualified teacher/caregiver; 7 = teacher/caregiver disliked by child; 8 = philosophy of program; 9 = religious orientation; 10 = facility/equipment; 11 = safety, sanitation, nutrition; 12 = negative atmosphere; 13 = other children; 14 = staff turnover; 15 = cost.

Table 5.14 Percentage distribution of service-using families according to major reason for using first setting

| | | | % of n Citing the Following Type[a] of Major Reason: | | | | | | | | | | | |
| | | | Parent-Related | | | | | Child-Related | | | | | | |
Country/ Territory	N	n Using at Least 1 Setting (% of N)	Wk	Ed	Ob	Oth	Total	Ed	S/E	Hlth	Oth	Total	Other	No Info
Belgium (Fr.)	424	416 (98)	—	—	—	—	—	—	—	—	—	—	—	—
China (PRC)+	12,835	5,468 (43)	—	—	—	—	—	—	—	—	—	—	—	—
Finland	576	431 (75)	76	—	—	—	80	—	14	—	—	19	1	0
Germany (FRG)	509	417 (82)	22	—	5	7	35	6	57	—	—	63	0	2
Hong Kong+	947	947 (100)	—	—	—	—	—	29	59	—	—	88	0	12
Italy	1,000	852 (85)	19	—	—	—	22	33	42	—	—	76	1	1
Nigeria+	1,295	435 (33)	46	12	—	6	66	15	—	—	—	22	8	4

Table 5.14 Percentage distribution of service-using families according to major reason for using first setting (continued)

Country/ Territory	N	n Using at Least 1 Setting (% of N)	% of n Citing the Following Type[a] of Major Reason:											
			Parent-Related					Child-Related					Other	No Info
			Wk	Ed	Ob	Oth	Total	Ed	S/E	Hlth	Oth	Total		
Portugal	581	410 (71)	52	—	—	—	57	—	22	—	—	28	14	1
Spain	480	379 (79)	28	—	—	—	36	43	12	—	8	63	1	0
Thailand	2,466	894 (36)	70	—	—	—	76	10	8	—	—	19	1	4
United States	432	264 (61)	36	—	6	—	51	19	21	—	—	42	6	1

Note. The symbol [+] indicates that weighted data were used for analysis. A dash indicates that no data were available or that the entry is less than 5 percent.

[a] Types of parent-related reasons: Wk = employment or job; Ed = education or training; Ob = obligations to family or community; Oth = other. Types of child-related reasons: Ed = preparation for school; S/E = social/emotional development; Hlth = physical health of child; Oth = other.

50 percent of parents indicated that a *child-related* reason led to their decision to use the first setting. In 3 of these 4 countries the most frequently cited child-related reason was the *social/emotional development* of the child, while in the remaining country (Spain) the most frequently cited child-related reason was the *education or training* of the child.

In the United States, the percentages citing *parent-related* and *child-related* reasons were similar to each other. However, if the percentage of American parents citing *education or training* of the child (19 percent) is added to the percentage citing *social/emotional development* of the child (21 percent), the combined percentage (40 percent) is greater than the percentage citing parental *employment or job* (36 percent).

INFLUENCES RELATED TO USE OF SERVICES

Based on information reported in the early childhood literature, researchers selected family and community variables (e.g., *mother's completed years of education, father's occupational level, marital status, urban/rural residence*) and examined the relationship between each variable and hours of use of early childhood services, in preparation for regression analyses. As a result of this examination, they selected a set of predictor variables for the analysis: (1) *urban/rural residence*, (2) *number of children in the family*, (3) *mother's completed years of education*, (4) *father's completed years of education*, (5) *mother's hours away from the child each week*, and (6) *father's hours away from the child each week.* Tables A.4 and A.5 in Appendix A, pp. 306–308, present the descriptive information for these six independent variables and for the criterion variable *total service hours* used each week, as well as the correlation matrix for these variables for each country.

Table 5.15 provides a summary of the results of the ordinary least squares regression analyses for the study's 11 participating nations. The coefficients of determination (R^2) reveal that the proportion of the criterion variable (*hours of use* of early childhood services) explained by the predictor variables in the regression model ranges from .01 (Hong Kong) to .69 (Thailand), with most values between .27 and .48. The standardized regression coefficients (Beta) listed in the table indicate that in each of the 10 countries with data for *mother's hours away,* this predictor variable has a statistically significant effect. The greater the number of hours that the mother is away from the 4-year-old, the greater the number of hours of extraparental care-education services used. *Father's hours away* as a predictor variable

Table 5.15   Results of regression analyses of hours of use
of early childhood services on various predictor variables

| Country/ Territory | n^a | Beta Values for Predictor Variables | | | | | | R^2 |
		Urban/ Rural	No. of Children	Educ., Mother	Educ., Father	Hours Away, Mother	Hours Away, Father	
Belgium (Fr.)	226	.04	−.20**	−.03	−.03	.34**	.03	.19
China (PRC)[+]	8,814	.19**	−.21**	.08**	.05**	.33**	.11**	.35
Finland	385	.07*	−.06	.00	.05	.76**	−.02	.63
Germany (FRG)	178	.00	−.14*	.10	.00	.46**	.10	.27
Hong Kong[+]	866	—	—	.02	.07**	—	—	.01
Italy	158	−.04	−.13	.02	−.07	.39**	.03	.17
Nigeria[+]	242	−.21**	—	−.20**	.46**	.27**	.14**	.32
Portugal	341	—	−.06	.00	.12*	.65**	−.00	.44
Spain	191	−.01	−.00	.05	−.01	.63**	.13*	.43
Thailand	986	−.04	−.06**	.03	.01	.82**	.02	.69
United States	209	.00	−.18**	.12	−.03	.65**	.12*	.48

Note. The symbol [+] indicates that weighted data were used for analysis. The use of weighted data for the multiple regressions analyses in China, Hong Kong, and Nigeria may have affected the findings. A dash indicates that no data were available.

[a]The regression analysis deleted cases with missing values (listwise).

*p < .05.   **p < .01

has a statistically significant effect in 4 countries (China, Nigeria, Spain, and the United States). In each of these countries, the greater the number of hours that the father is away from the child, the greater the number of hours of extraparental care/education services used.

For 3 countries (China, Finland, and Nigeria) the *urban/rural residence* predictor variable has a statistically significant effect. In China and Finland, *urban* families use services for a greater number of hours each week, while in Nigeria, *rural* families use services for a greater number of hours each week.

In each of 5 countries (Belgium, China, Germany, Thailand, and the

United States) the *number of children* predictor variable has a statistically significant effect. In every country, families with more children use extra-parental services for fewer hours each week.

Mother's years of education and/or *father's years of education* as predictor variables have statistically significant effects in 4 countries (China, Hong Kong, Nigeria, and Portugal). In China and Nigeria the educational levels of both parents have significant effects, while in Hong Kong and Portugal, only the father's educational level has a significant effect. In all cases where these predictor variables are significant (except that of Nigerian mothers), the greater the number of years of education completed by the parent, the greater the number of hours of extraparental care/education services used by the family.

In general, the results indicate that *mother's hours away* as a predictor variable has a statistically significant effect in the largest number of countries. In 10 countries, one or more predictor variables in addition to *mother's hours away* also has a statistically significant effect. However, these additional significant predictor variables vary from country to country, and no discernable pattern is evident across countries.

VI
STUDY FINDINGS:
USE OF ORGANIZED FACILITIES

Mikko Ojala, *Professor*
Department of Education
University of Joensuu
Joensuu, Finland

Sylvia Opper, *Senior Lecturer*
Department of Education
University of Hong Kong

Chapter 5 revealed that in every country studied in Phase 1, a certain percentage of 4-year-olds spend some time each week in an *organized facility*, such as a day care center or a kindergarten. This chapter presents the findings on children who experience an organized facility as their first or second setting (as the place where they spend the most or next-to-the-most extraparental time each week).[1]

Some of the topics reported in Chapter 5 — time children spend in their first settings, families' reasons for using extraparental services, problems encountered, and satisfaction with settings — will be examined again in this chapter, but with respect to *organized facilities in particular*. Other topics, such as service sponsors and auxiliary services, because they relate especially to programs in organized facilities, will now be explored in more detail. Also of particular interest in this chapter will be (1) the nature of any contacts parents have with the teachers/caregivers in the organized facilities their children attend, (2) the alternative arrangements parents make when organized facility care is occasionally not an option, and (3) children's and parents' satisfaction with organized facilities.[2]

Table 6.1 Percentage of all children attending organized facilities as the first or second setting[a]

Country/Territory	N	n No. of Children in Organized Facilities (% of N)
Belgium (Fr.)	424	396 (93)
China (PRC)[+]	12,835	4,127 (32)
Finland	576	202 (35)
Germany (FRG)	509	281 (55)
Hong Kong[+]	947	947 (100)
Italy	1,000	813 (81)
Nigeria[+]	1,295	106 (8)
Portugal	581	178 (31)
Spain	480	334 (70)
Thailand	2,466	296 (12)
United States	432	170 (39)

Note. The symbol [+] indicates that weighted data were used.

[a]The child's *first setting* was defined as the extraparental care/education setting he/she typically attended for the longest time each week; the *second setting* was the one he/she attended for the next-longest time. If a child's first and second settings were both organized facilities, data was collected for the most educational of the two settings, even if it was not the child's first (longest-attended) setting of the week.

Table 6.2 Percentage distribution of organized facility users (children) according to type of organized program they attend

Country/ Territory	n	% of n in the Following Type of Organized Program:			
		Child Care	Educational	Unclassified (General)	Miscellaneous
Belgium (Fr.)	396	0	100	0	0
China (PRC)[+]	4,127	14	86	0	0
Finland	202	0	67[a]	0	33[b]
Germany (FRG)	281	0	100	0	0
Hong Kong[+]	947	4	96	0	0
Italy	813	0	100	0	0
Nigeria[+]	106	9	51	40	0
Portugal	178	0	0	100	0
Spain	334	0	0	100	0
Thailand	296	36	64	0	0
United States	170	29	71	0	0

Note. The symbol [+] indicates that weighted data were used.

[a]Communal day care centers

[b]Day clubs, part-time

ORGANIZED FACILITIES – EXTENT OF USE AND NATURE OF PROGRAM

Information about the extent of children's attendance at organized facilities is given in Table 6.1. The table shows, for each of the study's countries, the percentage of sample children who experienced organized group care or group education as their first or second settings. Clearly, in most of the countries, organized group care or education plays an important role in the life of young children. Nigeria and Thailand are at one extreme with the lowest percentages (8 and 12 percent, respectively) in organized programs, and Belgium and Hong Kong are at the other extreme with the highest percentages (93 and 100 percent, respectively) in organized programs. The remaining countries are divided into three groups. In one group — China, Finland, Portugal, and the United States — about a third (31 to 39 percent) of children are in organized programs. In another group — Italy and Spain — about three fourths (70 to 81 percent) of children are in organized programs. Germany falls between the two groups, with about half (55 percent) of its children in such programs.

Having seen the important role of organized facilities in most countries, we might next ask, What types of programs do these organized facilities provide? As can be seen from Table 6.2, the basic orientation of organized facility programs in most countries is educational. In some countries (such as China, Hong Kong, Nigeria, Thailand, and the United States) a small proportion of programs (4 to 36 percent) are oriented toward child care. In Portugal and Spain it is difficult to distinguish between programs that are care- or education-oriented. (In Portugal preprimary programs may operate according to either an educational or a social-services model. Spain has no official curriculum for its preprimary programs, although the Ministry of Education and Science and some autonomous regions have educational plans for these programs.) Nigeria reports three kinds of programs provided by organized facilities: The majority (51 percent) are educational, 40 percent operate according to a "general model," and 9 percent have a child care orientation. In Finland the most frequently used organized facilities (67 percent) are day care centers, which have programs that are clearly educational in nature; the remaining organized settings are day clubs, which are sponsored by churches and which operate only about 5 hours per week.

Time Spent in Organized Facilities

One important issue that has educational, developmental, and practical implications is the amount of time children spend in organized facilities. As can be seen from Table 6.3, which shows how long children in different countries attend their organized programs over a typical week, the average time varies from country to country. Children in China and Portugal spend the longest time each week — averaging 47.2 and 45.4 hours, respectively —

Table 6.3 Average time children spend per week
in their organized facilities

Country/ Territory	n	Hours per Week			
		Minimum	Maximum	Mean	SD
Belgium (Fr.)	396	10.0	32.0	25.0	3.3
China (PRC)[+]	4,115	2.0	163.0	47.2	12.1
Finland	202	2.0	50.0	26.9	16.6
Germany (FRG)	281	2.0	48.0	19.8	8.9
Hong Kong[+]	947	14.0	55.0	17.2	7.0
Italy	813	2.0	53.0	32.5	8.8
Nigeria[+]	105	15.0	100.0	23.4	7.0
Portugal	168	14.0	80.5	45.4	12.1
Spain	333	12.5	64.5	29.1	8.2
Thailand	296	4.0	60.0	37.8	6.4
United States	169	2.0	65.0	22.1	15.4

Note. The symbol [+] indicates that weighted data were used.

in organized facilities. Next come children in Thailand and Italy, where children's weekly attendance averages 37.8 and 32.5 hours, respectively. In a third group (Belgium, Finland, Nigeria, Spain, and the United States) the average weekly attendance ranges from 22.1 to 29.1 hours. Children in Germany and Hong Kong — who average 19.8 and 17.2 hours, respectively — spend the least time each week in organized facilities.

Table 6.3 also gives information on the maximum and minimum hours per week that children in various countries spend in organized facilities. Inspection of the maximums reveals that some countries have children who spend great amounts of time in organized facilities. For

Table 6.4 Percentage distribution of children according to number of weekly hours spent in organized facilities

Country/ Territory	n	% of Children in Organized Facilities for:				
		2–10 Hr/Wk	10.1–20 Hr/Wk	20.1–30 Hr/Wk	30.1–40 Hr/Wk	Over 40 Hr/Wk
Belgium (Fr.)	396	1	10	89	0	0
China (PRC)[+]	4,115	0	1	5	17	77
Finland	202	32	7	9	26	26
Germany (FRG)	281	10	61	18	7	4
Hong Kong[+]	947	0	94	0	2	4
Italy	813	2	8	28	48	14
Nigeria[+]	105	0	64	32	3	1
Portugal	168	0	5	8	21	66
Spain	333	0	12	58	22	8
Thailand	296	0	1	12	69	18
United States	169	32	26	10	18	14

Note. The symbol [+] indicates that weighted data were used.

example, the highest maximum number of hours (163.0 hours) is found in China and includes children who attend boarding kindergartens for 6 or more days a week. Close behind is Nigeria, where there are children who spend as much as 100.0 hours per week in organized facilities. By contrast, the maximum weekly time in Belgium is only 32.0 hours. In the remaining countries (Finland, Germany, Hong Kong, Italy, Portugal, Spain, Thailand, and the United States) the maximum weekly hours range from 48.0 (in Germany) to 80.5 (in Portugal).

Some countries reported little variation in the weekly hours that chil-

dren spend in organized facilities, while others reported considerable variation. Table 6.4 shows that in Belgium, China, and Hong Kong, most children spend a similar amount of time in organized settings (in Belgium 89
percent spend 20.1 to 30 hours, in China 77 percent spend over 40 hours,
and in Hong Kong 94 percent spend 10.1 to 20 hours). At the other extreme,
in the United States at least 10 percent of the children are included in each
of the 10-hour categories listed in the table, indicating a wide variation in
weekly attendance. In Finland, the data indicate that children spend either
a few hours (32 percent spend 2 to 10 hours per week) or many hours (52
percent spend 30.1 hours per week or more) in organized facilities. In the
remaining countries, the majority of children are spread across two or three
of the 10-hour categories, indicating moderate variation.

Assuming that 20 hours or less per week in an organized facility represents a half-day program and that over 20 hours per week represents a
full-day program, we can describe two groups of countries. In the first —
Belgium, China, Finland, Italy, Portugal, Spain, and Thailand — the
majority of children are in full-day organized programs. In the second —
Hong Kong, Germany, Nigeria, and the United States — the majority of
children are in half-day organized programs.

The number of days children spend in organized facilities may vary
from country to country. For example, in some countries, children attend
their organized programs Monday through Saturday, whereas in others,
they attend only Monday through Friday. Consequently, researchers in
each country also obtained information on the average time children
spend each day in organized programs. This information appears in Table
6.5. From the table, we can see that children spend the longest average
daily times in organized facilities in China, Portugal, and Thailand (where
daily averages range from about 7.4 to 9.1 hours). The shortest average
daily time is found in Hong Kong (about 3.5 hours).

REASONS PARENTS GIVE FOR USING SPECIFIC ORGANIZED FACILITIES

What reasons do families give for using a particular organized facility as
their child's extraparental care or education setting? Do parents' reasons
differ from country to country? The major reasons given by parents can be
grouped into the seven general categories shown in Table 6.6: *convenience, positive information* about the setting, *physical characteristics* of the

Table 6.5 Children's daily hours in organized facilities

Country/ Territory	n	Hours in Organized Facility			
		Minimum	Maximum	Mean	SD
Belgium (Fr.)	396	2.5	6.4	5.0	0.6
China (PRC)[+]	4,062	0.3	24.0	7.8	1.9
Finland	201	0.7	15.0	6.1	2.9
Germany (FRG)	263	1.6	9.6	4.2	1.6
Hong Kong[+]	947	2.8	11.0	3.5	1.4
Italy	813	0.4	11.7	6.0	1.7
Nigeria[+]	105	2.9	9.0	4.5	1.1
Portugal	168	2.8	16.1	9.1	2.4
Spain	332	2.5	11.0	5.8	1.6
Thailand	296	0.8	11.2	7.4	1.1
United States	167	0.8	13.0	5.2	2.8

Note. The symbol [+] indicates that weighted data were used.

setting, *nonphysical characteristics* of the setting, *cost, no other alternative,* and *other.* (A category generally included several more-specific reasons, or subcategories).

As can be seen from Table 6.6, in general, reasons of *convenience* were the most frequently cited by parents who were asked the major reason for their organized facility choice. This was specifically the case (compared with all other categories) in China, Finland, Italy, Portugal, and Thailand. Also, although some other categories of reasons fared about as well as *convenience* in Germany, Nigeria, and Spain, about a third (32 to 38 percent) of parents in these 3 countries mentioned reasons falling in the *convenience* category.

Table 6.6 Percentage distribution of parents according to major reason for choice of a specific organized facility

Country / Territory	n	Convenience	Positive Information	Physical Characteristics	Nonphysical Characteristics	Cost	No Other Alternative	Other
Belgium (Fr.)[a]	—	—	—	—	—	—	—	—
China (PRC)[+]	4,112	60	22	2	2	2	10	2
Finland	201	30	12	6	27	1	24	0
Germany (FRG)	275	35	9	2	38	1	15	0
Hong Kong[+]	—	—	—	—	—	—	—	—
Italy	784	44	22	4	14	1	12	3
Nigeria[+]	61	38	50	0	7	0	0	5
Portugal	177	35	21	4	9	10	20	1
Spain	324	32	32	2	16	2	11	5
Thailand	289	53	13	2	16	3	13	0
United States	163	11	40	9	23	8	5	4

Note. The symbol [+] indicates that weighted data were used for analysis. A dash indicates that no information was available.

[a]Belgian researchers collected information about parents' reasons for choice but used a different format for the question. Their findings indicated that *convenience, positive information,* and *nonphysical characteristics* were given as the major reasons for facility choice.

In Finland, Germany, and Portugal, those who cited *convenience* usually mentioned *location* as the relevant subcategory of *convenience*.

In Nigeria and the United States, *positive information* about the setting was the most frequently cited reason category. In Spain this category was also very frequently cited — as frequently as *convenience* was. *Positive information* was also frequently cited in China, Italy, and Portugal, where about one fifth (21 to 22 percent) of parents gave this type of reason.

Nonphysical characteristics of the setting was the most frequently cited category in Germany, where parents mentioned these two *nonphysical characteristics* subcategories: the caregiver's *philosophy of childrearing*, and *personal characteristics of the caregiver/teacher*. In Finland and the United States *nonphysical characteristics* of the setting was parents' second-most frequently cited category.

In some countries, particularly Finland and Portugal, another reason frequently mentioned was *no other alternative* (this was cited by 24 and 20 percent of parents, respectively). *Physical characteristics* of the setting and *cost* were very rarely mentioned as the type of major reason for choosing a particular organized facility.

In brief, when parents cited the major reason behind their choice of a specific organized facility, three reason categories predominated. *Convenience* was the most frequently cited reason category in China, Finland, Italy, Portugal, and Thailand. *Positive information* about the setting was the most frequently cited in Nigeria and the United States. In Spain *convenience* and *positive information* were actually tied for "most frequent." *Nonphysical characteristics* of the setting was the most frequently cited in Germany.

Sponsors of Organized Facilities

Of the descriptors for the organized facilities attended by children in various nations, perhaps sponsorship shows the greatest variability across countries (see Table 6.7).[3] Among the 11 participating countries, we find 10 patterns of sponsorship, with only Finland and Italy having similar patterns (66 to 67 percent sponsorship by *government* and 23 to 29 percent sponsorship by *religious organizations*). In several countries the *government* sponsors the highest percentage of the organized facilities, either alone or in combination with one or more other sponsors (Finland, Italy, Portugal, Spain, and Thailand). In two countries *religious organizations* sponsor the greatest percentage of organized settings (Germany and Hong

Table 6.7 **Percentage distribution of children's organized facilities according to types of sponsors**

Country/ Territory	n	% of Organized Facilities With the Following Types[a] of Sponsors								
		1	2	3	4	5	6	7	8	9
Belgium (Fr.)	396	0	9	0	0	0	0	0	91[b]	0
China (PRC)[+]	4,127	16	16	0	28	9	2	2	0	27
Finland	202	1	66	29	2	1	1	0	0	0
Germany (FRG)	281	0	29	60	0	5	0	5	0	1
Hong Kong[+]	947	1	0	60	0	11	28	0	0	0
Italy	812	0	67	23	0	0	7	1	0	2
Nigeria[+]	195	0	0	18	0	4	26	3	0	49
Portugal	178	0	54	0	0	0	0	0	38[c]	8
Spain	334	0	24	2	1	1	2	1	0	69
Thailand	296	2	40	2	0	0	0	1	16[d]	39
United States	170	12	15	19	1	3	25	8	0	17

Note. The symbol [+] indicates that weighted data were used for analysis.

[a]1 = educational institution; 2 = government; 3 = religious organization; 4 = employer; 5 = voluntary organization; 6 = private organization; 7 = other; 8 = multiple sponsors; 9 = no information.

[b]2 + 7 = 50%; 2 + 3 = 41%.

[c]2 + 3 = 32%; 2 + 4 = 2%; 2 + 7 = 2%; other combinations combined = 2%.

[d]2 + 5 = 4%; 1 + 2 = 3%; 1 + 2 + 6 = 3%; 2 + 3 = 2%; other combinations combined = 4%.

with the percentage of settings sponsored by each falling within a fairly narrow range (the highest is *private organizations* at 25 percent and the lowest is *educational institutions* at 12 percent). Belgium displays a unique sponsorship situation: 100 percent of organized facilities are sponsored by the *government*, and most facilities have either an *educational institution* or *other* (i.e., a local authority) as an additional sponsor.

Auxiliary Services in Organized Facilities

It is often assumed that organized facility programs offer many kinds of auxiliary services to parents and children. The Phase 1 study of the IEA Preprimary Project examined this assumption with regard to health, special education, social services, and transportation. Information concerning the availability and use of these types of auxiliary services appears in Tables 6.8 through 6.11.

Health Services

Health services fared better than most other auxiliary services we looked into, yet Belgium is the only country whose organized facilities offer *extensive* health services (Table 6.8); there, 86 percent of children in organized facilities have families reporting health-service access through their programs. In 5 other countries more than a third of organized facility children are offered health services: In China and Spain health services are offered to 44 and 42 percent of the children, respectively, and in Hong Kong, Portugal, and the United States the corresponding percentages range from 33 to 37 percent of the children. In Finland, Italy, Nigeria, and Thailand, however, organized programs very rarely offer health services (only 2 to 21 percent of children in organized programs have health service access).

Although organized programs may *offer* health services, this does not necessarily mean that parents or children make use of the services. As can be seen from Table 6.8, the countries in which children make the most use of available health services are China, Finland, Nigeria, Thailand, and the United States, where the usage rates range from 75 to 100 percent. Though both Nigeria and Thailand have low rates of availability, the health services that are offered are used quite extensively. The lowest usage rates are found

Table 6.8 Availability and use of health services in
children's organized facilities

Country/ Territory	N	Children With Access to Services		Children Using Services		
		n	% of N	No. of Users	Users as % of n	Users as % of N
Belgium (Fr.)	396	339	86	225	66	57
China (PRC)[+]	4,126	1,795	44	1,425	79	35
Finland	202	43	21	34	79	17
Germany (FRG)	281	—	—	—	—	—
Hong Kong[+]	947	349	37	81	23	9
Italy	813	91	11	43	47	5
Nigeria[+]	105	2	2	2	100	2
Portugal	178	58	33	27	47	15
Spain	334	140	42	41	29	12
Thailand	296	52	18	44	85	15
United States	170	63	37	47	75	28

Note. The symbol [+] indicates that weighted data were used. N = number of children in organized facilities. Dashes mean the question was not asked.

in Hong Kong and Spain, where only 23 and 29 percent of children, respectively, actually make use of their available health services.

SPECIAL EDUCATION SERVICES

As can be seen from Table 6.9, the figures concerning special education services contrast with those concerning health services, with special education services being considerably less prevalent. Organized settings in

**Table 6.9 Availability and use of special education
services in children's organized facilities**

Country/ Territory	N	Children With Access to Services		Children Using Services		
		n	% of N	No. of Users	Users as % of n	Users as % of N
Belgium (Fr.)	396	100	25	11	11	3
China (PRC)[+]	4,126	35	1	14	40	< 1
Finland	202	56	28	9	16	5
Germany (FRG)	281	—	—	—	—	—
Hong Kong[+]	947	197	21	13	7	1
Italy	813	137	17	8	6	1
Nigeria[+]	106	2	2	1	50	1
Portugal	178	24	13	6	25	3
Spain	334	140	42	25	18	8
Thailand	296	12	4	3	25	1
United States	170	41	24	12	29	7

Note. The symbol [+] indicates that weighted data were used. N = number of children
in organized facilities. Dashes mean the question was not asked.

Spain are the likeliest to offer special education services (they are available to 42 percent of children in organized programs). In Belgium, Finland, Hong Kong, and the United States these services are available for 21
to 28 percent of children in organized programs. In Italy and Portugal
special education services are available to 13 to 17 percent of children in
organized programs. In China, Nigeria, and Thailand few organized settings offer special education services (only 1 to 4 per cent of children in
organized facilities have access).

Are special education services that are available actually used? The
data show that in China, Nigeria, Portugal, and Thailand, where only a

few organized settings offer special education services, the usage rates are higher than in some other countries with more availability of services (in the 4 countries just named, 25 to 50 percent of children make use of their available special education services). In Finland and Spain usage rates are 16 to 18 percent. In 3 countries — Belgium, Hong Kong, and Italy — available special education services are even less heavily used (by only 6 to 11 percent of the children who have access to them).

Social Services

Table 6.10 data show that in almost every country, a relatively small proportion of organized facilities offer social services. One exception is Belgium, where social services are available to 44 percent of children in organized facilities. In Hong Kong, Italy, Portugal, Spain, and the United States they are available to 13 to 27 percent of children in organized facilities. In China, Finland, Nigeria, and Thailand few organized facilities offer social services (only 2 to 11 percent of children in organized facilities have access).

Data about the use of available social services show that in Nigeria all of the small percentage of organized facility children who have access to services do make use of them. In China and Thailand the rate of usage is also quite high — 71 to 73 percent. In Finland and the United States the usage rates are 40 and 32 percent, respectively, and in Italy, Hong Kong, and Portugal usage of available social services ranges from 15 to 21 percent. Belgium and Spain report the lowest usage rates — only 13 and 7 percent, respectively.

Transportation

As Table 6.11 indicates, whereas 3 countries (China, Finland, and Nigeria) have very few organized facilities that offer children transportation, in 4 countries (Belgium, Hong Kong, Italy, and Thailand) transportation is offered for 32 to 40 percent of children in organized facilities. In Portugal, Spain, and the United States transportation services are offered for 21 to 26 percent of organized facility children.

In China, where organized settings very rarely offer transportation services, 65 percent of children use their available services. In Hong Kong, Portugal, Thailand, and the United States available transportation

Table 6.10   Availability and use of social services
in children's organized facilities

Country/ Territory	N	Children With Access to Services		Children Using Services		
		n	% of N	No. of Users	Users as % of n	Users as % of N
Belgium (Fr.)	396	176	44	23	13	6
China (PRC)[+]	4,126	440	11	321	73	8
Finland	202	15	7	6	40	3
Germany (FRG)	281	—	—	—	—	—
Hong Kong[+]	947	177	19	26	15	3
Italy	813	115	14	24	21	3
Nigeria[+]	105	2	2	2	100	2
Portugal	178	48	27	8	17	5
Spain	334	44	13	3	7	1
Thailand	296	21	7	15	71	5
United States	170	41	24	13	32	8

Note. The symbol [+] indicates that weighted data were used. N = number of children in organized facilities. Dashes mean the question was not asked.

services have 41 to 55 percent usage rates. In Belgium, Finland, Italy, and Spain the usage rates range from 22 to 34 percent. The lowest usage rate is seen in Nigeria, where no children use the limited transportation services that are available.

A CROSS-NATIONAL COMPARISON REGARDING AUXILIARY SERVICES

A cross-national comparison of rates of auxiliary-service usage among *all*

Table 6.11 Availability and use of transportation
services in children's organized facilities

Country/ Territory	N	Children With Access to Services		Children Using Services		
		n	% of N	No. of Users	Users as % of n	Users as % of N
Belgium (Fr.)	396	125	32	28	22	7
China (PRC)[+]	4,126	122	3	79	65	2
Finland	202	7	4	2	29	1
Germany (FRG)	281	—	—	—	—	—
Hong Kong[+]	947	375	40	185	49	20
Italy	813	288	35	99	34	12
Nigeria[+]	105	2	2	0	0	0
Portugal	178	37	21	15	41	8
Spain	334	77	23	26	34	8
Thailand	296	102	35	56	55	19
United States	170	44	26	22	50	13

Note. The symbol [+] indicates that weighted data were used. N = number of children in organized facilities. Dashes mean the question was not asked.

children attending organized facilities (users as a percent of the N in Tables 6.8–6.11) shows some interesting results. Considering this universe of children, we find that the pattern of percentages of organized facility children who benefit from *special education* and *social services* was similar across countries. For both types of services, "users-as-%-of-N" across all countries was no more than 8 percent — ranging from less than 1 percent benefiting in China (special education) to 8 percent benefiting in Spain (special education) and 8 percent benefiting in both China and the United States (social services).

For *health services*, we find a very different pattern — one that ranges

widely from only 2 percent benefiting in Nigeria to 57 percent benefiting
in Belgium. For health services, countries with the highest percentages
benefiting were Belgium (57 percent), China (35 percent), and the United
States (28 percent); those with the lowest percentages benefiting were
Hong Kong (9 percent), Italy (5 percent), and Nigeria (2 percent). In the
remaining countries, percentages ranged between 12 and 17 percent.

"Users-as-%-of-N" for *transportation* services also had a distinctive pattern. Hong Kong (20 percent) and Thailand (19 percent) showed the highest percentages of organized facility children benefiting from transportation; China (2 percent), Finland (1 percent) and Nigeria (0 percent) showed
the lowest. The remaining countries ranged between 7 and 13 percent.

In sum, most countries' organized facilities offer relatively few services beyond the regular care and education program. Belgium is the
country where auxiliary services are most commonly offered. Countries
offering a moderate amount of auxiliary services are Hong Kong, Portugal, Spain, and the United States. Countries offering few additional services are China, Finland, Italy, Nigeria, and Thailand. China does, however, offer health services to a substantial proportion of children, and
Thailand and Italy do offer transportation services to over a third of children in organized programs.

OCCASIONAL ALTERNATIVE ARRANGEMENTS FOR THE ORGANIZED SETTING

For children regularly attending organized settings, there may be occasions when parents must find alternatives. Some facilities close regularly
for vacations or holidays; others close occasionally in emergency situations; some are "closed" in that they are not the setting preferred (or perhaps allowed) when a child is ill. Table 6.12, on pages 160–161, which
indicates the alternative arrangements that parents make on such occasions, indicates that there are slightly different arrangements, depending
on whether the closing (or nonattendance) is planned and regular, or
unplanned and due to an emergency.

Generally, if the closing is planned, most parents arrange to take care
of their children at home. This is the case particularly in China, Finland,
Italy, Portugal, Thailand, and the United States (72 to 89 percent) and to a
lesser extent in Belgium and Spain (59 percent and 36 percent, respectively). Another common but less frequent arrangement used by fewer

than 10 percent of families in all countries except China is for the child to remain at home under the care of another relative. A third possibility, especially popular in Belgium and Spain (20 percent and 19 percent, respectively) is care in the home of another relative. Other arrangements, such as a (sick) child remaining in the organized setting, the child being cared for by a nonrelative in the home of one or the other, the child attending another organized setting, or the child attending the parent's workplace, are fairly uncommon in every country. Parents in most countries do make alternative arrangements for any regular closing (or nonattendance). In Spain and Thailand, however, 25 percent and 10 percent, respectively, report having no plan for such an occurrence.

The parent taking care of the child at home is also the most common arrangement during an emergency closing, although in almost all countries the percentage of families using this option for an emergency closing (which ranges from 26 percent in Spain to 72 percent in Germany) is considerably lower than the percentage using it for a planned closing. Parents presumably have difficulty changing their regular schedule to fit in with unexpected closings and consequently must rely more on relatives in these instances to take care of their children. For example, care in the child's home by another relative is an option used more frequently during an emergency than during a planned closing in Belgium, China, Finland, Italy, Spain, and the United States. Care in some other home by another relative is also more common during an emergency in Belgium, Italy, Portugal, and the United States. In each country, the percentages of parents making *other arrangements* were similar for planned and unplanned closings. The same can be said for the percentages having *no plans*. Finally, whereas relatively few countries provide care in an organized facility during planned closings, countries such as Finland, Germany, Spain, Thailand, and the United States still offer at least minimal services during an emergency closing — sometimes in a facility located nearby.

Contact Between Educators and Parents

It is increasingly recognized that a close partnership between parents and those who provide organized programs for their children results in benefits for all concerned. Parents benefit by becoming informed about program provisions for their children. In turn, these informed parents generally support the programs with which they have direct and meaning-

Table 6.12 Percentage distribution of service-using parents according to the alternative arrangement made during planned (P) and unplanned (UP) closings of facilities[a]

% of n Citing the Following Type[b] of Arrangement

Country/ Territory	n	1 P	(UP)	2 P	(UP)	3 P	(UP)	4 P	(UP)	5 P	(UP)	6 P	(UP)	7 P	(UP)	8 P	(UP)	9 P	(UP)	10 P	(UP)	No Info. P	(UP)
Belgium (Fr.)	396	0	(0)	59	(46)	7	(9)	2	(3)	20	(28)	4	(6)	4	(4)	1	(2)	3	(2)	0	(0)	0	(0)
China (PRC)+	4,420	3	(0)	89	(57)	0	(25)	0	(1)	7	(0)	0	(0)	0	(0)	0	(8)	0	(0)	1	(7)	0	(2)
Finland	202	8	(25)	72	(51)	3	(8)	0	(2)	3	(2)	0	(1)	9	(4)	0	(1)	2	(1)	0	(0)	3	(5)
Germany (FRG)	—	—	(8)	—	(72)	—	(3)	—	(0)	—	(14)	—	(3)	—	(0)	—	(0)	—	(0)	—	(0)	—	(0)
Hong Kong+	—	—	—	—	—	—	—	—	—	—	—	—	—	—	—	—	—	—	—	—	—	—	—
Italy	813	0	(1)	73	(63)	9	(15)	2	(3)	9	(10)	1	(1)	0	(0)	1	(1)	0	(1)	1	(0)	4	(5)
Nigeria+	—	—	—	—	—	—	—	—	—	—	—	—	—	—	—	—	—	—	—	—	—	—	—

Table 6.12 Percentage distribution of service-using parents according to the alternative arrangement made during planned (P) and unplanned (UP) closings of facilities[a] (continued)

% of n Citing the Following Type[b] of Arrangement

Country/Territory	n	1 P	(UP)	2 P	(UP)	3 P	(UP)	4 P	(UP)	5 P	(UP)	6 P	(UP)	7 P	(UP)	8 P	(UP)	9 P	(UP)	10 P	(UP)	No Info. P	(UP)
Portugal	178	2	(0)	78	(44)	8	(9)	1	(3)	7	(20)	1	(2)	0	(4)	2	(5)	0	(0)	0	(1)	1	(12)
Spain	334	3	(8)	36	(26)	8	(10)	7	(6)	19	(18)	0	(1)	0	(1)	1	(0)	25	(30)	0	(0)	1	(0)
Thailand	296	0	(15)	75	(64)	9	(8)	0	(0)	3	(1)	0	(0)	0	(1)	0	(1)	10	(6)	1	(2)	2	(2)
United States	170	1	(10)	86	(59)	3	(11)	2	(4)	2	(5)	4	(4)	0	(1)	0	(1)	0	(1)	0	(0)	2	(4)

Note. The symbol $^+$ indicates that weighted data were used for analysis. Dashes indicate that no data were available.

[a]Planned closing = holiday and staff inservice training; unplanned closing = emergency at setting or child is refused because of illness.

[b]Types of arrangements: 1 = (sick child) remaining in facility; 2 = own home with parent; 3 = own home with other relative; 4 = own home with nonrelative; 5 = other home with other relative; 6 = other home with nonrelative; 7 = other facility; 8 = parental workplace; 9 = no plan; 10 = other arrangement.

ful communication, and early childhood educators (both teachers and caregivers) benefit by receiving this active support from parents. Educators also benefit by becoming familiar with the child's experiences in the home and can then build curricular experiences on this knowledge. Most important, children benefit from the increased communication between program and parent.

Educators and parents, however, have been slow in promoting partnership and cooperation. In many countries parent involvement in organized programs still remains an ideal rather than a reality. This study examined the extent of educator-parent contact in the various countries by asking questions about certain types of contact parents had experienced during the past 3 months, such as informal meetings, formal meetings requested by either the educator or the parent, group meetings, telephone or written communications, and parent assistance in the organized program. Two aspects of educator-parent contacts were studied — availability and frequency.

Availability of Educator-Parent Contacts

Of the various types of educator-parent contacts reported in the study's countries (see Table 6.13), perhaps the most widespread is the *informal meeting* between parent and educator. This contact presumably takes place when the child arrives at or leaves the organized setting. *Informal meeting* is the most common type of contact in all but 3 countries — China, Hong Kong, and Nigeria.

Another common form of contact is the one-on-one *meeting requested by the educator or parent*. Such meetings, requested by the educator, were reported especially in China; they also occur fairly extensively in Belgium, Finland, Italy, and the United States. This type of contact also occurs, but less frequently, in Nigeria, Spain, and Thailand (where it was reported by 23, 15, and 24 percent of parents, respectively). One-on-one meetings requested by parents are universal in China and relatively frequent in Italy; they were also reported by about a third of the sample (organized facility parents) in both Finland and the United States. In Nigeria, Spain, and Thailand fewer than 10 percent of sample parents reported having such meetings.

Less common types of contact are *telephone or written communication*, the *group meeting*, or *parent assistance in the setting*. Although *tele-*

Table 6.13 **Percentages of organized facility users (parents) engaging in various kinds of educator-parent contacts**

Country/ Territory	n	% of Parents Reporting the Following Types[a] of Contact:						
		Inf. Mtg.	Mtg./ Ed.	Mtg./ Par.	Tel./ Writ.	Grp. Mtg.	Parent Assist.	Other
Belgium (Fr.)	396	95	44	—	—	—	33	—
China (PRC)[+]	4,127	61	100	100	13	32	—	1
Finland	202	85	54	34	64	71	13	14
Germany (FRG)	281	—	—	—	—	—	—	—
Hong Kong[+]	947	33	—	—	27	37	21	58
Italy	813	81	41	43	23	58	9	2
Nigeria[+]	106	20	23	6	8	4	5	3
Portugal	178	86	—	—	41	50	10	15
Spain	334	88	15	9	17	39	11	4
Thailand	296	60	24	9	9	20	6	0
United States	170	80	44	36	65	63	49	14

Note. The symbol [+] indicates that weighted data were used. Dashes mean the question was not asked.

[a]Inf. Mtg. = informal meeting; Mtg./Ed. = meeting requested by educator; Mtg./Par. = meeting requested by parent; Tel./Writ. = telephone/written communication; Grp. Mtg. = group meeting; Parent Assist. = parent assistance in setting.

phone or written communication is extremely common in Finland (64 percent) and the United States (65 percent) and relatively common in Portugal (41 percent), it is less so in Hong Kong and Italy and fairly uncommon in Spain, China, Thailand, and Nigeria. Contact through *group meetings* was reported by about two thirds of sample families in Finland, in Italy, and in the United States; by a third to a half of sample families in China, Hong Kong, Portugal, and Spain; and by only 20 percent of Thai and 4 percent of Nigerian sample families. In most countries of the study, *parent assistance in the setting* is not a common practice. About half of American parents, a third of Belgian parents, and a fifth of Hong Kong parents assist in the setting, but elsewhere, fewer than 14 percent of parents do so.

Alternative (*other*) types of contact are rare in most countries, with the exception of Finland, Hong Kong, Portugal, and the United States. In Hong Kong *other* contact consists of a handbook that the preschool sends regularly to the home. This contains reports on the child's progress, results of tests or exams (if these are a part of the curriculum), notices of special events, and so on. In Finland *other* contact consists of parents visiting the educator's home and parents participating in the same hobbies as the educator. In Portugal *other* contacts occur mostly because a mother works at her child's setting. In the United States *other* refers to various kinds of personal contact.

FREQUENCY OF EDUCATOR-PARENT CONTACTS

Not only is *informal meeting* the type of educator-parent contact that most parents experience, but it is also the type of contact that occurs most frequently for them, as can be seen in Table 6.14 on pages 166–167. It occurs *daily* in Finland for 51 percent of parents; in Italy, for 48 percent; in Spain, for 43 percent; in Portugal, for 39 percent; in Thailand, for 23 percent; and in the United States, for 21 percent. Of Belgian parents, 73 percent meet informally with the educator *weekly*, as do 23 percent of Finnish families and 19 percent of American families. At least half of sample parents in Belgium, Finland, Italy, Portugal, and Spain, and 40 percent in the United States, reported meeting with their children's educators at least *weekly*.

In China, Hong Kong, and Nigeria the *informal meeting* is less common. It occurs *once a month* for 26 percent of Chinese and for 15 percent of Nigerian families and *less than once a month* for 29 percent of Hong Kong families. In Thailand the situation is bimodal: 23 percent of parents meet the educator *daily*, whereas 41 percent *never* meet the educator.

Meetings requested by the educator are held infrequently except in Belgium (where they occurred *weekly* for 15 percent and *twice each month* for a further 16 percent of the sample) and in Nigeria (where they occurred *twice each month* for 14 percent of the sample). Parents who attend educator-requested meetings generally attend them *once a month* or *less than once a month* in China, Finland, Italy, Spain, Thailand, and the United States.

Of the 7 countries that report having *meetings requested by parents*,

Finland (12 percent) and Italy (14 percent) have the largest number of *daily* parent-requested meetings. Of United States parents, 15 percent request meetings at least *once a month*, and a further 16 percent request them *less than once a month*. In many countries a percentage of parents report at least *once-a month* parent-requested meetings (Finland, 22 percent; Italy, 33 percent; Nigeria, 2 percent; Spain, 4 percent; Thailand, 6 percent; United States, 20 percent).

Group meetings are not very frequent in most of the countries. They occur, but *less than once a month*, for 24 percent of families in China, 60 percent in Finland, 37 percent in Hong Kong, 39 percent in Italy, 3 percent in Nigeria, 38 percent in Portugal, 30 percent in Spain, 14 percent in Thailand, and 25 percent in the United States.

Telephone or written communications are also relatively rare. In most countries parents primarily reported them occurring *less than once a month*. Such communications occur most frequently in Finland and the United States. Of United States families, 5 percent have these contacts *daily*; 17 percent, *weekly*; and 12 percent, *twice each month*. In other words, about one third of the United States sample reported having telephone or written contacts at least *twice each month*. In Finland such contacts are also rather frequent: 1 percent of Finnish families have them *daily*; 13 percent, *weekly*; 11 percent, *twice each month*; and 20 percent, *once a month*. In the findings, no distinction was made between telephone and written communication, although these are very different types of contacts. In Hong Kong, for example, these contacts would be predominantly by telephone, whereas in the United States written communication, such as a newsletter, might be more popular.

Contact through *parent assistance in the setting* is infrequent in every country. Even in Belgium, where such contacts are the most common, only 14 percent of parents assist *weekly*; 12 percent, *twice each month*; and 66 percent, *never*. In the United States 30 percent of parents assist the educator at least *once a month*, but 47 percent *never* assist. In Finland 87 percent of parents *never* assist. Similarly large percentages of nonassisting parents exist in other countries: Hong Kong (79 percent), Italy (87 percent), Portugal (89 percent), Spain (88 percent), and Thailand (93 percent).

In brief, the two countries with the greatest variety and the highest frequency of contacts between organized programs and the home are Finland and the United States. Countries in which parents have access to the fewest types of contacts and where the various types of contacts have the lowest frequencies are Hong Kong, and Nigeria.

Table 6.14   Frequency of educator-parent contacts

Country/ Territory	% of Parents Reporting the Following Contact Frequency:						
	Daily	Weekly	2/Mo	1/Mo	Less than 1/Mo	Never	No Info.
Belgium (Fr.)							
Inf. Mtg.	0	73	12	0	10	4	1
Mtg./Ed.	0	15	16	0	13	54	2
Par. Assist.	0	14	12	0	7	66	1
China (PRC)[+]							
Inf. Mtg.	0	13	9	26	13	35	4
Mtg./Ed.	0	0	0	0	100	0	0
Mtg./Par.	0	0	0	0	100	0	0
Tel./Writ.	0	0	1	4	8	84	3
Grp. Mtg.	0	0	0	8	24	65	3
Finland							
Inf. Mtg.	51	23	2	2	7	15	0
Mtg./Ed.	3	3	2	8	39	45	0
Mtg./Par.	12	5	1	4	12	66	0
Tel./Writ.	1	13	11	20	19	35	1
Grp. Mtg.	0	0	2	9	60	28	1
Par. Assist.	2	0	1	2	8	87	0
Hong Kong[+]							
Inf. Mtg.	0	0	0	4	29	67	0
Tel./Writ.	0	0	1	5	21	73	0
Grp. Mtg.	0	0	0	0	37	63	0
Par. Assist.	0	0	0	0	21	79	0
Italy							
Inf. Mtg.	48	15	6	6	7	15	3
Mtg./Ed.	3	4	3	12	20	55	3
Mtg./Par.	14	9	3	7	9	54	4
Tel./Writ.	1	1	2	7	12	73	4
Grp. Mtg.	0	1	3	15	39	39	3
Par. Assist.	1	1	0	1	6	87	4
Nigeria[+]							
Inf. Mtg.	0	0	0	15	5	18	62
Mtg./Ed.	0	0	14	0	9	15	62
Mtg./Par.	0	0	0	2	4	31	63

Table 6.14 Frequency of educator-parent contacts (continued)

Country/ Territory	Daily	Weekly	2/Mo	1/Mo	Less than 1/Mo	Never	No Info.
% of Parents Reporting the Following Contact Frequency:							
Nigeria[+]							
Tel./Writ.	0	5	1	0	2	31	61
Grp. Mtg.	0	0	0	1	3	30	66
Par. Assist.	2	0	1	0	2	29	66
Portugal							
Inf. Mtg.	39	11	8	14	14	14	0
Tel./Writ.	3	3	3	12	20	57	2
Grp. Mtg.	0	0	1	11	38	50	0
Par. Assist.	1	1	1	3	4	89	1
Spain							
Inf. Mtg.	43	19	8	8	10	12	0
Mtg./Ed.	1	1	1	2	10	85	0
Mtg./Par.	1	0	1	2	5	91	0
Tel./Writ.	1	1	2	3	10	81	2
Grp. Mtg.	0	0	2	7	30	60	1
Par. Assist.	0	0	1	1	9	88	1
Thailand							
Inf. Mtg.	23	15	3	6	12	41	0
Mtg./Ed.	0	0	1	9	14	75	1
Mtg./Par.	2	1	1	2	3	90	1
Tel./Writ.	2	1	0	1	5	90	1
Grp. Mtg.	0	0	1	5	14	79	1
Par. Assist.	1	1	1	2	2	93	0
United States							
Inf. Mtg.	21	19	14	12	15	17	2
Mtg./Ed.	1	0	3	10	30	52	4
Mtg./Par.	1	3	1	15	16	59	5
Tel./Writ.	5	17	12	18	13	31	4
Grp. Mtg.	0	4	7	28	25	33	3
Par. Assist.	2	6	4	18	19	47	4

Note. The symbol [+] indicates that weighted data were used. No information was available for Germany. The *n* for each type of contact for each country can be calculated by using the percents and the *n* reported in Table 6.13.

PROBLEMS WITH ORGANIZED FACILITIES

Having seen some of the reasons parents give for choosing particular organized programs for their children, we can then ask whether parents are satisfied with the choices they have made. Do organized facilities meet parents' expectations? Once their children begin to attend on a regular basis, what are the problems parents encounter with these types of settings?

Examination of the problems reported by parents should provide some insight into what parents consider to be important dimensions of organized early education and care. The study of parent satisfaction will reveal parents' perceptions of the quality of the available programs. First of all, three main types of problems were identified by sample parents: problems pertaining to the *setting in general*, to the *program* within the setting, and to the *educator*.

PROBLEMS RELATED TO THE SETTING

Table 6.15 presents data about parents' problems pertaining to the setting. Inspection of the table shows that China, Germany, and Hong Kong reported the highest percentages of general problems. In China the main problems, in order of frequency, are *hours of operation* (for 10 percent of parents), *cost* (for 9 percent of parents), and *location* (for 8 percent of parents). In Germany the main problems are *hours of operation* (for 13 percent) and *cost* (for 5 percent), and in Hong Kong the main problems are *cost* (for 18 percent), and *location* (for 7 percent). In each of the remaining countries no more than 5 percent of parents cited any one type of problem related to the setting. The single category receiving the highest number of complaints overall was *cost*. In Finland and Spain *cost* was not cited as a problem; in the other countries the proportions of families reporting *cost* as a problem ranged from 18 percent (in Hong Kong) to 1 percent (in Belgium, Italy, Thailand, and the United States).

PROBLEMS RELATED TO THE PROGRAM

Table 6.16 shows the program-related problems sample parents cited. The major program-related problem concerns *facility/equipment* (particularly in China and Hong Kong, and less so in Belgium). This is followed by problems concerning *other children* (particularly in Hong Kong and Chi-

Table 6.15 **Percentages of organized facility users (parents) reporting problems related to setting**

		% of Parents Reporting the Following Type of Problem:				
Country/ Territory	n^a	Location	Hours of Operation	Exclusion of Sick Children	Cost	Other
Belgium (Fr.)	389	0	2	—	1	2
China (PRC)[+]	1,472	8	10	—	9	—
Finland	201	0	1	0	0	2
Germany (FRG)	281	—	13	—	5	—
Hong Kong[+]	932	7	—	—	18	—
Italy	807	1	2	0	1	0
Nigeria[+]	78	1	0	1	5	2
Portugal	177	1	1	1	5	0
Spain	332	0	1	0	0	0
Thailand	296	0	0	1	1	0
United States	168	1	0	1	1	1

Note. The symbol [+] indicates that weighted data were used. Dashes mean the question was not asked.

[a]This is the minimum number of parents who responded to these questions.

na, and to a lesser extent in Nigeria, Belgium, and Germany) and problems with the *philosophy of the program* (in Hong Kong). Staff turnover is a problem for only 8 percent of families in China, 6 percent in Hong Kong, and 2 percent in Belgium.

The two countries whose parents reported the most program-related problems are China — particularly for *facility/equipment* (29 percent), *other children* (10 percent), and *staff turnover* (8 percent) — and Hong Kong — for *philosophy* (20 percent), *facility/equipment* (21 percent), *other children* (13 percent), and *staff turnover* (6 percent). Some Belgian families also

Table 6.16 Percentages of organized facility users (parents) reporting problems related to program

Country/Territory	n^a	% of Parents Reporting the Following Type of Problem:							
		Philosophy of Program	Religious Orientation	Facility/ Equipment	Safety/ Sanitation/ Nutrition	Negative Atmosphere	Other Children	Staff Turnover	Others
Belgium (Fr.)	389	1	—	6	—	—	3	2	—
China (PRC)[+]	1,472	—	—	29	—	—	10	8	—
Finland	201	2	1	1	1	0	0	0	2
Germany (FRG)	281	3	—	—	—	—	3	—	1
Hong Kong[+]	932	20	—	21	—	—	13	6	—
Italy	807	1	0	2	1	1	1	0	1
Nigeria[+]	78	0	0	3	0	2	4	0	2
Portugal	177	1	0	4	4	0	1	0	2
Spain	332	0	0	0	0	0	0	0	0
Thailand	296	0	0	0	0	0	0	0	1
United States	168	0	1	1	1	1	1	0	3

Note. The symbol [+] indicates that weighted data were used. Dashes mean the question was not asked.
[a]This is the minimum number of parents who responded to these questions.

reported a problem with *facility/equipment*. In each of the other countries, no more than 4 percent of families reported any one type of problem. One program area that was reported as a problem in only 2 countries, Finland and the United States (1 percent each), was *religious orientation*.

Problems Related to the Educator

Table 6.17 presents data about problems related to the educator. Inspection of the table shows that except in China, Hong Kong, and Belgium, problems related to the educator are not a major concern for parents. Most countries reported fewer than 5 percent, and in many cases fewer than 1 percent, of parents having problems with any particular aspect of the educator. There also seems to be no common pattern to the educator problems that parents in various countries cited. In China the problems are that the educator is *unqualified* and the educator's *personal characteristics*. In Hong Kong it is mainly the *unreliability* of the educator, and in Belgium it is *other* unspecified educator problems.

In short, sample parents in most countries reported few problems with their children's organized facilities. Compared with those in other countries, sample parents in China and Hong Kong consistently reported more problems related to the programs, to the settings, and to the educators. In Belgium parents cited a few problems with educators and programs, and in Germany *hours of operation* (a facility-related problem) stood out among the problems cited. *Cost* is the single problem cited in almost all countries, but even that problem was reported with low frequency in every country but Hong Kong and China. Despite the reports about various problems, in every country, most parents reported few actual problems with the program, the setting, or the educator.

Satisfaction With Organized Facilities

The findings on satisfaction with organized facilities support the apparent lack of parental problems with these settings. Table 6.18 indicates that in every country a vast majority of parents are *somewhat* or *very satisfied* with their children's settings. The country with the highest degree of satisfaction is the United States (where 88 percent are *very satisfied*), followed by Finland (where 80 percent are *very satisfied*). Countries with the most

Table 6.17 Percentages of organized facility users (parents) reporting problems related to educators

Country/Territory	n^a	% of Parents Reporting the Following Type of Educator Problem:				
		Personal Characteristics	Unreliability	Unqualified	Disliked by Child	Other
Belgium (Fr.)	389	3	—	1	—	6
China (PRC)[+]	1,472	10	—	21	—	—
Finland	201	0	0	1	1	1
Germany (FRG)	281	—	—	—	—	3
Hong Kong[+]	932	—	10	3	—	—
Italy	807	1	1	1	1	1
Nigeria[+]	78	0	2	2	0	4
Portugal	177	2	1	1	1	1
Spain	332	0	0	0	2	0
Thailand	296	0	0	0	0	1
United States	168	1	0	1	0	1

Note. The symbol [+] indicates that weighted data were used. Dashes mean the question was not asked.

[a] This is the minimum number of parents who responded to these questions.

Table 6.18   Percentage distribution of parents according to degree
of satisfaction with their child's organized facility

Country/ Territory	n	% of Parents Reporting the Following Degree of Satisfaction				
		Very	Some-what	Not Very	Not at All	No Answer
Belgium (Fr.)	396	56	38	4	1	1
China (PRC)[+]	4,126	46	46	7	1	0
Finland	202	80	18	1	1	0
Germany (FRG)	—	—	—	—	—	—
Hong Kong[+]	947	14	82	0	0	4
Italy	813	61	32	5	1	1
Nigeria[+]	105	59	31	7	0	3
Portugal	178	53	45	2	0	0
Spain	334	77	19	2	1	1
Thailand	296	68	30	1	0	1
United States	170	88	9	2	0	1

Note. The symbol [+] indicates that weighted data were used for analysis. Dashes indicate that no information was available.

dissatisfaction (sizable percentages of *not very* or *not at all satisfied*) are Italy (6 percent), China (8 percent), and Nigeria (7 percent).

The findings about children's enjoyment while attending organized facilities, shown in Table 6.19, are similar to the findings for parental satisfaction with these settings. In all 10 countries reporting findings for this item, at least 85 percent of parents reported that their children enjoyed participating in these settings. When *enjoys* and *sometimes enjoys* are combined, in every country, at least 95 percent of parents indicated that these categories would describe their children's experiences in the organized facilities.

Table 6.19 Percentage distribution of children according to their
degree of enjoyment of their organized setting

| Country/ Territory | n | | % of Children Exhibiting to Parents the Following Degree of Enjoyment | | |
		Enjoys	Sometimes Enjoys	Does Not Enjoy	No Information
Belgium (Fr.)	396	92	5	1	12
China (PRC)[+]	4,127	93	6	1	0
Finland	202	94	6	0	0
Germany (FRG)	281	96	2	1	1
Hong Kong[+]	947	88	9	1	2
Italy	813	85	10	2	3
Nigeria[+]	106	—	—	—	—
Portugal	178	90	6	3	1
Spain	334	89	7	4	0
Thailand	296	85	14	1	0
United States	170	91	5	1	3

Note. The symbol [+] indicates that weighted data were used for analysis. Dashes
indicate that no information was available.

NATIONAL SUMMARIES

The findings on the various aspects of organized facilities show that
whereas some features are common to all countries, other features vary.
Perhaps the most consistent finding is the high degree of satisfaction that
sample parents of all countries reported with organized settings. Eighty-
two to 100 percent of parents are either somewhat or very satisfied with
organized settings. Similarly, in almost all countries, a very large proportion of children, ranging from 89 percent in Spain to 96 percent in Germany, appear to enjoy the time they spend in organized settings. In Hong

Kong, Spain, Italy, and Thailand, however, from 10 to 15 percent of children do not or only sometimes enjoy these settings. Other characteristics, such as the amount of time children spend in organized facilities, facility sponsors, or the type and frequency of educator-parent contacts, show wide variations across countries. These have been discussed separately by topic in the previous sections of this chapter. This final section presents for each country a brief summary of the distinctive organized facility characteristics that exhibit a range of variation across countries. The purpose is to highlight the unique pattern of services that each country adopts to provide organized early education and care for their young children.

Belgium (Fr.)

Belgium is exceptional among the study's European countries in that organized facilities, all of which are educational, are available for all 4-year-old children and attended by 93 percent of them. Children spend, on average, 5 hours a day, or 25 hours a week, in these settings, with the majority being there 20 to 30 hours a week. During facility closings children are cared for at home by their parents (planned closing, 59 percent; unplanned closing, 46 percent) or cared for at another home by a relative (planned closing, 20 percent; unplanned closing, 28 percent).

All organized facilities are sponsored by the government. Most of them have additional support from local authorities or religious organizations. As reported by Belgian parents, health services are provided and used extensively; 86 percent of Belgian children attending organized facilities have this type of service available, and 66 percent of those make use of it. Also, social services are provided for 44 percent, special education for 25 percent, and transportation for 32 percent of Belgium's organized facility users.

The most common educator-parent contact reported by 95 percent of the organized facility sample is the informal meeting, which occurs weekly for 73 percent of parents. Two other types of contact reported by Belgian parents are the meeting requested by the educator (44 percent) and parent assistance in the setting (33 percent). Parents report very few problems with the organized facilities their children attend.

China (PRC)

China is characterized by moderate provision but heavy use of organized facilities, particularly of facilities with an educational program. Almost one third of China's total study sample attended organized facilities, with the majority of these (86 percent) enrolled in educational programs and the rest of them (14 percent) enrolled in care-oriented programs. China's children spend a great deal of time in these programs, an average of 8 hours daily, or 47 hours weekly. The majority (77 percent) spend more than 40 hours each week in such settings. Most of the children attending organized facilities stay at home with their parents during planned closings (89 percent) or unplanned closings (57 percent), and another 25 percent stay in their own home with a relative during unplanned closings.

Organized facilities are sponsored by a variety of organizations, in particular, by employers (28 percent), government, and educational institutions (each 16 percent). The most important criterion that parents use when choosing an organized facility is convenience (60 percent), although positive information about the program is also an important deciding factor for 22 percent of organized facility parents, and having no other alternative is the deciding factor for 10 percent. Health care is the most widespread auxiliary service provided by China's organized facilities; it is available for 44 percent of children and is also used quite extensively (by 79 percent of those for whom it is available). The social services that organized facilities offer are available for 11 percent of organized facility children.

The most frequent educator-parent contact consists of informal meetings (reported by 61 percent of parents), and these occurred weekly for 13 percent of the organized facility sample. Meetings requested by either the educator or the parent are universally available, though they are held less than once a month. Parents feel that the major problems with organized facilities have to do with equipment and materials (29 percent), staff qualifications (21 percent), hours of operation, and the personal characteristics of the educator (each 10 percent). China and Nigeria are the countries reporting the highest degree of parental dissatisfaction (7 percent) with the organized facilities their children attend.

FINLAND

In Finland, the only Scandinavian country of the study, organized facilities were used by 35 percent of the total study sample. Of these children, 67 percent attended educational programs (day care centers), and the remaining 33 percent attended part-time day clubs. Although Finnish children average 6 hours a day, or 27 hours a week, in their organized programs, the amount of time individuals spend in such programs varies widely. About one third of the children attend for 1 to 10 hours; one third, for 30 to 40 hours; and one third, for over 40 hours. During facility closings, the most common alternative (72 percent for planned, 51 percent for unplanned) is care in the child's own home. However, 25 percent of children are able to be accommodated by another organized facility in the event that their own program announces an unplanned closing.

Organized facilities for the most part are sponsored by the government (66 percent) and religious organizations (29 percent). Parents indicate a variety of reasons for choosing their child's particular program, such as convenience (30 percent), the nonphysical characteristics of the setting (27 percent), and having no other alternative (24 percent). Organized facilities offer a moderate level of health services (21 percent) and special education services (28 percent), but few social services (7 percent). Of these, health services are the most widely used (by 79 percent of those families with access to them).

Various types of educator-parent contacts occur, and these are frequent. The most common are informal meetings (85 percent), group meetings (71 percent), telephone/written communication (64 percent), and meetings requested by the educator (54 percent) or the parent (34 percent). Informal meetings took place daily for 51 percent of the organized facility sample. Finnish parents reported almost no problems with organized settings.

Germany (FRG)

About half of all German children (55 percent) attend organized facilities. In line with a long tradition of Froebelian kindergartens, all such settings are educational in orientation. The average time children spend in these settings is shorter than that spent by children in most other countries in the study — 4 hours a day, or 20 hours a week. Most children (61 percent) spend 10 to 20 hours each week in their kindergartens. Although 29 percent spend more time than this, their attendance is rarely for more than 30 hours per week. The most common alternatives during unplanned facility closings are care by parents at home (72 percent) and care at a relative's home (14 percent).

Most of Germany's organized facilities are sponsored by religious organizations (60 percent); an additional 29 percent are sponsored by government. Sample parents reported that they chose their child's organized facility because of nonphysical characteristics of the setting (38 percent) and convenience (35 percent); some parents (15 percent) had no other alternative. German parents' problems with organized settings are hours of operation (for 13 percent) and cost (for 5 percent).

HONG KONG

The distinctive features of organized facilities in Hong Kong are extensive provision and widespread use. Almost every 4-year-old child attends either an educational setting (96 percent) or a care setting (4 percent). However, as in Germany, the average time children attend these settings is relatively short — 4 hours daily, or 17 hours weekly; most children attend for only 10 to 20 hours each week.

Organized facilities are sponsored by either religious (60 percent), private (28 percent), or voluntary (11 percent) organizations — government plays no part. On the whole, these settings provide a moderate level of auxiliary services. The most widespread is transportation (for 40 percent of the sample), followed by health services (37 percent), special education (21 percent), and social services (19 percent). With the exception of transportation, which is used by 49 percent of families having access to this service, most of the services provided are underutilized (used by only 7 to 23 percent of the families with access).

The most common forms of educator-parent contact are use of a handbook (for 58 percent of organized facility parents), group meetings (for 37 percent), informal meetings (for 33 percent), and telephone/written communication (for 27 percent). Most contacts occur less than once a month. Parents report having problems with a number of aspects of their children's programs: the facility and equipment (21 percent), philosophy of the program (20 percent), cost (18 percent), other children (13 percent), and educator unreliability (10 percent).

ITALY

A high proportion (81 percent) of Italy's 4-year-old children attend organized settings, all of which are educational. On average, children attend their educational programs 6 hours each day, or 33 hours each week. A large number (48 percent) attend 30 to 40 hours weekly, and 28 percent attend 20 to 30 hours. In the event of a facility closing, most children are cared for at home by their parents (planned closing, 73 percent;

unplanned closing, 63 percent), although some children stay with a relative at home (9 percent and 15 percent, respectively) or at a relative's home (9 percent and 10 percent, respectively).

As in Finland, the major sponsors of organized facilities are government (67 percent) and religious organizations (23 percent). Parents select their child's facility mainly for convenience (44 percent) or because of positive information about the setting (22 percent). The facilities offer a moderate level of auxiliary services: The most widespread is transportation (offered for 35 percent of organized facility children), followed by special education (for 17 percent), social services (for 14 percent), and health services (for 11 percent). Use of health and transportation services by children who have access is moderate (47 percent and 34 percent, respectively), but the percentages of all organized facility users who benefit from auxiliary services are low, only 1 to 12 percent.

Italian parents engage in a variety of educator-parent contacts, such as informal meetings (81 percent), group meetings (58 percent), and meetings requested by the educator or by the parent (each 41 to 43 percent). Informal meetings occurred daily for 48 percent of the organized facility sample, but other types of contact were relatively infrequent. Meetings requested by the educator generally took place once a month or less, and meetings requested by the parents ranged from daily meetings (for 14 percent) to less than once a month (for 9 percent). The vast majority of sample parents reported few or no problems with their children's organized facilities.

NIGERIA

Nigeria is characterized by low (only 8 percent) usage of organized facilities. Of the organized programs attended, 51 percent are educational, 9 percent are care-oriented, and 40 percent provide a "general" setting. Children spend, on average, 5 hours daily, or 23 hours weekly, in these settings, with the majority (64 percent) attending 10 to 20 hours a week.

Information available on half the sample parents shows that organized facilities are sponsored by a variety of organizations, the most common being private (26 percent), religious (18 percent), and voluntary (4 percent). Parents base their choice of a setting primarily on having heard positive information about the facility (50 percent) and also on convenience (38 percent). Very few organized settings (1 to 2 percent) offer health, social, and special education services.

The most common educator-parent contacts are meetings requested by the educator (reported by 23 percent of parents) about once every 2 weeks, and informal meetings (reported by 20 percent) once a month or less. Sample parents cited few specific problems with organized settings, the most common having to do with cost (5 percent) and other children (4 percent). However, Nigeria, along with China, reported one of the highest degrees of parental dissatisfaction with organized settings (7 percent).

PORTUGAL

In Portugal, as in China, Finland, and the United States, there is moderate use of organized facilities (31 percent), and all of these facilities provide programs that are "general" in nature. Compared with children in most other countries of the study, Portuguese children spend a long time in their organized programs — an average of 9 hours a day, or 45 hours a week. As in China, the majority (66 percent) attend more than 40 hours each week. During facility closings most children stay at home with their parents (planned closing, 78 percent; unplanned closing, 44 percent) or in a relative's home (7 percent and 20 percent, respectively).

Of the organized facilities, 54 percent are government-sponsored, and a further 38 percent have multiple sponsors, usually government together with religious organizations. Sample parents indicated a variety of reasons for their selection of a setting: convenience (35 percent), positive information about the setting (21 percent), and having no other alternative (20 percent). Children attending organized facilities have a moderate level of auxiliary services provided for them. Health services (available for 33 percent) are most common; next come social services (for 27 percent), transportation (for 21 percent), and special education (for 13 percent). Among children with access to the services, usage ranges from 17 percent for social services to 47 percent for health services.

The most widespread educator-parent contacts are informal meetings (reported by 86 percent of parents), group meetings (50 percent), and telephone/written communication (41 percent). Informal meetings take place daily for 39 percent of parents, but other types of contacts occur less than once a month. The vast majority of sample parents (90 percent) reported that their children enjoyed their organized facilities. With the exception of problems with cost, which was mentioned by 5 percent of the sample, parents appeared to have few problems with organized settings.

Spain

The majority of Spanish children (70 percent) attend organized facilities. As in Portugal, these settings are described as "general," presumably covering both education and care. Average daily attendance is 6 hours, and average weekly attendance, 29 hours, with the majority of children (58 percent) attending 20 to 30 hours per week. Although parents use a variety of alternatives during facility closings, the most usual ones are for children to stay at home with their parents (planned closing, 36 percent; unplanned closing, 26 percent), or at a relative's home (19 percent and 18 percent, respectively). Relatively high proportions of parents have no plan for either planned (25 percent) or unplanned closings (30 percent).

Of those sample parents who responded to the question on facility sponsorship (31 percent), the majority (24 percent) indicated government sponsorship. Most parents choose their children's settings on the basis of *convenience* or *positive information* about the setting (each 32 percent), or they base their decision on the *nonphysical characteristics* of the setting (16 percent). Organized facilities in Spain offer quite extensive auxiliary services for children. The most widely available are health services and special education services (each 42 percent), and transportation (23 percent). Available health and transportation services are the most used (by 29 percent and 34 percent of the children, respectively).

As is true in many other countries, the most common educator-parent contact is through informal meetings (for 88 percent of parents); 43 percent of parents reported having this type of contact daily. Other parents cited group meetings (39 percent), telephone/written communication (17 percent), and meetings requested by the educator (15 percent), although all of these occurred less than once a month. Parents reported few problems with organized settings, and a large majority (89 percent) believed that their children enjoyed the facilities they were attending.

Thailand

In Thailand, as in Nigeria, there is relatively low use of organized facilities. Only 12 percent of sample parents reported that their children attended organized facilities. Of these children, 64 percent were in an educational setting, and 36 percent, in a care setting. Thai children attend their settings for a relatively long time — an average of 7 hours daily, or 38 hours weekly, with the majority (69 percent) attending 30 to 40 hours each week. During facility closings the majority of children stay at home with their parents.

However, a small minority of parents reported having no plans for either planned (10 percent) or unplanned (6 percent) closings.

The major sponsors of organized facilities are government (40 percent), or government combined with other institutions (16 percent). The most important criteria that parents use when choosing a facility are convenience (53 percent) and nonphysical characteristics of the setting (16 percent). The most widely offered auxiliary services are transportation (35 percent), and health care (18 percent); these are used by 55 percent and 85 percent of children with access, respectively.

The most common educator-parent contacts are informal meetings (60 percent), which occurred daily for about one quarter of the sample. Other types of contacts are meetings requested by the educator and group meetings, both of which usually occur less than once a month. Thai parents reported very few problems with their children's organized settings.

THE UNITED STATES

Organized facilities in the United States are used to a moderate extent — by 39 percent of the total sample, with 71 percent of these children attending an educational setting, and 29 percent, a care setting. Although the average time children attend organized facilities is 5 hours daily, or 22 hours weekly, there is wide variation among children. Attendance ranges from 2 to 10 hours (for 32 percent) to more than 40 hours (for 14 percent). As is the case in most other countries, the common arrangement during facility closings is for children to stay at home with their parents (planned closings, 86 percent; unplanned closings, 59 percent). During unplanned closings a few children (11 percent) are cared for at home by relatives.

A variety of organizations sponsor organized facilities: these are mainly private (25 percent), religious (19 percent), government (15 percent), and educational (12 percent). The criteria parents usually consider when choosing an organized facility are positive information about the setting (40 percent) and nonphysical characteristics of the setting (23 percent). Organized facilities in the United States offer a moderate level of auxiliary services: health (37 percent), transportation (26 percent), special education, and social services (each 24 percent). Health care and transportation are the two most widely used (used by 75 percent and 50 percent, respectively, of the children with access to these services).

Informal meetings between educators and parents occur quite extensively (80 percent); 21 percent of these are daily, and 19 percent, weekly.

Also widespread are telephone/written contact (65 percent), group meetings (63 percent), parents helping in the setting (49 percent), and meetings requested either by the educator (44 percent) or the parent (36 percent). With the exception of telephone/written communication, which occurs weekly for 17 percent and every 2 weeks for a further 12 percent, most contacts occur less than once a month. Parents in the U.S. report almost no problems with their children's organized settings.

* * *

This chapter and the previous one have reported study findings about the various kinds of settings families reported using for their children, with a special emphasis on the features of organized facilities. The next chapter reports findings on the daily routines of study children.

Endnotes

1. If a child's first and second settings were both organized facilities, researchers collected data for the *more educational* of the two settings, even if it was not the child's first (longest-attended) extraparental setting of the week.

2. *Organized facility* settings comprise both group care programs and group education programs and thus employ different terms to refer to adults working in these settings. Adults in child care centers are usually called *caregivers*, whereas adults in educational programs are called *teachers*. For purposes of simplification, this chapter about organized facilities refers to adults in both of these categories as *educators*. Since researchers chose to gather data about the more educational of a child's two longest-attended organized programs, the term *educator* is appropriate more often than not.

3. Countries defined sponsor types as follows: *Educational institution* — In almost all cases, this means sponsorship by a school system (e.g., a preprimary program affiliated with the formal educational system). In a very few instances, it means sponsorship by an institution of higher education (e.g., a preprimary program that is affiliated with a college or university). *Government* — Sponsorship by a national, regional, or local governmental agency. *Religious Organization* — Sponsorship by a specific church or religious group (e.g., the Catholic church in Italy). *Employer* — Sponsorship by the company employing one or both parents. *Voluntary Organization* — Sponsorship by a charitable organization (e.g., Save the Children) or group (e.g., a

women's organization for education of young children). *Private Organization* — Sponsorship by a proprietary group (e.g., Kindercare in the United States) or private individual. Sponsorship may combine two or more of these sponsor types (e.g., the preprimary programs affiliated with government and religious organizations in Portugal).

VII
STUDY FINDINGS:
CHILDREN'S DAILY ROUTINES

Arlette Delhaxhe, *Researcher*
University of Liège

Genevieve Hindryckx, *Researcher*
University of Liège

Patricia P. Olmsted, *Senior Research Associate*
High/Scope Educational Research Foundation
Ypsilanti, Michigan

Zhenkui Ma, *Research Associate*
University of Montana
Missoula, Montana

In the Phase 1 household survey, parents in each country were asked to provide a detailed description of a typical day in their child's life. The daily routines that parents outlined for their children's waking hours yielded such country-specific findings as these:

- A typical 4-year-old in Portugal may spend up to 2 hours a day with grandparents.
- In the United States, mothers usually supervise their preschool-aged children for 10 to 11 hours a day.
- In China, it is common for a 4-year-old to spend nearly 3 hours a day without direct adult supervision.

This chapter examines the daily routine part of the household survey in greater detail, explaining development of the daily routine questionnaire, data collection procedures, and findings from 10 countries.[1]

Methodology

The Daily Routine Chart

The daily routine (DR) chart was jointly developed by the National Research Coordinators (NRCs) from the participating countries. The chart contains spaces for an interviewer to record the parent/guardian's recollections about the child's routine on the day before the interview. The interviewer asked for three types of information for each of 24 hours, beginning at midnight. These three types of information were (1) the child's primary caregiver, (2) the child's location, and (3) the number of other adults/adolescents present and the number of other children present (i.e., the social context of the child). The Parent/Guardian Interview in Appendix B includes a copy of the daily routine chart.

As a group, the NRCs developed the following 10 categories of primary caregivers:

Category	Definition of Category
1. Mother	Mother, stepmother, or female guardian
2. Two parents	Mother and father, equally responsible
3. Father	Father, stepfather, or male guardian
4. Sibling	Brother, sister, stepbrother, stepsister
5. Grandparent	Grandmother, grandfather, or both
6. Other relative	Aunt, uncle, cousin, and so forth
7. Friend/neighbor	Friend or neighbor of the family
8. Other adult	Family child care provider, nurse, baby sitter, maid, childminder, paraprofessional in organized facility
9. Teacher/caregiver	Regular staff person in an organized early childhood facility
10. Nobody	No direct supervisor

They also developed these 9 categories for the location of the child:

Category	Definition of Category
1. Home	Home of the child/family
2. Relative's home	Home of grandparent(s), aunt, cousin, and so forth
3. Friend/neighbor's home	Home of friend or neighbor of child's family

4. Child care home   Private home in which child care is pro-
                            vided, on a regular basis, to at least one
                            child unrelated to the child care provider

5. School/center   Organized facility in which staff provide
                            early childhood services to a group of
                            children

6. Parent's workplace   Location where mother or father works,
                            including such locations as a factory, hos-
                            pital, educational institution, and market-
                            place

7. Play area   Locations, formal or informal, where
                            children play

8. Shops/stores   Locations where family buys things,
                            transacts business, or meets with others
                            (i.e., city hall, community center)

9. In transition   In-transit locations, when child moves
                            from one setting to another (e.g., on foot,
                            by car, by public transportation)

The NRCs agreed to use a 1-hour interval on the DR chart. When the parent/guardian reported more than one location, caregiver, or social context for a given hour, the interviewer was instructed to enter the information that best represented (i.e., described the longest portion of) the 1-hour time interval. For example, if the child was at home alone with the mother for 20 minutes and then went with a grandparent to a nearby public park to play for 40 minutes, the latter situation (grandparent/play area) would be the information recorded for that hour.

Each national research center pilot-tested the DR chart to check the appropriateness of the system of categories, the design of the chart, and the feasibility of the proposed data collection procedures. As a result of this national pilot-testing, minor changes were made in the DR chart.

The International Coordinating Center (ICC) pilot-tested the DR procedures to insure that parents' recollections about their 4-year-olds' care providers and locations on the previous day were sufficiently accurate. The method used for the pilot test included researchers observing ten 4-year-old children for a minimum of 6 hours each on a single day and recording all caregivers, locations, and others present. On the following day, an ICC staff member administered the Parent/Guardian Interview to each child's family and then compared the information parents provided in the daily routine chart with the researcher's observations of each child's daily routine on the previous day. The results indicated that parents' recollections of their children's daily routines were extremely accurate. Also, with the exception of cases in which a parent was not present and thus could not know about changes in the number of adults or children in a child's setting (e.g., while the child was in an extrafamilial setting), the parental information regarding children's social contexts was accurate.

Data Collection Procedures

As noted earlier, interviewers collected three types of daily routine information (caregiver, location, and social context for each hour of a child's typical day) while they were administering the Parent/Guardian Interview. The NRCs decided that whenever possible, to minimize the amount of recall required, the parent should be asked about the day immediately previous to the day of interview. So this would produce information about a typical weekday, the Parent/Guardian Interview was to be administered on Tuesday through Friday. (In Belgium, where preschools are not open on Wednesday, interviewers administered the Parent/Guardian Interview on Tuesday, Wednesday, or Friday only.) If the parent indicated that the previous day had not been typical (e.g., if the child had been ill), then the interviewer was to ask for information for either the day *before* the previous day or for some other recent typical day.

Each NRC instructed the interviewers to use one of two recording procedures: (1) writing the information on the DR chart during the interview with the parent/guardian or (2) writing the information on a running-record form and later transferring the data to the DR chart. Using either procedure, the interviewer produced a DR chart containing the three types of information described earlier.

Limitations

The DR chart information has several limitations that should be noted. First, the data refer only to a typical weekday and not to Saturday or Sunday. Second, the data refer only to a single day. Finally, only one set of information (the hour's most representative information) was recorded for each 1-hour period, even though the child may have changed caregiver, location, or social context within that hour. Within this 1-hour period, locations, or caregivers, or contexts of short duration are not specifically identified in the data set.

THE DAILY ROUTINE DATA

This examination of the data is limited to analyzing only the child's waking hours. Each NRC designated the 16-hour period that best represented the waking hours for 4-year-old children in his or her country, and this period was used for all children in that country, regardless of individual waking-sleeping patterns. Seven NRCs (in Belgium, China, Finland, Germany, Hong Kong, Nigeria, and the United States) selected 6:00 a.m. to 10:00 p.m. as the waking-hour period, while the NRCs from Portugal and Spain selected 8:00 a.m. to 12:00 midnight, and Thailand's NRC selected 5:00 a.m. to 9:00 p.m.

CAREGIVERS

Table 7.1 lists, for 10 nations, the mean number of waking hours that 4-year-olds spend with each type of caregiver. The table shows that despite some differences from nation to nation, in every country the *mother* is the care provider for the greatest number of hours. Mothers in Belgium serve in this role for the shortest time each day (5.2 hours), while mothers in the United States serve for the longest time (10.7 hours). Belgium is the only nation with any caregiver having hours of supervision close to those of the mother (the *teacher/caregiver*, 4.8 hours). In all other countries, the mother's supervisory time is much longer than that of any other type of caregiver.

Figure 7.1 shows that when the data are limited to types of caregivers who provide at least 1 hour of supervision, each country has three or four such caregivers. For example, *mother* meets this criterion in every country, and *teacher/caregiver* meets this criterion in 8 countries. The category of *two parents* meets the criterion in 7 countries, and the categories *grandparent* and *other adult* (e.g., family child care provider, baby sitter) meet it in 4 countries.

In recent decades, many countries have witnessed a growing interest in involving fathers in childrearing; so it is interesting to note in Table 7.1 that no country reported supervision by *father* exceeding 1 hour daily. There is, however, some variation from nation to nation in the amount of

Table 7.1   Number of waking hours that 4-year-old children spend with various caregivers

Country/Territory	N	Mother Mean (SD)	Two Parents Mean (SD)	Father Mean (SD)	Sibling Mean (SD)	Grand-Parent Mean (SD)	Other Relative Mean (SD)	Friend/Neighbor Mean (SD)	Other Adult Mean (SD)	Teacher/Caregiver Mean (SD)	Nobody Mean (SD)	Missing/No Info. Mean (SD)
Belgium (Fr.)	424	5.2 (3.8)	3.2 (3.3)	0.5 (1.2)	0.1 (0.4)	0.7 (1.8)	0.2 (0.9)	0.1 (0.6)	1.2 (1.3)	4.8 (1.6)	0.0 (0.2)	0.0
China (PRC)+	12,835	6.8 (4.7)	—	0.9 (2.2)	0.1 (0.9)	1.3 (3.2)	0.1 (1.0)	0.1 (0.8)	0.0 (0.5)	3.0 (4.0)	2.9 (4.2)	0.8 (0.0)
Finland	576	7.7 (5.1)	2.1 (3.2)	0.8 (1.7)	0.1 (0.8)	0.3 (1.5)	0.1 (0.7)	0.1 (0.5)	2.7 (3.9)	2.0 (3.5)	0.1 (0.4)	0.0
Germany (FRG)	509	10.0 (4.8)	1.9 (3.2)	0.6 (1.8)	0.1 (0.7)	0.9 (2.4)	0.1 (0.6)	0.2 (0.8)	0.2 (1.0)	1.9 (2.5)	0.1 (0.6)	0.0
Hong Kong+	947	7.5 (5.5)	0.8 (2.0)	0.1 (0.7)	0.0 (0.4)	1.4 (3.6)	0.3 (1.8)	0.1 (1.1)	0.6 (2.3)	3.3 (1.5)	0.0 (0.2)	1.9 (0.0)
Nigeria+	1,295	10.0 (5.0)	1.0 (2.5)	0.7 (1.1)	0.7 (1.5)	0.2 (1.6)	0.3 (1.2)	0.2 (0.9)	1.8 (3.0)	0.5 (1.9)	0.2 (0.9)	0.4 (0.0)
Portugal	581	8.2 (5.7)	1.6 (2.9)	0.4 (1.4)	0.2 (1.2)	1.9 (3.7)	0.5 (2.0)	0.0 (0.4)	0.8 (2.5)	2.3 (3.8)	0.1 (0.6)	0.0
Spain	480	7.6 (4.9)	2.3 (3.0)	0.3 (1.2)	0.2 (0.7)	0.7 (2.0)	0.1 (0.9)	0.1 (0.7)	0.3 (1.2)	4.3 (3.2)	0.1 (0.5)	0.0
Thailand	2,466	8.0 (5.9)	3.3 (4.2)	0.2 (1.3)	0.2 (1.3)	2.1 (4.3)	0.4 (1.9)	0.0 (0.4)	0.4 (1.8)	0.6 (2.0)	0.8 (2.1)	0.0
United States	432	10.7 (4.9)	0.9 (2.2)	0.7 (1.9)	0.1 (0.4)	0.5 (2.3)	0.2 (1.2)	0.1 (0.5)	1.0 (2.6)	1.8 (3.1)	0.0 (0.1)	0.0

Note. The symbol + indicates that weighted data were used for analysis. A dash indicates that no data were available. Entries are in hours and total to 16.0.

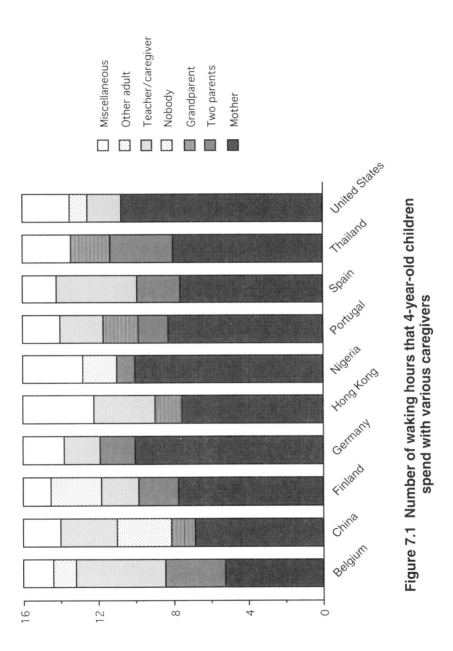

Figure 7.1 Number of waking hours that 4-year-old children spend with various caregivers

daily supervision by *father* (e.g., 0.1 hour in Hong Kong; 0.9 hour in China). If the time that fathers serve as the primary caregivers for 4-year-old children is actually increasing in parts of the world, the increase may be occurring only for subpopulations of families, or the increase may be so small that it is not reflected in an aggregated data set with a 1-hour coding interval. Also, fathers may indeed be providing more care, but it may be in the presence of the mothers and thus recorded under the category *two parents* rather than the category *father*.

LOCATIONS

Table 7.2 presents, for 10 countries, the mean number of hours that 4-year-old children spend in various locations. In all nations, *home* is the location where children spend the greatest part of their waking hours. Belgium reported the least time in this location (8.6 hours), while Nigeria reported the most time (13.0 hours). In 8 nations, an organized facility (*school/center*) is where 4-year-old children spend the second-longest amount of time daily. The exceptions to this situation are Finland, where the time spent in a *child care home* (2.4 hours) is longer than the time spent in a *school/center* (2.0 hours), and Nigeria, where the time spent in a *friend/neighbor home* (0.8 hour) is longer than the time spent in a *school/center* (0.6 hour).

As Figure 7.2 shows, there are only 3 locations other than the family's own *home* (in 10 nations) and the *school/center* (in 9 nations) where children in any nation typically spend more than 1 hour a day. In Finland and the United States 4-year-old children average at least 1 hour a day in a *child care home*, and in Germany and Portugal they average at least 1 hour a day in a *relative's home*. In China and Spain at least 1 hour daily is spent in a *play area*.

CAREGIVER/LOCATION COMBINATIONS

Figures 7.3 to 7.12 on pages 196–205 present the percentages of time that 4-year-old children in each nation experience various caregiver/location combinations. The findings reported in the figures were obtained using the following steps: First, the total number of waking child-hours was calculated for each country (e.g., for the United States, 432 children × 16 hours = 6,912 child-hours). For each hour during the 16-hour waking

Table 7.2 Number of waking hours that 4-year-old children spend in various locations

Country/Territory	N	Home Mean (SD)	Relative's Home Mean (SD)	Friend/Neighbor Home Mean (SD)	Child Care Home Mean (SD)	School/Center Mean (SD)	Parent's Workplace Mean (SD)	Play Area Mean (SD)	Shops/Stores Mean (SD)	In Transition Mean (SD)	Missing/No Info. Mean (SD)
Belgium (Fr.)	424	8.6 (2.4)	0.9 (1.9)	0.1 (0.6)	0.0 (0.3)	6.0 (2.3)	0.0 (0.3)	0.1 (0.5)	0.0	0.3 (0.8)	0.0
China (PRC)[+]	12,835	8.7 (4.2)	0.3 (1.5)	0.6 (1.8)	0.4 (1.9)	3.0 (4.0)	0.4 (1.6)	1.4 (2.7)	0.2 (1.1)	0.3 (0.9)	0.7 (0.0)
Finland	576	10.1 (3.8)	0.3 (1.3)	0.2 (0.8)	2.4 (3.7)	2.1 (3.5)	0.0 (0.3)	0.7 (1.3)	0.2 (0.6)	0.0 (0.2)	0.0
Germany (FRG)	509	11.0 (3.4)	1.0 (2.4)	0.3 (1.0)	0.1 (0.8)	2.0 (2.4)	0.0	0.7 (1.4)	0.4 (0.9)	0.5 (1.2)	0.0
Hong Kong[+]	947	11.3 (3.6)	0.5 (2.3)	0.1 (1.1)	0.1 (0.7)	3.3 (1.5)	0.1 (0.8)	0.1 (0.4)	0.0 (0.1)	0.0	0.5 (0.0)
Nigeria[+]	1,295	13.0 (4.7)	0.5 (1.1)	0.8 (1.4)	0.1 (1.2)	0.6 (2.1)	0.3 (1.9)	0.2 (0.8)	0.0 (0.1)	0.0	0.5 (0.0)
Portugal	581	10.1 (4.5)	1.6 (3.4)	0.1 (0.7)	0.5 (2.2)	2.5 (3.9)	0.5 (1.7)	0.5 (1.6)	0.1 (0.6)	0.1 (0.4)	0.0
Spain	480	8.9 (3.0)	0.5 (1.5)	0.1 (0.5)	0.0 (0.3)	4.3 (3.1)	0.1 (0.9)	1.7 (1.6)	0.3 (0.8)	0.1 (0.4)	0.0
Thailand	2,466	12.6 (4.1)	0.9 (2.6)	0.8 (2.0)	0.1 (0.9)	1.0 (2.4)	0.2 (1.4)	0.3 (1.4)	0.0 (0.4)	0.1 (0.5)	0.0
United States	432	12.1 (3.7)	0.3 (1.0)	0.1 (0.7)	1.0 (2.6)	1.9 (3.1)	0.0 (0.4)	0.2 (0.6)	0.3 (0.8)	0.1 (0.4)	0.0

Note. The symbol [+] indicates that weighted data were used for analysis. Entries are in hours and total to 16.0

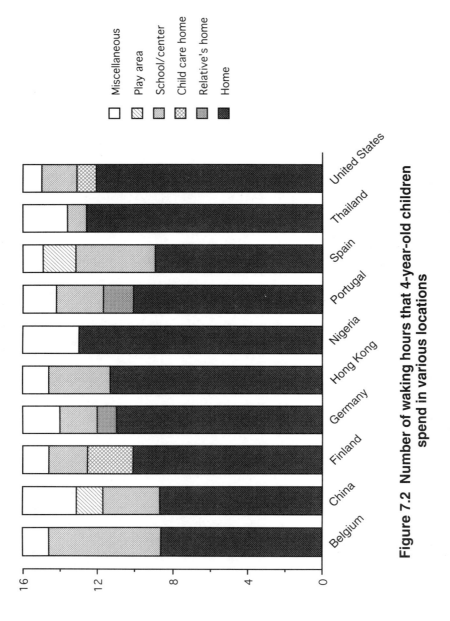

Figure 7.2 Number of waking hours that 4-year-old children spend in various locations

period, the number of children experiencing each combination of caregiver/location was tallied (e.g., 7:00–8:00 a.m.: 378 children with mother in own home = 378 child-hours in *mother/home* cell). Then, these cell-specific child-hours were aggregated across the 16-hour waking period (i.e., 378 + . . . = 4,288), and a percentage was calculated for the child-hours by dividing the child-hours in the *mother/home* cell by the total child-hours (e.g., 4,288/6,912 = 62 percent).

The figures show that in most countries, *mother, father,* or *two parents* nearly always supervise the 4-year-olds at *home*. Only in Spain is any other single caregiver/location combination involving a parent experienced more than 5 percent of the time (Spanish children experience *mother/play area* 7 percent of waking time). In many countries *grandparent* supervision occurs in two different locations — in the child's home (the *grandparent/home* cell) and in the grandparent's home (the *grandparent/relative's home* cell). *Teacher/caregiver* supervision generally occurs in organized facilities (*teacher/caregiver* in the *school/center*). In some countries (e.g., Belgium and Thailand) *other adult* supervision is in *schools/centers*, while in other countries (e.g., Finland and Portugal) it occurs in a *child care home*.

Across the 10 figures, the number of cells containing entries varies from 6 (for Belgium, Finland, Hong Kong, and Spain) to 10 (for China and Portugal), indicating that the total number of caregiver/location combinations that 4-year-old children encounter during a typical day is relatively small. (Note: A minimum 1-hour interval was used). In any one country, supervision by a given type of caregiver generally occurs in a single location. The exceptions to this include *grandparent* (who provides care in both the child's *home* and the *relative's* [grandparent's] *home*) and *other adult* (who provides care in the *child care home* and *school/center*).

GROUPINGS OF CAREGIVERS AND LOCATIONS

It is also possible to combine the information presented in Tables 7.1 and 7.2 with the data in Figures 7.3–7.12 to develop five general groupings of caregivers and locations. Table 7.3 on page 207 presents the five groupings, with each defined by the nature of the relationship between the caregiver and the child as well as by the nature of the location:

■ **Parental care in all locations**, which includes the caregiver categories of *mother, father,* and *two parents*. For this grouping, all

Caregiver

Location	Mother	Two Parents	Father	Sibling	Grand-parent	Other Relative	Friend/Neighbor	Other Adult	Teacher/Caregiver	Nobody
Home	31	19	3							
Relative's home					4					
Friend/neighbor home										
Child care home										
School/center								7	30	
Parent's workplace										
Play area										
Shops/stores										
In transition										

Total % for 16 hours = 100%. Total % in figure = 94%. Minimum % entered in figure = 2%.

Figure 7.3 Percentage of waking hours that 4-year-old children in Belgium experience various caregiver/location combinations (N = 424)

Location	Mother	Two Parents	Father	Sibling	Grand-parent	Other Relative	Friend/Neighbor	Other Adult	Teacher/Caregiver	Nobody
Home	37		4		4					9
Relative's home										
Friend/neighbor home										2
Child care home					2					
School/center									19	
Parent's workplace	2									
Play area	2									5
Shops/stores										
In transition										

Total % for 16 hours = 100%. Total % in figure = 86%. Minimum % entered in figure = 2%. Missing Data = 4%.

Figure 7.4 Percentage of waking hours that 4-year-old children in China experience various caregiver/location combinations (N = 12,835)

Caregiver

Location	Mother	Two Parents	Father	Sibling	Grand-parent	Other Relative	Friend/Neighbor	Other Adult	Teacher/Caregiver	Nobody
Home	44	13	4							
Relative's home										
Friend/neighbor home										
Child care home								15		
School/center									13	
Parent's workplace										
Play area	2									
Shops/stores										
In transition										

Total % for 16 hours = 100%. Total % in figure = 91%. Minimum % entered in figure = 2%.

Figure 7.5 Percentage of waking hours that 4-year-old children in Finland experience various caregiver/location combinations (N = 576)

Caregiver

Location	Mother	Two Parents	Father	Sibling	Grand-parent	Other Relative	Friend/Neighbor	Other Adult	Teacher/Caregiver	Nobody
Home	52	10	3							
Relative's home					4					
Friend/neighbor home										
Child care home										
School/center									11	
Parent's workplace										
Play area	3									
Shops/stores	2									
In transition	2									

Total % for 16 hours = 100%. Total % in figure = 87%. Minimum % entered in figure = 2%.

Figure 7.6 Percentage of waking hours that 4-year-old children in Germany experience various caregiver/location combinations ($N = 509$)

Caregiver

Location	Mother	Two Parents	Father	Sibling	Grand-parent	Other Relative	Friend/Neighbor	Other Adult	Teacher/Caregiver	Nobody
Home	46	5			7			3		
Relative's home					2					
Friend/neighbor home										
Child care home										
School/center									21	
Parent's workplace										
Play area										
Shops/stores										
In transition										

Total % for 16 hours = 100%. Total % in figure = 84%. Minimum % entered in figure = 2%. Missing data = 11%.

Figure 7.7 Percentage of waking hours that 4-year-old children in Hong Kong experience various caregiver/location combinations (N = 947)

Caregiver

Location	Mother	Two Parents	Father	Sibling	Grand-parent	Other Relative	Friend/ Neighbor	Other Adult	Teacher/ Caregiver	Nobody
Home	57	6	4	3				8		
Relative's home										
Friend/neighbor home										
Child care home										
School/center									3	
Parent's workplace	2									
Play area										
Shops/stores										
In transition										

Total % for 16 hours = 100%. Total % in figure = 83%. Minimum % entered in figure = 2%. Missing data = 3%.

Figure 7.8 Percentage of waking hours that 4-year-old children in Nigeria experience various caregiver/location combinations (N = 1,295)

Caregiver

Location	Mother	Two Parents	Father	Sibling	Grand-parent	Other Relative	Friend / Neighbor	Other Adult	Teacher / Caregiver	Nobody
Home	45	9	2		5					
Relative's home					6	2				
Friend / neighbor home										
Child care home								3		
School / center									14	
Parent's workplace	2									
Play area	2									
Shops / stores										
In transition										

Total % for 16 hours = 100%. Total % in figure = 90%. Minimum % entered in figure = 2%.

Figure 7.9 Percentage of waking hours that 4-year-old children in Portugal experience various caregiver/location combinations (*N* = 581)

Caregiver

Location	Mother	Two Parents	Father	Sibling	Grand-parent	Other Relative	Friend/Neighbor	Other Adult	Teacher/Caregiver	Nobody
Home	38	13			2					
Relative's home					2					
Friend/neighbor home										
Child care home										
School/center									27	
Parent's workplace										
Play area	7									
Shops/stores										
In transition										

Total % for 16 hours = 100%. Total % in figure = 89%. Minimum % entered in figure = 2%.

Figure 7.10 Percentage of waking hours that 4-year-old children in Spain experience various caregiver/location combinations ($N = 480$)

Caregiver

Location	Mother	Two Parents	Father	Sibling	Grand-parent	Other Relative	Friend/Neighbor	Other Adult	Teacher/Caregiver	Nobody
Home	45	19			9	2				
Relative's home					3					
Friend/neighbor home	2									2
Child care home										
School/center								2	4	
Parent's workplace										
Play area										
Shops/stores										
In transition										

Total % for 16 hours = 100%. Total % in figure = 88%. Minimum % entered in figure = 2%.

Figure 7.11 Percentage of waking hours that 4-year-old children in Thailand experience various caregiver/location combinations (N = 2,466)

Caregiver

Location	Mother	Two Parents	Father	Sibling	Grand-parent	Other Relative	Friend/Neighbor	Other Adult	Teacher/Caregiver	Nobody
Home	62	5	4		2					
Relative's home										
Friend/neighbor home										
Child care home								5		
School/center									12	
Parent's workplace										
Play area										
Shops/stores	2									
In transition										

Total % for 16 hours = 100%. Total % in figure = 92%. Minimum % entered in figure = 2%.

Figure 7.12 Percentage of waking hours that 4-year-old children in the United States experience various caregiver/location combinations ($N = 432$)

locations in which parental supervision occurs (e.g., *home, play area*) are included.

- **Relative care in all locations,** which includes the caregiver categories of *sibling, grandparent,* and *other relative.* For this grouping, all locations in which relative supervision occurs (e.g., *home, play area*) are included.
- **Nonfamilial care in informal locations,** which includes the caregiver categories of *friend/neighbor, other adult,* and *teacher/caregiver.* For this grouping, all locations except *school/center* are included.
- **Nonfamilial care in formal locations,** which includes the caregiver categories of *friend/neighbor, other adult* and *teacher/caregiver.* Only the *school/center* location is included in this grouping.
- **Nobody caring for the child in all locations,** which includes only the caregiver category of *nobody.* In this grouping, all locations are included.

The data for these five groupings, as presented in Table 7.3, reveal the following:

Parental care in all locations
China reported the lowest number of hours of parental care (7.7), while Germany reported the highest number of hours (12.5). For 5 nations, parents are the caregivers for 10 to 12 hours of the child's waking time. In Belgium, China, and Hong Kong, parental care covers less than 10 hours; in Germany and the United States, parental care covers more than 12 hours.

Relative care in all locations
In most countries, supervision of 4-year-old children by relatives typically occurs for only a short time each day. In 8 of the 10 countries, relatives supervise for periods ranging from 0.5 hour to 1.7 hours. Only in Portugal and Thailand do relatives supervise young children for more than 2 hours a day (2.6 hours and 2.7 hours, respectively).

Nonfamilial care in informal locations
Only 3 nations reported more than 1 hour per day for this caregiver and location grouping. In 2 of these 3 countries, (Finland, 2.8 hours; the United States, 1.1 hours) the care usually involves a caregiver in a child care home. In the third country (Nigeria, 2.0 hours), the care is generally provided by a maid or childminder in the child's own home.

Table 7.3 Hours of care of 4-year-old children during waking hours by various caregivers in various locations

Country/ Territory	N	Caregiver/Location Group					
		Parental,[a] All Locations	Relative,[b] All Locations	Nonfamilial,[c] Informal[d] Locations	Nonfamilial, Formal[e] Locations	Nobody, All Locations	Missing/ No Information
Belgium (Fr.)	424	8.9	1.0	0.1	6.0	0.0	0.0
China (PRC)+	12,835	7.7	1.5	0.1	3.0	2.9	0.8
Finland	576	10.6	0.5	2.8	2.0	0.1	0.0
Germany (FRG)	509	12.5	1.1	0.2	2.1	0.1	0.0
Hong Kong+	947	8.4	1.7	0.7	3.3	0.0	1.9
Nigeria+	1,295	11.7	1.2	2.0	0.5	0.2	0.4
Portugal	581	10.2	2.6	0.8	2.3	0.1	0.0
Spain	480	10.2	1.0	0.1	4.6	0.1	0.0
Thailand	2,466	11.5	2.7	0.0	1.0	0.8	0.0
United States	432	12.3	0.8	1.1	1.8	0.0	0.0

Note. The symbol + indicates that weighted data were used for analysis. Entries are in hours and total to 16.0.

[a]Mother, father, or two parents.
[b]Sibling, grandparent, or other relative.
[c]Friend/neighbor, other adult, or teacher/caregiver.
[d]All locations except school/center.
[e]School/center.

Nonfamilial care in formal locations

Nigeria reported the least time in this type of care (0.5 hour), while Belgium reported the most time (6.0 hours). In the remaining nations, 4-year-old children experience from 1.0 to 4.6 hours of this type of supervision in formal locations.

Nobody caring for the child in all locations

China is the only nation reporting more than 0.8 hour in this grouping. *Nobody* as a caregiver occurs primarily in the rural areas of China (80 percent of the country), where it is commonly considered safe to leave a 4-year-old child unattended near the family's home while the parents are away for several hours, working in the fields.

On the basis of these five groupings, it is possible to identify some countries where children typically experience similar **daily patterns of caregivers and location**. For example, young children in Belgium and Spain have several hours of nonfamilial care in formal locations and parental supervision for most of their remaining waking hours. Children in Germany and the United States spend a great amount of time under parental supervision, with their remaining waking hours divided between relative care and nonfamilial care in both informal and formal locations. Finally, children in Portugal and Thailand share a pattern that includes more than 2 hours of relative care daily.

PATTERNS OF CAREGIVERS AND LOCATIONS

Behind the general descriptions just presented, it is useful to look for groups of children within each nation who have similar patterns of caregivers and locations during their waking hours. Researchers applied cluster analysis procedures (BMDP, k-means clustering) using 19 variables (10 caregivers, 9 locations) to each set of national data to identify the groups of children who share common patterns. For the countries in which weighted data were used for the analysis, a Fortran program was additionally prepared to produce weighted cluster analysis results. This book's chapter authors chose to follow a standard procedure to determine the number of clusters to represent the patterns in each nation and selected the largest number of clusters in which the smallest cluster contained at least 5 percent of the sample children.

Tables 7.4 to 7.13 on pages 210–228 present **detailed information for each pattern** identified from the sets of national data (note that *pat-*

terns are also called *clusters*). The tables give, for each country, the number and percentage of children in each cluster (immediately under the column head) as well as the average number of hours children spend with each type of caregiver and in each location. The data for those variables deemed to characterize the cluster are indicated in bold type.[2] In each figure, the clusters for that country are ordered according to the number of children in each, in decreasing order.

As already mentioned, the findings presented in Figures 7.3 through 7.12 indicate that most caregivers provide supervision in a single location. Consequently, Figures 7.13 through 7.22 depict just the caregiver portions of each nation's cluster information (from Tables 7.4–7.13). The width of each bar represents the percentage of the sample (*N*) included in the cluster (i.e., a wide bar represents a large percentage of the sample, whereas a narrow bar indicates a small percentage).

A cluster that is found in most countries is a combination *mother-teacher/caregiver* cluster, defined by a minimum of 12 hours of supervision provided by these caregivers. The pattern is present in 8 of 10 countries and is generally one of the larger groupings of children. Only Nigeria and Thailand do not have such a cluster. In some countries there are two or three *mother-teacher/caregiver* clusters that are differentiated by the addition of one other category (e.g., *grandparent* in Spain's fourth cluster). Also, the groupings vary in the proportion of time that mothers or teachers/caregivers serve as supervisors for the children.

Another cluster found in 8 of the 10 nations is a *mother-only* pattern, that is, a group of children for whom the mother serves as the only caregiver for nearly the entire waking period. In most countries, this cluster contains the highest or the second-highest percentage of children, and most of the mother's supervision takes place in the family *home*. Belgium and Hong Kong do not have this pattern. Nigeria has two *mother* groupings, one characterized by mother care in the *home* and another characterized by mother care in two locations, the *workplace* (e.g., the marketplace) and the *home*. Portugal also has two *mother* groupings, one cluster characterized by mother care in the *home* and another cluster characterized by mother care in the *workplace* and *play area* as well in the *home*.

Six countries have a *grandparent* cluster, that is, a grouping in which a grandparent typically supervises the child for a minimum of 5 hours a day. This cluster often contains only a small percentage of the 4-year-old children (i.e., 8 to 15 percent), but the proportion of the child's waking hours that the grandparent serves as caregiver is generally very large (more than 60 percent in 4 of the 6 countries).

Table 7.4 Hours of caregivers and locations for 4-year-old children in Belgium (N = 424)

| | Pattern (Cluster) | | | | | | | | | |
| | 1 Mother in Home; T/C, OA in S/C; n = 157; 37% of N | | 2 2 Parents in Home; T/C, OA in S/C; n = 153; 36% of N | | 3 Mother in Home; T/C in S/C; n = 54; 13% of N | | 4 GP in GP Home; T/C in S/C; n = 41; 9% of N | | 5 2 Parents in Home; n = 19; 5% of N | |
Category										
Caregiver										
Mother	**7.4**		2.2		**10.9**		2.5		1.3	
Father		0.4		0.5		0.4		0.6	1.1	
2 parents		0.6	**5.7**		1.2		2.6		**10.4**	
Sibling		0.1		0.0		0.1				0.1
Grandparent (GP)		0.3		0.2		0.4	**5.0**			0.2
Other relative (OR)		0.1		0.1		0.2		0.3	1.3	
Friend/neighbor (F/N)		0.2		0.1		0.0		0.0		0.0
Other adult (OA)	**1.5**		**1.7**			0.0		0.3		0.0
Teacher/caregiver (T/C)	**5.4**		**5.5**		2.7		**4.7**		1.3	
Nobody		0.0		0.0		0.0		0.0		0.3
Location										
Home	**8.3**		**8.2**		**12.1**		5.6		**10.9**	
Relative's home		0.4		0.2		0.4	**5.1**		1.8	
F/N home		0.1		0.1		0.1		0.0		0.0
Child care home (CCH)		0.0		0.1		0.0		0.0		0.1
School/center (S/C)	**6.8**		**7.1**		2.7		**5.0**		1.3	
Workplace (WP)		0.0		0.0		0.0		0.0		0.2
Play area (PA)		0.1		0.1		0.1		0.0		0.4
Shops/stores		0.0		0.0		0.0		0.0		0.0
In transition		0.2		0.2		0.5		0.3	1.3	

Note. Guidelines for interpreting table: (1) The smallest cluster contains at least 4.5% (≈ 5%) of the sample children. (2) Entries are in hours and total to 16.0. (3) All times greater than 1.0 hour are listed in left column under cluster. (4) All times less than 1.0 hour are listed in right column under cluster. (5) The numbers critical to understanding the uniqueness of the cluster are boldfaced.

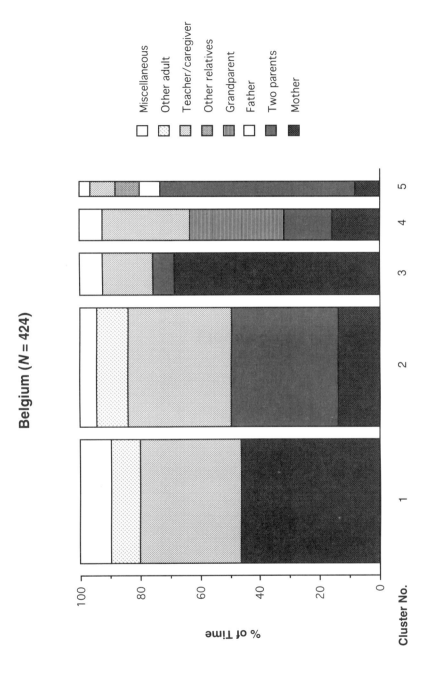

Figure 7.13 Patterns of time spent with different caregivers between 6:00 a.m. and 10:00 p.m.

Table 7.5 Hours of caregivers and locations for 4-year-old children in China (N = 12,835)

	Pattern (Cluster)							
Category	1 — T/C in S/C; Mother in Home — n = 2,567 — 20% of N	2 — T/C in S/C; Father in Home — n = 2,181 — 17% of N	3 — Mother in Home — n = 1,669 — 13% of N	4 — Nobody or Mother in Home or PA — n = 1,540 — 12% of N	5 — Mother in Home, PA, or WP — n = 1,412 — 11% of N	6 — Nobody or Mother in Home — n = 1,284 — 10% of N	7 — GP or Mother in Home — n = 1,155 — 9% of N	8 — Father in Home — n = 1,027 — 8% of N
Caregiver								
Mother	7.1	3.1	**14.4**	4.4	**12.6**	4.6	4.0	3.6
Father	0.4	**1.5**	0.4	0.5	0.4	0.6	0.4	**4.3**
2 parents	—	—	—	—	—	—	—	—
Sibling	0.0	0.0	0.1	0.1	0.1	0.2	0.0	0.7
Grandparent (GP)	0.3	0.6	0.2	0.4	0.3	0.4	**10.2**	0.3
Other relative (OR)	0.0	0.1	0.1	0.1	0.1	0.1	0.0	1.1
Friend/neighbor (F/N)	0.0	0.0	0.1	0.0	0.2	0.1	0.1	0.7
Other adult (OA)	0.1	0.1	0.0	0.0	0.0	0.0	0.0	0.1
Teacher/caregiver (T/C)	**7.1**	**8.9**	0.1	0.1	0.1	0.2	0.2	0.2
Nobody	0.7	1.4	0.5	**10.1**	1.5	**9.8**	0.8	0.9
Location								
Home	**7.4**	5.2	**14.8**	6.7	8.2	**13.1**	**9.3**	**7.0**
Relative's home	0.1	0.3	0.1	0.4	0.4	0.2	1.0	0.8
F/N home	0.2	0.1	0.4	1.5	1.2	0.7	0.7	1.4
Child care home (CCH)	0.0	0.2	0.0	0.3	0.1	0.0	2.8	0.4
School/center (S/C)	**7.3**	**9.1**	0.1	0.2	0.1	0.3	0.2	0.5
Workplace (WP)	0.1	0.0	0.1	0.4	**2.1**	0.3	0.2	0.8
Play area (PA)	0.3	0.4	0.3	**5.4**	**2.9**	0.8	1.4	1.4
Shops/stores	0.0	0.0	0.1	0.5	0.3	0.3	0.1	0.6
In transition	0.5	0.4	0.1	0.4	0.3	0.2	0.2	0.3

Note. A dash indicates no data were available. Guidelines for interpreting table: (1) The smallest cluster contains at least 4.5% (= 5%) of the sample children. (2) Entries are in hours and total to 16.0. (3) All times greater than 1.0 hour are listed in left column under cluster. (4) All times less than 1.0 hour are listed in right column under cluster. (5) The numbers critical to understanding the uniqueness of the cluster are boldfaced.

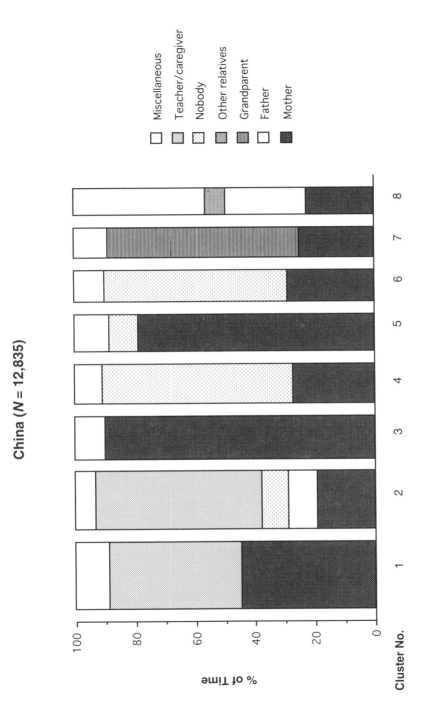

Figure 7.14 Patterns of time spent with different caregivers between 6:00 a.m. and 10:00 p.m.

Table 7.6 Hours of caregivers and locations for 4-year-old children in Finland (N = 576)

	Pattern (Cluster)						
	1	2	3	4	5	6	7
Category	Mother in Home; n = 134; 23% of N	T/C in S/C; Mother in Home; n = 123; 21% of N	OA in CCH; Mother in Home; n = 118; 20% of N	Mother or 2 Parents in Home; n = 76; 13% of N	OA in CCH; 2 Parents in Home; n = 54; 10% of N	Mother in Home; T/C in S/C; GP in GP Home; n = 46; 8% of N	2 Parents in Home; GP in GP Home; n = 25; 5% of N
Caregiver							
Mother	**15.0**	4.2	6.9	7.9		9.5	1.0
Father	0.4	0.7	0.5	1.5	0.8	1.0	1.4
2 parents	0.2	2.4	0.1	**4.3**	**5.4**		**9.4**
Sibling	0.0	0.0	0.1	0.5	0.0	0.3	
Grandparent (GP)	0.1	0.0	0.0	0.6	0.0	**1.5**	**2.2**
Other relative (OR)	0.0	0.0	0.0	0.0	0.0	0.8	0.2
Friend/neighbor (F/N)	0.1	0.1	0.0	0.0	0.0	0.2	0.1
Other adult (OA)	0.0	0.1	**8.2**	0.8	**8.6**	0.5	1.0
Teacher/caregiver (T/C)	0.2	**8.4**	0.1	0.3	0.0	**1.8**	0.3
Nobody	0.0	0.1	0.0	0.1	0.0	0.2	0.0
Location							
Home	**14.1**	7.0	7.2	**14.2**	7.2	**9.2**	**13.0**
Relative's home	0.1	0.0	0.0	0.0	0.0	**2.6**	**1.1**
F/N home	0.3	0.0	0.1	0.1	0.0		
Child care home (CCH)	0.0	0.0	**7.7**	0.1		0.5	0.1
School/center (S/C)	0.2	**8.4**	0.1	0.4	**8.2**	0.2	0.2
Workplace (WP)	0.0	0.0	0.0	0.1	0.0	0.0	0.2
Play area (PA)	0.9	0.3	0.6	0.8	0.2	0.9	0.8
Shops/stores	0.3	0.1	0.2	0.3	0.1	0.3	0.2
In transition	0.0	0.0	0.1	0.0	0.0	0.1	0.0

Note. Guidelines for interpreting table: (1) The smallest cluster contains at least 4.5% (= 5%) of the sample children. (2) Entries are in hours and total to 16.0. (3) All times greater than 1.0 hour are listed in left column under cluster. (4) All times less than 1.0 hour are listed in right column under cluster. (5) The numbers critical to understanding the uniqueness of the cluster are boldfaced.

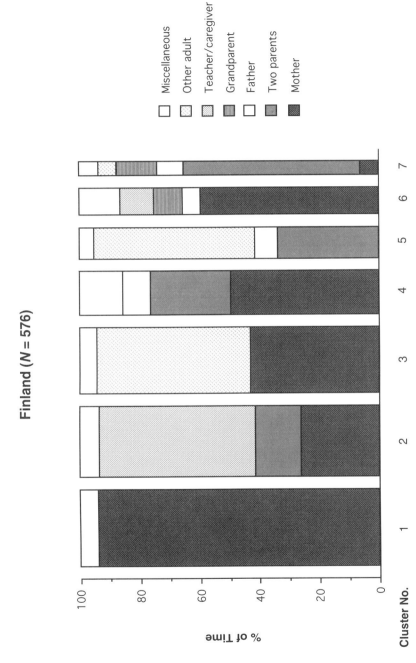

Figure 7.15 Patterns of time spent with different caregivers between 6:00 a.m. and 10:00 p.m.

Table 7.7 Hours of caregivers and locations for 4-year-old children in Germany (N = 509)

| | Pattern (Cluster) | | | | | | | |
| | 1 Mother in Home; n = 255; 50% of N | | 2 Mother in Home; T/C in S/C; n = 167; 33% of N | | 3 2 Parents in Home; T/C in S/C; n = 45; 9% of N | | 4 GP in GP Home; Mother in Home; n = 42; 8% of N | |
Category								
Caregiver								
Mother	**13.5**		8.1		1.8		4.5	
Father		0.3		0.7	1.6			0.6
2 parents		0.9	1.5		**8.9**		1.6	
Sibling		0.1		0.1		0.2		0.0
Grandparent (GP)		0.5		0.3		0.5	**6.2**	
Other relative (OR)		0.1		0.1		0.2		0.3
Friend/neighbor (F/N)		0.1		0.4		0.4		0.0
Other adult (OA)		0.1		0.2		0.6		0.0
Teacher/caregiver (T/C)		0.4	**4.4**		**1.7**			0.5
Nobody		0.0		0.2		0.1		0.0
Location								
Home	**13.0**		9.3		**11.0**		5.5	
Relative's home		0.4		0.4		0.6	**6.6**	
F/N home		0.2		0.4		0.3		0.0
Child care home (CCH)		0.0		0.1		0.2		0.0
School/center (S/C)		0.6	**4.4**		**1.8**			0.6
Workplace (WP)		0.0		0.0		0.0		0.0
Play area (PA)		0.8		0.6		0.8		0.4
Shops/stores		0.5		0.2		0.3		0.4
In transition		0.5		0.5		0.9		0.2

Note. Guidelines for interpreting table: (1) The smallest cluster contains at least 4.5% (≈ 5%) of the sample children. (2) Entries are in hours and total to 16.0. (3) All times greater than 1.0 hour are listed in left column under cluster. (4) All times less than 1.0 hour are listed in right column under cluster. (5) The numbers critical to understanding the uniqueness of the cluster are boldfaced.

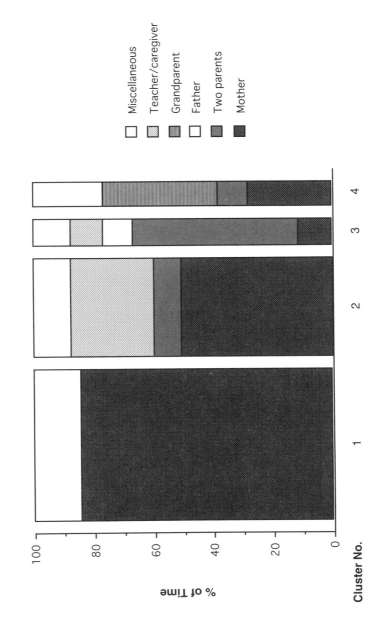

Figure 7.16 Patterns of time spent with different caregivers between 6:00 a.m. and 10:00 p.m.

Table 7.8 Hours of caregivers and locations for 4-year-old children in Hong Kong (N = 947)

| | Pattern (Cluster) | | | | | | | | | |
| | 1 | | 2 | | 3 | | 4[a] | | 5 | |
Category	Mother in Home; T/C in S/C; n = 511 54% of N		T/C in S/C; 2 Parents in Home; n = 180 19% of N		GP in Multiple Home Settings; T/C in S/C; n = 133 14% of N		OR, F/N, OA in Multiple Home Settings; T/C in S/C; n = 66 7% of N		OA in Home; T/C in S/C; n = 57 6% of N	
Caregiver										
Mother	**12.2**		2.9	0.3	1.3	0.1	1.2	0.1	1.5	0.0
Father		0.0				0.7		0.5		0.6
2 parents		0.4	2.5			0.0		0.0		0.0
Sibling		0.0		0.1		0.0		0.2		0.0
Grandparent (GP)		0.0		0.1	**9.8**					0.0
Other relative (OR)		0.0		0.4		0.0	3.2			0.0
Friend/neighbor (F/N)		0.0		0.0		0.0	1.7			0.0
Other adult (OA)		0.0		0.1		0.0	1.5		**8.1**	
Teacher/caregiver (T/C)	3.1		4.9		3.0		2.2		3.1	
Nobody		0.0		0.0		0.0		0.0		0.0
Location										
Home	**12.7**		**10.6**		**10.9**		1.8		**12.7**	
Relative's home		0.0		0.0	**2.0**		3.2			0.0
F/N home		0.0		0.0		0.0	1.5			0.0
Child care home (CCH)		0.0		0.0		0.0		0.6		0.2
School/center (S/C)	3.1		4.9		3.0		2.2		3.1	
Workplace (WP)		0.1		0.3		0.0		0.0		0.0
Play area (PA)		0.1		0.1		0.1		0.0		0.0
Shops/stores		0.0		0.1		0.0		0.0		0.0
In transition		0.0		0.0		0.0		0.0		0.0

Note. Guidelines for interpreting table: (1) The smallest cluster contains at least 4.5% (= 5%) of the sample children. (2) Entries are in hours and total to 16.0. (3) All times greater than 1.0 hour are listed in left column under cluster. (4) All times less than 1.0 hour are listed in right column under cluster. (5) The numbers critical to understanding of the uniqueness of the cluster are boldfaced.

[a]Because of the large amount of missing data, no entries are highlighted.

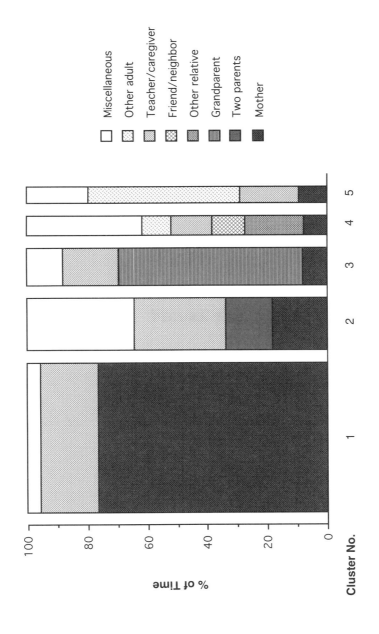

Figure 7.17 Patterns of time spent with different caregivers between 6:00 a.m. and 10:00 p.m.

Table 7.9 Hours of caregivers and locations for 4-year-old children in Nigeria (N = 1,251)

	Pattern (Cluster)			
	1	2	3	4
Category	Mother in Home $n = 587$; 47% of N	Mother, 2 Parents, or Sibling in Home; T/C in S/C $n = 356$; 28% of N	Mother or OA in Home $n = 249$; 20% of N	Mother in Home or WP $n = 59$; 5% of N
Caregiver				
Mother	**14.2**	**5.5**	**5.9**	**13.7**
Father	0.5	0.8	0.7	0.4
2 parents	0.3	**2.7**	0.4	0.5
Sibling	0.2	**1.6**	0.6	0.5
Grandparent (GP)	0.0	0.8	0.0	0.0
Other relative (OR)	0.1	0.9	0.1	0.0
Friend/neighbor (F/N)	0.0	0.5	0.0	0.2
Other adult (OA)	0.2	0.3	**8.2**	0.0
Teacher/caregiver (T/C)	0.1	1.6	0.0	0.2
Nobody	0.1	0.4	0.0	0.5
Location				
Home	**14.8**	**10.4**	**13.9**	**6.6**
Relative's home	0.3	0.7	0.7	0.0
F/N home	0.4	1.2	0.9	0.7
Child care home (CCH)	0.0	0.4	0.1	0.1
School/center (S/C)	0.2	**1.8**	0.1	0.1
Workplace (WP)	0.0	0.2	0.0	**6.0**
Play area (PA)	0.1	0.4	0.2	0.9
Shops/stores	0.0	0.0	0.1	0.0
In transition	0.0	0.0	0.0	0.0

Note. Guidelines for interpreting table: (1) The smallest cluster contains at least 4.5% ($\approx$ 5%) of the sample children. (2) Entries are in hours and total to 16.0. (3) All times greater than 1.0 hour are listed in left column under cluster. (4) All times less than 1.0 hour are listed in right column under cluster. (5) The numbers critical to understanding the uniqueness of the cluster are boldfaced.

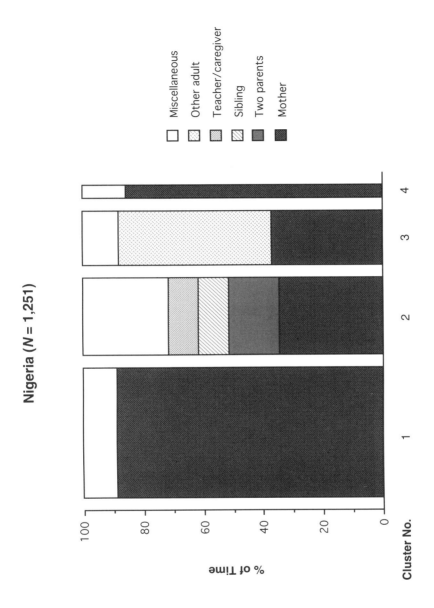

Figure 7.18 Patterns of time spent with different caregivers
between 6:00 a.m. and 10:00 p.m.

Table 7.10 Hours of caregivers and locations for 4-year-old children in Portugal (N = 581)

Category	Pattern (Cluster)											
	1		2		3		4		5		6	
	Mother in Home n = 174; 30% of N		T/C in S/C; Mother in Home n = 160; 28% of N		GP in Multiple Home Settings n = 87; 15% of N		2 Parents, Mother, OR, Sibling in Multiple Home Settings n = 70; 12% of N		Mother in Home, WP, PA n = 58; 10% of N		OA in CCH n = 32; 5% of N	
Caregiver												
Mother	**14.0**		4.5		3.7		4.0		**15.2**		3.4	
Father		0.2		0.3		0.5	1.2			0.0		0.5
2 parents		0.7	1.8		1.5		**4.4**			0.2	1.9	
Sibling		0.2		0.1		0.1	1.1			0.0		0.1
Grandparent (GP)		0.5		0.6	**9.9**			0.7		0.1		0.1
Other relative (OR)		0.1		0.1		0.1	**3.0**			0.1		0.0
Friend/neighbor (F/N)		0.1		0.0		0.0		0.1		0.0		0.0
Other adult (OA)		0.1		0.5		0.0		0.3		0.3	**9.7**	
Teacher/caregiver (T/C)		0.1	**8.1**			0.2		0.2		0.0		0.2
Nobody		0.0		0.0		0.0		0.3		0.1		0.1
Location												
Home	**14.9**		6.6		9.0		**10.3**		9.2		6.3	
Relative's home		0.3		0.4	**6.0**		**2.9**			0.8		0.0
F/N home		0.0		0.0		0.2		0.1		0.1		0.0
Child care home (CCH)		0.0		0.0		0.0		0.1		0.1	**9.3**	
School/center (S/C)		0.1	**8.4**			0.2		0.2		0.2		0.2
Workplace (WP)		0.1		0.2		0.1		0.5	**2.9**			0.0
Play area (PA)		0.3		0.1		0.2	1.1		**2.2**			0.2
Shops/stores		0.2		0.0		0.1		0.1		0.3		0.0
In transition		0.1		0.2		0.0			0.1		0.1	

Note. Guidelines for interpreting table: (1) The smallest cluster contains at least 4.5% (= 5%) of the sample children. (2) Entries are in hours and total to 16.0. (3) All times greater than 1.0 hour are listed in left column under cluster. (4) All times less than 1.0 hour are listed in right column under cluster. (5) The numbers critical to understanding the uniqueness of the cluster are boldfaced.

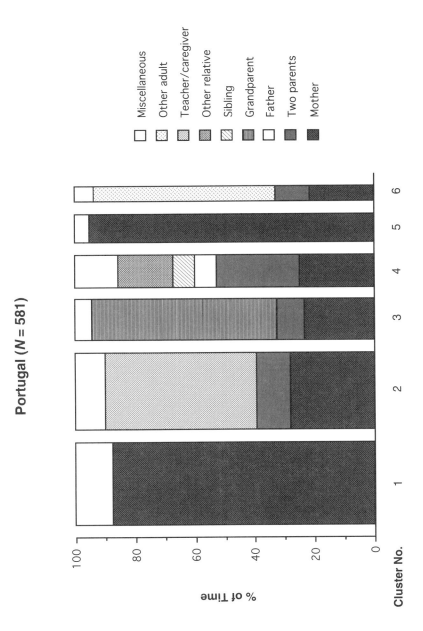

Figure 7.19 Patterns of time spent with different caregivers between 8:00 a.m. and 12:00 midnight

Table 7.11 Hours of caregivers and locations for 4-year-old children in Spain ($N = 480$)

	Pattern (Cluster)				
Category	1 Mother in Home; T/C in S/C $n = 129$; 27% of N	2 T/C in S/C; 2 Parents in Home $n = 123$; 26% of N	3 Mother in Home or PA $n = 97$; 20% of N	4 T/C in S/C; Mother or GP in Home $n = 77$; 16% of N	5 Mother in Home or PA; 2 Parents in Home; GP in Multiple Home Settings $n = 54$; 11% of N
Caregiver					
Mother	**9.5**	2.5	**14.7**	5.2	5.8
Father	0.1	0.4	0.0	0.1	1.1
2 parents	0.4	**5.9**	0.2	0.5	**5.0**
Sibling	0.1	0.2	0.3	0.3	0.0
Grandparent (GP)	0.3	0.2	0.2	1.7	**2.3**
Other relative (OR)	0.1	0.0	0.1	0.1	0.5
Friend/neighbor (F/N)	0.1	0.0	0.2	0.1	0.2
Other adult (OA)	0.1	0.5	0.1	0.1	0.8
Teacher/caregiver (T/C)	**5.3**	**6.3**	0.1	**7.8**	0.2
Nobody	0.0	0.0	0.1	0.1	0.1
Location					
Home	8.8	7.3	**12.3**	6.0	**11.0**
Relative's home	0.3	0.2	0.5	0.9	**1.0**
F/N home	0.0	0.0	0.1	0.0	0.3
Child care home (CCH)	0.0	0.0	0.0	0.0	0.1
School/center (S/C)	**5.3**	**6.3**	0.1	**7.7**	0.2
Workplace (WP)	0.1	0.0	0.3	0.1	0.3
Play area (PA)	1.4	1.9	**2.1**	1.1	**2.4**
Shops/stores	0.1	0.1	0.6	0.1	0.7
In transition	0.0	0.2	0.0	0.1	0.0

Note. Guidelines for interpreting table: (1) The smallest cluster contains at least 4.5% (= 5%) of the sample children. (2) Entries are in hours and total to 16.0. (3) All times greater than 1.0 hour are listed in left column under cluster. (4) All times less than 1.0 hour are listed in right column under cluster. (5) The numbers critical to understanding the uniqueness of the cluster are boldfaced.

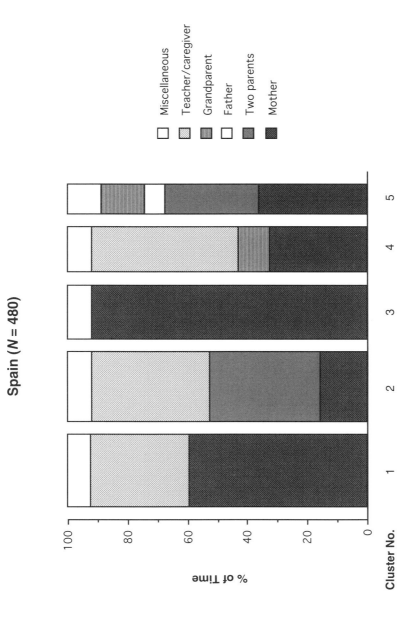

Figure 7.20 Patterns of time spent with different caregivers between 8:00 a.m. and 12:00 midnight

Table 7.12 Hours of caregivers and locations for 4-year-old children in Thailand (N = 2,466)

| | Pattern (Cluster) | | | | | | | | | | | | | | | |
| | 1 | | 2 | | 3 | | 4 | | 5 | | 6 | | 7 | | 8 | |
Category	Mother in Home n = 593; 24% of N		Mother or 2 Parents in Home n = 481; 20% of N		T/C or OA in S/C; Mother or 2 Parents in Home n = 317; 13% of N		GP in Home n = 251; 10% of N		Mother in Multiple Home Settings or WP n = 250; 10% of N		Nobody, Mother, 2 Parents, OR in Multiple Home Settings or PA n = 225; 9% of N		2 Parents in Home or WP n = 196; 8% of N		GP or 2 Parents in Multiple Home Settings n = 153; 6% of N	
Caregiver																
Mother	**15.2**		8.5		4.2		1.8		**13.1**		4.4			0.8	2.2	
Father		0.0		0.4		0.2		0.0		0.1		0.7		0.3		0.1
2 parents		0.3	**5.5**		2.5		1.5		1.3		2.0		13.7		3.4	
Sibling		0.0		0.4		0.1		0.0		0.1		0.4		0.6		0.3
Grandparent (GP)		0.2		0.3		0.8	**12.2**			0.5		0.7		0.3	**8.5**	
Other relative (OR)		0.0		0.5		0.3		0.2		0.1	**1.6**			0.2		0.9
Friend/neighbor (F/N)		0.0		0.0		0.1		0.0		0.0		0.1		0.0		0.0
Other adult (OA)		0.0		0.1	**3.1**			0.0		0.0		0.1		0.0		0.1
Teacher/caregiver (T/C)		0.0		0.0	**4.4**			0.0		0.0		0.0		0.0		0.1
Nobody		0.1		0.3		0.2		0.2		0.8	**5.8**			0.1		0.3
Location																
Home	**15.7**		**15.4**		7.5		14.7		9.3		9.9		14.3		5.5	
Relative's home		0.1		0.2		0.2		0.2	**1.0**			0.7		0.2	**9.5**	
F/N home		0.1		0.3		0.1		0.9	**3.4**		2.7			0.1		0.4
Child care home (CCH)		0.0		0.0		0.3		0.0		0.1		0.1		0.0		0.2
School/center (S/C)		0.0		0.0	**7.0**			0.0		0.0		0.0		0.0		0.2
Workplace (WP)		0.0		0.0		0.1		0.0	**1.0**		**2.0**		**1.2**			0.0
Play area (PA)		0.0		0.1		0.1		0.1		0.9		0.2		0.1		0.0
Shops/stores		0.0		0.0		0.0		0.0		0.0		0.2		0.0		0.0
In transition		0.0		0.0		0.7		0.0		0.1		0.0		0.1		0.2

Note. Guidelines for interpreting table: (1) The smallest cluster contains at least 4.5% (= 5%) of the sample children. (2) Entries are in hours and total to 16.0. (3) All times greater than 1.0 hour are listed in left column under cluster. (4) All times less than 1.0 hour are listed in right column under cluster. (5) The numbers critical to understanding the uniqueness of the cluster are boldfaced.

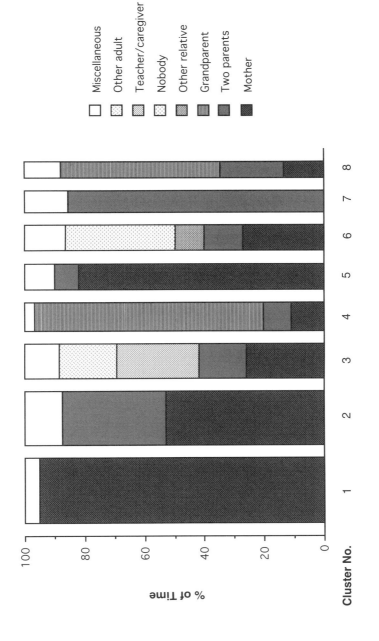

Figure 7.21 Patterns of time spent with different caregivers between 5:00 a.m. and 9:00 p.m.

Table 7.13 Hours of caregivers and locations for 4-year-old children in the United States (N = 428)

	Pattern (Cluster)					
	1		2		3	
Category	Mother in Home $n = 252$; 59% of N		Parents or GP in Home; OA in CCH $n = 95$; 22% of N		T/C in S/C; Mother in Home $n = 81$; 19% of N	
Caregiver						
Mother	**14.1**		5.3		6.2	
Father		0.5	**1.3**			0.7
2 parents		0.6	**1.7**		1.0	
Sibling		0.0		0.1		0.1
Grandparent (GP)		0.1	**1.9**			0.1
Other relative (OR)		0.0		0.8		0.0
Friend/neighbor (F/N)		0.1		0.2		0.0
Other adult (OA)		0.1	**4.1**			0.2
Teacher/caregiver (T/C)		0.5		0.6	**7.7**	
Nobody		0.0		0.0		0.0
Location						
Home	14.4		9.7		7.7	
Relative's home		0.2		0.5		0.1
F/N home		0.1		0.2		0.0
Child care home (CCH)		0.0	**4.2**			0.1
School/center (S/C)		0.5		0.7	**7.7**	
Workplace (WP)		0.0		0.0		0.0
Play area (PA)		0.3		0.2		0.1
Shops/stores		0.4		0.3		0.1
In transition		0.1		0.1		0.2

Note. Guidelines for interpreting table: (1) The smallest cluster contains at least 4.5% (≈ 5%) of the sample children. (2) Entries are in hours and total to 16.0. (3) All times greater than 1.0 hour are listed in left column under cluster. (4) All times less than 1.0 hour are listed in right column under cluster. (5) The numbers critical to understanding the uniqueness of the cluster are boldfaced.

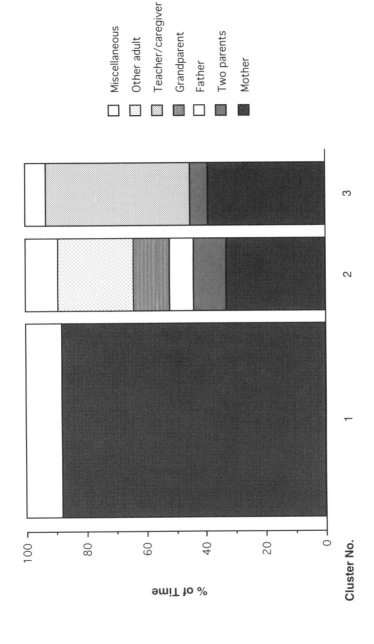

Figure 7.22 Patterns of time spent with different caregivers between 6:00 a.m. and 10:00 p.m.

A *mother/other adult* cluster is found in 3 countries. In 2 of these countries (Finland and the United States) many families use *child care homes* for their 4-year-old children, whereas in Nigeria many families have a maid or childminder come into their *homes* to supervise the preschool-aged children during the day.

Although there are similarities among countries in the types of clusters found, each country presents a distinct pattern of clusters with regard to the percentage of children represented by each cluster, the combinations of caregivers and locations included in each cluster, and the presence of unique clusters. For example, even among the countries that have a *mother* cluster, the percentages of children represented by this cluster range from 13 percent (in China) to 59 percent (in the United States). Also, Germany and Portugal each have a *grandparent* cluster, but this cluster in Portugal includes 15 percent of the children, while the same cluster in Germany includes 8 percent of the children.

In some countries (e.g., Belgium, Hong Kong) nearly all clusters include a *teacher/caregiver* category, whereas in other countries (e.g., Nigeria, Portugal) only a single cluster includes the *teacher/caregiver* category. Also, in some nations (e.g., Belgium, Thailand) the category *two parents* appears in nearly all clusters, while in others (e.g., Hong Kong, Nigeria) it appears in only a single cluster.

Perhaps the most unique clusters among the 10 countries are those that include *nobody* as a caregiver. When the NRCs were developing the categories of caregivers, some of the directors from industrialized nations questioned the usefulness of including this category, noting that parents might be reluctant to report that nobody was supervising their child, even when this was the case. However, NRCs from other nations considered this to be a realistic category and thought that parents in their countries would report it accurately. The category of *nobody* as a caregiver (for at least 1 hour) does indeed appear in Thailand's sixth cluster and in China's second, fourth, fifth, and sixth clusters. Another unique type of cluster includes the *sibling* as caregiver — Nigeria's second cluster and Portugal's fourth cluster are examples of this type.

The Daily Routine Data in a Weekly Context

Are the daily routine findings congruent with the findings reported in previous chapters? To answer this question, this section will briefly examine each country's daily routine clusters in relationship to findings presented earlier about that country's sample characteristics (e.g., the percentage of mothers active in the labor force) and families' weekly use of various types of early childhood services.

BELGIUM (FR.)

As the findings in Chapter 5 indicated, 98 percent of Belgium's sample children attended an extraparental care or education setting, with 93 percent attending an organized facility and the remaining children participating in home settings. Forty-one percent of sample children attended at least a second setting, with 70 percent of second settings being organized facilities (schools/centers) and 30 percent being home settings.

Belgium's cluster findings indicate that as expected, school/center as a location (for at least 1 hour a day) occurs in all five clusters. In the two largest (first and second) clusters, children remain in an organized facility for additional hours in the care of some other adult. Belgium's fourth cluster includes grandparent care in the grandparent's home, indicating that the second setting referred to in the previous paragraph is a home setting. As noted in Table 7.4, care in the child's own home is provided mainly by the mother or the two parents.

CHINA (PRC)

According to earlier chapters, in China, almost half (43 percent) of 4-year-old children attend an extraparental setting, with most of those (33 percent) enrolled in an organized facility; the remaining 10 percent are divided nearly equally between own-home settings and other-home settings, where the care is provided almost entirely by relatives. While 98 percent of mothers of 4-year-olds are active in the labor force, over half work in agriculture and consequently may be able to care for their own children during at least part of their working day.

Table 7.5 and Figure 7.14 show that children attending schools/centers are included in the first and second clusters, and that these children are in schools/centers 7 to 9 hours a day; their remaining waking hours are spent in the care of one or both parents at home. Five clusters (the third through sixth and the eighth) contain children in a parental-care-only category; these clusters include two that are primarily mother care and that are differentiated by the location in which the mother care occurs (home in the third cluster and home, workplace, and play area in the fifth cluster). The eighth cluster includes care mainly by mother or father in several locations. The two remaining clusters (the fourth and sixth) are the "nobody" clusters, and each includes approximately 10 hours when "nobody" cares for the child, with supervision provided by the mother for the remaining waking hours. These clusters would seem to indicate that as noted elsewhere, parents in rural areas leave their young children playing near the family home without direct adult supervision while they are working in the fields during the day. China's final, seventh, cluster represents extraparental care in a home setting, with grandparents providing supervision.

FINLAND

The findings reported in previous chapters were that approximately 25 percent of 4-year-old Finnish children are cared for exclusively by their parents, while the other 75 percent participate in extraparental settings (own-home settings, 5 percent; other-home settings, 35 percent; organized facilities, 35 percent). In Finland, when an other-home setting is selected by parents, the care is nearly always provided by a nonrelative (e.g., by some other adult).

In view of the information just summarized from earlier chapters, it is not surprising that of Finland's seven clusters, two are organized facility clusters, two are other-home clusters, two are parental-care-only clusters, and the smallest cluster includes relative care in a home setting. The first and fourth clusters contain children in parental care and are differentiated by which parent is the caregiver (the mother in the first cluster, and the mother, father, or both parents in the fourth cluster). The second and sixth clusters include children attending a school/center as well as being cared for in-home by different combinations of parents and relatives. The third and fifth clusters are characterized by other-home care, with children spending approximately 8 hours a day in home-based settings.

GERMANY (FRG)

An earlier chapter related that only 18 percent of Germany's total sample of 4-year-olds were cared for exclusively by parents, while 82 percent attended at least one extraparental setting (own-home settings, 15 percent; other-home settings, 18 percent; organized facilities, 49 percent). Slightly over half of the sample children attended more than one setting, and their second setting was usually the family home or some other home.

As Table A.1 (Appendix A, p. 301) indicates, when a child's first setting was either an own-home or other-home setting, the caregiver was usually a relative. This was also likely to be the case when a home setting was the child's second, third, or fourth setting.

Of Germany's four daily routine clusters in Table 7.7 and Figure 7.16, two (the first and third) are characterized by either mother or two-parent care in the child's home. Two other clusters (the second and third) include care by teachers/caregivers in schools/centers, and a very small amount of time in school/centers is noted in the remaining two clusters (0.4 and 0.5 hour). Grandparent care predominates in the fourth cluster, supporting the information provided by parents about relative care in either own-home or other-home settings.

HONG KONG

As noted in Chapter 3, since nearly all 4-year-olds in Hong Kong attend organized facilities, the sample children were selected from these settings. One would therefore expect each of Hong Kong's clusters to include at least a few hours in schools or centers. In fact, all five clusters do indicate that children spend time in such settings, with the minimum time being 2.2 hours daily (in the fourth cluster). When children are not in schools or centers, in all but one cluster (the fifth), they are generally in home settings being cared for mainly by one or more of the following: mother, two parents, a grandparent. In the fifth cluster, some other adult (e.g., a maid) provides supervision in the child's home.

NIGERIA

Nigeria reported the lowest percentages of children cared for in extra-parental settings (33 percent); this included 22 percent cared for at home by someone other than a parent (see Table A.1 in Appendix A, p. 301), 3 percent cared for in other homes, and 8 percent cared for in organized facilities. Also in Nigeria, although 67 percent of mothers of the sample children were active in the labor force, one third worked in agriculture and consequently might have been able to have their children with them during working hours.

Nigeria's daily routine clusters are in close agreement with the findings just reviewed. As Table 7.9 and Figure 7.18 indicate, there are two mother-care clusters in Nigeria (the first and fourth), one characterized by home as the location and one characterized by two locations — home and the parent's workplace. Another cluster (Nigeria's third) includes a large amount of time (8.2 hours) during which some other adult cares for the preschool-aged child in the child's own home. Still another cluster (Nigeria's second) includes care by mother, two parents, and sibling in various home settings, as well as a small amount of time spent in schools/centers.

PORTUGAL

Earlier chapters related that 29 percent of Portugal's 4-year-olds are cared for exclusively by their parents, while the remaining 71 percent attend extraparental settings (own-home settings, 16 percent; other-home settings, 25 percent; organized facilities, 29 percent; other, 1 percent). As noted in Table A.1 (Appendix A, p. 301) the care in own-home extraparental settings is provided primarily by relatives, while the care in other-home settings is sometimes provided by nonrelatives.

Portugal's daily routine clusters include two parental care clusters (the first and fifth); the home is the primary location in the first cluster, whereas the home, parental workplace, and play areas are the locations in the fifth cluster. Children attending school/centers are represented in Portugal's second cluster, with children in mother care or two-parent care at home making up the remainder of the child's time. Relative care is included in the third and fourth of Portugal's clusters; grandparents provide the majority of this care, either in the child's home or in their home. The final, sixth, cluster includes the small percentage of children cared for in other-home settings by nonrelatives.

SPAIN

There is almost perfect agreement between Spain's daily routine clusters and the findings reported earlier for the weekly use of early childhood services in Spain. For example, Chapter 5 indicated that approximately 20 percent of Spain's sample children were cared for exclusively by their parents, and these children are represented in Spain's third cluster. Also, about 69 percent of the total sample of families reported that their children attended organized facilities, and these children are represented in Spain's first, second, and fourth clusters. Finally, as noted in Chapter 5, about 10 percent of Spain's 4-year-olds are served by extraparental home-based caregivers, either in own-home settings or in other-home settings. The country's fifth cluster includes these children, with grandparents providing the extraparental supervision in either the child's home or their own home.

THAILAND

In Thailand, 36 percent of sample families reported that their 4-year-old children attended extraparental care or education settings (own-home, 15 percent; other-home, 9 percent; organized facilities, 12 percent). For children participating in home-based settings, Table A.1 (Appendix A, p. 301) indicates that the supervision was nearly always provided by relatives. Slightly over half (57 percent) of the mothers in the sample were active in the labor force, but 60 percent of those mothers worked in agriculture and may have been able to supervise their young children during at least some of their working hours. This would suggest that Thailand's daily routine clusters might include large amounts of supervision by parents and relatives.

Of Thailand's eight national clusters, four are predominantly parental clusters (the first, second, fifth, and seventh). The first two clusters include parental supervision primarily in the child's home, with the mother serving as care provider in the first cluster and the mother and both parents sharing these responsibilities in the second cluster. The fifth and seventh clusters are characterized by parental supervision in the home, the workplace, and other-home settings; the mother is supervisor in the fifth cluster, and both parents provide care in the seventh cluster.

The fourth and eighth clusters contain children in relative care; grandparents provide nearly all of this care in either the child's home or their own home. The third cluster includes the small percentage of 4-year-olds in Thailand who attend a school/center. Finally, the sixth cluster is characterized by children who have nobody supervising them for approximately 6 hours a day.

THE UNITED STATES

Chapter 5 reported that 39 percent of the U.S. sample children were cared for exclusively by parents, 35 percent attended schools/centers, 17 percent were cared for in other homes, and 9 percent were cared for by others in the child's own home. Twenty-nine percent of the sample attended two or more settings, and these additional settings were either own-home, other-home, or organized facility settings.

As Table 7.13 and Figure 7.22 show, U.S. daily routine data yielded three national clusters. Not surprisingly, the first, or largest, cluster is predominantly mother care in the child's home. The number of children included in this first cluster is larger than expected (252 children, or 59 percent of the total). However, considering that the cluster includes 0.5 hour of school/center time, it is possible to conclude that it may contain some children who attend organized facilities for a short time each week (e.g., a 2-hour preschool program, 2 to 3 days a week). The second U.S. cluster contains the children who attend child care homes for approximately one-half day as well as those children cared for by grandparents in their own homes for a few hours a day. The final, third, cluster consists of children who attend schools or centers, usually for the entire day.

* * *

In nearly every country researchers discovered a good correspondence between the information reported by parents/guardians about their weekly use of early childhood services and the information reported in the daily routine section of the household survey. Each set of information provides a different perspective from which to look at the lives of young children in various nations around the world.

ENDNOTES

1. This chapter presents findings for only 10 countries because Italy chose not to have its daily routine data included in the cross-national analysis.

2. The column headings in Tables 7.4 to 7.13 describe the various clusters by listing the major caregivers and major locations of children in each cluster. The boldfacing of data within each column of the table highlights what is *unique* to a given cluster — what sets it apart from the other clusters of that country. In general, each column heading comprehensively includes (1) any caregivers and locations utilized for several hours a day and (2) any unique elements of the cluster.

    Examples of how the above guidelines were followed can be seen in Table 7.4 (Belgium). The *teacher/caregiver*, who supervises the child for at least 1 hour in every cluster, is only included in the headings of the first four clusters (i.e., the clusters with longer periods of *teacher/caregiver* time). Even though *teacher/caregiver* is in the heading of the third cluster, it does not have highlighted data in that cluster, since the *teacher/caregiver* category appears in all clusters and thus is not unique to the third cluster. In the fifth cluster, the *teacher/caregiver* supervises for only a short period of time, so *teacher/caregiver* does not appear in the heading nor does it have highlighted data.

By scanning Belgium's clusters and looking at the highlighted data, it is possible to see how the five Belgian clusters differ from one another. For example, in two clusters, the category *mother* is highlighted, while in two others, the category *two parents* is highlighted. In the fourth cluster, only *grandparent* and *teacher/caregiver* data are highlighted, even though there are short periods during which the *mother* and *two parents* supervise the child. The combination of *grandparent* and *teacher/caregiver* is what makes this cluster unique among Belgium's clusters.

VIII
A Nation-by-Nation Look at the Findings

Patricia P. Olmsted, *Senior Research Associate*
High/Scope Educational Research Foundation
Ypsilanti, Michigan

Previous chapters — on families' use of services, on use of organized facilities, and on children's daily routines — have looked at data cross-nationally. This chapter considers the findings in another way, summarizing each nation's findings individually and comparing those national findings to the information that the National Research Coordinators (NRCs) provided at the outset of the study, in *How Nations Serve Young Children: Profiles of Child Care and Education in 14 Countries* (Olmsted & Weikart, 1989; Chapter 2 summarized the profiles.) Much of what is presented here corroborates and clarifies the initial profile that each nation provided in 1989, based on statistics available at that time. In some cases, the IEA data for a particular country enable us to update or supplement the earlier profile, or even to refute some part of it. This chapter also provides an opportunity to describe findings for subregions or subpopulations within an individual country, whenever such findings are of interest.

Belgium(Fr.) — Part-day Services and Full-day Needs

Belgium, like some other Western developed countries, entered the IEA Preprimary Project with fairly extensive, government-sponsored early childhood services already in place. These excerpts from Arlette Delhaxhe's

1989 profile of those services indicate how, at the outset of the IEA study, she described the situation in French-speaking Belgium:

> ... 98 percent of the children aged 2½ to 6 years are in nursery school (p. 27).

> There is no charge for a child to attend nursery school in Belgium. Private schools with a charge for admission are rare; there are perhaps, at most, only five in Belgium (p. 26).

> [Nursery school] activities usually take place from 8:30 to 12:00 in the morning and from 1:30 to 3:30 in the afternoon for 5 days a week during the school year. (Schools are closed on Wednesday afternoons) (p. 27).

> Today, ... if one considers those employed full-time, employed part-time, and actively seeking employment, 66 percent of mothers of children under age 10 are "economically active" in Belgium. Thus the nation's network of extrafamilial child care is of more importance than ever (p. 14).

Delhaxhe's initial description of early childhood services in Belgium revealed a situation in which nursery school services are available to and used by nearly all families; nevertheless, for many families — especially those in which all adults are "economically active" — there would appear to be a mismatch between when services are available and when they are needed. For this reason, many families typically seek out additional care/education services for their 4-year-olds each week. This summary of Belgium's IEA/PPP Phase 1 study methods and findings looks at the family survey results to see (1) how they compare with Delhaxhe's 1989 description and (2) how families address any disparity between services offered and services needed.

The Families Surveyed in Belgium

Belgian IEA researchers collected information from 424 families in 73 communes located throughout French-speaking Belgium. They obtained a response rate of 67 percent and a refusal rate of 18 percent. Sample parents were in their early 30s and averaged 12 to 13 years of education. Ninety-two percent of sample fathers were employed, while the corresponding figure for mothers was 57 percent. In general, fathers were away from their 4-year-olds for 49 hours per week, and mothers were away for 32 hours per week. Nearly all households (95 percent) had both parents present.

The Findings About Belgium's Preprimary Care/Education

The IEA family survey generally confirmed the information in the 1989 profile by Delhaxhe. Survey findings were these: (1) Of sample children (who were 3½ to 4½ years old), 95 percent attended organized facilities (nursery schools), (2) very few parents paid for these services, and (3) the majority of families (73 percent) typically used two or more care/education settings for their 4-year-olds each week. Of sample families, 98 percent reported using extraparental care/education services — 95 percent making use of nursery schools and 3 percent utilizing home-based settings as the *first setting* (the care/education setting attended for the longest time each week). As just noted, 73 percent of families used a *second setting* (the setting attended for the second-longest time each week). This 73 percent included 51 percent using an organized facility (usually care services provided in the nursery school building) and 22 percent using a home-based setting (generally care by a relative in the relative's home or in the child's own home).

The IEA family survey found that Belgian 4-year-olds average 34 hours per week in care/education settings, a figure that is very close to the length of time that mothers typically spend away from their children each week (32 hours) but much less than the length of time fathers spend away (49 hours). These findings support those of an earlier research study reported by Delhaxhe on page 32 of her 1989 profile: "A research study by V. Pieltain shows that the time spent outside the home by a child correlates with the time spent outside the home by the mother. The daily schedule for the father does not influence that of the child."

In the information presented in Chapter 6 about the organized facilities used by families in various countries, all organized facilities used by Belgian parents were categorized as *educational*, which would be consistent with Delhaxhe's 1989 characterization of the prevailing services. Children were reported to spend an average of 25 hours per week in these organized facilities. If we consider children's weekly total of 34 hours spent in care/education settings, this indicates approximately 9 hours per week spent in one or more additional settings.

The IEA household survey found that while all nursery schools are sponsored by the government, 50 percent of them are also sponsored by local authorities and 41 percent are additionally sponsored by the Roman Catholic church — findings very much in agreement with the 1989 profile's breakdown of 53 percent and 37 percent, respectively, which was based on national statistics.

One finding of the family survey, in particular, runs contrary to what one would anticipate from the information provided in Delhaxhe's 1989 profile. When sample parents were asked about the problems they experienced with the nursery schools, *very few identified any problem at all*. For example, 6 percent of parents cited *facility/equipment* as a problem, while smaller but equal percentages of parents (3 percent in each case) noted problems with the *personal characteristics of the teacher/caregiver* and with *other children* in the setting. Only 2 percent of parents mentioned either *hours of operation* or *staff turnover* as a problem. The low percentage of parents citing *hours of operation* is surprising, since both Delhaxhe's 1989 profile and family survey results seem to indicate a need for weekly care/education services over and above those offered by nursery schools. Possibly parents do not consider it to be the role of the nursery school to provide all the service needs they have. Rather, they may see the nursery school as focusing on one or more particular aspects of their children's development, and they may believe that other solutions need to be found to meet the need for any additional hours of supervision for their children.

If nursery schools operate for only the limited hours indicated in Delhaxhe's 1989 profile, looking at the caregivers for 4-year-olds during the nursery school lunch-break and during the late afternoon hours should provide information about the solutions parents have found to supplement nursery school services. A report of Belgian IEA Preprimary Project findings prepared by Delhaxhe and Hindryckx (1991) provided this information: Between 12:00 noon and 1:00 p.m., 49 percent of sample children were with caregivers (at school), 34 percent were with parents, and 10 percent were with grandparents. Between 4:00 and 5:00 p.m., 65 percent of children were with their parents, 13 percent were with extrafamilial caregivers (either at the school or at another location), and 13 percent were with their grandparents. Thus it would seem that for 4-year-olds from homes in which parents are not available at noon and after nursery school, there are two major groups of supervisors — grandparents and caregivers at the nursery schools. Delhaxhe and Hindryckx examined the relationship between family characteristics and the child's daily pattern of caregivers and noted the following:

> The socio-economic status of the family is related to the child's daily routine: children who are cared for by relatives [generally grandparents] belong to families with lower income, where fathers have a lower professional level. . . . children who attend care services [either at school or in another location] belong to families with higher income . . . (p. 61).

As Delhaxhe noted in her 1989 profile, a major concern in Belgium is the *quality* of the services provided for children who remain at the nursery school outside of official curriculum hours:

> There is no overall care policy for these children to date (regarding caregivers, activities, child-adult ratio, quality of care, and organization of meals). . . . Thus, at the end of the 20th century, we find in the child care services organized during the extracurricular time some characteristics reminiscent of the first preschool setting that sheltered young children in the 19th century — low wages for staff, unqualified staff, excessive noise, inadequate facilities, and grouping together of children of different ages (p. 34).

Having gotten from the IEA survey a sense of how great the need is, early childhood professionals and policymakers in Belgium eventually hope to work on improving the services outside of nursery school hours. Their goal will be to provide a high-quality environment for 4-year-olds whenever it is needed by Belgium's families. From the results of future phases of the IEA Preprimary Project, Belgium hopes to be able to assess the variability between practices adults use with children — both in and out of nursery school — and the consequences for child development.

CHINA (PRC) — STRIVING FOR MODERNIZATION

In the People's Republic of China, the IEA Preprimary Project has been the first large-scale survey study in many years involving families with preschool-aged children. These words from a 1990 speech delivered in Beijing by Professor Shi Hui Zhong, the NRC of the IEA Preprimary Project in China, convey how important the study is to China's overall progress as a nation:

> In a country with a population of 1.1 billion and a territory of 9.6 million square kilometers, one of the urgent tasks in its realization of Four Modernizations is to enhance the quality of the nation. Therefore, it is an important objective for us early childhood educators to lay a good foundation for this cause. . . . [The IEA Preprimary Project] has enabled us to get a clear understanding of the care and educational situation of young children of the country and to provide our policy makers with a scientific basis for the reform of our early childhood education (p. 1).

Chinese researchers looked at the IEA study not only as an opportunity to cooperate with other nations in a cross-national project but also as a chance to collect needed information for planning future policies and programs for China's children and families. This summary of China's Phase 1 findings presents basic data of cross-national interest and also highlights those findings that were of particular interest nationally.

The Families Surveyed in China

Project researchers developed 10 strata from the total set of provinces in China and then selected 1 province from each stratum for the present study. Within each chosen province, they then selected urban areas (cities) and rural areas (towns and townships). The final sample consisted of 12,835 families (4,000 urban and 8,835 rural) across the 10 provinces. Approximately 1,000 data collectors interviewed the families, with a 99 percent response rate and no refusals. To ensure that the household survey would include even very remote rural families, interviewers were required to collect data from any family selected that was within a 24-hour walking distance. The result of this unusual effort has been that this study may be the first in recent times to include those Chinese families living in very primitive conditions in mountainous regions. Later in this summary, detailed family and household characteristics of the sample are given, with differentiation between urban and rural families.

The Findings About China's Preprimary Care/Education

As Shi Hui Zhong (1989) noted in China's profile written at the outset of Phase 1 of the IEA study, since the founding of the People's Republic of China in 1949, early childhood institutions have experienced extensive and rapid growth. The state (national government) developed guidelines and requirements for kindergartens to serve children 3 to 6 years old and called for factories, the military, governmental and academic institutions, neighborhoods, and villages to operate kindergartens as need dictated. According to Shi, this development effort produced, by 1985, enough kindergartens to accommodate approximately 20 percent of China's preschool-aged children.

Updating this 20 percent statistic are the findings from the IEA Phase

1 survey, which indicate that 43 percent of Chinese families with 4-year-old children use extraparental care/education services each week — including 33 percent using the services provided by an organized facility (kindergarten), 5 percent having another adult come into the home, and 4 percent using an "other-home" care setting (also, 1 percent who reported using "other" types of arrangements). Since the sample families were representative of the nation's population, the findings suggest that since 1985, fairly rapid growth of kindergartens has continued, so organized settings are now available for a considerably larger percentage of China's children.

Response to the household survey indicated that most of the sample children who were service-users typically attended only one setting each week, while a small number attended two or more settings. Children's second and third settings were always home settings — with this additional care being provided either in the child's own home or in another person's home. Children attending extraparental settings did so for an average of 55 to 56 hours per week; this care time agrees with the length of time that parents were typically away from the child. Sample parents were generally satisfied with their children's care/education settings, and the problems they identified (regarding qualifications of teachers/caregivers, equipment and facilities) were the types one would expect to find in a nation that is rapidly increasing availability of services.

If we look only at those sample children in China who attended organized facilities, we find that the average weekly time children spent in such settings was 47 hours, with the maximum weekly time being 163 hours. This maximum refers to a small number of 4-year-olds, mostly in urban areas, who attended boarding, or residential, kindergartens for 24 hours a day, 5 or 6 days each week.

Because China's urban and rural areas involve considerable contrast, Table 8.1 presents the sample's family and household characteristics separately for the two kinds of areas. Whereas in urban areas both parents had completed an average of 9 to 10 years of education, in rural areas fathers had completed 7 to 8 years, and mothers, 6 years. Urban mothers typically spent an average of 57 hours away from their preschool-aged child each week, while the corresponding number for rural mothers was 50 hours. In both urban and rural areas, fathers typically spent 60 to 65 hours away from the child each week. Also, in both urban and rural areas, nearly all parents with preschool-aged children participated in the labor force.

Survey results reveal further urban-rural contrasts. As Table A.2 (in Appendix A, p. 303) indicates, a much higher proportion of rural families

Table 8.1 China's urban/rural information for selected family and household characteristics

Characteristic	Total Sample		Urban Sample		Rural Sample	
	N	Mean	N	Mean	N	Mean
Mother's yr of ed	12,363	6.9	3,884	9.4	8,483	6.0
Father's yr of ed	12,370	8.1	3,872	9.7	8,499	7.5
Mother's hr away	9,255	52.2	3,513	57.3	5,833	49.6
Father's hr away	10,428	65.1	3,636	63.0	6,848	66.0
Number of children	—	—	4,000	1.2	8,835	1.8
	N	%	N	%	N	%
Mother works for pay	12,835	98	4,000	98	8,835	97
Father works for pay	12,835	98	4,000	99	8,835	98
Indoor water	12,835	35	4,000	81	8,835	17
Television	12,835	56	4,000	88	8,835	43

Note. A dash indicates that no data were available.

(70 percent) than of urban families (22 percent) reported caring for their young children by themselves. However, a closer look at the actual care situations for rural children (Shi & Xiang, 1990) reveals that a fairly large proportion of parents in rural areas reported that their preschool-aged children spent several hours a day without direct adult supervision. This situation is considered safe in rural areas, where there are thought to be few dangers (such as traffic, or adults who abduct children). A larger percentage of urban families (67 percent) than of rural families (19 percent) reported using organized facilities for their children, but equal percentages in the two areas utilized home-based settings (10 percent).

Because Chinese IEA researchers were interested in gathering information about parents' educational perceptions and practices, they included a set of interview questions covering these topics: (1) parents' expectations concerning the child's level of education and future occupation, (2) parents' views of their children's strong points, (3) parental praise of children (frequency and reasons), and (4) educational activities that parents engage in with their children. The researchers were surprised and disquieted by the types of parental responses, especially in rural areas. As a result, the government decided to develop a widespread training program involving parent-education classes to be held in various areas of the country for parents of young children. Shi and Xiang (1990) stressed the importance China places on the cooperative effort of families, early childhood educators, and society:

> The views and practices of parents are an important factor which will exert a great influence on the development of the child. Early childhood educators should realize that parent education is an indispensable part of their work and worth their great effort on it. On the other side, the parents should be aware of their responsibility of . . . child education. Only when the family, early childhood educators, and the whole society are united, will there become a better environment for our child development (p. 1).

In the speech referred to at the beginning of this summary, Shi (1990) explained how the data from Phase 1 of the IEA Preprimary Project should expand her country's thinking about *early childhood care and education*. Rather than being merely synonymous with *kindergarten*, the phrase refers also to the many children being cared for exclusively by their parents and to those receiving extraparental care in "other-home" settings. Shi called for a broadening of the curriculum of teacher-training institutions to increase awareness of and training in several types of early childhood care and education, including parent education:

> In our point of view, although it is necessary to bring every positive factor into play so as to run organized settings of various type[s], it seems more important and feasible at present economic conditions to strengthen parent education and improve the parental practice of care and education for their young children. Early childhood educators must realize that "early childhood education" consists of both organized and unorganized care and education. Similarly, "family education" means work [with] the parents whose children are in organized settings and the parents whose children are not in organized settings. "Early childhood education" can no longer be regarded as "kinder-

garten education." It is the time for our early childhood educators to establish a correct point of view of early childhood education on the basis of our
national situation and demand. This is also an important subject to be put forward in front of our policy makers . . . (p. 10).

FINLAND — AIMING AT INTEGRATED NATIONAL POLICIES

Finland, positioned in the northernmost region of Europe, is another
country with considerable urban-rural contrast. Most of the population is
concentrated in the South, where the climate is relatively mild, while the
rest of the population is sparsely distributed throughout the North. Finland's urban/rural contrasts are reflected in its IEA Preprimary Project
data, as will be explained in this summary of Phase 1 findings. In addition
to presenting a general picture of Finland's findings from the household
survey, we describe here Finland's current efforts at integrating national
policies affecting families, employment, and education.

THE FAMILIES SURVEYED IN FINLAND

Finnish IEA researchers selected 80 geographical regions located in 68
counties throughout Finland and conducted the household survey with a
total of 576 families in these regions. The survey response rate was 85 percent, which is a higher rate than that usually attained in Finnish survey
studies. The refusal rate was only 5 percent.

Compared with sample families in other participating nations, Finland's sample families were slightly older (the average age for mothers was
32.8 years, and for fathers, 35.5 years). They had also completed slightly
more education (mothers averaged 12.4 years of education, and fathers,
12.1 years). Seventy-five percent of mothers were active in the labor force,
and mothers were away from their children for approximately 34 hours a
week; nearly all of the fathers (98 percent) were employed, and they averaged 47 hours away from their children each week. When comparisons
were made between sample families and the general population in Finland, all differences found were in anticipated directions, so the sample
was representative of families with preschool-aged children in Finland.

THE FINDINGS ABOUT FINLAND'S PREPRIMARY CARE/EDUCATION

When questioned about the weekly use of care/education services for their 4-year-olds, 75 percent of Finnish parents indicated that their children were in some kind of extraparental care. This included 5 percent who had a care provider come into the child's own home, 35 percent whose children were cared for in another person's home, and 35 percent whose children attended organized facilities. Only a small number of families reported that their children attended two or three settings, and of those using two or more settings, about half selected an organized facility for the second setting, and half selected home settings. Very little of the home-based extraparental care in Finland was provided by relatives. Reporting few problems, parents were generally satisfied with the care/education services their children received.

When Finnish parents were asked to state the major reason for their use of extraparental care/education services, 76 percent said that *parental employment* was the major reason, while 14 percent said that they considered the services to be important for *the child's social-emotional development*. A more detailed analysis of these findings by Ojala (1990) indicated that compared with families using home-based settings, a higher percentage of organized facility users gave a reason related to the child's social-emotional development.

One interesting finding about Finnish children, as compared with sample children in the other participating nations, was the high percentage receiving various types of health examinations during the year prior to the survey. In response to interviewer questions, 98 percent of families reported a medical exam, while 95 percent reported a dental exam. The percentages of children receiving vision exams and hearing exams were 93 and 91 percent, respectively. (Based on the data in Table 6.8, it would seem that these exams were not connected to early childhood services, since only 21 percent of Finnish families reported that health services were available at their children's organized facilities.)

A striking feature of organized facility care in Finland was the diversity and amount of home-setting contact. Over 50 percent of sample parents reported having four different types of home-setting contact during the past 3 months (informal meetings, group meetings, telephone/written communication, and meetings requested by the teacher/caregiver), and many families had more than one type of contact weekly or monthly.

In his 1990 report on the Finnish IEA Preprimary Project, Ojala exam-

Table 8.2 Finland's urban/rural information for selected family and household characteristics

Characteristic	Total Sample		Urban Sample		Rural Sample	
	N	Mean	N	Mean	N	Mean
Mother's yr of ed	568	12.4	341	12.7	227	12.0
Father's yr of ed	527	12.1	311	12.8	216	11.1
Mother's hr away	457	33.9	288	35.6	169	31.1
Father's hr away	491	47.2	289	46.9	202	47.7
	N	%	N	%	N	%
Mother works for pay	576	75	344	79	228	69
Father works for pay	576	98	317	99	223	96

Note. For 4 of the 6 characteristics in this table, urban/rural differences, when tested by *t* test or chi square, were significant at *p* < .05 (*father's hr away* and *father works for pay* were the 2 exceptions).

ined the relationship between the use of extraparental care/education services and family-background variables. He found that the use of extraparental services is related to the level of education of both mother and father. Families in which parents have fewer years of education are less likely to use extraparental care/education services for their child. Also, the number of care/education settings used is related to the father's years of education: A family in which the father has a higher level of education is more likely to use multiple care/education settings for their child.

Table 8.2 compares data for selected family and household characteristics for urban and rural areas. The findings indicate that compared with their rural counterparts, urban mothers and fathers have completed more years of education. Also, a higher percentage of urban mothers than rural mothers are active in the labor force, and urban mothers typically spend more time away from their preschool-aged children each week. Table A.2

(Appendix A, p. 303) which presents urban/rural information on the use or nonuse of extraparental services, indicates that rural families are less likely than urban families to use such services. Also, urban families are more likely to use organized facilities than other-home settings, while for rural families, the reverse is true. The data presented in Table A.2 are consistent with statements made in the 1989 profile by Ojala.

In discussing early childhood issues for the 1990s, Ojala's 1989 profile mentioned needing to improve availability of services as well as provide more trained care/education staff, which are issues echoed by many of the participating countries. Ojala summarized some of efforts under way in Finland to integrate the national policies for early childhood services, families, employment, and education — efforts that only a few nations in the world are undertaking at the present time. For example, Finland's government is studying the relationships between family policies (e.g., extended maternity leave, home care benefits, the assured right to return to work) and provision of early childhood services. Also, measures concerning flexible working hours for parents with preschool-aged and first-grade children are gaining support; such measures would, of course, affect parents' needs for early childhood services. Finally, the nature of the preschool training that some Finnish 6-year-olds currently receive may eventually lead to lowering the country's school-entry age to 6 years, leaving early childhood settings to serve predominantly 3- to 5-year-old children. Since Finland is at the forefront of nations working to integrate all the various aspects of social policy, other nations developing early childhood policies would do well to stay informed of developments in Finland.

GERMANY(FRG) — MEETING THE NEEDS OF A CHANGING POPULATION AND A CHANGING NATION

Since the writing of Germany's 1989 profile of early childhood services, undreamed-of transformations have occurred in that country. Phase 1 of the IEA Preprimary Project has been carried out, nonetheless. As in many other countries, Germany's assumption of the IEA Project was an attempt to address a growing national concern about coordinating early education services and other aspects of family life — employment, education, social services — to meet the changing needs of families with young children.

The 1989 profile of early childhood services in the Federal Republic of Germany, by Tietze, Rossbach, and Ufermann, described the situation at the time this way:

> Most recently, kindergarten has again been brought to public notice. Changes in the structure of the family, the increase in single-parent families, the improvement in the standard of education of young mothers and their desire for employment outside the family, as well as the remaking of woman's image that has resulted from the feminist movement, all appear to be causes for the appeal for institutions that are more capable of responding to the changing needs and lifestyles of families and children (p. 51).

This response to changing needs and lifestyles may involve expanding early childhood services in many geographic regions of Germany and providing more-flexible hours of operation — both efforts aimed at increasing the supply, based on an accurate assessment of the demand. This summary attempts to clarify current demand by comparing Phase 1 findings from the IEA Preprimary Project as it was conducted in the Federal Republic of Germany with information presented in that country's 1989 profile. We also discuss recent changes in Germany that will be placing extra demands on its early childhood education/care system.

THE FAMILIES SURVEYED IN GERMANY

Germany's IEA Preprimary Project research team collected data from 509 families in 525 electoral districts throughout the Federal Republic. Interviewers included a household in the study if (1) it was maintained by a German-surnamed householder and (2) it contained the child's genetic or social mother. Consequently, the study did not include any household of foreign nationals living and working in the country, even if the household contained children in the appropriate age-range. The response rate for the study was 67 percent, and the refusal rate was 15 percent.

The general characteristics of sample families were these: (1) parents were generally in their early 30s and averaged 10 to 11 years of general education, (2) 43 percent of mothers and 98 percent of fathers were employed, and (3) mothers typically spent 18 to 19 hours away from their children each week, and fathers, 52 hours away. When the sample was compared with the population of the Federal Republic on several characteristics, the two groups were sufficiently similar for the sample to be considered representative of the German population.

THE FINDINGS ABOUT GERMANY'S PREPRIMARY CARE/EDUCATION

Phase 1 results indicate that 82 percent of families with children 4 years (± 6 months) of age typically use early childhood education/care services each week, with 49 percent enrolling their children in an organized facility (kindergarten) and 33 percent utilizing home-based services. Since families with both 3- and 4-year-old children were included in the study, the percentage enrolled in kindergartens can be compared with the kindergarten enrollment rates reported in the 1989 profile for 3-year-olds (38 percent) and 4-year-olds (71 percent); the two sets of figures (the Phase 1 percentages and the 1989 percentages) are indeed similar.

In the Federal Republic, 39 percent of 3- and 4-year-olds typically attend one extraparental care/education setting each week, and 43 percent attend two or more such settings. Among the 11 nations participating in Phase 1 of the IEA Preprimary Project, Germany was found to have the second-highest percentage of young children in multiple early childhood care/education settings. Data consistent with this IEA Project finding come from a special study (Rossbach, 1988) of the daily and weekly routines of young children in the Federal Republic. Rossbach found that on the average, a child typically experiences 2.5 changes in caregivers/teachers in a day.

When we examine other organized facility data from Germany's Phase 1 findings, we note that 60 percent of facilities were sponsored by religious organizations; 29 percent, by government (public) agencies; and 10 percent, by voluntary or other organizations. These findings are very similar to those presented in the 1989 profile (religious sponsorship, 57 percent; public sponsorship, 31 percent; other welfare-organization sponsorship, 11 percent).

The IEA Phase 1 researchers found that on average, young children in Germany spend 20 hours per week in kindergartens, with 11 percent of the children in such settings for 30 hours or more each week. The 1989 profile essentially concurred with this latter figure in noting that "only 12 percent of kindergarten children are cared for over and beyond midday" (p. 72). When IEA interviewers asked parents to cite any problems they encountered with kindergartens, the problem identified by the highest percentage of parents (13 percent) was *hours of operation*; the problem identified by the second-highest percentage of parents (5 percent) was *cost*. Thus, the Phase 1 findings summarized here would seem to support the contention that Germany needs to better fit services — both the availability and the cost — to the needs of families with young children.

As noted at the beginning of this summary, during recent years, the Federal Republic of Germany has been experiencing the types of family and societal changes that have occurred in many industrialized nations (e.g., changes in family structure, in employment of mothers with young children). In addition, 1990 brought a major change — the unification of the Federal Republic of Germany and the German Democratic Republic and the subsequent immigration of large numbers of Eastern Europeans to unified Germany. Besides introducing new issues of assimilation as well as new quantitative demands on educational systems already in place, unification also juxtaposed two early childhood systems (from former West and East Germany) that to this day continue to have strong differences.

At the time of unification, the former West Germany had kindergarten places for barely 70 percent of children aged 3 and older and *krippe* (day care center) places for fewer than 2 percent of children under age 3. By comparison, the former East Germany provided places for 95 percent of children aged 3 and older and for 56 percent of children under age 3. Moreover, *all* early childhood services in the former East Germany are usually available for the entire day (10 to 12 hours); in the former West Germany, this is true of krippen (serving children under age 3), but not of most kindergartens (only 14 percent are full-day). Sponsorship also differs: In the former West Germany, early childhood programs are mostly operated by churches or other voluntary organizations, with a few operated by municipalities; former East German programs are operated almost entirely by municipalities.

This dichotomous situation is expected to eventually change. For example, spreading unemployment among women in the former East Germany could lead to krippen services there decreasing to approach the under-age-3 service situation now prevalent in the Western part of Germany. For children aged 3 and older (including immigrant children in this age-range), a new law of the unified Germany now guarantees universal kindergarten coverage by the year 1996. This will provide for all children aged 3 and older a service that children in former East Germany have had available for many years.

Hong Kong — Adding Quality to Quantity

Hong Kong entered the IEA Preprimary Project well aware that its population has a somewhat unique attitude toward preprimary education.

Hong Kong families, taking the long view, see preschool as the first step along the road to economic and social success. Though this attitude has assured that preschool provisions exist, it has not always assured the quality of those provisions. In her 1989 profile on early childhood services in Hong Kong, Opper described the situation as follows:

> In 1986, kindergarten enrollment represented 89 percent of the relevant population. This high proportion reflects the value that the Chinese traditionally attach to education, but it also reflects the economic and educational situation. Although a university degree has distinct economic advantages in Hong Kong, university places are only available for 2 percent of the population. Consequently university entrance competition is very keen, and success in previous schooling becomes a crucial factor. Formal schooling is an important avenue to social and economic mobility, and preschool is perceived as the first step along this avenue (pp. 119–120).

> On the positive side, Hong Kong is fortunate in having universal preschool education and care for all children between ages 3 and 6.... This high enrollment rate reflects both parents' recognition of the benefits of preschool and the positive response of private enterprise to their demand for preschools (p. 139).

> The other side of the coin, however, is that the system is being "stretched" to serve the large number of children that use it. In many cases, quantity is emphasized at the expense of quality (p. 139).

Evidence to support Opper's profile description can be seen in Hong Kong's Phase 1 findings.

THE FAMILIES SURVEYED IN HONG KONG

The IEA Preprimary Project collected Phase 1 data from 947 families with 4-year-old children in the three administrative districts of the Hong Kong Territory (Hong Kong Island, Kowloon, and the New Territories). Since nearly all of Hong Kong's 4-year-olds attend preschools (kindergartens or nurseries), researchers first selected a sample of the preschools and then selected children from each of these settings. The response rate was 95 percent, and there were no refusals. Researchers found that parents in the sample generally had 9 to 10 years of education; nearly all the fathers and approximately half of the mothers were employed.

The Findings About Hong Kong's Preprimary Care/Education

Study results indicated that 96 percent of sample children attended kindergartens (educational organized facilities) and 4 percent attended nurseries (care-oriented organized facilities). These findings roughly agree with the percentages given in the 1989 profile (90 percent in kindergarten, 10 percent in nurseries). The study further found that sample children spent an average of 17 hours per week, or approximately 3½ hours per day, in their extraparental settings. The settings were close to families' homes, so that 81 percent of children traveled only 15 minutes or less to reach them, and 64 percent of children were able to walk to their kindergartens or nurseries.

When families were asked to give their major reason for using early childhood services, their replies were predominantly child-related. Of the more than 800 parents who responded, 67 percent said that *social/emotional development of the child* was the major reason, while the remaining 33 percent gave *educational development of the child* as the major reason. These percentages support the statements from the national profile that were presented at the beginning of this summary. In addition, in another discussion of the Hong Kong IEA Preprimary Project findings, Opper (1990) wrote,

> It is clear that the majority of parents feel that preschool, even for only half a day, is an essential component of the life of young children in Hong Kong. This is substantiated by the large number of nonworking mothers who do not require care for their children during the day, [but] nevertheless voluntarily choose to send their children to preschool. The majority of preschools in Hong Kong do not appear to fulfil a need for day care but are serving some other function for young children and their families (pp. 22–23).

The Phase 1 study found that of the care/education settings identified by sample families, 28 percent were sponsored by private organizations, 60 percent were sponsored by religious organizations, and 11 percent were sponsored by voluntary agencies. Educational institutions sponsored 1 percent of the settings, and no setting was sponsored by the government. This information corroborates the 1989 profile's contention that private and voluntary organizations are the primary sponsors of organized settings for young children.

In discussing the early childhood services in Hong Kong, Opper's

1989 profile noted the following pressing needs: improved facilities and equipment, improved teacher training, curriculum improvement, and an expanded program of fee assistance for low-income families. One might have expected parents interviewed in the Phase 1 study to overwhelmingly mention similar needs, but this was not the case. When Phase 1 researchers asked parents about problems they had encountered with their children's services, only a minority of parents answered by citing one or more specific problems. However, among this minority of parents, the most cited problems did support the needs listed earlier by Opper: Twenty-one percent of parents noted equipment and facilities as a problem, 20 percent saw the academic orientation (i.e., the philosophy) of the setting as a problem, and 18 percent said cost was a problem. Despite the specific problems they cited, those parents who responded to the satisfaction item seemed to be generally satisfied with the settings they had selected (14 percent *very satisfied*, and 86 percent *somewhat satisfied*).

In her 1990 report on Hong Kong's Phase 1 findings, Opper suggested that the high degree of satisfaction and the small percentage of parents citing problems may be due either to parents' relatively low expectations of teachers/caregivers or to parents' limited contact with settings and their consequent lack of awareness of what actually happens in the settings. Regarding her latter point — parents' limited contact with settings — we can go back to information presented in Chapter 6 of this volume. There, the cross-national data about various types of home-setting contacts do indeed show very limited *in-person* or *within-setting* contact between Hong Kong parents and their children's caregivers/teachers.

However, one type of home-setting contact that is not included in the Chapter 6 data needs to be mentioned here to provide a more complete picture of the parental role in Hong Kong. Nearly all of the Territory's kindergartens and nurseries use a handbook that, according to Opper's 1990 report, "the child takes home at the end of a preschool session and returns to the preschool the next day with the parents' written response. This handbook usually contains comments from the teacher, often includes homework or suggested activities for the child to do at home, and provides an end-of-term and end-of-year report on the child's progress in the preschool" (pp. 33–34). Consequently, there is often daily *written* communication between parents and educators about children's work, despite the limited amount of other types of educator-parent contact.

Opper's 1989 profile noted that one major problem of Hong Kong's preschool situation was the existence of two separate service systems — child care centers (nurseries) and kindergartens. She described ways that the two systems differ, including the following: supervision by different government agencies, different staff requirements and training programs, different staff-child ratios, different operating hours, and different curriculum guidelines. Though the Phase 1 study did not collect information from families specifically related to the operation of the two separate systems, some of the problems that sample families identified could be indirectly related to differences between the systems.

Considering that the *quantity* of early childhood services offered in the Hong Kong Territory is nearly sufficient to meet the needs of its population, it is likely that early childhood professionals and policymakers in Hong Kong will concentrate next on improving the *quality* of services. As Opper (1989) noted, the major issues to be focused on will probably include improvements in the training of teachers/caregivers, increased support by the government to stabilize the teaching staff and increase the proportion of experienced teachers/caregivers, new guidelines for curriculum development and for implementation of developmentally appropriate teaching methods, and unification of standards and delivery of early childhood services within the dual system. One final overarching question, of course, that looms for the Hong Kong early childhood community concerns what will happen to early childhood services in 1997, when Hong Kong reverts to China.

ITALY — TWO SYSTEMS, REGIONAL AND URBAN-RURAL VARIATIONS

The existence of two nursery school systems and great variations in service availability from region to region — in particular in urban versus rural areas — characterize early childhood provisions in Italy. In her 1989 profile of early childhood services in Italy, Pistillo said it this way:

> Serving the educational needs of 3- to 6-year-olds, nursery schools in Italy are divided into state institutions (run directly by a ministry or agency of the national government) and non-state institutions (run by other kinds of government bodies or by private organizations) (p. 166).

> Since non-state nursery schools concentrate primarily on urban areas, outer suburbs and rural areas are being progressively abandoned, at least until the state decides to take action. Agricultural and needy areas may have one or

two state nursery schools, at times with only one or two classes; they will have no others (p. 185).

One must also denounce the grave disparity still existing between preschool services in the North and those in the South [including the Islands], in spite of the development of nursery education over the last few years (p. 193).

This summary of Italy's Phase 1 findings presents information relevant to this characterization. Italy's Phase 1 study, to determine what early childhood services families used, was directed by Lucio Pusci of the Centro Europeo dell' Educazione (CEDE).

THE FAMILIES SURVEYED IN ITALY

The IEA research team first defined 4 geographic strata (northern, central, and southern Italy, and the Islands) and then divided each of these into 4 substrata representing different population densities. From the 16 substrata that resulted, researchers selected 50 communes. The final sample contained 1,000 families; data collection resulted in a response rate of 85 percent and a refusal rate of 7 percent.

THE FINDINGS ABOUT ITALY'S PREPRIMARY CARE/EDUCATION

Phase 1 researchers found that 85 percent of families typically use at least one extraparental early childhood care/education setting each week. This 85 percent comprises the 80 percent whose children attend nursery schools and the 5 percent whose children are cared for in home settings. In her 1989 profile, Pistillo reported that according to official records, the nursery school coverage rate for 1985–86 was 88 percent, a percentage slightly higher than the one found in the IEA study.[1]

The IEA study also revealed that 60 percent of sample children attend only one setting, while 25 percent attend two or more settings. When we examine children's second and third settings, we see that they are usually home settings — either the child's own home or someone else's home. As shown in Table A.1 (Appendix A, p. 301), all of Italy's home-based care is provided by relatives. Indeed, in a detailed analysis of the Italian IEA study findings (1990), Pusci found that grandparents provide most of the extraparental home-based care for preschool-aged children:

> Since nursery school and grandparents prove to be the two prominent settings, . . . this also turns out to be the most significant and best represented combination. Usually nursery school is the first setting, and grandparents the second one, but there are a few cases (6%) in which grandparents are the first setting (according to the number of hours of weekly attendance) and nursery school is the second (pp. 52–53).

When we examine the findings for organized facilities (nursery schools) in Italy, we note that children spend an average of 6 hours a day in such settings, a finding consistent with the hours of operation reported for these settings in Pistillo's 1989 profile. Regarding sponsorship, the Italian IEA study found that various levels of the government sponsor 67 percent of the settings, with the *state* sponsoring 52 percent and regional and communal governments sponsoring the remainder. Religious organizations (primarily the Roman Catholic church) sponsors 23 percent of the nursery schools, and private agencies sponsor 7 percent. When these percentages are combined, they reveal a picture of 52 percent *state* sponsorship and approximately 45 percent *non-state* sponsorship, findings very close to those reported in the 1989 profile — 51 percent *state* and 48 percent *non-state* sponsorship.

In his 1990 report of the results of the Italy's Phase 1 study, Pusci presented usage rates of extraparental services for the 16 substrata mentioned earlier (the intersection of 4 geographical regions and 4 levels of demographic density). These rates, given in Table 8.3, indicate greater extraparental service usage in the northern and central regions of Italy than in the southern region and the Islands. In her 1989 profile, Pistillo noted a similar disparity in availability of services between the North (including the northern and central regions) and the South (including the southern region and the Islands). Her observations of the situation are in agreement with the data from the IEA Preprimary Project.

Another finding of the Phase 1 study is that service usage is higher in urban areas than in rural areas in all regions except the Islands. Pistillo's 1989 profile noted that non-state nursery schools were more likely to be located in urban areas, and the greater usage indicated in the table may correspond to the greater availability of such settings in urban areas.

Pistillo's profile listed seven current issues related to the provision of early childhood care/education services in Italy, some of which were discussed in Chapter 2 of this volume. Two of these issues — forming a single national system of nursery schools and improving services in certain regions — are directly related to the service-usage focus of Phase 1 of the

Table 8.3 Percentages of families in Italian communes using extraparental care/education services, by commune location and density

Demographic Density of Commune	Geographical Region of Commune				
	North	Central	South	Islands	Total
Very high	95	94	90	69	88
High	100	96	78	62	83
Moderate	95	87	79	78	84
Low	83	89	87	88	86
All communes	89	92	83	77	85

Note. The extraparental care/education used is primarily nursery school (94 percent). *Very high* indicates communes with more than 1,500 target-age children; *high* indicates communes with 501–1,500 target-age children; *moderate* indicates communes with 101–500 target-age children; *low* indicates communes with 1–100 target-age children.

IEA Preprimary Project.

As we have noted, Italy has two systems of nursery schools, a state system and a non-state system. The systems differ in their operating guidelines, personnel requirements, and methods of financing. In discussing the organization of the state and non-state nursery schools into a single national system, Pistillo (1989) wrote,

> Everyone accepts the idea of a national system capable of overseeing relations between the various managements and of unifying nursery education, but diversity and the principle of institutional pluralism must be respected, as provided by the Constitution. . . . [One] proposal could be summed up in the following terms: a national public system (state plus local-authority nursery schools), backed up by a set of national-level guidelines . . . that would regulate state, regional, and local authority measures to support autonomous schools and that would set certain conditions for the autonomous schools (p. 191).

Pistillo also proposed that there be state involvement in improving nursery school services in the South of Italy, including the Islands. She noted not only that there are fewer nursery schools in operation in these areas but also that many of those operating have one or more serious problems (temporary quarters, inability to provide hot meals, lack of support services).

Between the state and non-state systems, nursery schools are available for a large proportion of Italy's 3- to 6-year-old children. However, the IEA Phase 1 study substantiates that services are not equally available in all regions of the country. Moreover, the quality of services in some regions needs attention. During the next few years, both the quantity and the quality of services for young children will be the focus of early childhood professionals and policymakers in Italy.

Nigeria — Mostly Home-Based Care

Of all the nations undertaking Phase 1 of the IEA Preprimary Project, Nigeria perhaps found itself the most lacking in national statistics concerning early childhood services. In her 1989 profile of early childhood services in Nigeria, using what statistics could be found at the time, Olayemi Onibokun painted this picture of the need for and availability of care/education for young children:

> The vast majority (95 percent) of Nigerian women, whether in urban or in rural areas, whether educated or illiterate, are economically active (p. 221).

> Currently the federal government . . . does not participate directly in early childhood education (p. 225).

> The states . . . leave responsibility for provision of preprimary education in private/corporate hands (p. 225).

> No institutions in Nigeria provide free child care, and no law limits the fees that may be charged by the institutions (p. 231).

> Most Nigerian families do not earn the income to support their children in preprimary institutions (p. 231).

Based on Onibokun's statements, we might formulate the following hypotheses: (1) since a large percentage of Nigerian women are economically active, many families need early childhood care and education services and (2) because of the type of sponsorship and the cost of many organized early childhood facilities, Nigerian families of limited income may have to use other forms of child care. The IEA Preprimary Project in Nigeria collected information to test these hypotheses.

The Families Surveyed in Nigeria

Nigerian Phase 1 researchers collected data from 1,295 families in 5 states located throughout the country. In each of the 5 states, interviewers for the Federal Office of Statistics who were native to that state surveyed families face to face, with an estimated response rate of 96 percent. Although Chapter 4 presented characteristics of the sample families, because Nigerian national statistics are virtually nonexistent, it was not possible to compare the sample characteristics with those of the general population. However, the quality of the survey information is considered to be above average, since the Federal Office of Statistics supervised the data collection.

The Findings About Nigeria's Preprimary Care/Education

Survey researchers questioning Nigerian mothers of 4-year-old children found that 67 percent of the mothers were employed for pay. It is not surprising that the percentage of "economically active" women reported in Onibokun's profile was higher than 67 percent, because Onibokun's estimate referred to all adult women, whereas the Phase 1 study's percentage includes only mothers of 4-year-olds. Other factors explaining the difference might include some distinction between "working for pay" and "being economically active," or respondents' reluctance, for various reasons, to admit their employment to a federal interviewer.

Despite the reported large percentage of mothers of 4-year-old children employed, the family survey found that only 33 percent of sample families typically used extraparental care/education services each week. The most common form of service (used by 22 percent of sample families) involved having a person come into the child's home; nonrelatives provided nearly 90 percent of this type of care. Children attending an organized facility was less common (reported by 8 percent of sample families); care-oriented settings, education-oriented settings, and "unclassified" settings are all included in the term *organized facility*. The type of extraparental service least used (by 3 percent of families) was care in another person's home, with nonrelatives once again providing the majority of this type of care.

What we see from these findings is less-than-expected extraparental care use, and among families using such services, a reliance on home-based settings rather than organized facilities. This is understandable when we consider that the population (and sample) in Nigeria is predominantly rural, while the few organized facilities that do exist are located in the urban areas of the country.

When interviewers asked families using extraparental care/education services their reasons for using these services, nearly half cited *parental employment* as the major reason, while another 12 percent gave *parental educational commitments* as a response. Only 15 percent of parents stated that the major reason they used extraparental services was to provide *early educational experiences* for their 4-year-old children. These findings confirm Onibokun's assertion that parental employment is an important factor in the use of early childhood care/education services.

Onibokun's 1989 profile noted that over 90 percent of preprimary institutions were run by private individuals, religious groups, or voluntary organizations. The findings of the IEA Preprimary Project support this statement. Of the organized facilities for which researchers obtained sponsorship information, 94 percent were sponsored by private organizations/individuals, religious groups, or voluntary organizations. Phase 1 findings indicated that fewer than 1 percent of organized facilities were sponsored by governmental agencies.

Since Onibokun, in her profile of Nigerian early childhood services, discussed the differential between services in urban and in rural areas, it may also be useful to examine the IEA study's urban and rural findings separately. Table 8.4 presents the sample characteristics for urban families, for rural families, and for the total group. In general, parents living in urban areas have more years of education than do parents living in rural areas. Compared with rural mothers, those living in urban areas spend more hours away from their 4-year-old children each week. The corresponding figures for fathers, however, are comparable for urban and rural areas. Of urban mothers, 56 percent work for pay, and of rural mothers, 69 percent work for

**Table 8.4 Nigeria's urban/rural information for selected family and
household characteristics**

Characteristic	Total Sample		Urban Sample		Rural Sample	
	N	Mean	N	Mean	N	Mean
Mother's yr of ed	677	6.2	238	7.7	470	5.9
Father's yr of ed	711	7.5	225	9.2	505	4.9
Mother's hr away	713	31.0	187	42.7	525	29.1
Father's hr away	810	53.9	233	55.7	586	53.6
	N	%	N	%	N	%
Mother works for pay	1,295	67	267	56	662	69
Father works for pay	1,295	78	248	79	599	78

pay. The percentages of fathers working for pay are nearly equal in rural and urban areas (78 percent and 79 percent, respectively).

Table A.2 (Appendix A, p. 303) presents the percentages of families in urban and rural areas typically using various types of extraparental early childhood services each week. In urban areas 43 percent of families use such services, while in rural areas the corresponding figure is 36 percent — a fairly small difference. However, when we examine the findings for the urban and rural areas separately, some differences in service usage appear. In urban areas 19 percent of families enroll their children in organized facilities, whereas in rural areas only 7 percent of families use this type of setting. This finding supports Onibokun's contention that the organized facilities are located largely in urban areas. Having a person come into the family's home to care for the child is the type of care arrangement used by 17 percent of urban families and 26 percent of rural families — a difference almost equal to the rural/urban difference regarding use of organized facilities. Care by a person in another home is rarely used by families in either type of area, urban (7 percent) or rural (3 percent).

In her profile Onibokun stated: "Mothers working in the informal sector of the economy (on the farms, in the markets) often work and care for their children at the same time" (p. 221). Assuming that this type of employment occurred largely in rural areas, we examined the daily routine information separately for the two subsamples of 4-year-old children, urban and rural. We expected the data to indicate that rural children spend a larger proportion of their waking time in the parental workplace than urban children do. However, whereas urban children spend an average of only 0.3 hour in the parental workplace, the corresponding figure for rural children is not much greater, only 0.4 hour per day. So the parent's workplace appears to be a significant location for only a very small number of children in either urban or rural areas. Perhaps, in rural areas, families only consider their children to be "in the workplace" when they travel with their parents to the market; otherwise, children are considered to be at home, even if they accompany their parents into the farm fields. The study's finding that Nigeria's rural 4-year-olds spend approximately 2 more hours per day at home (13.5 hours) than do urban 4-year-olds (11.4 hours), would appear to support this explanation.

As Onibokun wrote in her 1989 profile:

> Early childhood care and education today is largely a family responsibility in Nigeria. . . . The existing child care arrangements [organized facilities] appear elitist, because they are available only to those who can pay for them (pp. 237–238).

The IEA Preprimary Project findings appear to confirm this statement.

In such a country as Nigeria it would seem that government involvement will be necessary if there is to be any significant increase in the provision of early childhood services either to children at the lower socioeconomic levels or to children in rural areas. In 1987 the Nigerian government launched the Mass Mobilization Program for Social and Economic Recovery (MAMSER), a program that encompasses social justice, economic recovery, and self-reliance. MAMSER is "directed at improving the conditions in rural areas and elevating the status of women" (Onibokun, 1989, p. 238), and the expansion of the government sponsorship of preprimary services would increase the availability of these services and assist women in combining their roles of mother and wage earner. The findings from the IEA Preprimary Project can now serve as an important source of information for the government as it plans early childhood policies and programs as part of the MAMSER program.

Portugal — Kindergartens and Grandparents

In most countries, because statistics about preprimary care and education
are generally compiled by government agencies, the information available
pertains largely to care in *organized facilities*, such as preschools and child
care centers. Because it is outside of government aegis, care by relatives,
which is what a considerable number of families in some countries use,
goes undocumented. Portugal is a case in point. Portugal's IEA Phase 1
findings have been able to at last provide statistics about the incidence and
frequency of grandparent care, a common phenomenon in that country.

Prior to the Phase 1 family survey, in their 1989 profile of Portugal's
early childhood services, authors Bairrão, Barbosa, Borges, Cruz, and
Macedo-Pinto presented information about the organized facilities
(kindergartens) available to 3-, 4-, and 5-year-old children. Bairrão and
colleagues noted that in 1984, across Portugal, approximately one third of
the children in this age-range attended kindergartens. These facilities, run
by both private and public agencies, were sponsored either by the Ministry of Education (ME) or by the Ministry of Work and Social Security
(MWSS). The ME kindergartens operated for 6 hours per day and were
open during the academic year, while the MWSS kindergartens were open
for 10–12 hours per day and operated year-round. The 1989 profile mentioned a government goal to increase kindergarten enrollment to approximately 80 percent of preprimary-aged children by early 1991–92. The
IEA Preprimary Project's Phase 1 findings not only clarify how Portugal is
doing in reaching this goal, but they shed some interesting light on where
children are who are not in ME or MWSS kindergartens.

The Families Surveyed in Portugal

Portugal's researchers located the sample of families to be interviewed for
the Phase 1 study by a search of 4-year-olds' birth records (a method
proved by pilot-testing to yield an 87 percent location rate). The sample of
families thus located was found to be representative of the general population of Portugal. Researchers, experiencing a response rate of 76 percent
and a refusal rate of only 3 percent, interviewed 581 families from 57
counties throughout Portugal. Sample parents were generally in their early 30s, with both mothers and fathers having an average of 5 to 6 years of
full-time education. Approximately 65 percent of mothers were employed
in the labor force; the corresponding figure for fathers was 98 percent. In

a typical week, mothers spent 43 hours away from their 4-year-olds, and fathers spent 64 hours away.

The Findings About Portugal's Preprimary Care/Education

The Phase 1 family survey in Portugal revealed that 71 percent of Portuguese families with 4-year-old children use extraparental early childhood services. This 71 percent is made up of 29 percent who use organized facilities (kindergartens) and 41 percent who use either own-home or other-home care/education settings (1 percent are classified as using "other" types of settings). This finding of 29 percent kindergarten attendance agrees closely with the 32 percent kindergarten attendance reported in the 1989 profile by Bairrão and colleagues.

Phase 1 researchers found that Portugal's 4-year-old children are typically in extraparental settings for 44 hours per week, a figure very similar to the number of hours that mothers spend away from their 4-year-olds each week (i.e., the 43 hours mentioned earlier).

For the sizable group of 171 families (29 percent) choosing *not* to use extraparental care/education services, the most frequently given reason for this choice was the mother's nonemployment (i.e., availability to care for her 4-year-old child; 45 percent of mothers gave this explanation). Two other reasons for this choice were cited by nearly equal percentages of families: (1) 24 percent said that no service was available or the available service was too expensive and (2) 22 percent said they received personal satisfaction either from caring for the child or from teaching the child at home.

As mentioned earlier, the Phase 1 findings allow a closer look at the caregiving role that Portuguese grandparents play, which is a subject that Portugal's 1989 profile, based on government statistics, was unable to shed light on. The findings presented here were drawn from supplemental analyses of Phase 1 data either by the ICC or by the Portuguese NRC (Barbosa et al., 1990).

The method that Portuguese researchers used to locate their survey sample — a search of children's birth records — is a method that can only be used in a country with a very low rate of family mobility. Its successful use implies that families rarely move and that succeeding generations of the same family either live in the same household or live near each other. Among the 581 households surveyed in Phase 1 of the Portuguese Preprimary Project, interviewers found grandparents present in 21 percent. However, even when grandparents do not live in the household of a Portuguese 4-year-old, there is a good chance that they live nearby and consequently may be available to serve as the child's caregiver.

As noted earlier, Phase 1 findings indicate 41 percent of families using own-home or other-home care as their child's first setting (i.e., the extraparental setting attended for the longest time week). Table A.1 (Appendix A, p. 301) shows that nearly all this home care is provided by relatives. Further examination of the data indicates that nearly *all* care by relatives is provided by grandparents; very little is provided by siblings or other relatives. When we examine the data for children's second settings (i.e., the extraparental setting attended for the second-longest time each week), we note that for a second setting, 15 percent of families use relative (i.e., grandparent) care either in the child's home or in the relative's home, while only 2 percent make use of organized facility care.

If we consider all settings selected by Portuguese families for the care/education of their 4-year-olds, we conclude from the Phase 1 findings that more families use grandparents as caregivers/educators than use teachers. Of sample children, 207 were typically cared for by grandparents each week, while 177 attended kindergartens. Some of this care/education by grandparents took place in children's own homes, and some of it took place in the grandparent's home. The children in grandparent care spent 30 hours per week (median) in that setting; the median time spent with teachers was 40 hours per week. Thus, though more families entrust their children to grandparents than to teachers, the weekly time children spend with grandparents is less than that spent with teachers.

These Phase 1 findings, obtained in the late 1980s, show Portugal to be short of its 1991–92 goal of 80 percent kindergarten enrollment, which was mentioned at the beginning of this summary. Large percentages of 4-year-olds, at the time of the household survey, still remained at home with their mothers (29 percent) or in mostly relative-tended home-care settings (40 percent). Less than a third of sample children attended kindergartens. Although a fourth of the mothers keeping their children at home said they did so because of the personal satisfaction they derived from it, another fourth expressed the opinion that programs in organized facilities were unavailable or too expensive. If the government hopes to reach its 80 percent enrollment goal, they will need to increase the availability of kindergartens to families with 4-year-old children and look for solutions to make kindergartens financially accessible to more families. Also, if the proportion of women active in the labor force continues to increase in

Portugal, as it has in so many countries, the result may be a decreased availability of grandparents to serve as caregivers — a situation that would drastically alter life for families in Portugal.

Spain — From Schoolmasters and "Friendly Women" to Public and Private Preprimary Centers

Though evidence of early childhood services in Spain goes back as far as the fifteenth through seventeenth centuries, when young children were taught by town-hall-hired schoolmasters or by "friendly women" paid by mothers to look after their children, it is particularly in the last 20 years that the country has aimed at providing school places for *all* 4- and 5-year-olds. Palacios, in his 1989 profile of Spain's early childhood services, described increasing government involvement in this area, as Spain's 17 regions go about assuming more and more responsibilities from the central government.

Palacios's profile, noting that the country's ongoing process of decentralization made it difficult to present "national" statistics, presented data from both government reports and research studies about families and their early childhood services. Also, as Palacios explained and as in many other countries, preprimary situations falling outside of government control are underrepresented in the profile's statistics. Phase 1 of the IEA Preprimary Project supplies some of these missing statistics. This summary of Spain's Phase 1 findings compares selected IEA Preprimary Project results with Palacios's earlier figures.

The Families Surveyed in Spain

For their IEA project, Spanish researchers together with the project's international sampling referee developed a sampling plan that would result in surveying a total of 480 families with 4-year-old children throughout 45 provinces. In most data collection sites, local registers of households were available, and the researchers followed careful guidelines in selecting prospects for the household survey from these registers. In a few sites, however, because household registers were not available, researchers used random-route procedures to locate children for the project. The response rate for the study was 29 percent, and the refusal rate, 35 percent. When the ICC explored with the Spanish research team the reasons for the low response and the high refusal rates, they learned that when a family could not easily be contacted, the interviewer had replaced that family with another one, with little effort at repeated attempts to contact the "original" family. This extensive use of "replacement" families, as well as the unavailability of national population characteristics, makes it difficult, if not impossible, to assess the representativeness of the achieved sample in Spain. Consequently, the reader should approach the Phase 1 findings of the IEA Preprimary Project in Spain with a certain degree of caution.

Two similarities can be noted between the families reported by Palacios (1989) and those surveyed by the Phase 1 study: (1) Palacios reported that 24 percent of mothers with children under 6 years of age were employed, while the employed-mothers figure from the IEA study was 35 percent. The moderate difference in these two percentages can be explained by the fact that Palacios included even mothers of infants and toddlers, whereas the IEA survey focused on mothers of somewhat older children (aged 3 and 4), a maternal population that is more likely to be employed. (2) Both the 1989 profile and the Phase 1 study found approximately 90 percent of households having two parents. Despite these two similarities in study samples, it is still important to remember that with the interviewers' liberal substitution of households that were easy to contact, and in the absence of any other comparisons between the achieved sample and the population of Spain, the reader should use caution in interpreting Spain's Phase 1 findings.

THE FINDINGS ABOUT SPAIN'S PREPRIMARY CARE/EDUCATION

Phase 1 researchers in Spain found 79 percent of families with 3- and 4-year-old children to be using extraparental care and education services. This included 69 percent who enrolled their children in preprimary centers and 10 percent whose children were cared for in home settings. The 1989 profile reported that in 1986, approximately 16 percent of 3-year-olds and 85 percent of 4-year-olds were enrolled in preprimary centers; so the profile's statistics and the recent findings seem to be in general agreement. About one quarter of the sample families in the present study typically used two or more settings each week, and the second and third settings were nearly always home settings.

With 79 percent of sample families using extraparental services and

35 percent of sample mothers employed, maternal employment must be only one of several reasons families use early childhood services. Thus, it is interesting to examine the reasons that families gave for turning to extraparental services. When families in the IEA study were asked their major reason for service use, 63 percent cited child-related reasons, including 43 percent who mentioned *education of the child* as the specific reason; *social/emotional development of the child* was the next-most-common specific reason. Only 28 percent of families said that *parental employment* was their major reason for using early childhood services. Palacios, in his 1989 profile, reported the findings of a similar survey conducted with urban Spanish families having children under 6 years of age. In this 1983 study, 70 percent of families cited child-related reasons (*education, social/emotional development*) for using extraparental services, while only 3 percent cited *parental employment*.

The IEA Phase 1 findings and the findings included in the Palacios profile are in general agreement on the following matters regarding Spain's preprimary centers: (1) Children spend 5–6 hours per day in these settings; (2) a moderate proportion of the settings (40–60 percent) offer health services for children, while a smaller proportion have transportation services; and (3) there is little educator-parent contact beyond informal meetings. However, the two studies reported different findings regarding how children travel between their home and the care/education setting. In the IEA study, 74 percent of families reported that their children traveled by foot, while in the 1983 study included in the Palacios profile, 97 percent of families indicated that they used either private or public transportation to convey their children to their settings. This difference in percentages may be explained by the fact that the earlier study was limited to urban areas, whereas the Phase 1 study included rural areas, small towns, and urban sites.

Since the 1989 profile also included data (from the 1983 study) about the amount of time fathers spend with their children daily, these data can be compared with the daily caregiver findings of the IEA Preprimary Project. In the IEA study, families reported that alone, fathers supervised their 4-year-olds for approximately 20 minutes daily, and together with mothers, they supervised for approximately 2 hours 20 minutes a day. In the 1983 study, families reported that 46 percent of fathers played with the child for 1 hour or less per day and 29 percent engaged in this activity for 2 to 3 hours per day. The findings of both studies seem to indicate that there is limited involvement of fathers in the care or education of young children in Spain.

Among the group of countries participating in Phase 1 of the IEA Preprimary Project, Spain belongs to a subgroup in which organized facilities are available to and utilized by the majority of families. Spain is also one of only 4 countries in which parents citing child-related reasons for using extraparental services outnumbered those citing parent-related reasons. These findings suggest that Spanish parents are generally aware of the importance of preprimary education and therefore a large proportion of them enroll their children in preprimary centers.

Considering the current state of early childhood education in Spain (i.e., general availability of services, parent awareness of the importance of early childhood education), the nation's early childhood policymakers and professionals may now begin to focus on how the quality of existing services affects children, families, professional staff, and society. It is time to explore such questions as these: What is the quality of experiences for children in these preprimary centers? Do these centers adequately meet the needs of families trying to integrate early childhood services with other segments of their lives (e.g., employment)? Are the equipment and facilities in the preprimary centers sufficient to allow professionals to plan and execute a variety of developmentally appropriate activities for young children? How does the preprimary education system fit into the overall educational goals for the various regions of Spain, and are sufficient resources allocated to this system?

THAILAND — WORKING TOWARD A GOAL

Thailand, a Southeast Asian country with over 1 million 4-year-old children, has had early childhood care and education programs since the late-nineteenth-century reign of King Rama V. As recounted in Thailand's 1989 profile (Passornsiri, Kutintara, & Suwannapal, 1989), during the country's 100-year history with early childhood services, the government has initiated different types of programs in both urban and rural areas. The *Sixth National Education Development Plan (1987–1991)* set a goal of expanding preprimary programs to serve at least 37 percent of 3-, 4-, and 5- year-old children. About the same time, the government approved the expansion of preprimary classes annexed to primary schools, a project called The Rural Kindergarten. Since the data collection for Phase 1 of the IEA Preprimary Project took place in 1989, this summary examines the Phase 1 statistics in the light of government goals and efforts.

The Families Surveyed in Thailand

It is important to note that the Phase 1 household survey in Thailand was conducted with a large number of families (2,466) from 33 provinces located throughout the country. The response rate was 99 percent, and the comparison of key characteristics of the sample and the population indicated that the sample was generally similar to the population. Considering all these factors — the large sample-size, the distribution of the sample throughout Thailand, the high response-rate, and the representativeness of the sample — a comparison of Phase 1 findings with Sixth Plan goals seems indeed appropriate.

Among the sample households, 57 percent of mothers and 95 percent of fathers were employed for pay. These parents typically spent a great deal of time away from their 4-year-olds each week (mothers averaged 44 hours a week away; fathers, 76 hours).

The Findings About Thailand's Preprimary Care/Education

Researchers working on Phase 1 of the IEA Preprimary Project found that in 1989, 12 percent of Thailand's 4-year-old children were enrolled in preprimary programs in organized facilities. Making up this 12 percent were the 8 percent who attended educational programs and the 4 percent who attended programs that were primarily care-oriented. The researchers also found that a total of 36 percent of 4-year-old children were cared for by extraparental caregivers in all major types of settings (own-home, other-home, and organized facility). If one considers the 12 percent in organized facilities, this leaves 24 percent receiving extraparental care/education in home settings (either their own home or someone else's home). In these two kinds of home settings, relatives provided nearly all of the extraparental care. This finding was not surprising, since adult family members often live near one another in Thailand, especially in the rural areas.

The government's Sixth Plan goal (for 37 percent of 3-, 4-, and 5-year-olds to be in preprimary programs) referred only to organized facilities, therefore the Phase 1 finding (12 percent of 4-year-olds attending organized facilities) would seem to fall short of the goal — at least if the 37 percent goal meant equal percentages of each age group (3-, 4-, and 5-year-olds). If coverage for 5-year-olds was intended to be almost universal, with lower percentages for the younger age groups, the goal might well have been met at the time of the Phase 1 survey.

Considering the large percentages of sample mothers and fathers employed for pay and the long hours parents spent away from their children, it was not surprising to find that 4-year-old children in Thailand typically received extraparental care/education services for an average of 56 hours each week. Of the total group of families in the Thailand study who regularly made use of extraparental care/education services, 70 percent gave *parental employment* as the major reason.

If we examine Phase 1 findings about the organized facilities attended by Thailand's 4-year-olds, we see that the government is frequently a sponsor of these settings, either as the sole sponsor or as one of multiple sponsors along with educational institutions, religious institutions, and so forth. Approximately 20 percent of organized facilities offer health services to children, but fewer than 10 percent offer special education services or social services. While only 25 percent of families to whom special education services are available actually use these services, a large percentage of families use the available health services (85 percent) or social services (71 percent).

Sixty percent of Phase 1 sample families reported that they had at least one informal meeting with the teacher/caregiver in the organized facility during the previous 3 months, and 38 percent reported that they had this type of contact at least weekly. Meetings requested by the teacher/caregiver and parent group meetings were other types of parent-setting contact reported by the parents, but these meetings occurred infrequently (less than once per month).

Since approximately two thirds of Thailand's sample children were cared for solely by their parents/guardians, it is interesting to look at the daily routine data for these children. The findings indicate that for the average child, the mother was the caregiver for 8 of the child's 16 waking hours each day. Only two other categories of persons (both parents, grandparents) served as caregivers for more than 1 hour of the child's waking time. Thus, the largest proportion of the 4-year-old child's time was spent with a parent or grandparent, a finding that is consistent with Thailand's Phase 1 data about family use or nonuse of extraparental care/education settings.

Because of the nature of Thailand, it is interesting to examine some major findings separately for urban areas (16 percent of the sample) and for rural areas (84 percent of the sample). Table 8.5 presents data separately for urban and rural areas for several selected family and household variables.

Table 8.5 Thailand's urban/rural information for selected family and household characteristics

Characteristic	Total Sample		Urban Sample		Rural Sample	
	N	Mean	*N*	Mean	*N*	Mean
Mother's yr of ed	2,249	4.8	349	6.6	1,899	4.5
Father's yr of ed	2,194	5.4	340	7.9	1,853	5.0
Mother's hr away	1,116	43.7	170	47.9	945	42.9
Father's hr away	1,873	76.4	302	70.8	1,570	77.4
Number of children	—	—	386	2.2	2,079	2.4
	N	%	*N*	%	*N*	%
Mother works for pay	2,466	57	353	58	1,921	57
Father works for pay	2,466	95	345	97	1,868	94
Indoor water	2,466	18	385	81	2,071	7
Television	2,466	44	386	81	2,079	37

Note. A dash indicates no data were available.

The two groups of families — rural and urban — look similar in the number of hours that mothers and fathers are away from the child and in the number of children in the household. However, urban mothers and fathers have more years of education (6.6 and 7.9, respectively) than do rural mothers and fathers (4.5 and 5.0, respectively). Table 8.5 presents the percentages of urban and rural families who have running water and who own a television set. (These variables were of interest because availability of running water is one of several factors that determines how much time family members spend in routine daily household activities, while the presence of television is an indicator of the young child's access to the world beyond his or her immediate surroundings.) In urban areas,

81 percent of sample families have running water, and an equal percentage own at least one television set. In rural areas, only 7 percent of sample families have running water, while 37 percent have a television set.

Table A.2 (Appendix A, p. 303) presents separate urban and rural percentages for 4-year-old children in extraparental care/education settings. The percentages of children cared for solely by their parents/guardians are similar for urban (57 percent) and rural (65 percent) areas. However, in urban areas, 28 percent of children attend organized facility preprimary programs, while in rural areas, the comparable figure is 9 percent.

The Phase 1 findings present a picture of Thailand as a country in which the majority of parents use exclusively parent/guardian at-home care for their 4-year-olds. The reasons that families gave for choosing this type of care were largely parent/guardian-related and included such responses as the parent enjoys having the child around and thinks it is important for parents to be the major persons in the child's life during this period. Also, many families had not considered using extraparental early childhood services. The families who did use extraparental care/education services tended to choose home settings (own-home or other-home) rather than organized facilities, and in these home settings, relatives provided the care/education.

With the Phase 1 results as a basis, Thailand must now consider the next steps in the government's involvement with early childhood care and education services. Questions that emerge from the results of this study include the following: Are the government's goals and purposes for early childhood programs consistent with the lifestyles and preferences of families? If the government views early childhood education in an organized facility as important, how can it communicate this information effectively to parents to increase their use of these programs?

THE UNITED STATES — A MULTIFACETED SYSTEM OF PREPRIMARY SERVICES

If one word could characterize early childhood services in the United States, it would be *diversity*. Services have various sponsors (government, church, private enterprise), different forms (care-oriented, education-oriented), and varying hours of operation (part-day, full-day, extended-day). The U.S. profile (Olmsted, 1989) described the variety of early childhood services available to families and reported on service usage as reported in government documents. This summary of the United States' IEA/PPP Phase 1 study methods and findings looks at the family survey results to see how they compare with information in the 1989 profile and to present findings for subgroups of families.

The Families Surveyed in the United States

American Phase 1 researchers collected data from families in 11 sites located throughout the country. As a group, the 11 sites covered all four U.S. census regions. They included both urban and rural areas and included families from all major racial/cultural and socioeconomic groups. For each site, researchers used PPS procedures to select 12 area segments, and in most segments (except extremely large ones) all households with children in the target age-range were included in the sample. The final sample contained 432 families; data collection resulted in a response rate of 85 percent and a refusal rate of 6 percent.

The general characteristics of the sample families were these: (1) parents were generally in their early 30s and averaged 12 to 14 years of education, (2) 94 percent of fathers and 50 percent of mothers were employed, (3) fathers typically spent 52 hours away from their children each week, and mothers, 27 hours away, and (4) approximately 70 percent of the sample families resided in "married, spouse-present" households. When the sample was compared with the population of the United States on several characteristics, the two groups were sufficiently similar for the sample to be considered representative of the population.

The Findings About United States Preprimary Care/Education

The Phase 1 family survey revealed that 61 percent of American families with 4-year-old children use extraparental early childhood services. This 61 percent is made up of 35 percent who use organized facilities, 17 percent who use other home arrangements, and 9 percent whose children are cared for in their own homes by others. Table 8.6, summarizing service usage as reported in the 1989 profile and as found in the present study, reveals a close correspondence between the two sets of findings.

Phase 1 researchers found that American 4-year-olds are typically in

Table 8.6 U.S. care and education for children aged 3–4
in 1987 and in present study

Category	Percent of Age Group	
	1987 (Population)	Present Study (N = 424)
Children with mothers in labor force	**54**	**50**
Parental care during work	12	11
In-home care	14[a]	7
Other-home care	10[b]	14
Centers or schools	18	18
Children with mothers not in labor force	**46**	**50**
Parental care only	30	28
Centers or schools	16	17
In-home care	—	2
In other-home care	—	3
Children in any form of extrafamilial out-of-home care or education	**45**	**52**

Note: A dash indicates that no data were available.

[a]This category in 1987 findings also included relative care in other-home setting.

[b]This category in 1987 findings also included nonrelative care in child's own home.

extraparental settings for 28 hours per week. This closely agrees with the weekly hours mothers spend away from their 4-year-olds. Also, 43 percent of American 4-year-olds typically attend one extraparental care/education setting each week, and 18 percent attend two or more such settings. Reporting few problems, American parents are generally satisfied with the care/education services their children receive.

When American parents were asked to state the major reason for their use of extraparental services, 51 percent cited parent-related reasons (such as *employment, family obligations*), while 42 percent cited child-related reasons (such as *education, social-emotional development*). Of the 9 countries reporting data for this question, the United States is the only one in which nearly equal percentages of parents cited parent-related and child-related reasons. These findings suggest that both the "care strand" and the "education strand" of services described in Olmsted's 1989 U.S. profile continue to exist.

Regarding average annual service costs in the United States, Phase 1 findings were these: $1,200 per year for in own-home care, $1,440 per year for other-home care, and $1,728 per year for organized facility care (in a child care center, preschool). In general, American families pay 5 to 7 percent of monthly household income for care/education services for their 4-year-olds. These figures are lower than those reported in the 1989 profile, perhaps because the earlier figures came from studies in predominantly large urban areas.

The Phase 1 study found that of the organized care/education facilities identified by sample families ($n = 170$), 25 percent were sponsored by private organizations, 19 percent were sponsored by religious organizations, 15 percent were sponsored by the government, and 12 percent were sponsored by educational institutions. These data support the 1989 profile's information about the multiplicity of sponsors of American early childhood care/education settings.

Phase 1 findings indicated that 37 percent of organized facilities in the United States offer health services, while approximately a quarter offer each of the other categories of service — special education services, social services, and transportation services. Whereas a large proportion (75 percent) of children to whom health services are available use these services, about half use available transportation services, and only a third use available special education and social services.

When organized facility users in each country were asked about types and frequencies of home-setting contact in the previous 3 months, American parents were among those reporting the most contact. Over 60 percent of U.S. sample parents reported having three different types of home-setting contact (informal meetings, group meetings, telephone/written communication). The most striking finding was that nearly 50 percent of parents reported having assisted in the setting. Also, 44 percent noted that they had attended a meeting requested by the teacher/caregiver.

When we examine the daily routine information for 4-year-olds in the United States, we find that the mother serves as caregiver for 10 to 11 hours of the child's daily waking hours; the organized facility teacher/caregiver serves for the second-longest period (1.8 hours daily). The American father typically provides little primary supervision of the young child, either alone (0.7 hours daily) or in the presence of the mother (0.9 hours daily). In the United States, other relatives tend to serve as caregivers for only a small portion of the child's day. Findings about the various settings attended by the 4-year-old child during his/her waking hours are consistent with findings about the persons serving as caregivers. American 4-year-olds typically spend about 12 hours a day in their own homes and 1 to 2 hours a day in either an organized facility or another home (e.g., a family day care home).

Since both *family structure* (two-parent or one-parent) and *employment status of parents* could be related to use/nonuse of extraparental services and to type of services used, it is useful to examine the data separately for the four categories of families formed by these two characteristics (see Table 8.7). Among families with both parents or the sole parent in the labor force (i.e., *no unemployed parent*), it is not surprising that only a small percentage of 4-year-olds in one-parent households are in *parental care only*; however, in a two-parent household where both parents are employed outside the home, a sizable percentage of 4-year-olds are in *parental care only*. This may be because it is sometimes possible for two parents to work alternating schedules in order to provide the child's total care between them.

From Table 8.7 data this further observation about families with *no unemployed parent* can be made: When the one-employed-parent family uses extraparental services, they are more likely than the two-employed-parent family to use a single care/education setting.

Another interesting conclusion from Table 8.7 is that when we examine the use of extraparental services for two-parent, one-unemployed-parent families (third column in the table) and one-parent, unemployed-parent families (fourth column in the table), we see very similar patterns regarding both numbers and types of settings used. Comparable pattern-similarity cannot be found in comparing the two kinds of two-parent households (the table's first and third columns) or the two kinds of one-parent households (the table's second and fourth columns). The data in Table 8.7 would thus suggest that in the U.S., *parental employment status is more related to service usage than family structure is*.

In the Phase 1 family survey, U.S. researchers added questions about medical and dental insurance coverage. The findings indicate that 85 percent of children are covered by medical insurance, with employer-provid-

Table 8.7   U.S. early childhood care and education service usage
for families with various characteristics

Service Usage	No Unemployed Parent		At Least 1 Unemployed Parent	
	% of 2-Parent Households ($n = 163$)	% of 1-Parent Households ($n = 49$)	% of 2-Parent Households ($n = 131$)	% of 1-Parent Households ($n = 81$)
Parental care only	24	14	56	58
1 extraparental setting per week				
Own-home care	9	14	2	5
Other-home care	15	27	4	3
Organized facility	26	19	28	25
Subtotal	50	60	34	33
2 or more extraparental settings per week				
Own-home and other(s)	3	4	2	0
Other-home and other(s)	13	8	2	2
Organized facility and other(s)	10	14	6	7
Subtotal	26	26	10	9
Total	100	100	100	100

ed insurance accounting for 55 percent, family-purchased insurance accounting for 13 percent, and Medicaid accounting for 12 percent (5 percent responded with "other"). The findings also indicate that 56 percent of children are covered by dental insurance, and this agrees with the percentage of children receiving dental examinations in the year previous to the survey.

In summary, the U.S. Phase 1 findings confirm recently reported government statistics about the use of extraparental care/education services by families with preschool-aged children. The additional information that was obtained through the family survey, however (about family reasons for service usage, hours spent in settings, and problems with services), enriches the total data set and facilitates more in-depth analyses. The U.S. findings about organized facility use both confirm 1989 profile data about the setting diversity and add information about availability of special services. An interesting finding is that among all nations reporting on home-setting contact, the United States shows the strongest contact. Also of interest is the U.S. finding about the mother being the primary caregiver for 10 to 11 hours of the child's day, with the father and other relatives providing only very small amounts of primary supervision.

* * *

IEA studies are valuable both for shedding light on policies, practices, and outcomes in individual countries (as summarized in this chapter) and for bringing into focus issues of international concern. The next chapter, which summarizes the Phase 1 study, discusses these global issues.

ENDNOTES

1. It is worth noting that the official statistics are based on the actual *enrollment* rates, whereas the IEA study records only the data on actual *attendance*. A number of children enroll in nursery school but do not really attend, or attend only for a few months. So the gap between official statistics and the IEA study may be due to the percentage of children who fail to attend nursery school for the entire school year.

REFERENCES

Bairrão, J., Barbosa, M., Borges, I., Cruz, O., & Macedo-Pinto, I. (1989). Care and education for children under age 6 in Portugal. In P.P. Olmsted & D.P. Weikart (Eds.), *How nations serve young children: Profiles of child care and education in 14 countries* (pp. 273–302). Ypsilanti, MI: High/Scope Press.

Barbosa, M., Cruz, O., Abreu-Lima, I., Rangel-Henriques, M., Bairrão, J., & Borges, M. I. (1990). *IEA Preprimary Project Phase 1 findings report for Portugal.* Porto: University of Porto.

Delhaxhe, A. (1989). Early childhood care and education in Belgium. In P. P. Olmsted & D. P. Weikart (Eds.), *How nations serve young children: Profiles of child care and education in 14 countries* (pp. 13–37). Ypsilanti, MI: High/Scope Press.

Delhaxhe, A., & Hindryckx, G. (1991). *IEA Preprimary Project Phase 1 findings report for Belgium.* Liège: University of Liège.

Ojala, M. (1989). Early childhood training, care, and education in Finland. In P. P. Olmsted & D. P. Weikart (Eds.), *How nations serve young children: Profiles of child care and education in 14 countries* (pp. 87–118). Ypsilanti, MI: High/Scope Press.

Ojala, M. (1990). *IEA Preprimary Project Phase 1 findings report for Finland.* Joensuu: University of Joensuu.

Olmsted, P. P. (1989). Early childhood care and education in the United States. In P. P. Olmsted & D. P. Weikart (Eds.), *How nations serve young children: Profiles of child care and education in 14 countries* (pp. 365–400). Ypsilanti, MI: High/Scope Press.

Olmsted, P. P. & Weikart, D. P. (Eds.), (1989). *How nations serve young children: Profiles of child care and education in 14 countries.* Ypsilanti, MI: High/Scope Press.

Onibokun, O. (1989). Early childhood care and education in Nigeria. In P. P. Olmsted & D. P. Weikart (Eds,). *How nations serve young children: Profiles of child care and education in 14 countries* (pp. 219–240). Ypsilanti, MI: High/Scope Press.

Opper, S. (1989). Child care and early education in Hong Kong. In P. P. Olmsted & D. P. Weikart (Eds.), *How nations serve young children: Profiles of child care and education in 14 countries* (pp. 119–142). Ypsilanti, MI: High/Scope Press.

Opper, S. (1990). *IEA Preprimary Project Phase 1 findings report for Hong Kong.* Hong Kong: University of Hong Kong.

Palacios, J. (1989). Child care and early education in Spain. In P. P. Olmsted & D. P. Weikart (Eds.), *How nations serve young children: Profiles of child care and education in 14 countries* (pp. 303–341). Ypsilanti, MI: High/Scope Press.

Passornsiri, N., Kutintara, P., & Suwannapal, A. (1989). Child care and early education in Thailand. In P. P. Olmsted & D. P. Weikart (Eds.), *How nations serve young children: Profiles of child care and education in 14 countries* (pp. 343–363). Ypsilanti, MI: High/Scope Press.

Pistillo, F. (1989). Preprimary education and care in Italy. In P. P. Olmsted & D. P. Weikart (Eds.), *How nations serve young children: Profiles of child care and education in 14 countries* (pp. 151–202). Ypsilanti, MI: High/Scope Press.

Pusci, L. (1990). *IEA Preprimary Project Phase 1 findings report for Italy.* Frascati: European Center for Education.

Rossbach, H.-G. (1988, April). *Daily routines of young children.* Paper presented at the annual meeting of the American Educational Research Association, New Orleans, LA.

Shi, H. Z. (1989). Young children's care and education in the People's Republic of China. In P. P. Olmsted & D. P. Weikart (Eds.), *How nations serve young children: Profiles of child care and education in 14 countries* (pp. 241–254). Ypsilanti, MI: High/Scope Press.

Shi, H. Z. (1990, September). *Some implications for China's early childhood education from Phase 1 of IEA Preprimary Project.* Paper presented at the IEA General Assembly Meeting, Beijing, China.

Shi, H. Z. & Xiang, Z. P. (1990). *IEA Preprimary Project Phase 1 findings report for China (PRC).* Beijing: China Central Institute of Educational Research.

Tietze, W., Rossbach, H.-G., & Uferman, K. (1989). Child care and early education in the Federal Republic of Germany. In P. P. Olmsted & D. P. Weikart (Eds.), *How nations serve young children: Profiles of child care and education in 14 countries* (pp. 39–85). Ypsilanti, MI: High/Scope Press.

IX

QUESTIONS ANSWERED, QUESTIONS RAISED — A SUMMARY

David P. Weikart, *President*
High/Scope Educational Research Foundation
Ypsilanti, Michigan

With the worldwide increase in out-of-home care and education of young children, the issues involved in developing and providing such services have become the subject of much debate. Information to guide this debate and to serve as a basis for public policy formation, though scarce at first, is increasingly available.

To begin with, the United Nations (UNESCO, 1989) provides statistical information related to early child development from 150 countries. In addition, Robert Myers (1992) in *The Twelve Who Survive* provides a comprehensive summary of policy and research in developing countries. Moncrieff Cochran (1993) and authors from 29 countries, in the *International Handbook of Child Care Policies and Programs*, also supply information from a wide range of countries, including modern, industrialized states such as Sweden and Italy as well as struggling Third World countries such as Vietnam and Zimbabwe. What is notable is that *none of these sources examines the use of child care and education services from the family's perspective.* That investigation is the goal of the IEA Preprimary Project reported here.

Initially, Phase 1 of the multiphase IEA project documented what 14 nations' official government policies have historically been toward early childhood services for families. This documentation took the form of the book *How Nations Serve Young Children: Profiles of Child Care and Education in 14 Countries* (Olmsted & Weikart, 1989). Phase 1 researchers then went on to their major task of surveying families in each country about their use, or nonuse, of the services that are available. The aim has been to let families speak — to learn firsthand how parents accommodate family needs and beliefs in light of the child care/education services they are offered by the public and private sectors. Such information, because it has been obtained in as accurate a manner as possible, should serve as a sound basis for national decision making. By gathering identical types of data from a wide range of countries — those with comprehensive, well-formed child care/education systems and those with patchwork or nonexistent systems, those with large-scale private-sector services and those with predominantly government provision — the IEA study provides a picture of the full range of policy options.

Until now, the field of child service has been clouded with extensive statements about what families need or want, as expressed by advocates of various points of view. Often these statements are not research-based, and even government statistics — narrow as they are — are of little use in validating them. The purpose of the Phase 1 study, then, is to provide reliable information, comparable across countries, that can be used for careful discussion of the issues. It should set a standard for other studies as well as contribute to the understanding of the problems families face in this age of new opportunities.

THE CONTEXT OF THE IEA PREPRIMARY PROJECT

The IEA Preprimary Project comes at a good time. In addition to parents' growing need for out-of-home care for their preschool-aged children, there is growing recognition that the early childhood period establishes the foundation for later adult performance. That high-quality early childhood education can significantly improve the life chances of children from poor homes and environments is confirmed by such longitudinal studies as the (American) High/Scope Perry Preschool Project (Schweinhart, Barnes, & Weikart, 1993) and the Turkish Early Enrichment Project (Kağitçibaşi, Sunar, & Bekman, 1988). While there is little or no comparable research showing that preprimary programs can benefit nonpoor children to the same extent, policymakers as well as parents recognize the importance of adequate support for all children during this crucial period of development. In short, need for child care and realization of the value of early childhood education converge to generate today's extensive support for the provision of preprimary programs. The information that the three phases of the IEA Preprimary Project will provide should guide development of programs to meet the needs of both families and children in the twenty-first century.

The most important aspect of this study was the commitment to searching out a representative sample of parents of 4-year-olds in each country and asking them what early childhood services they used, if any, and their opinions about them. So often, studies in the early childhood field start with the care/education setting and select parents whose children already participate in that setting. This practice makes a project easier to carry out but does not survey an unbiased sample of users and does not give information about those who elect *not* to entrust their children to the out-of-home setting.

Also, until now, most of the studies conducted in this area of research have focused on the "structural" characteristics of settings and/or have limited themselves to studying just one type of setting. Those studies that have included some on-site observation or assessment of children have typically limited the scope of their investigation to children's development as it relates to the care/education program's structural features. In the United States, for example, one can cite several such studies:

The National Day Care Study (Ruopp, Travers, Glantz, & Coelen, 1979) was a study of U.S. center-based day care only. Using child observation and assessment, it explored the relationships among three structural features (staff-child ratio, group size, and caregiver qualifications), program quality and cost, and effects on children. Similarly, the considerable amount of research documenting the impact of U.S. National Head Start programs on children's development (e.g., cognitive, socioemotional), has been limited to only one type of center-based program and has evaluated the relationship between structural features of Head Start programs and children's development during and after Head Start participation (Hubbell, 1983; McKey et al., 1985).

Another U.S. study concerned with just one type of setting, the Public School Early Childhood Study (Mitchell, 1988a, 1988b; Marx & Seligson, 1988), gathered descriptive data at the state, district, and program levels on issues in early childhood education and characteristics of public school preschool programs for children under the age of 5. However, once again, this study produced information focusing on structural features, such as the classroom setup and types of activities provided for children.

A second study concerned with day care in the United States, the National Day Care Home Study (Singer, Fosburg, Goodson, & Smith, 1980), explored a wide range of characteristics of family day care homes by conducting limited observations of individual children and adults to collect data about such behaviors as children's involvement in activities, interactions with other children and adults, and expressions of emotion. These observations provided researchers with behavioral data to assist in determining the influence of structural characteristics (e.g., caregiver training, enrollment) on adult and child behaviors.

While each of the studies just mentioned may have determined that within a single type of early childhood care/education setting, certain structural characteristics are *necessary* to produce specific developmental outcomes, that is not to say what characteristics are *sufficient* to do so. For this latter type of conclusion, a study across a wide range of settings, encompassing more than structural characteristics of settings, is called for. This is the multiphase IEA Preprimary Project.

WHAT MAKES THIS IEA PROJECT UNIQUE?

From the first meeting of the Preprimary Project's National Research Coordinators (NRCs), it was clear that the participating countries would need to survey a wide range of formal and informal systems that had been developed for child care/education both in and out of the home. Thus the preprimary study is taking great care to incorporate both formal and informal, both in-home and out-of-home care systems. Not just the official care/education policies in participating countries, but the care/education arrangements that parents piece together to meet child and family needs is what this study has set out to document.

Designers of the IEA Preprimary Study decided to include all types of early childhood settings, so comparisons across all settings can be made. As various countries reported their data, it became clear that this decision was a good one. While it might have been relatively simple within a given country to distinguish between what are considered "care" and what are considered "education" settings, across countries it made no sense. For instance, Hong Kong's day care settings literally look more like Hong Kong's education settings than they do like day care settings in Finland or the United States.[1]

Another aspect of the IEA study that lends it special value is that it includes information on the total care and education of the child throughout the week. While most children in most countries attend only one major setting outside the home, significant numbers in many countries attend a second setting, and in some countries (such as Belgium and Germany) they attend more than two. From the point of view of public policy, creating and financing a system to provide one major setting for children is task enough, but where two or more settings a week are required, how are these settings supported and monitored? What is their quality? How are they staffed? Finally, what is the overall public policy regarding adequacy of service if families must seek out so many different forms of support in caring for their children?

While there are several international early childhood studies, the IEA preprimary study is the largest household survey with internationally devised and agreed-upon data collection procedures and instruments. One of the principal decisions in creating the study was that it would represent a cross-national consensus regarding the types of information to be collected. Because childrearing, a subject close to each country's cultural life and national temperament, cannot be forced into any externally devised mold, it was important that the instruments not be unilaterally developed (by the ICC) and then "imposed upon" participating countries. Instead, instruments were developed by cooperating national planning teams. Then, once the instruments were approved by all countries on an item-by-item basis, local field trials were employed in each country to assess item response and time required for administration. While this consensus method often made steady progress in a timely fashion difficult, all participants agreed that it was the only method that would respect each country's needs and sensitivities.

A special goal of the project was to obtain a representative sample of parents in each country. Aside from the difficulties encountered in doing so in Spain, this goal was reached. In cooperation with the project's sampling referee, different but equivalent sampling procedures were devised for each country (as described in Chapter 3). Thus the data give a representative picture of families' views and use of care and education services in each participating country.

In an effort to reach a sample of all parents, an entire country was included in the study in nearly every case. Though it would have been tempting and certainly easier to include only the city where a particular National Research Center was located or just a neighboring province or state, IEA researchers strove to achieve a good balance between, for example, urban and rural populations. This was true in vast countries, such as China and the United States, as well as in countries/territories of more manageable size, such as Hong Kong and Belgium.

A final point of uniqueness is this: The IEA Phase 1 study was able to obtain high response rates from the nationally selected samples. Whereas high refusal rates have negatively affected the quality of the findings of many studies both nationally and internationally, this project was able to minimize such a problem (the response rate in Spain was the exception). Through the household survey method used, the national data collection teams were able to convey to parents a sense of purpose and responsibility that encouraged them to cooperate with the study. This accomplishment, which attests to the careful supervision that NRCs provided during the survey, has greatly added to the quality of the data obtained.

A small number of well-done international comparisons of early education services have been conducted in recent years. One of these, an intensive study of specific preschool settings, used video and other methods to gain insight about how teachers viewed their own preschool and a preschool in each of two other countries (Tobin, Wu, & Davidson, 1989). However, we must be wary of the fact that studies using this approach frequently mention "Chinese preschools" or "U.S. preschools" as though a single case represents the whole system.

Other approaches to international studies have brought together a number of reports by experts on individual countries to describe the state of early childhood care and education internationally (Kamerman & Kahn, 1978; Cochran, 1993). The IEA Preprimary Project's initial Phase 1 report, *How Nations Serve Young Children*, used this latter approach to document official policy and data from governmental sources in 14 nations. Only when public records are accurate is this approach sufficient.

Both the case-study and expert-report methods stand in contrast to the method used in the IEA Preprimary Project to gather its major Phase 1 data. As described in Chapters 3 and 4, this project surveyed a representative sample of households to discover what kinds of settings preschool-aged children in each country experience on a daily or weekly basis. Therefore the findings are an indication of what typically happens in each country rather than an in-depth study of a single selected preschool setting or a summary of government data.

THE PHASE 1 FINDINGS

Earlier chapters of this book presented country-specific data from the Phase 1 survey. The following sections of this chapter lift out from that data some overarching issues concerning all the participating nations.

WORKFORCE PARTICIPATION AND UTILIZATION OF CARE/EDUCATION SERVICES

One of the principal policy findings from this study is that the trend from parent care to out-of-home (or at least extraparental) care/education for preschool-aged children is linked to the movement of women into the formal, paid workforce. In all countries, this trend is stronger in urban than in rural areas, as might be expected. Indeed, the only countries recording a majority of children exclusively in home care by parents are China (55 percent), Nigeria (65 percent), and Thailand (63 percent) — all countries where rural populations predominate. No other country reported more than 40 percent of 4-year-olds exclusively under parental care.

PERSEVERANCE OF THE TREND

The second principal policy finding is that for two major reasons, this trend toward extraparental care/education is unlikely to be reversed. First, the majority of parents using extraparental services (most parents in 5 of the 9 countries reporting data) cite their employment as the reason. Where service usage is approximately 80 percent or higher, as in Germany, Hong Kong, Italy, and Spain, the child's need for education or for social-emotional development is cited.

Second, the one issue that might cause a halt or shift in the trend — parental concern about the quality of extraparental care/education the child receives — did not surface in any country. Indeed, at least 92 percent of parents in every country reported that they were "somewhat satisfied" or "very satisfied" with the services their children were receiving. Furthermore, when asked for specific problems encountered with services, most parents in most countries reported few or none.

There were some exceptions. Hong Kong parents reported a range of concerns, including problems with program philosophy (20 percent), with facilities and equipment (21 percent), with other children who attend (13 percent), and with cost (18 percent). Parents in China reported problems with facilities and equipment (10 percent), and with qualifications of staff (9 percent). Otherwise, the 10,913 parents using extraparental services were largely uncomplaining. For example, no problem area (including "sick child not accommodated") merited even 1 percent mention across all those interviewed.

This lack of parental dissatisfaction does not mean that from a professional point of view, there is no room for improvement in program quality or delivery. It also does not mean that from the regulatory perspective, no health or safety shortcomings can be found. It means that while a few families, especially those with special needs, may experience problems, the average parent, found through a household survey, either truly has adequate, problem-free services or does not perceive any inadequacies. This finding may be one reason why advocates for meeting the needs of special subpopulations of young children and their families find it difficult to gain widespread support for their causes.

The Number of Settings Attended

A third finding from this study is that most children (a majority in 8 countries) who experience extraparental care/education each week are served in only one extraparental setting. However a considerable number of children — ranging from 5 percent in Nigeria to 41 percent in Belgium — attend a second setting, as well. In two countries, small to moderate numbers of children typically attend third and fourth settings each week (Belgium reported 23 percent in a third and 5 percent in a fourth setting; Germany reported 8 percent in a third and 8 percent in a fourth setting). Thus, since the principal "cause" of extraparental care/education is the need for child care while parents work, the need to resort to more than one setting was reported by significant numbers of families in countries where children's services do not cover the full parental work day. Belgium, Germany, Italy, and the United States are instances of this phenomenon.

Extent of Time in Extraparental Settings

A fourth finding is that when children are in extraparental care/education, they spend significant time in such settings. While Hong Kong (17 hours per week), Germany (25 hours), and the United States (28 hours) represent the low end of the scale, more typical are the 35 hours found in Spain, Nigeria, and Italy and the 55 hours found in Thailand and China. This time in extraparental care/education settings represents a large proportion of a child's life — in the case of a child in Thailand or China, more than half the child's waking hours during the five or six parental workdays each week. Thus, in many countries, the extraparental settings the child experiences play a large part in forming the child's physical, intellectual, and social-emotional growth. Leaving the conduct of these settings to chance, whim, or even unquestioned tradition, would seem an unwise course for a nation. Phase 2 of the IEA Preprimary Project will examine, through direct observation, the quality of the settings where children spend much of their time — including the quality of home settings.

EDUCATION, A GOAL FOR THE HOME SETTING

A fifth finding is that in all countries, parents electing to keep their children at home overwhelmingly cited parent-related reasons for doing so. Primarily, these reasons involved parent goals — for example, the goal of being the child's "first" teacher or educator. (Education of the child in the service setting is a reason cited by parents who use extraparental settings.) Noteworthy, however, is the fact that a number of parents who keep their children at home do so because they lack an alternative — services either are unavailable or are unsatisfactory in some way. *Lack of an alternative* was cited especially in China (where 32 percent of "home-care" mothers gave this reason) and to a lesser extent in Finland (7 percent), Germany (8 percent), Italy (9 percent), Nigeria (9 percent), and the United States (10 percent).

SPONSORS OF OUT-OF-HOME CHILD CARE AND EDUCATION

A sixth finding from the study is that across the 11 participating countries, the out-of-home child care and education services that families use are sponsored primarily by governmental or religious organizations. In Finland, Italy, and Portugal at least 50 percent of all programs are under government auspices, whereas religious organizations sponsor the majority (60 percent) of programs in Germany and Hong Kong. In Belgium all settings have multiple sponsors, with the government always being one of those sponsors, and religious organizations being another for 41 percent of settings. Private organizations also play some role, providing 25 to 28 percent of programs in Hong Kong, Nigeria, and the United States. In spite of the extensive interest in and discussions about employer-provided care, only China reported a significant percentage of programs with such sponsorship (28 percent), while Finland, Spain, and the United States reported only 2 percent or less; no other countries reported any employer sponsorship. Clearly, corporate- or workplace-sponsored care, while an interesting alternative, is relatively rare.

These findings about service sponsorship suggest that governments and religious organizations will continue to be the primary funders and administrators of early childhood care and education programs. They are also the likeliest source of funds for the vast early childhood service expansion envisaged in most countries. While private institutions will continue to play their part, it appears unlikely that families will have their service needs met through corporate or workplace sponsorship.

AUXILIARY SERVICES TO CHILDREN

A seventh finding of the Phase 1 study is that few group settings offer families and children comprehensive services such as health care, special education services, social services, and transportation. The most offered and best used service is health care. But services offered are not necessarily used. Only 6 countries reported health service usage by more than 50 per cent of those to whom it was available. Only Belgium reported health care usage by more than half of all children in its survey sample.

Special education and social services, when provided, are lightly used. As a percent of total sample, fewer than 8 percent of children in any country receive special education or social services through their early education and care programs. These findings are in spite of the fact that the usual service providers — governmental or religious agencies — are ones likely to promote and encourage auxiliary service usage (as does the national Head Start program in the United States). Fewer than half of the 4-year-olds in any country are offered transportation to their early childhood programs. Among those to whom transportation is offered, usage ranges from 22 per cent in Belgium to 65 percent in China. However, since the survey found that most children live within a few minutes of the facility they attend, availability of transportation does not appear to be an issue.

MOTHERS AS PRINCIPAL CAREGIVERS

An eighth finding concerns who takes principal responsibility for children's care. In every participating country, regardless of its stage of economic development, mothers take the most responsibility for young children's care and supervision. Of the 4-year-old's 16-hour waking day, the time spent with mother (alone or with father) ranges from 8.4 hours (or 53 percent of the day) in Belgium to 11.9 hours (or 74 percent of the day) in

Germany. This contrasts sharply with the hours that fathers are present (with or without mothers), which ranges from 0.9 hour (or 6 percent of the day) in China and Hong Kong to 3.7 hours (23 percent of the day) in Belgium and 3.5 hours (22 percent of the day) in Thailand. Indeed, no country reports "father only care" amounting to even an hour a day; father's daily time alone with the child ranges from 0.1 hour (6 minutes) in Hong Kong to 0.9 hour (54 minutes) in China. Child care, in spite of the rhetoric about equality and role sharing in the Western countries, is still very much the responsibility of mothers in all participating countries, regardless of the various cultures and levels of development involved.

NONFAMILIAL CAREGIVERS OR TEACHERS

A ninth finding relates to caregivers other than parents. Further investigation of children's daily routines indicates that the time children spend with caregivers/teachers other than their parents or relatives varies greatly from country to country. While Belgium reported children spending 6 hours per day in nonfamilial care, Germany — also a developed European country — reported only 2.1 hours (though more than Thailand's 1.0 hour, this is below the United States' 2.8 hours). One of the most interesting facts to come out of the daily routine information is that preschool-aged children in a few countries are left alone for extended periods of time without direct adult supervision. This occurs in China, where "alone time" constitutes 2.9 hours of the child's day, and in Thailand, where it is 0.8 hour of the child's day. (See Chapter 7 for more information on children spending time alone.) Another fact worth noting is this: While Belgium comes closest to having nonfamilial services (in multiple settings) cover a full workday for parents (6 hours), across all participating countries, the average early childhood service coverage is only a portion of the full workday.

LOCATION OF CHILDREN'S SERVICES

A tenth and final finding is that the majority of children spend most of their waking hours either at home (with their mothers) or at a school or organized care center. An interesting exception is found in Finland, where children average more time in a family day care home (2.4 hours) than in an organized facility (2.1 hours). Time spent in all other settings is minimal. The wide variety of locations that this study hypothesized *does* exist — parks and playgrounds, family day care homes, workplace arrangements, neighbors' homes — but to a far lesser extent than a worldwide survey might be expected to uncover. Worthy of special note is the finding that transition times (traveling to and from education/care settings) are not a problem, since the average travel time is no more than 15 minutes in most countries. However, there are some children who travel more than 15 minutes, which is the case in China for 27 percent of children. Most countries reported an average of 5 minutes travel time, and since for many children this is walking time, we can conclude that settings are generally close at hand. Private auto use is high in the United States (74 percent) and also typical in Belgium (57 percent) and Finland (55 percent).

FINAL COMMENTS

The IEA Preprimary Project has undertaken a difficult Phase 1 task — the documentation of care/education service usage in 11 participating countries, based on a household survey of parents who have 4-year-olds. The international research team was committed to developing survey instruments that represented the best ideas that were acceptable to all. By working as a team, the NRCs achieved this goal without compromising the quality of information attained. Through teamwork, the problems in data collection were resolved, and the complex work was carried out.

Perhaps the most noteworthy finding of this study to date is this: Although preschool-aged children in all countries are in extraparental or out-of-home care in significant numbers (in most countries, over 60 percent typically experience more than 2 hours of care each week from someone other than a parent), mothers still provide the greatest share of children's care. While the national patterns of early childhood services differ considerably, mothers and paid nonfamily adults provide the most supervision, and fathers, the least — everywhere. There appear to be two reasons for the increasing use of child services: Mothers are entering the paid workforce in increasing numbers throughout the world, and families are seeking advantages for their children in a world they see as highly competitive.

Some social policy analysts may see the spread of the feminist movement or the economic pressures of industrialized society as the issues behind the worldwide demand for early childhood services. Such views only draw the focus away from children. The very real out-of-home care situation that the world's children face demands our careful attention: Children are right now being raised by young people or adults paid to undertake the task rather than by parents or family members. How qualified are these caregivers and educators? What is the content of the settings in which these children find themselves? What is the quality of children's social interactions in these settings? Are children having the kinds of early childhood experiences that lead to sound child development? Do children's early childhood settings provide the appropriate framework for the development of good workers and good citizens? Are families better-off for having such settings to turn to?

The second phase of the IEA preprimary project asks these questions by addressing the quality of life of the child in care and education settings both inside and outside of home. Finding the answers to such questions is vital to the life of every nation involved.

ENDNOTES

1. In connection with Phase 2 of the IEA Preprimary Project, High/Scope Educational Research Foundation has prepared a set of videotapes showing typical early childhood settings in the countries participating in Phase 2, including Hong Kong, Finland, and the United States. For information about the videotapes, contact High/Scope Press.

REFERENCES

Cochran, M. (Ed.). (1993). *International handbook of child care policies and programs*. Westport, CT: Greenwood Press.

Hubbell, R. (1983). *A review of Head Start research since 1970 (Head Start Evaluation, Synthesis, and Utilization Project)*. Washington, DC: CSR.

Kağitçibaşi, Ç., Sunar, D., & Bekman, S. (1988). *Comprehensive Preschool Education Project: Final report*. Ottawa: International Development Research Center

Kamerman, S. and Kahn A. (Eds.). (1978). *Family policy: Government and families in 14 countries*. New York: Columbia University Press.

Marx, F. & Seligson, M. (1988). *The Public School Early Childhood Study: The state survey*. New York: Bank Street College of Education.

McKey, R. H., Condelli, L., Ganson, H., Barrett, B. J., McConkey, C., & Plantz, M. C. (1985). *The impact of Head Start on children, families, and communities (Final report of the Head Start Evaluation, Synthesis, and Utilization Project)*. Washington, DC: CSR.

Mitchell, A. (1988a). *The Public School Early Childhood Study: The case studies*. New York: Bank Street College of Education.

Mitchell, A. (1988b). *The Public School Early Childhood Study: The district survey*. New York: Bank Street College of Education.

Myers, R. (1992). *The twelve who survive*. London: Routledge.

Olmsted, P. P., & Weikart, D. P. (Eds.). (1989). *How nations serve young children: Profiles of child care and education in 14 countries*. Ypsilanti, MI: High/Scope Press.

Ruopp, R., Travers, J. Glantz, F., & Coelen, C. (1979). *Children at the center: Summary findings and their implications* (Final Report of the National Day Care Study, Vol. 1). Cambridge, MA: Abt Associates.

Schweinhart, L. J., Barnes, H. V., & Weikart, D. P. (1993). *Significant Benefits: The High/Scope Perry Preschool Study Through Age 27*. Ypsilanti, MI: High/Scope Press.

Singer, J., Fosburg, S., Goodson, B., & Smith, J. (1980). *Final Report of the National Day Care Home Study*. Cambridge, MA: Abt Associates.

Tobin, J. J., Wu, D. Y. H., & Davidson, D. H. (1989). *Preschool in three cultures: Japan, China and the United States*. New Haven, CT: Yale University Press

United Nations Educational, Scientific, and Cultural Organization (UNESCO). (1989, September). *1988 world survey on early childhood care and education (ECCE): Summary of findings*. Paris: Author.

Appendix A: Supplementary Tables

Table A.1 Percentage distribution of 4-year-old service-users according to type of first setting

Country/Territory	N	n Who Attend 1 or More Settings (% of N)	% of n in Own Home		% of n in Other Home		% of n in Organized Facility				% of n in Other Settings
			Relative	Non-relative	Relative	Non-relative	Care	Edu-cation	Unclassi-fied	Miscel-laneous	
Belgium (Fr.)	424	416 (98)	1	0	3	1	0	95	0	0	0
China (PRC)[+]	12,835	5,469 (43)	12	0	10	0	11	65	0	2	0
Finland	576	431 (75)	4	3	4	43	0	31	0	15	0
Germany (FRG)	509	417 (82)	14	4	18	4	0	60	0	0	0
Hong Kong[+]	947	947 (100)	—	—	—	—	4	96	0	0	0
Italy	1,000	852 (85)	3	0	3	0	0	94	0	0	0
Nigeria[+]	1,295	435 (33)	6	60	1	8	2	13	10	0	0

Table A.1 Percentage distribution of 4-year-old service-users according to type of first setting (continued)

Country/ Territory	N	n Who Attend 1 or More Settings (% of N)	% of n in Own Home		% of n in Other Home		% of n in Organized Facility				% of n in Other Settings
			Relative	Non-relative	Relative	Non-relative	Care	Education	Unclassified	Miscellaneous	
Portugal	581	410 (71)	21	2	26	9	0	0	41	0	1
Spain	480	379 (79)	4	2	5	1	0	0	87	0	1
Thailand	2,466	894 (36)	41	1	24	1	12	21	0	0	0
United States	432	264 (61)	9	5	10	18	18	40	0	0	0

Note. The symbol $^{+}$ indicates that weighted data were used for analysis.

Table A.2 Percentage distribution of urban/rural 4-year-olds according to use or nonuse of first settings

Country/Territory	N		n	% of N	Own Home, Parent Care Only	Own Home (Nonparent)	Other Home	Organized Facility	Other
Belgium (Fr.)	—		—	—	—	—	—	—	—
China (PRC)[+]	12,591	U	3,540	28	22	4	6	67	1
		R	9,051	72	70	6	4	19	1
Finland	576	U	345	60	18	6	32	44	
		R	231	40	37	4	39	20	
Germany (FRG)	509	U	396	78	19	13	17	51	
		R	113	22	17	19	21	43	
Hong Kong[+]	—		—	—	—	—	—	—	—
Italy	1,000	U	551	55	11	3	3	83	
		R	449	45	20	2	2	76	
Nigeria[+]	1,172	U	191	16	57	17	7	19	
		R	981	84	64	26	3	7	
Portugal	—		—	—	—	—	—	—	—
Spain	480	U	273	57	18	3	4	75	0
		R	207	43	26	7	4	62	1
Thailand	2,448	U	381	16	57	10	5	28	0
		R	2,067	84	65	16	10	9	0
United States	432	U	401	93	38	9	16	37	
		R	31	7	52	6	29	13	

Note. The symbol [+] indicates that weighted data were used for analysis. *U* indicates urban, and *R* indicates rural. Dashes indicate that no urban/rural comparison data were available.

Table A.3 Median hourly cost and median weekly cost to parents in U.S. dollars for services in extraparental care/education settings

Country/ Territory	N	Own Home (Nonparent)				Other Home				Organized Facility			
		No. Using	Median Cost Per Hr	Mean Hr Used Per Wk (SD)	Median Cost Per Wk	No. Using	Median Cost Per Hr	Mean Hr Used Per Wk (SD)	Median Cost Per Wk	No. Using	Median Cost Per Hr	Mean Hr Used Per Wk (SD)	Median Cost Per Wk
Belgium (Fr.)	424	—	—	—	—	2	1.85	19.0 (4.2)	33.00	65	0.04	25.3 (2.8)	1.14
China (PRC)[+]	12,835	—	—	—	—	—	—	—	—	—	—	—	—
Finland	576	19	2.24	31.2 (8.7)	57.50	170	1.11	37.4 (9.0)	34.21	148	1.07	30.2 (15.1)	33.92
Germany (FRG)	509	10	2.97	23.5 (11.4)	68.00	12	1.44	30.0 (11.9)	41.50	242	0.44	20.5 (8.9)	8.75
Hong Kong[+]	947	—	—	—	—	—	—	—	—	947	0.40	17.2 (7.0)	6.63
Italy	1,000	2	0.06	15.0 (8.9)	0.97	—	—	—	—	15	0.02	32.7 (9.1)	0.80

Table A.3 Median hourly cost and median weekly cost to parents in U.S. dollars for services in extraparental care/education settings (continued)

Country/ Territory	N	Own Home (Nonparent)				Other Home				Organized Facility			
		No. Using	Median Cost Per Hr	Mean Hr Used Per Wk (SD)	Median Cost Per Wk	No. Using	Median Cost Per Hr	Mean Hr Used Per Wk (SD)	Median Cost Per Wk	No. Using	Median Cost Per Hr	Mean Hr Used Per Wk (SD)	Median Cost Per Wk
Nigeria[+]	1,295	214	0.05	41.4 (8.9)	1.79	32	0.04	37.4 (11.5)	2.04	80	0.03	23.8 (5.5)	0.51
Portugal	—	—	—	—	—	—	—	—	—	—	—	—	—
Spain	480	—	—	—	—	2	0.55	28.8 (5.3)	15.89	212	0.30	29.6 (8.9)	7.77
Thailand	2,466	33	0.08	73.6 (42.0)	4.47	29	0.05	61.4 (47.9)	1.95	277	0.01	38.1 (6.7)	0.58
United States	432	20	1.50	21.3 (17.2)	25.00	53	1.11	28.5 (14.7)	30.00	114	1.61	24.4 (16.3)	36.00

Note. The symbol [+] indicates that weighted data were used for analysis. Dashes indicate that no information was available.

Table A.4 Mean and standard deviation of variables used for regression analysis on hours of use of early childhood services

Country/ Territory	n^a	Hr Per Week (SD)	Urban/ Rural[b] (SD)	No. of Children (SD)	Educ., Father (SD)	Educ., Mother (SD)	Hr Away, Mother (SD)	Hr Away, Father (SD)
							Variables	
Belgium (Fr.)	226	36.8 (11.8)	2.2 (.8)	2.2 (.8)	13.1 (3.0)	13.2 (3.6)	32.5 (15.3)	48.4 (14.4)
China (PRC)[+]	8,814	33.0 (32.6)	.3 (.5)	1.5 (.9)	7.4 (3.9)	8.4 (3.3)	51.8 (24.6)	63.5 (32.8)
Finland	385	29.1 (17.2)	.6 (.5)	2.3 (1.1)	12.9 (3.3)	12.3 (3.3)	33.4 (16.6)	47.5 (16.5)
Germany (FRG)	178	22.0 (16.4)	.7 (.4)	1.8 (.7)	10.3 (2.3)	10.9 (3.1)	17.2 (16.7)	50.7 (12.4)
Hong Kong[+]	866	17.2 (7.0)	— —	— —	9.1 (2.7)	10.0 (3.1)	— —	— —
Italy	158	36.8 (10.8)	.7 (.5)	1.9 (1.0)	10.7 (4.5)	11.3 (4.8)	30.7 (12.2)	47.5 (12.5)
Nigeria[+]	242	34.6 (12.9)	.2 (.4)	— —	9.0 (4.9)	11.0 (4.3)	42.2 (16.6)	54.8 (15.6)
Portugal	341	45.2 (20.6)	— —	1.9 (1.1)	6.3 (3.4)	6.2 (3.4)	43.9 (20.3)	62.9 (26.0)
Spain	191	36.6 (18.4)	.7 (.5)	1.9 (1.0)	13.0 (4.8)	13.4 (5.0)	31.3 (16.5)	50.4 (16.7)
Thailand	986	36.6 (34.5)	.2 (.4)	2.4 (1.4)	5.2 (3.2)	5.8 (3.6)	42.6 (30.0)	73.0 (39.1)
United States	209	21.5 (18.5)	.9 (.2)	2.6 (1.3)	13.6 (3.3)	14.1 (3.7)	26.5 (16.4)	52.7 (22.0)

Note. The symbol [+] indicates that weighted data were used for analysis.

[a]The regression analysis deleted cases with missing values (listwise).

[b]Rural is coded as 0 and urban is coded as 1, except for Belgium, for which rural area is coded as 1, middle (combined urban and rural) area as 2, and urban area as 3.

Table A.5 Correlation between the variables used for regression analysis on hours of use of early childhood services

Country/Territory	n^a	Hr/Wk & Urban/Rural[b]	Hr/Wk & No. of Children	Hr/Wk & Educ, Mother	Hr/Wk & Educ, Father	Hr/Wk & Hr Away, Mother	Hr/Wk & Hr Away, Father	Urban/Rural & No. of Children	Urban/Rural & Educ, Mother	Urban/Rural & Educ, Father	Urban/Rural & Hr Away, Mother	Urban/Rural & Hr Away, Father
Belgium (Fr.)	226	-.072	-.267*	-.094	-.098	.378*	.076	-.133*	.024	.032	.010	.084
China (PRC)[+]	8,814	.351*	-.359*	.332*	.254*	.434*	.229*	-.309*	.403*	.318*	.155*	-.020*
Finland	385	.172*	-.339*	.077	.085*	.786*	.058	-.173*	.120*	.260*	.110*	.012*
Germany (FRG)	178	.026	-.264*	.116	.008	.483*	-.012	-.162*	-.005	.012	.038	-.148*
Hong Kong[+]	866	—	—	.069*	.081*	—	—	—	—	—	—	—
Italy	158	-.034	-.106	.018	-.057	.387*	.062	-.045	.104	.149*	.011	.119
Nigeria[+]	242	-.164*	—	-.016	.374*	.273*	.245*	—	.140*	.037	.195*	.065*
Portugal	341	—	-.206*	.059	.083	.649*	.082	—	—	—	—	—
Spain	191	.131*	-.036	.095	-.001	.639*	.178*	.037	.295*	.175*	.204*	.006
Thailand	986	.003	-.151*	.101*	.099*	.829*	.248*	-.101*	.326*	.391*	.028	-.088
United States	209	-.025	-.219*	.098	-.023	.653*	.068	.026	.089	.053	-.041	-.026

Table A.5 Correlation between the variables used for regression analysis on hours of use of early childhood services (continued)

Country/Territory	n^a	No. of Children & Educ. Mother[b]	No. of Children & Educ. Father	No. of Children & Hr Away, Mother	No. of Children & Hr Away, Father	Educ., Mother & Educ., Father	Educ., Mother & Hr Away, Mother	Educ., Mother & Hr Away, Father	Educ., Father & Hr Away, Mother	Educ., Father & Hr Away, Father	Hr Away, Mother & Hr Away, Father
Belgium (Fr.)	226	.108	.165*	-.179*	.052	.615*	-.073	-.120 *	-.063	-.055	.151*
China (PRC)+	8,814	-.447*	-.322*	-.112*	-.035*	.521*	.143*	.052*	.085*	.044*	.340*
Finland	385	-.090*	-.075	-.347*	-.024	.573*	.047	-.006	.021	.051	.095*
Germany (FRG)	178	-.006	.045	-.284*	.071	.465*	.059	-.098	-.060	-.038	-.202*
Hong Kong+	866	—	—	—	—	.720*	—	—	—	—	—
Italy	158	-.151*	-.127	.039	-.050	.737*	.093	-.009	-.029	-.013	.065
Nigeria+	242	—	—	—	—	.433*	.071*	-.044	.015	.024	.379*
Portugal	341	-.259*	-.198*	-.195*	.048	.718*	-.066	-.129*	-.077	-.163*	.164*
Spain	191	-.080	-.038	-.054	.025	.605*	.083	.036	-.007	-.093	.076
Thailand	986	-.205*	-.192*	-.107*	-.059*	.705*	.084*	-.071*	.091*	-.059*	.279*
United States	209	-.149*	-.188*	-.058	.063	.670*	-.050	.037	-.185*	.137*	-.057

Note. The symbol $^+$ means that weighted data were used for analysis.

[a]Regression analysis deleted cases with missing data (listwise).

[b]Rural is coded as 0 and urban is coded as 1, except for Belgium, for which rural area is coded as 1, middle area as 2, and urban area as 3.

*p ≤ .05

Appendix B:
Parent/Guardian Interview

Part A: Child's Present Caretaking Experiences

A1. Does anyone other than you [or your (spouse/partner)] take care of (*child's name*) at any time during a typical week?

☐ 1. Yes

☐ 5. No → Go to A100

↓

A1a. About how many total hours during a typical week is (*child's name*) cared for by someone other than yourself [or your (spouse/partner)]?

_____ Hours per Week

A2. *Interviewer Checkpoint*

☐ 1. Child is in child care less than 2 hours per week. → Go to A100

☐ 2. All others

↓

A3. Could you tell me the name of the place or individual that takes care of (*child's name*) for the *longest* period of time during a typical week?

_____
Name of Caregiver

A3a. About how many hours a week is (*child's name*) cared for by (*caregiver*)?

_____ Number of Hours

A3b. *Interviewer Checkpoint*

☐ 1. Child is cared for at this setting 2 hours or more per week. → Go to A4

☐ 2. All others → Go to A99

↓

A4. *Interviewer Checkpoint*

☐ 1. Caregiver named in A3 is an individual.

☐ 2. Caregiver named in A3 is a facility.

↓

1

IEA/PP/31
Dec. 1987

PARENT/GUARDIAN INTERVIEW

(United States Version)

IEA Preprimary Project

Respondent ID #: _____

Date of Interview: _____

Length of Interview: _____

IWER Instruction: Probe for all starting and ending times for each day mentioned. If it is impossible for the R to give you those times, obtain the total number of hours per day during a typical week, and enter that total in the blank provided.

A9. Day of Week	A10. Hours of Day	Total Hours
a. Monday	_____ A.M. P.M. to _____ A.M. P.M.	_____
b. Tuesday	_____ A.M. P.M. to _____ A.M. P.M.	_____
c. Wednesday	_____ A.M. P.M. to _____ A.M. P.M.	_____
d. Thursday	_____ A.M. P.M. to _____ A.M. P.M.	_____
e. Friday	_____ A.M. P.M. to _____ A.M. P.M.	_____
f. Saturday	_____ A.M. P.M. to _____ A.M. P.M.	_____
g. Sunday	_____ A.M. P.M. to _____ A.M. P.M.	_____

A11. Do you pay money for (*child's name*)'s care that is provided by (*caregiver*)?

1. Yes ↓　　5. No → Go to A12

A11a. How much money do you pay for this care? Please do not include any extra money you may pay for meals.

_____ per | Hour | Day | Week | Month |

Amount　　Monetary Unit

A12. Do you provide goods or help (*caregiver*) in any way to help pay for (*child's name*)'s care?

1. Yes ↓　　5. No → Go to A13

A12a. What type of goods or service do you provide?

_____

A12b. What do you estimate to be the value of the goods or services you provide?

_____ per | Day | Week | Month |

Amount　　Monetary Unit

3

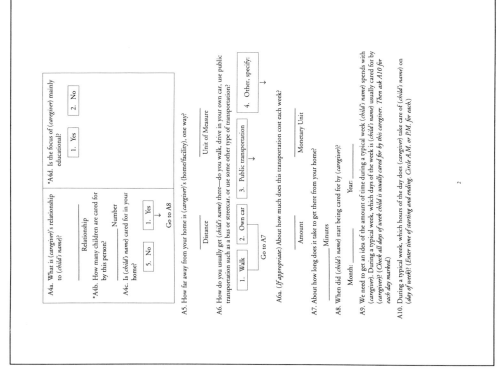

A4a. What is (*caregiver*)'s relationship to (*child's name*)?

_____ Relationship

*A4d. Is the focus of (*caregiver*) mainly educational?
1. Yes　2. No

*A4b. How many children are cared for by this person?
_____ Number

A4c. Is (*child's name*) cared for in your home?
5. No　1. Yes ↓
Go to A8

A5. How far away from your home is (*caregiver*)'s (home/facility), one way?

_____ Distance　　_____ Unit of Measure

A6. How do you usually get (*child's name*) there—do you walk, drive in your own car, use public transportation such as a bus or streetcar, or use some other type of transportation?

1. Walk　2. Own car　3. Public transportation ↓　4. Other, specify: →
Go to A7

A6a. (*If appropriate*) About how much does this transportation cost each week?

_____ Amount　　_____ Monetary Unit

A7. About how long does it take to get there from your home?

_____ Minutes

A8. When did (*child's name*) start being cared for by (*caregiver*)?
Month: _____　Year: _____

A9. We need to get an idea of the amount of time during a typical week (*child's name*) spends with (*caregiver*). During a typical week, which days of the week is (*child's name*) usually cared for by (*caregiver*)? (*Check all days of week child is usually cared for by this caregiver. Then ask A10 for each day marked.*)

A10. During a typical week, which hours of the day does (*caregiver*) take care of (*child's name*) on (*day of week*)? (*Enter time of starting and ending. Circle A.M. or P.M. for each.*)

2

A15a. (*If more than one reason:*) Which of those reasons is the most important?

IWER Instruction: Code the most important reason into one of the categories below. Probe if you don't have enough information to categorize.

10. Reasons Relating to Parent/Guardian
___ 11. Work/job
___ 12. Education/training of parent
___ 13. Personal/social obligations of parent
___ 14. Other reason relating to parent/guardian, specify: _____

20. Reasons Relating to Child
___ 21. Education of child
___ 22. Social/emotional needs of child
___ 23. Health of child
___ 24. Other reason relating to child, specify: _____

30. Other, specify: _____

A16. Do you have any problems with (*caregiver*)?
[1. Yes] → [5. No → Go to A17]

A16a. What problems do you have? (*Allow for three problems.*)
1. _____
2. _____
3. _____

IWER Instruction: As before, code below after obtaining response. For this question, only three responses are allowed and may be coded below.

10. Inconvenience
___ 11. Location
___ 12. Hours
___ 13. Sick child care not provided
___ 14. Other inconvenience, specify: _____

20. Characteristics Relating to CG
___ 21. CG's personal characteristics, e.g., personality, personal habits, language, hygiene, etc.
___ 22. Unreliability of CG
___ 23. Qualifications of CG
___ 24. Child does not like CG
___ 25. Other problem with characteristics of CG, specify: _____

5

A13. Does (*caregiver*) receive payment from a government agency, such as social services, that helps pay for (*child's name*)'s care?
[1. Yes] [5. No → Go to A14]

A13a. From which agency? _____

A13b. Do you have any idea how much this payment is?
[1. Yes] [5. No → Go to A14]

A13c. About how much is it?
Amount _____ Monetary Unit _____ per [Day] [Week] [Month]

A14. Are meals or snacks provided for your child by (*caregiver*)?
[1. Yes] [5. No → Go to A15]

A14a. During a typical day, which meals or snacks are provided by (*caregiver*)? Please do not include meals or snacks that (*child's name*) brings with (him/her) from home. (*Check all that apply*)
| A. Morning meal | B. A.M. snack | C. Midday meal | D. P.M. snack | E. Evening meal | F. Bedtime snack |

A14b. Do you pay extra for these meals or snacks?
[1. Yes] [5. No → Go to A15]

A14c. How much extra do you pay?
Amount _____ Monetary Unit _____ per [Day] [Week] [Month]

A15. Parents have others care for their children for various reasons. Please tell me your reasons for having (*caregiver*) provide care for (*child's name*).

4

A20a. What is (*caregiver*)'s relationship to (*child's name*)?

_____
Relationship

*A20b. How many children are cared for by this person?

_____
Number

A20c. Is (*child's name*) cared for in your home?

| 5. No | 1. Yes |
↓
Go to A24

*A20d. Is the focus of (*caregiver*) mainly educational?

| 1. Yes | 2. No |

A21. How far away from your home is (*caregiver*)'s (home/facility), one way?

_____   _____
Distance   Unit of Measure

A22. How do you usually get (*child's name*) there—do you walk, drive in your own car, use public transportation such as a bus or streetcar, or use some other type of transportation?

| 1. Walk | 2. Own car | 3. Public transportation | 4. Other, specify: |
↓
Go to A23

A22a. (*If appropriate.*) About how much does this transportation cost each week?

_____   _____
Amount   Monetary Unit

A23. About how long does it take to get there from your home?

_____
Minutes

A24. When did (*child's name*) start being cared for by (*caregiver*)?

Month: _____   Year: _____

A25. We need to get an idea of the amount of time during a typical week (*child's name*) spends with (*caregiver*). During a typical week, which days of the week is (*child's name*) usually cared for by (*caregiver*)? (*Check all days of week child is usually cared for by this caregiver. Then ask A26 for each day marked.*)

A26. During a typical week, which hours of the day does (*caregiver*) take care of (*child's name*) on (*day of week*)? (*Enter time of starting and ending. Circle A.M. or P.M. for each.*)

7

---

30. Characteristics of Setting

_____ 31. Philosophy of child care
_____ 32. Religious/ethnic orientation
_____ 33. Problem with facility and/or equipment
_____ 34. Nutrition/sanitation/safety conditions
_____ 35. Negative atmosphere
_____ 36. Problem with other children
_____ 37. High CG turnover rate
_____ 38. Other problem relating to characteristics of setting, specify:

_____ 40. Cost, i.e., too expensive
_____ 50. Other, specify: _____

*A17. On the whole, how satisfied are you with the care your child receives from (*name of caregiver*)—very satisfied, somewhat satisfied, not very satisfied, or not at all satisfied?

| 1. Very satisfied | 2. Somewhat satisfied | 3. Not very satisfied | 4. Not at all satisfied |

A18. Is there another person or place that provides care for your child during a typical week?

| 1. Yes | 5. No |
↓   → Go to A82

A19. Could you tell me the name of the place or individual taking care of (*child's name*) for the *next longest* period of time during a typical week?

_____
Name of Caregiver

A19a. About how many hours a week is (*child's name*) cared for by (*caregiver*)?

_____
Number of Hours

A19b. *Interviewer Checkpoint*

☐ 1. Child is cared for at this setting 2 hours or more per week. → Go to A20
☐ 2. All others → Go to A82

A20. *Interviewer Checkpoint*

☐ 1. Caregiver named in A19 is an individual. →

☐ 2. Caregiver named in A19 is a facility. →

6

A29. Does (*caregiver*) receive payment from a government agency, such as social services, that helps pay for (*child's name*)'s care?

[1. Yes]   [5. No] → Go to A30
↓

A29a. From which agency?

_____

A29b. Do you have any idea how much this payment is?

[1. Yes]   [5. No] → Go to A30
↓

A29c. About how much is it?

_____   _____   per [Day] [Week] [Month]
Amount   Monetary Unit

A30. Are meals or snacks provided for your child by (*caregiver*)?

[1. Yes]   [5. No] → Go to A31
↓

A30a. During a typical day, which meals or snacks are provided by (*caregiver*)? Please do not include meals or snacks that (*child's name*) brings with (him/her) from home. (*Check all that apply*)

[A. Morning meal] [B. A.M. snack] [C. Midday meal] [D. P.M. snack] [E. Evening meal] [F. Bedtime snack]

A30b. Do you pay extra for these meals or snacks?

[1. Yes]   [5. No] → Go to A31
↓

A30c. How much extra do you pay?

_____   _____   Per [Day] [Week] [Month]
Amount   Monetary Unit

A31. Parents have others care for their children for various reasons. Please tell me your reasons for having (*caregiver*) provide care for (*child's name*).

_____

9

IWER Instruction: Probe for all starting and ending times for each day mentioned. If it is impossible for the R to give you those times, obtain the total number of hours per day during a typical week, and enter that total in the blank provided.

A25. Day of Week	A26. Hours of Day		Total Hours
a. Monday	_____ A.M. P.M. to	_____ A.M. P.M.	_____
b. Tuesday	_____ A.M. P.M. to	_____ A.M. P.M.	_____
c. Wednesday	_____ A.M. P.M. to	_____ A.M. P.M.	_____
d. Thursday	_____ A.M. P.M. to	_____ A.M. P.M.	_____
e. Friday	_____ A.M. P.M. to	_____ A.M. P.M.	_____
f. Saturday	_____ A.M. P.M. to	_____ A.M. P.M.	_____
g. Sunday	_____ A.M. P.M. to	_____ A.M. P.M.	_____

A27. Do you pay money for (*child's name*)'s care that is provided by (*caregiver*)?

[1. Yes]   [5. No] → Go to A28
↓

A27a. How much money do you pay for this care? Please do not include any extra money you may pay for meals.

_____   _____   per [Hour] [Day] [Week] [Month]
Amount   Monetary Unit

A28. Do you provide goods or help (*caregiver*) in any way to help pay for (*child's name*)'s care?

[1. Yes]   [5. No] → Go to A29
↓

A28a. What type of goods or service do you provide?

_____

A28b. What do you estimate to be the value of the goods or services you provide?

_____   _____   per [Day] [Week] [Month]
Amount   Monetary Unit

8

30. Characteristics of Setting

_____ 31. Philosophy of child care

_____ 32. Religious/ethnic orientation

_____ 33. Problem with facility and/or equipment

_____ 34. Nutrition/sanitation/safety conditions

_____ 35. Negative atmosphere

_____ 36. Problem with other children

_____ 37. High CG turnover rate

_____ 38. Other problem relating to characteristics of setting, specify:

_____ 40. Cost, i.e., too expensive

_____ 50. Other, specify:

*A33. On the whole, how satisfied are you with the care your child receives from (*name of caregiver*)—very satisfied, somewhat satisfied, not very satisfied, or not at all satisfied?

| 1. Very satisfied | 2. Somewhat satisfied | 3. Not very satisfied | 4. Not at all satisfied |

A34. Is there another person or place that provides care for your child during a typical week?

1. Yes   5. No → Go to A82

A35. Could you tell me the name of the place or individual taking care of (*child's name*) for the next *longest* period of time during a typical week?

Name of Caregiver

A35a. About how many hours a week is (*child's name*) cared for by (*caregiver*)?

Number of Hours

A35b. *Interviewer Checkpoint*

☐ 1. Child is cared for at this setting 2 hours or more per week. → Go to A36

☐ 2. All others → Go to A82

A36. *Interviewer Checkpoint*

☐ 1. Caregiver named in A35 is an individual.   ☐ 2. Caregiver named in A35 is a facility.

11

A31a. (*If more than one reason.*) Which of those reasons is the most important?

IWER Instruction: Code the most important reason into one of the categories below. Probe if you don't have enough information to categorize.

10. Reasons Relating to Parent/Guardian

_____ 11. Work/job

_____ 12. Education/training of parent

_____ 13. Personal/social obligations of parent

_____ 14. Other reason relating to parent/guardian, specify:

20. Reasons Relating to Child

_____ 21. Education of child

_____ 22. Social/emotional needs of child

_____ 23. Health of child

_____ 24. Other reason relating to child, specify:

30. Other, specify:

A32. Do you have any problems with (*caregiver*)?

1. Yes   5. No → Go to A33

A32a. What problems do you have? (*allow for three problems*)

1.

2.

3.

IWER Instruction: As before, code below after obtaining response. For this question, only three responses are allowed and may be coded below.

10. Inconvenience

_____ 11. Location

_____ 12. Hours

_____ 13. Sick child care not provided

_____ 14. Other inconvenience, specify:

20. Characteristics Relating to CG

_____ 21. CG's personal characteristics, e.g., personality, personal habits, language, hygiene, etc.

_____ 22. Unreliability of CG

_____ 23. Qualifications of CG

_____ 24. Child does not like CG

_____ 25. Other problem with characteristics of CG, specify:

10

IWER Instruction: Probe for all starting and ending times for each day mentioned. If it is impossible for the R to give you those times, obtain the total number of hours per day during a typical week, and enter that total in the blank provided.

A41. Day of Week	A42. Hours of Day		Total Hours
a. Monday	___ A.M. P.M. to	___ A.M. P.M.	___
b. Tuesday	___ A.M. P.M. to	___ A.M. P.M.	___
c. Wednesday	___ A.M. P.M. to	___ A.M. P.M.	___
d. Thursday	___ A.M. P.M. to	___ A.M. P.M.	___
e. Friday	___ A.M. P.M. to	___ A.M. P.M.	___
f. Saturday	___ A.M. P.M. to	___ A.M. P.M.	___
g. Sunday	___ A.M. P.M. to	___ A.M. P.M.	___

A43. Do you pay money for (*child's name*)'s care that is provided by (*caregiver*)?

1. Yes →

5. No → Go to A44

A43a. How much money do you pay for this care? Please do not include any extra money you may pay for meals.

___ per [Hour] [Day] [Week] [Month]
Amount   Monetary Unit

A44. Do you provide goods or help (*caregiver*) in any way to help pay for (*child's name*)'s care?

1. Yes →

5. No → Go to A45

A44a. What type of goods or service do you provide?

_____

A44b. What do you estimate to be the value of the goods or services you provide?

___ per [Day] [Week] [Month]
Amount   Monetary Unit

13

A36a. What is (*caregiver*)'s relationship to (*child's name*)?

___ Relationship

*A36b. How many children are cared for by this person?

___ Number

A36c. Is (*child's name*) cared for in your home?

5. No

1. Yes → Go to A40

*A36d. Is the focus of (*caregiver*) mainly educational?

1. Yes   2. No

A37. How far away from your home is (*caregiver*)'s (home/facility), one way?

___ Distance   ___ Unit of Measure

A38. How do you usually get (*child's name*) there—do you walk, drive in your own car, use public transportation such as a bus or streetcar, or use some other type of transportation?

1. Walk   2. Own car   3. Public transportation   4. Other, specify: →
Go to A39

A38a. (*If appropriate.*) About how much does this transportation cost each week?

___ Amount   ___ Monetary Unit

A39. About how long does it take to get there from your home?

___ Minutes

A40. When did (*child's name*) start being cared for by (*caregiver*)?

Month: ___   Year: ___

A41. We need to get an idea of the amount of time during a typical week (*child's name*) spends with (*caregiver*). During a typical week, which days of the week is (*child's name*) usually cared for by (*caregiver*)? (*Check all days of the week child is usually cared for by this caregiver. Then ask A42 for each day marked.*)

A42. During a typical week, which hours of the day does (*caregiver*) take care of (*child's name*) on (*day of week*)? (*Enter time of starting and ending. Circle A.M. or P.M. for each.*)

12

A47a. (*If more than one reason:*) Which of those reasons is the most important?

IWER Instruction: Code the most important reason into one of the categories below. Probe if you don't have enough information to categorize.

10. Reasons Relating to Parent/Guardian
___ 11. Work/job
___ 12. Education/training of parent
___ 13. Personal/social obligations of parent
___ 14. Other reason relating to parent/guardian, specify:

20. Reasons Relating to Child
___ 21. Education of Child
___ 22. Social/emotional needs of child
___ 23. Health of child
___ 24. Other reason relating to child, specify:

30. Other, specify: _____

A48. Do you have any problems with (*caregiver*)?
1. Yes →
5. No → Go to A49

A48a. What problems do you have? (*Allow for three problems.*)
1.
2.
3.

IWER Instruction: As before, code below after obtaining response. For this question, only three responses are allowed and may be coded below.

10. Inconvenience
___ 11. Location
___ 12. Hours
___ 13. Sick child care not provided
___ 14. Other inconvenience, specify:

20. Characteristics Relating to CG
___ 21. CG's personal characteristics, e.g., personality, personal habits, language, hygiene, etc.
___ 22. Unreliability of CG
___ 23. Qualifications of CG
___ 24. Child does not like CG
___ 25. Other problem with characteristics of CG, specify:

15

A45. Does (*caregiver*) receive payment from a government agency, such as social services, that helps pay for (*child's name*)'s care?
1. Yes →
5. No → Go to A46

A45a. From which agency?

A45b. Do you have any idea how much this payment is?
1. Yes →
5. No → Go to A46

A45c. About how much is it?
___ Amount ___ Monetary Unit per [Day] [Week] [Month]

A46. Are meals or snacks provided for your child by (*caregiver*)?
1. Yes →
5. No → Go to A47

A46a. During a typical day, which meals or snacks are provided by (*caregiver*)? Please do not include meals or snacks that (*child's name*) brings with (him/her) from home. (*Check all that apply*)

A. Morning meal | B. A.M. snack | C. Midday meal | D. P.M. snack | E. Evening meal | F. Bedtime snack

A46b. Do you pay extra for these meals or snacks?
1. Yes →
5. No → Go to A47

A46c. How much extra do you pay?
___ Amount ___ Monetary Unit per [Day] [Week] [Month]

A47. Parents have others care for their children for various reasons. Please tell me your reasons for having (*caregiver*) provide care for (*child's name*).

14

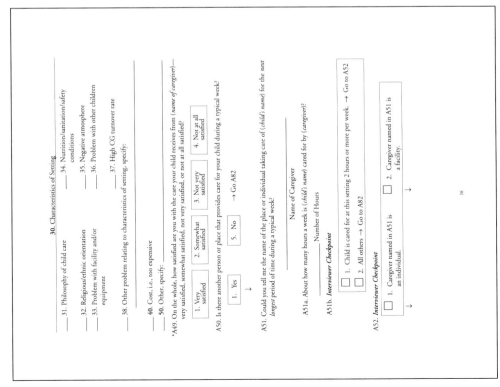

30. Characteristics of Setting

_____ 31. Philosophy of child care

_____ 32. Religious/ethnic orientation

_____ 33. Problem with facility and/or equipment

_____ 34. Nutrition/sanitation/safety conditions

_____ 35. Negative atmosphere

_____ 36. Problem with other children

_____ 37. High CG turnover rate

_____ 38. Other problem relating to characteristics of setting, specify:

_____ 40. Cost, i.e., too expensive

_____ 50. Other, specify:

*A49. On the whole, how satisfied are you with the care your child receives from (_name of caregiver_)—very satisfied, somewhat satisfied, not very satisfied, or not at all satisfied?

| 1. Very satisfied | 2. Somewhat satisfied | 3. Not very satisfied | 4. Not at all satisfied |

A50. Is there another person or place that provides care for your child during a typical week?

| 1. Yes | 5. No → Go to A82 |

A51. Could you tell me the name of the place or individual taking care of (_child's name_) for the _next longest_ period of time during a typical week?

_____
Name of Caregiver

A51a. About how many hours a week is (_child's name_) cared for by (_caregiver_)?

_____
Number of Hours

A51b. _Interviewer Checkpoint_

☐ 1. Child is cared for at this setting 2 hours or more per week. → Go to A52

☐ 2. All others → Go to A82

A52. _Interviewer Checkpoint_

☐ 1. Caregiver named in A51 is an individual. →

☐ 2. Caregiver named in A51 is a facility. →

A52a. What is (_caregiver_)'s relationship to (_child's name_)?

_____
Relationship

*A52b. How many children are cared for by this person?

_____
Number

A52c. Is (_child's name_) cared for in your home?

| 5. No | 1. Yes ↓ Go to A56 |

*A52d. Is the focus of (_caregiver_) mainly educational?

| 1. Yes | 2. No |

A53. How far away from your home is (_caregiver_)'s (home/facility), one way?

_____   _____
Distance   Unit of Measure

A54. How do you usually get (_child's name_) there—do you walk, drive in your own car, use public transportation such as a bus or streetcar, or use some other type of transportation?

| 1. Walk | 2. Own car | 3. Public transportation ↓ | 4. Other, specify: ↓ |

Go to A55

A54a. (_if appropriate_): About how much does this transportation cost each week?

_____   _____
Amount   Monetary Unit

A55. About how long does it take to get there from your home?

_____
Minutes

A56. When did (_child's name_) start being cared for by (_caregiver_)?

Month: _____   Year: _____

A57. We need to get an idea of the amount of time during a typical week (_child's name_) spends with (_caregiver_). During a typical week, which days of the week is (_child's name_) usually cared for by (_caregiver_)? (Check all days of week child is usually cared for by this caregiver. Then ask A58 for each day marked.)

A58. During a typical week, which hours of the day does (_caregiver_) take care of (_child's name_) on (_day of week_)? (Enter time of starting and ending. Circle A.M. or P.M. for each.)

A61. Does (*caregiver*) receive payment from a government agency, such as social services, that helps pay for (*child's name*)'s care?

1. Yes   5. No   → Go to A62

A61a. From which agency?

A61b. Do you have any idea how much this payment is?

1. Yes   5. No   → Go to A62

A61c. About how much is it?

_____   _____   per   Day   Week   Month
Amount   Monetary Unit

A62. Are meals or snacks provided for your child by (*caregiver*)?

1. Yes   5. No   → Go to A63

A62a. During a typical day, which meals or snacks are provided by (*caregiver*)? Please do not include meals or snacks that (*child's name*) brings with (him/her) from home. (*Check all that apply.*)

A. Morning meal   B. A.M. snack   C. Midday meal   D. P.M. snack   E. Evening meal   F. Bedtime snack

A62b. Do you pay extra for these meals or snacks?

1. Yes   5. No   → Go to A63

A62c. How much extra do you pay?

_____   _____   per   Day   Week   Month
Amount   Monetary Unit

A63. Parents have others care for their children for various reasons. Please tell me your reasons for having (*caregiver*) provide care for (*child's name*).

_____

19

IWER Instruction: Probe for the starting and ending times for each day mentioned. If it is impossible for the R to give you those times, obtain the total number of hours per day during a typical week, and enter that total in the blank provided.

A57. Day of Week	A58. Hours of Day	Total Hours
a. Monday	_____ A.M. P.M. to _____ A.M. P.M.	
b. Tuesday	_____ A.M. P.M. to _____ A.M. P.M.	
c. Wednesday	_____ A.M. P.M. to _____ A.M. P.M.	
d. Thursday	_____ A.M. P.M. to _____ A.M. P.M.	
e. Friday	_____ A.M. P.M. to _____ A.M. P.M.	
f. Saturday	_____ A.M. P.M. to _____ A.M. P.M.	
g. Sunday	_____ A.M. P.M. to _____ A.M. P.M.	

A59. Do you pay money for (*child's name*)'s care that is provided by (*caregiver*)?

1. Yes   5. No   → Go to A60

A59a. How much money do you pay for this care? Please do not include any extra money you may pay for meals.

_____   _____   per   Hour   Day   Week   Month
Amount   Monetary Unit

A60. Do you provide goods or help (*caregiver*) in any way to help pay for (*child's name*)'s care?

1. Yes   5. No   → Go to A61

A60a. What type of goods or service do you provide?

_____

A60b. What do you estimate to be the value of the goods or services you provide?

_____   _____   per   Day   Week   Month
Amount   Monetary Unit

18

A63a. (If more than one reason:) Which of those reasons is the most important?

IWER Instruction: Code the most important reason into one of the categories below. Probe if you don't have enough information to categorize.

10. Reasons Relating to Parent/Guardian
___ 11. Work/job
___ 12. Education/training of parent
___ 13. Personal/social obligations of parent
___ 14. Other reason relating to parent/guardian, specify: _____

20. Reasons Relating to Child
___ 21. Education of child
___ 22. Social/emotional needs of child
___ 23. Health of child
___ 24. Other reason relating to child, specify: _____

30. Other, specify: _____

A64. Do you have any problems with (caregiver)?

[1. Yes →]   [5. No → Go to A65]

A64a. What problems do you have? (Allow for three problems.)

1. _____
2. _____
3. _____

IWER Instruction: As before, code below after obtaining response. For this question, only three responses are allowed and may be coded below.

10. Inconvenience
___ 11. Location
___ 12. Hours
___ 13. Sick child care not provided
___ 14. Other inconvenience, specify: _____

20. Characteristics Relating to CG
___ 21. CG's personal characteristics, e.g., personality, personal habits, language, hygiene, etc.
___ 22. Unreliability of CG
___ 23. Qualifications of CG
___ 24. Child does not like CG
___ 25. Other problem with characteristics of CG, specify: _____

20

---

30. Characteristics of Setting
___ 31. Philosophy of child care
___ 32. Religious/ethnic orientation
___ 33. Problem with facility and/or equipment
___ 34. Nutrition/sanitation/safety conditions
___ 35. Negative atmosphere
___ 36. Problem with other children
___ 37. High CG turnover rate
___ 38. Other problem relating to characteristics of setting, specify: _____
___ 40. Cost, i.e., too expensive
___ 50. Other, specify: _____

*A65. On the whole, how satisfied are you with the care your child receives from (name of caregiver)— very satisfied, somewhat satisfied, not very satisfied, or not at all satisfied?

[1. Very satisfied]   [2. Somewhat satisfied]   [3. Not very satisfied]   [4. Not at all satisfied]

A66. Is there another person or place that provides care for your child during a typical week?

[1. Yes →]   [5. No → Go to A82]

A67. Could you tell me the name of the place or individual taking care of (child's name) for the next longest period of time during a typical week?

Name of Caregiver _____

A67a. About how many hours a week is (child's name) cared for by (caregiver)?

Number of Hours _____

A67b. Interviewer Checkpoint

[] 1. Child is cared for at this setting 2 hours or more per week. → Go to A68
[] 2. All others → Go to A82

A68. Interviewer Checkpoint

[] 1. Caregiver named in A67 is an individual →
[] 2. Caregiver named in A67 is a facility. →

21

IWER Instruction: Probe for the starting and ending times for each day mentioned. If it is impossible for the R to give you those times, obtain the total number of hours per day during a typical week, and enter in the blank provided.

A73. Day of Week	A74. Hours of Day		Total Hours
a. Monday	___ A.M. P.M. to	___ A.M. P.M.	___
b. Tuesday	___ A.M. P.M. to	___ A.M. P.M.	___
c. Wednesday	___ A.M. P.M. to	___ A.M. P.M.	___
d. Thursday	___ A.M. P.M. to	___ A.M. P.M.	___
e. Friday	___ A.M. P.M. to	___ A.M. P.M.	___
f. Saturday	___ A.M. P.M. to	___ A.M. P.M.	___
g. Sunday	___ A.M. P.M. to	___ A.M. P.M.	___

A75. Do you pay money for (*child's name*)'s care that is provided by (*caregiver*)?

1. Yes →   5. No → Go to A76

A75a. How much money do you pay for this care? Please do not include any extra money you may pay for meals.

___ ___ per [Hour] [Day] [Week] [Month]
Amount   Monetary Unit

A76. Do you provide goods or help (*caregiver*) in any way to help pay for (*child's name*)'s care?

1. Yes →   5. No → Go to A77

A76a. What type of goods or service do you provide?

___ →

A76b. What do you estimate to be the value of the goods or services you provide?

___ ___ per [Day] [Week] [Month]
Amount   Monetary Unit

23

A68a. What is (*caregiver*)'s relationship to (*child's name*)?

___ Relationship

*A68b. How many children are cared for by this person?

___ Number

A68c. Is (*child's name*) cared for in your home?

5. No →   1. Yes → Go to A72

*A68d. Is the focus of (*caregiver*) mainly educational?

1. Yes   2. No

A69. How far away from your home is (*caregiver*)'s (home/facility), one way?

___ Distance   ___ Unit of Measure

A70. How do you usually get (*child's name*) there—do you walk, drive in your own car, use public transportation such as a bus or streetcar, or use some other type of transportation?

1. Walk   2. Own car   3. Public transportation →   4. Other, specify: →
Go to A71

A70a. (*If appropriate*) About how much does this transportation cost each week?

___ Amount   ___ Monetary Unit

A71. About how long does it take to get there from your home?

___ Minutes

A72. When did (*child's name*) start being cared for by (*caregiver*)?

Month: ___   Year: ___

A73. We need to get an idea of the amount of time during a typical week (*child's name*) spends with (*caregiver*). During a typical week, which days of the week is (*child's name*) usually cared for by (*caregiver*)? (*Check all days of week child is usually cared for by this caregiver. Then ask A74 for each day marked.*)

A74. During a typical week, which hours of the day does (*caregiver*) take care of (*child's name*) on (*day of week*)? (*Enter time of starting and ending. Circle A.M. or P.M. for each.*)

22

A79a. (*If more than one reason.*) Which of those reasons is the most important?

IWER Instruction: Code The most important reason into one of the categories below. Probe if you don't have enough information to categorize.

10. Reasons Relating to Parent/Guardian
___ 11. Work/job
___ 12. Education/training of parent
___ 13. Personal/social obligations of parent
___ 14. Other reason relating to parent/guardian, specify:

20. Reasons Relating to Child
___ 21. Education of child
___ 22. Social/emotional needs of child
___ 23. Health of child
___ 24. Other reason relating to child, specify:

30. Other, specify:

A80. Do you have any problems with (*caregiver*)?
| 1. Yes | 5. No → Go to A81 |
→

A80a. What problems do you have? (*Allow for three problems.*)
1.
2.
3.

IWER Instruction: As before, code below after obtaining response. For this question, only three responses are allowed and may be coded below.

10. Inconvenience
___ 11. Location
___ 12. Hours
___ 13. Sick child care not provided
___ 14. Other inconvenience, specify:

20. Characteristics Relating to CG
___ 21. CG's personal characteristics, e.g., personality, personal habits, language, hygiene, etc.
___ 22. Unreliability of CG
___ 23. Qualifications of CG
___ 24. Child does not like CG
___ 25. Other problem with characteristics of CG, specify:

25

A77. Does (*caregiver*) receive payment from a government agency, such as social services, that helps pay for (*child's name*)'s care?
| 1. Yes | 5. No → Go to A78 |
→

A77a. From which agency?

A77b. Do you have any idea how much this payment is?
| 1. Yes | 5. No → Go to A78 |
→

A77c. About how much is it?
_____ _____ per [Day] [Week] [Month]
Amount Monetary Unit

A78. Are meals or snacks provided for your child by (*caregiver*)?
| 1. Yes | 5. No → Go to A79 |
→

A78a. During a typical day, which meals or snacks are provided by (*caregiver*)? Please do not include meals or snacks that (*child's name*) brings with (him/her) from home. (*Check all that apply.*)
[A. Morning meal] [B. A.M. snack] [C. Midday meal] [D. P.M. snack] [E. Evening meal] [F. Bedtime snack]

A78b. Do you pay extra for these meals or snacks?
| 1. Yes | 5. No → Go to A79 |
→

A78c. How much extra do you pay?
_____ _____ per [Day] [Week] [Month]
Amount Monetary Unit

A79. Parents have others care for their children for various reasons. Please tell me your reasons for having (*caregiver*) provide care for (*child's name*).

24

A83a. Are health services, such as hearing or vision screening or a nurse on site, available from (*caregiver*)?

  5. No →

  1. Yes → A83b. Has your child used any of these health services?

    1. Yes   5. No

A83c. Is special education, such as speech or physical therapy or assistance with learning difficulties, available?

  5. No →

  1. Yes → A83d. Has (*child's name*) used these special education services?

    1. Yes   5. No

A83e. Is transportation *to and from the setting* available from (*caregiver*)?

  5. No →

  1. Yes → A83f. Does your child use this transportation?

    1. Yes   5. No

A83g. Are any social services available from (*caregiver*)?

  5. No →

  1. Yes → A83h. Have you or your child used these social services?

    1. Yes   5. No

  Go to A84

A84. Now we are interested in contact you may have had with (*name of individual caregiver*/people who work at (*caregiver*)) about (*child's name*) during the past 3 months.

A84a. How often during the past 3 months have you had a *scheduled meeting* that was *requested by you*? Would you say daily, weekly, twice a month, once a month, less than once a month, or never?

  1. Daily | 2. Weekly | 3. Twice a month | 4. Once a month | 5. Less than once a month | 6. Never/no contact

A84b. How often during the past 3 months have you had a *scheduled meeting* that was *requested by the caregiver*? Would you say daily, weekly, twice a month, once a month, less than once a month, or never?

  1. Daily | 2. Weekly | 3. Twice a month | 4. Once a month | 5. Less than once a month | 6. Never/no contact

27

---

30. Characteristics of Setting

___ 31. Philosophy of child care

___ 32. Religious/ethnic orientation

___ 33. Problem with facility and/or equipment

___ 34. Nutrition/sanitation/safety conditions

___ 35. Negative atmosphere

___ 36. Problem with other children

___ 37. High CG turnover rate

___ 38. Other problem relating to characteristics of setting, specify:

___ 40. Cost, i.e., too expensive

*___ 50. Other, specify:

*A81. On the whole, how satisfied are you with the care your child receives from (*name of caregiver*)—very satisfied, somewhat satisfied, not very satisfied, or not at all satisfied?

  1. Very satisfied | 2. Somewhat satisfied | 3. Not very satisfied | 4. Not at all satisfied

A82. *Interviewer Checkpoint*

  □ 1. Child is not cared for outside the home. → Go to A99)

  □ 2. All others

  →

IWER Instruction: Questions A83–A98 need to be asked about the most organized, educational setting where the child goes, even if that is not the place where the child spends the most time during the week. If more than one setting is educational, ask A83–A98 about the setting where the child spends the most time. If there is only one setting, ask A83–A98 about that setting.

  Please determine which setting these questions should be asked about, and enter the name here:

  A82a. _____ Name of Child Care Setting

A82b. Now I would like to ask you a few more questions about (*name of caregiver*)?

First, does (*child's name*) like to go there?

  1. Yes | 3. Sometimes | 5. No

A83. I'm going to read you a list of special services that are sometimes provided by people or organizations who care for children. For each one, please tell me if the service is available to your child and, if so, whether you have used the service.

26

A85. *Interviewer Checkpoint*

☐ 1. Child is cared for by a baby sitter or in a family day care facility. → Go to A94

☐ 2. All others →

A86. Is (*caregiver*) run or sponsored by an educational institution?

1. Yes   5. No   → Go to A87

→

A86a. What is the name of the educational institution?

_____

Go to A94

A87. Is (*caregiver*) run or sponsored by a government agency?

1. Yes   5. No   → Go to A88

A87a. Which government agency?

_____

Go to A94

A88. Is (*caregiver*) run or sponsored by a religious group?

1. Yes   5. No   → Go to A89

A88a. What is the name of the religious group?

_____

Go to A94

A89. Is (*caregiver*) run or sponsored by a military institution?

1. Yes   5. No   → Go to A90

→

29

---

*A84c. How often during the past 3 months have you had an *informal, unscheduled meeting* either at the setting or somewhere else? Would you say daily, weekly, twice a month, once a month, less than once a month, or never?

| 1. Daily | 2. Weekly | 3. Twice a month | 4. Once a month | 5. Less than once a month | 6. Never/no contact |

A84d. How often during the past 3 months have you *talked* to the caregiver on the phone, *written a note* to (them/him/her), or *received a note* from (them/him/her)? Would you say daily, weekly, twice a month, once a month, less than once a month, or never?

| 1. Daily | 2. Weekly | 3. Twice a month | 4. Once a month | 5. Less than once a month | 6. Never/no contact |

A84e. How often during the past 3 months has there been a *group meeting* of any type, including business or social gatherings? Would you say daily, weekly, twice a month, once a month, less than once a month, or never?

| 1. Daily | 2. Weekly | 3. Twice a month | 4. Once a month | 5. Less than once a month | 6. Never/no contact |

A84f. How often during the past 3 months have you *assisted* (*caregiver*), for example, by helping with the children, going on a field trip, or helping with paperwork? Would you say daily, weekly, twice a month, once a month, less than once a month, or never?

| 1. Daily | 2. Weekly | 3. Twice a month | 4. Once a month | 5. Less than once a month | 6. Never/no contact |

A84g. Has there been any other type of contact with the caregiver during the past 3 months that I haven't asked you about?

1. Yes   5. No   → Go to A85
→

A84h. What kind of contact was that?

_____

_____

28

A94a. (*If more than one reason*.) Of those you've mentioned, that is the most important reason why (*child's name*) goes to this (person/place) rather than somewhere else?

IWER Instruction: Code the most important reason into one of the categories below. Probe if you don't have enough information to categorize.

10. Convenience
_____ 11. Location
_____ 12. Hours
_____ 13. Sick child care not provided

_____ 14. Other reason relating to
convenience, specify: _____

20. Positive Information About Setting
_____ 21. Personal knowledge of setting
_____ 22. Recommended or has good reputation
_____ 23. Other reason relating to positive
information, specify: _____

30. Characteristics of Setting
_____ 31. Physical attributes of setting
_____ 32. Group size or child-CG ratio
_____ 33. Other reasons relating to physical
characteristics, specify: _____

40. Nonphysical Characteristics of Setting
_____ 41. Philosophy of childrearing
_____ 42. Religious/ethnic orientation
_____ 43. Personal characteristics of CG

_____ 44. Preference for particular kind of setting
_____ 45. Preference for public/private setting
_____ 46. Parent involvement
_____ 47. Other reason relating to nonphysical
characteristics, specify: _____

50. Cost

60. No Other Alternative Available
_____ 61. No other arrangement available/only opening
_____ 62. Assigned by government agency

_____ 70. Other, specify: _____

A95. When you were choosing caregivers for your child, did you consider any arrangements other than the ones we have talked about?

| 1. Yes | 5. No | → Go to A96 |

→

31

A89a. What is the name of the military institution?

Go to A94

A90. Is (*caregiver*) run or sponsored by your (or your [spouse's/partner's]) employer?

| 1. Yes | 5. No | → Go to A91 |

Go to A94

A91. Is (*caregiver*) run or sponsored by some type of volunteer parent or neighborhood organization?

| 1. Yes | 5. No | → Go to A92 |

→

A91a. What is the name of the organization?

Go to A94

A92. Is (*caregiver*) run or sponsored by some private organization or foundation?

| 1. Yes | 5. No | → Go to A93 |

→

A92a. What is the name of the group?

Go to A94

A93. Is (*caregiver*) run or sponsored by some other organization or group that I haven't asked you about?

| 1. Yes | 5. No | → Go to A94 |

→

A93a. What is the name of that group?

Go to A94

A94. Why did you choose this particular (person/place) to provide care for your child instead of a different (person/place)?

_____

30

A95a. What other types of arrangements did you consider?

_____

A95b. (*If more than one arrangement considered.*) Which one of these alternatives did you consider most seriously?

_____

IWER Instruction: Record R's answer in the space above, then mark the category below that best matches the response. Probe until you have enough information to categorize.

10. Care in Child's Home by Individual	20. Care in Another Home by Individual
___ 11. By parent/guardian	___ 21. By relative
___ 12. By other relative	___ 22. By nonrelative
___ 13. By nonrelative	

30. Care in Organized Facility
___ 31. Primarily child care facility
___ 32. Primarily educational
___ 40. Other, specify: _____

A96. What plans have you made for (*child's name*)'s care when (he/she) is supposed to be cared for at (*primary caregiver*), but (*child's name*) is ill?

_____

_____

A96a. (*If more than one plan.*) Which one of these alternatives do you use most often?

_____

IWER Instruction: Record R's answer in the space above, then mark the category below that best matches the response. Probe until you have enough information to categorize.

20. Child Stays Home	30. Child in Another Home
___ 21. With parent/guardian	___ 31. With relative
___ 22. With other relative	___ 32. With nonrelative
___ 23. With nonrelative	

___ 40. Child goes to another organized facility
___ 50. Parent/guardian takes child to work/school with them
___ 60. Child is left alone at home
___ 70. No plan
___ 80. Other, specify: _____

A97. What about when a short-term emergency comes up (for the caregiver/at the center) or when the person who takes care of (*child's name*) is ill—what plans have you made for (*child's name*)'s care?

_____

A97a. (*If more than one plan.*) Which one of these alternatives do you use most often?

_____

IWER Instruction: Record R's answer in the space above, then mark the category below that best matches the response. Probe until you have enough information to categorize.

20. Child Stays Home	30. Child in Another Home
___ 21. With parent/guardian	___ 31. With relative
___ 22. With other relative	___ 32. With nonrelative
___ 23. With nonrelative	

___ 40. Child goes to another organized facility
___ 50. Parent/guardian takes child to work/school with them
___ 60. Child is left alone at home
___ 70. No plan
___ 80. Other, specify: _____

A98. What plans have you made for (*child's name*)'s care on holidays (and other times when the center is not open)?

_____

A98a. (*If more than one plan.*) Which one of these alternatives do you use most often?

_____

Part B: Daily Routine of Child

Now I'd like to ask some questions that will give us a picture of (*child's name*) typical weekday. Think about yesterday (the last working day).

Was (*child's name*) asleep at midnight?

(*If yes*) What time did (*child's name*) wake up?

(*If no*) What was (he/she) doing at midnight?

Where was (*child's name*) at the time? And who was taking care of (him/her)? How many other adults were present? How many other children?

And what did (*child's name*) do after that?

Record answers on the worksheet on next page. For the person who was taking care of the child at each point, obtain the relationship to the child and write that in. (If person is not related to child, write in a description, such as friend, teacher, etc.) If both parents/guardians could be considered the "main" caregiver, write in "both parents." Probe for transitions from one place to another if the transition is not mentioned. For example, if the child is at the grandmother's and then goes to a day care center, but the transition (who took the child and how long it took) isn't mentioned, probe for that information.

Continue questioning to obtain information about the child's whole day. If mealtimes are not mentioned, ask specifically about them using questions B1–B3.

IWER Instruction: Record R's answer in the space above, then mark the category below that best matches the response. Probe until you have enough information to categorize.

20. Child Stays Home

___ 21. With parent/guardian

___ 22. With other relative

___ 23. With nonrelative

30. Child in Another Home

___ 31. With relative

___ 32. With nonrelative

___ 40. Child goes to another organized facility

___ 50. Parent/guardian takes child to work/school with them

___ 60. Child is left alone at home

___ 70. No plan

___ 80. Other, specify:

A99. Interviewer Checkpoint

See A1a

[ ] 1. Child is in some type of child care situation (in home or outside the home) *more than 10 hours a week.* → Go to Part B

[ ] 2. All others

↓

A100. Why did you decide to care for your child yourself (most of the time)?

A100a. (*If more than one reason mentioned.*) Which of those reasons was the most important?

IWER Instruction: Record R's answer in the space above, then mark the category below that best matches the response. Probe until you have enough information to categorize.

10. Reasons Relating to Parent/Guardian

___ 11. Personal/emotional

___ 12. Wants to teach child himself/herself

___ 13. Other reasons relating to P/G, specify:

20. Reasons Relating to Child

___ 21. Personal/emotional

___ 22. Physical/developmental needs

___ 23. Other reasons relating to child, specify:

30. Reasons Relating to Available Care Arrangements

___ 31. Problems with physical aspects of facility

___ 32. Problems with nonphysical aspects of facility

___ 33. Other problems with available facilities, specify:

___ 40. Other, specify:

Daily Routine Chart

I.D. Number: _____

		A.M.												P.M.											
		12:00 1:00	1:00 2:00	2:00 3:00	3:00 4:00	4:00 5:00	5:00 6:00	6:00 7:00	7:00 8:00	8:00 9:00	9:00 10:00	10:00 11:00	11:00 12:00	12:00 1:00	1:00 2:00	2:00 3:00	3:00 4:00	4:00 5:00	5:00 6:00	6:00 7:00	7:00 8:00	8:00 9:00	9:00 10:00	10:00 11:00	11:00 12:00
Where is the child? Indicate time with a line.	At home																								
	Home of relatives																								
	Home of neighbors/friend																								
	Family day care home																								
	Day care setting/preschool																								
	Working place of mother/father																								
	Public park/playground/street																								
	Shops/stores/public buildings																								
	Transition/on the road																								
Who is the main caretaker? Indicate time with a line.	Mother																								
	Father																								
	Both parents																								
	Sibling																								
	Grandparent																								
	Other relative																								
	Friend/neighbor																								
	Day care mother/nurse/babysitter/ bus driver/maid																								
	Teacher																								
	Nobody																								
How many others are present?*	Other adults/adolescents																								
	Other children																								
	Meal times																								

*Estimate if necessary.

Daily Activities Worksheet

Time Span	Activity & Location	Main Caregiver(s)	# Other Adults Present	# Other Children Present
12:00 a.m.–				

37

Daily Activities Worksheet

Time Span	Activity & Location	Main Caregiver(s)	# Other Adults Present	# Other Children Present
12:00 a.m.–				

38

Interviewer Checkpoint

☐ 1. Mealtimes were recorded on the previous page → Go to Part C

☐ 2. All others

→

B1. What time did (*child's name*) have (his/her) morning meal? (*circle A.M. or P.M.*)

_____ A.M.   P.M.

B1a. And when was (his/her) morning meal over?

_____ A.M.   P.M.

B1b. Where was (*child's name*) when (he/she) had (his/her) morning meal?

_____ Location

B1c. Who was taking care of (him/her) at the time?

_____ Relationship

B1d. How many other adults were present?

_____ Number of adults

B1e. How many other children were present?

_____ Number of children

B2. What time did (*child's name*) have (his/her) midday meal? (*circle A.M. or P.M.*)

_____ A.M.   P.M.

B2a. And when was (his/her) midday meal over?

_____ A.M.   P.M.

B2b. Where was (*child's name*) when (he/she) had (his/her) midday meal?

_____ Location

B2c. Who was taking care of (him/her) at the time?

_____ Relationship

B2d. How many other adults were present?

_____ Number of adults

B2e. How many other children were present?

_____ Number of children

B3. What time did (*child's name*) have (his/her) evening meal? (*circle A.M. or P.M.*)

_____ A.M.   P.M.

B3a. And when was (his/her) evening meal over?

_____ A.M.   P.M.

B3b. Where was (*child's name*) when (he/she) had (his/her) evening meal?

_____ Location

B3c. Who was taking care of (him/her) at the time?

_____ Relationship

B3d. How many other adults were present?

_____ Number of adults

B3e. How many other children were present?

_____ Number of children

Part C: Household Description

C1. Now I need to list the people who live here. Please include people who usually live here but may be away temporarily, such as people who are in school, travelling, in the hospital, etc. Include any boarders or roomers who may live with you only if they have contact with (*child's name*).

First, let me write down (*child's name*) and (his/her) age. Next, how old are you?

Now, I need the age, sex and relationship to (*child's name*) of the other people who live here.

	(a) Relationship to Child	(b) Sex	(c) Age
1. Child			
2. Informant			
3.			
4.			
5.			
6.			
7.			
8.			
9.			
10.			

C1a. So, there are (*number of occupants from listing*) who live here. Is that right?

IWER Instruction: If R says that is right, proceed with the interview; if not, review listing and pick up any missing people.

*C2. Do you rent or own your home?

1. Own	2. Live in someone else's home	3. Housing provided by employer	4. Rent →
↓	↓	↓	

*C2a. Do you rent from a private individual or firm, or is this public housing?

1. Private	2. Public

C3. How many rooms are there in your home, not counting the bathroom, the utility room, or any other rooms which are not finished and usable?

_____ Number of rooms

41

C4. Do you have your own private kitchen?

1. Yes	5. No

C5. Do you have a source of heat where you live?

1. Yes	5. No → Go to C6
↓	

C5a. What type of heat is that?

_____

C6. Do you have a source of lights where you live?

1. Yes	5. No → Go to C7
↓	

C6a. What type of lighting is that?

_____

C7. Do you have running water?

1. Yes	5. No

C8. Do you have an indoor toilet?

1. Yes	5. No

C9. Do you have a bathtub or shower?

1. Yes	5. No

C10. Do you have some type of arrangement for helping to cool your home?

1. Yes	5. No → Go to C11

C10a. What type of arrangement is that?

_____

*C11. I am going to read a list of items. For each one I read, please let me know if you have that particular item. Do you have an automobile that is in working condition?

42

*C15. Now I'm going to ask a few more questions about (*child's name*). Would you say (*child's name*)'s general health is excellent, good, fair, or poor?

| 1. Excellent | 2. Good | 3. Fair | 4. Poor |

Go to C17

*C15a. What type of health problem does (*child's name*) have? _____

C16. Has (*child's name*)'s health influenced (your choice of care arrangement for [him/her]/your decision to care for [him/her] yourself)?

| 1. Yes | 5. No | → Go to C17 |

↓

C16a. In what way? _____

*C17. I am going to read you a list of common health problems for children. Please indicate how often each one has been a problem for (*child's name*) during the past 6 months.

Common Health Problems	Often (1)	Sometimes (2)	Rarely (3)	Never (4)
*C17a. First, headaches. How often have headaches been a problem for (*child's name*) during the past 6 months—often, sometimes, rarely, or never?				
*C17b. How often have stomachaches been a problem?				
*C17c. How often has diarrhea been a problem?				
*C17d. How often have ear infections been a problem?				
*C17e. How often have asthma or allergies been a problem during the past 6 months				
*C17f. How often have fevers been a problem?				
*C17g. How often have colds been a problem?				
*C17h. How often has not eating well been a problem?				

44

*C12. (*If yes*) How many working automobiles do you have?

	No (5)	Yes (1)	C12. Number
a. Automobile			
b. Do you have a working bicycle?			
c. A motor scooter that works?			
d. A motorcycle that works?			
e. A telephone that is hooked up?			

*C13. Do you have a clothes washer that is in working condition?
*C14. (*If yes*) How many?

	No (5)	Yes (1)	C14. Number
a. Clothes washer			
b. Do you have a clothes dryer that works?			
c. A refrigerator that works?			
d. A vacuum cleaner that works?			
e. Do you have a working microwave oven?			
f. A working radio?			
g. A working tape recorder?			
h. A phonograph/record player?			
j. A working television?			
k. (*If R owns working television*) Do you own a working video cassette recorder (VCR)?			
m. A working computer?			
n. (*If yes*): What brand(s) of computers(s)?			
p. Do you have a dictionary?			
q. Do you have an encyclopedia?			

43

*C18. During the past year has your child been examined by a medical person such as a nurse or a doctor?

1. Yes   5. No

*C19. During the past year has your child been examined by a dentist?

1. Yes   5. No

*C20. During the past year has your child had any serious illness or bad accident?

1. Yes   5. No   → Go to C21

*C20a. What type of illness or accident?

_____

*C21. During the past year has your child stayed overnight in a hospital?

1. Yes   5. No   → Go to C22

*C21a. What was the problem?

_____

*C21b. How long did (child's name) stay in the hospital?

_____

*C22. Has (child's name) had (his/her) vision checked?

1. Yes   5. No   → Go to C23

*C22a. Were any problems found?

1. Yes

*C22b. What type of problem?

_____

45

*C23. Has (child's name) had (his/her) hearing checked?

1. Yes   5. No   → Go to C24

*C23a. Were any problems found?

1. Yes   5. No   → Go to C24

*C23b. What type of problem?

_____

*C24. Has (child's name) been vaccinated or immunized?

1. Yes   5. No   9. Don't know

*C25. Is (child's name) covered by any form of health insurance?

1. Yes   5. No   → Go to C26

*C25a. What type of insurance is that?

1. Medicare   2. Health insurance provided by employer   3. Health insurance paid for by parent/guardian

4. Other, specify: _____

*C26. Is (child's name) covered, either partially or fully, by dental insurance?

1. Yes   5. No

*C27. How many people in your household smoke on a regular basis?

_____ Number

*C28. Do any of the child's caregivers smoke on a regular basis while they are caring for your child?

1. Yes   5. No   9. Don't know

*C29. Are outside areas easily available where (child's name) can play?

1. Yes   5. No   → Go to C30

46

Section CN: Child Care Needs Assessment

For the next few questions we will be talking about what you feel is needed in the area of child care. Since the needs for child care differ quite a bit depending on the age of the child, as we ask these questions, we would like you to think about the child care needs of children aged 2 to 5.

CN1. Do you feel that quality child care for your child(ren) between the ages of 2 and 5 is readily available to you?

| 1. Yes | | 5. No | → Go to CN2 |

CN1a. Why do you feel that way?

_____

_____

_____

Go to CN5

CN2. If quality child care were readily available to you, would that change things for you?

| 1. Yes | | 5. No | → Go to CN3 |

↓

CN2a. What would change for you?

_____

_____

CN2b. (*If appropriate*) About how many hours per week would you use child care if it were readily available?

_____ Hours per week

CN3. Have you ever looked for child care for your child(ren)?

| 1. Yes | | 5. No | → Go to CN5 |

↓

CN4. I'm going to read a list of problems some parents run into when they are looking for child care settings. Please tell me if each one is a problem you've had within the last 2 years.

CN4a. Have you had a problem with being unable to *find* child care?

| 1. Yes | | 5. No |

48

C29. What types of play areas are easily available?

_____

C30. How safe is it for your child to play outside your home—is it very safe, somewhat safe, not very safe, or not at all safe?

| 1. Very safe | 2. Somewhat safe | 3. Not very safe | 4. Not at all safe |

Go to C31   ↓   ↓

C30a. In what ways is it not safe?

C31. Has (*child's name*) always lived at this address?

| 5. No | | 1. Yes | → Go to Section D |

↓

C32. How long has (*child's name*) lived (here/there)?

| Less than 1 year |

_____ Number of Years

C33. Before you moved (here/there), where did (*child's name*) live?

_____ _____
City/Town/Village   State/Province

_____
Country

C34. How many time has (*child's name*) moved in the past 3 years?

_____ Number of Times

47

CN4b. Has the *quality* of the child care that's available been a problem?

1. Yes   5. No

CN4c. Has *cost* been a problem?

1. Yes   5. No

CN4d. Has it been a problem finding child care that the hours of operation fit your schedule?

1. Yes   5. No

CN4e. Has it been a problem finding child care that is near your home (or where you work)?

1. Yes   5. No

CN5. What do you think, in general, is the best type of child care for 3½- to 4½-year-old children? (*Probe, if necessary:* This can be any type of arrangement you can think of, without regard to whether or not it is available to you at the present time. Examples would be home care, family day care, and care in some type of center.)

CN6. Would the type of child care you just described be the best type of care for (*child's name*)?

1. Yes   5. No
Go to CN7   ↓

CN6a. What would be the best type of child care for (*child's name*)?

CN7. Head Start is a program with appropriate learning activities for young children. It encourages parent participation in the program, and it offers support to families as needed. If a program like Head Start were available to you and you could enroll (*child's name*), would you place (him/her) in the program?

1. Yes   5. No

CN7a. Why?

CN8. What do you think are the most important experiences in terms of preparing a 3½- to 4½-year-old child for school?

CN9. Based on the care (*child's name*) is receiving, do you feel that (he/she) will be prepared for school?

1. Yes   5. No

CN9a. Why do you feel that way?

CN10. If you could tell your elected officials what should be done during the next 5 years to best improve the quality and availability of child care for you, what would you suggest?

CN11. We hear a lot of talk about spending "quality time" with children. What types of activities do you think would qualify as spending "quality time" with (*child's name*)?

CN12. Using that definition, about how much quality time do you spend with (*child's name*) during a typical day?

_____ Per day

CN13. (*If R lives with spouse/partner.*) Using that definition, about how much quality time does your (husband/wife/partner) spend with (*child's name*) during a typical day?

_____ Per day

Part D: Personal Information About Family

D1. How many years of full-time education have you completed, starting with first grade?

_____ Number of years

D2. Are you working now for pay?

1. Yes →   5. No →

D2a. Do you usually work in your home or outside of your home?

1. In home   2. Outside home

D2b. Are you retired, on a pension, on permanent disability leave, a student, (a homemaker,) or unemployed?

1. Retired   2. Pension

3. Disability leave

4. Student   5. Homemaker

6. Unemployed

D2c. What was your last job for pay? (What did you do?) _____

D2d. Are you currently looking for work?

1. Yes   5. No

Go to D9

D3. What is your job title? _____

D4. What are your most important duties? (Probe for two duties.)

_____

_____

51

D5. What type of business or industry is that in? (*Please be as specific as possible—the name of the company is not enough. For example, government office, hospital, gas station, farm, department store.*)

D6. Are you self-employed, or do you work for someone else?

1. Self-employed   2. Work for someone

D7. Is this work relatively permanent, or is it temporary or seasonal?

1. Permanent   2. Temporary   3. Seasonal   4. Other, specify: _____

*D8. Do you currently hold more than one job?

1. Yes   5. No

D9. During a typical week, which days of the week are you away from your home without (*child's name*) for activities such as work, classes or community activities?

D10. (*For each day mentioned*) During a typical week, how many hours are you away from your child on (*day of week*)?

D9. Day of week	D10. Number of hours
a. Monday	
b. Tuesday	
c. Wednesday	
d. Thursday	
e. Friday	
f. Saturday	
g. Sunday	

52

D13. Is (he/she) working now for pay?

1. Yes →   5. No →

D13a. Does (he/she) usually work in your home or outside of your home?

1. In home   2. Outside home

D13b. Is (he/she) retired, on a pension, on permanent disability leave, a student, (a homemaker,) or is (he/she) unemployed?

1. Retired   2. Pension

3. Disability leave

4. Student   5. Homemaker

6. Unemployed

D13c. What was (his/her) last job for pay? What did (he/she) do?

D13d. Is (he/she) currently looking for work?

1. Yes   5. No
          Go to D20

D14. What is (his/her) job title?

D15. What are (his/her) most important duties? (*Probe for two duties.*)

D16. What type of business or industry is that in? (*Please be as specific as possible—the name of the company is not enough. For example, government office, hospital, gas station, farm, department store.*)

D17. Is (he/she) self-employed or does (he/she) work for someone else?

1. Self-employed   2. Works for someone

54

D11. Are you currently married?

1. Yes →   5. No →

D11a. Are you living with your spouse, is your spouse temporarily absent, or are you separated?

1. Living with spouse

2. Spouse absent

3. Separated

D11b. Are you divorced, widowed or have you never been married?

1. Divorced   2. Widowed

3. Never married

D11c. Are you currently living with a partner?

1. Yes →   5. No →
          Go to D22

D12. How many years of full-time education has your (spouse/partner) completed, starting with first grade?

_____ Number of years

53

D18. Is this work relatively permanent, or is it temporary or seasonal?

1. Permanent   2. Temporary   3. Seasonal   4. Other, specify: _____

*D19. Is (he/she) currently hold more than one job?

1. Yes   5. No →

D20. During a typical week, which days of the week is (he/she) away from home without (*child's name*) for activities such as work, classes or community activities?

D21. (*For each day mentioned.*) During a typical week, how many hours is (he/she) away from (*child's name*) on (*day of week*)?

D20. Day of week	D21. Number of hours
a. Monday	
b. Tuesday	
c. Wednesday	
d. Thursday	
e. Friday	
f. Saturday	
g. Sunday	

D22. Does most of your household money come from your (and your [spouse's/partner's]) work?

5. No →   1. Yes → Go to D27

D23. Does most of your household money come from relatives?

5. No →   1. Yes → Go to D27

55

D24. Does most of your household money come from welfare?

5. No   1. Yes → Go to D27

D25. Does most of your household money come from your pension or disability income?

5. No   1. Yes → Go to D27

D26. Where does your household money come from?

D27. Approximately how much money did you (and your family living [there/here]) receive last year, before taxes, from all sources?

_____ Amount   _____ Monetary Unit

D28. Which language do you use in your own home? _____ Language

D29. Is the language spoken in your home the same as the language spoken in your community?

1. Yes   5. No

D30. Are any other languages or dialects spoken in your home?

1. Yes   5. No → Go to D31

D30a. Which other languages?

D31. These are all the questions we have. Is there anything else that you would like to tell us?

_____

Thank you for your time.

56

Appendix C:
IEA Preprimary Project Phase 1
National Research Centers and
Coordinators

Belgium
    Service de Pédagogie Expérimentale
    Faculte de Psychologie et Sciences de l'Education
    B 32 Université de Liège au Sart-Tilman
    B 4000 Liège

    Coordinators: Arlette Delhaxhe
        Genevieve Hindryckx

China (PRC)
    China Central Institute of Educational Research
    Beisanhuan zhong lu 46
    100088 Beijing

    Coordinators: Shi Hui Zhong
        Xiang Zong Ping

Finland
    Early Childhood Education Department
    University of Joensuu
    P.O. Box 111
    80101 Joensuu

    Coordinator: Mikko Ojala

Germany (FRG)
    Universität Münster
    FB Erziehungswissenschaft Institut III
    GeorgsKommende 33
    4400 Münster

    Coordinator: Hans-Günther Rossbach

Hong Kong
    Department of Education
    University of Hong Kong
    Pokfulam Road

    Coordinator: Sylvia Opper

Italy
Centro Europeo dell'Educazione
Villa Falconieri
I-00044 Frascati
Rome

Coordinator: Lucio Pusci

Nigeria
Institute of Education
University of Ibadan
Ibadan

Coordinator: Olayemi Onibokun

Portugal
Faculdade de Psicológia e de Ciências da Educaçáo
Universidade do Porto
Rua das Taipas, 76
4000 Porto

Coordinator: Joaquim Bairrão

Spain
Departamento Psicologia Evolutiva
Universidad de Sevilla
Apartado 3128
41071 Sevilla

Coordinator: Jesús Palacios

Thailand
School of Educational Studies
Sukhothai Thammathirat Open University
Jaengwattana Road, Bangpood, Pakkred
Nonthaburi 11120

Coordinator: Nittaya Passornsiri

United States
>   High/Scope Educational Research Foundation
>   600 North River Street
>   Ypsilanti, Michigan 48198
>
>   Coordinators: Patricia P. Olmsted, Helena Hoas

International Coordinating Center
>   High/Scope Educational Research Foundation
>   600 North River Street
>   Ypsilanti, Michigan 48198
>
>   International Coordinator: David P. Weikart
>   Deputy International Coordinator: Patricia P. Olmsted

COMMENTARIES

Perspectives on the IEA Preprimary Project

Çiğdem Kağitçibaşi, *Professor*
Department of Psychology
Boğaziçi University
Istanbul, Turkey

Overview of the Project

The IEA Preprimary Project is an impressive long-term comparative research endeavor that is ongoing at the time of this writing and that spans extensive space and time. Fifteen countries in four different continents, displaying a variety of cultures and economic development levels, have participated in at least one phase of the study. The multiphase work spans a period of almost a decade, the first phase being completed with this second published volume, and the work of the second and third phases being now under way. Because detailed information about the project and its background is available both in this volume and in its predecessor, *How Nations Serve Young Children: Profiles of Child Care and Education in 14 Countries* (Olmsted & Weikart, 1989), I will not reiterate it here. I would like to start, however, by listing some important features of the IEA Preprimary Project that, in combination, attest to its uniqueness. They are the features of Phase 1 of the ongoing study.

■ The IEA Preprimary Project is essentially an empirical research study utilizing individual-level data collected through surveys conducted directly with parents. This characteristic sets it apart from reports and documents that are based on aggregate statistics regarding the existence and distribution of preprimary care/education services for young children or that collect information from teachers and institutions.

■ The samples drawn for surveys are nationally representative, with the sampling being done appropriately for each country, in line with the demographic and socioeconomic characteristics of each. This is a notable achievement, especially in view of the large population sizes in some countries and their great diversity in terms of rural-urban and socioeconomic development levels. The national representativeness of the findings allows for their international comparisons

■ Both developed and developing countries are included in the study. This allows for several types of comparisons, both within each group and between groups. This can, for example, allow researchers to find out about variations within developed countries and to look for differences between them and the developing countries

■ The data gathered are sufficiently detailed and fine-tuned to allow for analysis that goes beyond mere description. For example, it is possible to look not only for the extent of use but also for the reasons underlying parents' use of child care/education services. This can reveal, for example, if there is a relationship between the underlying reasons for use and the extent of use of services.

■ Similarly, the data allow for an examination of the links between the use of child care/education services and such important characteristics of families and parents as their urban-rural standing, education, income, job status, labor force participation, and the like.

■ This international study is a good example of truly collaborative research; at every phase of the study there is shared decision making, responsibility, and contribution on the part of all the various national investigators. What is more commonly seen in international research is unequal participation by the various research partners, with the developed countries usually doing the conceptualization and instrument development, and the developing countries doing only the data collection.

■ Having international-option items as well as national-option items in the Phase 1 parent/guardian interview, in addition to the international core items, provides flexibility and independence for country researchers. They can investigate their own national issues of interest and importance while still allowing for international comparison.

- The study encompasses all the advantages of the cross-cultural approach that is so badly needed in the study of human development, socialization, and the family. Cross-cultural comparison enables the researcher to examine the generalizability of the patterns, relationships, and regularities observed in any one sociocultural context. Through cross-cultural research, then, the limitations and strengths of our models can be tested, leading toward their improvement. Such an approach is especially welcome in the study of preprimary care and education, to help us unravel the variables that may be confounded within single-culture settings.
- Good models have strong policy implications. This study promises to have significant policy relevance. Armed with cross-culturally valid findings regarding the need for and use of child care services, policymakers have valuable information to use in building or reviewing their policies.
- Finally, though the focus of the IEA Preprimary Project is on child care/education services, the study also provides cross-cultural information and insights regarding the family, childhood, child-rearing orientations, societal values about women's roles, and variations in all these. Thus its potential contribution to basic knowledge and understanding in these areas is considerable.

The above features of the IEA Preprimary Project point to its unique value and status as a comparative study in the field of education. Obviously, the study also has its limitations, and these are mainly dictated by the constraints of organizational structure, time, and money. Specifically, the research participation is biased toward developed countries, with the bias reflecting the international structure of the IEA. Since some large areas of the world are conspicuously missing — notably, Latin America, the Middle East, and the Indian subcontinent — the findings can hardly be considered globally representative. Furthermore, certain national samples (especially in Nigeria but also, for example, in Belgium) appear to be somewhat biased toward representing an urban and high socioeconomic-status population. This can be seen, for example, from the distribution of such variables as *number of rooms in the house, mother's education*, and *parental employment status* (Tables 4.2, 4.3, 4.5, 4.7). The youthfulness of the sample parents also plays a role in this bias, as explained in Chapter 4. Nevertheless, the effort put into drawing nationally representative samples is admirable, and such biases are inevitable in a large-scale study like this one, where building of the sampling frame must rely on existing local statistics/information.

PERSPECTIVE OF THE FAMILY AND SEX ROLES

Having ventured a brief overview of Phase 1 of the IEA Preprimary Project by pointing out its important features, I would now like to discuss the findings from the perspective of the changing family and sex roles in the world. As the researchers note in Chapter 1, the general focus of the study is on the socialization of the young child. Socialization is a complex process occurring through a myriad of interactions that extend over time and space. The family constitutes a focal point in this process. Thus the findings of the IEA Preprimary Project, which shed light on the family, can be better understood when considered with reference to the family in the context of socioeconomic change and development in the world.

Assumptions, perhaps myths, about the family abound in popular usage, affecting at times even academic accounts. One tenacious assumption, based on the modernization theory, is that the traditional family prevalent in developing countries is an extended family in which the non-working mother cares for the children. This is contrasted with the modern nuclear family in Western society, with its high levels of maternal employment and therefore lower levels of maternal child care.

This assumption is not warranted. Extensive evidence from developing countries shows that while women do carry the main responsibility for the care of infants and young children everywhere, they are most often *not* children's sole caretakers. In particular, it is the exception rather than the rule for mothers in developing countries to do most of the child care unaided (Mueller, 1982; Oppong, 1982; Myers & Indriso, 1987; Myers, 1992). Furthermore, in both rural and urban settings in both developed and developing countries, the nuclear family structure is widespread, since maintaining an extended household often requires affluence, which is not common (Drinkwater, 1985; Duben, 1982; Yang, 1988). However, nuclear families that are related to one another as kin while each family lives in its own nuclear household often function as if they *were* an extended family. For example, several related nuclear families may share household chores and child care, and thus they may be called "functionally extended" (Kağitçibaşi, 1985, p. 133). The persistence of such support functions of the family have led some researchers to suggest that the extended family is continuing to exist, for example, in Colombia (Rosenberg, 1984). It has even been rediscovered in the United States as the "modified extended" family (Cohler & Geyer, 1982, p. 197). Thus the assumed contrasts between "traditional" and "modern" families are too simplistic to reflect the great complexity in family patterns around the world, including both the diversity and the similarity. Ironically, as pointed out by Engle (1986), some Western, especially American, views stressing the role of the mother in the development of the child, influenced by Freudian theory, have helped to *assign* to the woman the sole-caregiver role.

Some of the findings of the IEA Preprimary Project provide evidence to help correct some of the unwarranted assumptions. It is noteworthy, for example, that children's care by mothers is *not* more prevalent in the less developed countries. On the contrary, in the most developed and richest countries, Germany and the United States, mothers are absent from home the least amount of time (18 and 27 hours per week, respectively, Table 4.5). While Germany reports the highest average number of hours of parental care for children per day (12.5 hours), China reports the lowest average number (7.7 hours, Table 7.3).

Pursuing women's work further, whether it reflects the need for income to survive or for professional involvement and self-actualization, it is widespread. Also contrary to common assumptions regarding higher women's employment in the developed, "modern" contexts, the Preprimary Project findings reveal the highest percentage of maternal employment in China (98 percent), with Nigeria ranking third (67 percent) — and they are both developing countries (Table 4.3). Women's work brings with it the need for extraparental child care. Spousal sharing is in most cases not a viable alternative; as also shown in the Preprimary Project, nowhere does care by father reach 1 hour a day (Table 7.1). This is in line with much research around the world showing that spousal help in child care is negligible, regardless of whether the wife is a wage earner (see Engle, 1986, for case studies from several Latin American and Asian countries, and see Ybarra, 1982, Hoffman, 1975, and Hiller, 1984, for American research findings). Again contrary to the stereotypical conceptualization of "modern" and "traditional" family and sex roles, in the Preprimary Project the highest frequency of two-parent care (thus father care) is found in Thailand, and sole father care is highest in China; both of these are developing ("traditional") countries (Table 7.1).

Nonmaternal care/education takes many forms, as demonstrated by the IEA Preprimary Project findings (Table A.1). In the words of the author of Chapter 1, *"variety is the rule."* When informal nonparental care is examined, we find that it is not at all negligible, and in fact, in some countries it is quite substantial. Specifically, when the categories of *sibling*, *grandparent*, and *other relative* are combined, we find that 1.7 to 2.7 hours of daily care of children is provided by the family in Hong Kong, Portugal, and Thailand, and in no country is it less than 0.5 hour a day (Table 7.3). *The family*, as broadly defined here, appears to be an important support-mechanism, especially for the working mother.

In terms of the amount of time care is provided, family support is not as significant in societies where organized care/education is almost universally available (thus the large amount of care by "teacher" in Belgium and Spain, Table 7.1) or in societies where "other-home" care is prevalent (Finland). Nevertheless, family is still the main source of support to bridge the gap between the mother's work hours and the hours of organized care, even if organized care is universally available, as in Hong Kong.

Where family care is substantial, as in Portugal, Thailand, China, and Hong Kong, grandparents' role in the care of children is considerable (Table 7.1). This finding emphasizes the support function of the closely knit family. Even in China, in spite of official policies undermining the role of the family for decades, "familism" is found to be strong (Yang, 1988, p. 94), and recent surveys have portrayed close networks among the elderly and their adult offspring "indicative of the traditional parental protection of children until their [parents'] death" (Yang, 1988, p. 109). Similar family interdependencies are reported in many cultural contexts (e.g., Sinha, 1981, 1988, for India; Kağitçibaşi 1982, 1990, for Turkey; Bond, 1986, for China; and Sinha & Kao, 1988, for several Asian countries) as well as for some ethnic groups in the posttechnological society, such as Asian-American (Iwasaki-Mass, 1984; Suzuki, 1985) and Hispanic (Mirande, 1985) families in the United States and various ethnic groups in Australia (Storer, 1985).

Even in the United States, despite widespread commitment to individualism, independence, and self-sufficiency (Berger & Berger, 1984), a great deal of interdependence is observed among generations, kin, and families (e.g., Bronfenbrenner & Weiss, 1983; Cohler & Grunebaum, 1981; Fu, Hinkle, & Hanna, 1986; Cohler & Geyer, 1982). Indeed, a discrepancy is noted between the "myth of family independence" (Keniston, 1985) and the reality of interdependence. However, because self-sufficiency is a cultural ideal, such interdependence is often problematic, accompanied by feelings of ambivalence (Cohler & Geyer, 1982). This may be one reason underlying both the search for nonfamilial care options and the great diversity of care options available in the United States, as evidenced by the Preprimary Project.

CONCLUSIONS AND POLICY IMPLICATIONS

The foregoing discussion attests to the great value of cross-cultural comparative research in providing insights that challenge assumptions based on rather ethnocentric orientations. To reach global perspectives, broader comparative coverage is needed, and this is what the second and the third phases of the Preprimary Project promise to achieve. Specifically, the findings show that we cannot talk about a developing-country pattern (or a "traditional society" pattern) and a developed-country pattern, with a linear shift from the former to the latter. The picture is much more complex than that.

Nevertheless, some trends may be detectable from the findings of the Preprimary Project. For example, it appears that as mother's participation in the labor force, parental education, and parental occupational levels increase, there is greater use of extraparental care/education, and an organized facility is more likely to be used for this purpose (Table 5.15). Even though there is much variability — as evidenced, for example, by the preference for other-home informal care in Finland or by the diversity of care settings in the United States — this finding may point to some common pattern or trend. However, whether such a trend surfaces in a country is mediated by that country's availability of organized facilities. For example, when in-home child care is more readily available than organized-facility care, as in Nigeria, the trend may not be seen. Clearly, policies and priorities regarding social services and education are determining factors in this. These policies and priorities often, but not always, reflect a country's economic resources and wealth. Even when resources are available, where social norms and conventions favor other options (as in Finland) or where there are no explicit policies and many options are available (as in the United States), the trend toward organized facilities may also be blurred.

Given the diversity of care/education services in the countries participating in the Preprimary Project, it probably makes more sense to talk about *complementarity* of the different care/education settings rather than to try to determine the *best* model among alternatives. Indeed, no country was found to use only one extraparental care/education setting; combination of settings/caregivers is the rule. Which combination is used is a complex joint-outcome of the many interacting factors discussed above and extensively examined in this book.

As for improving the care/education for children, there needs to be recognition that different models may be suitable in different circumstances and that "quality" care/education can be provided in several different models or in a combination thereof. Furthermore, what is the most suitable care/education service in a particular locality needs to be locally decided, taking into consideration both children's and parents' (especially mothers') needs and the available resources.

However, this is not to say that we should be content with whatever is available. On the contrary, in every country much work is needed to educate parents, to raise their expectations concerning services for children, to encourage them to demand better services, and in general, to create public awareness of the importance of early childhood care and education. The Phase 1 Preprimary Project finding of overall parental satisfaction with child care/education services probably results from many factors other than or in addition to the quality of the services. It may reflect low levels of parental awareness of children's needs; low parental expectations concerning the care settings; satisfaction at having been lucky enough to secure scarce services, or "cognitive dissonance" (if parents had a choice and need to feel they have made the right choice).

The expectation expressed in the beginning — that families (or countries) believing in the educational value of preprimary extraparental/out-of-home care/education would demand high-quality settings is probably a sound one, though it is not directly examined in this Phase 1 study. We would further expect this process to be facilitated by the level of (parental) education and general socioeconomic development of the country. The main policy implication of the Preprimary Project would appear to be the need to increase the demand for high-quality settings in cultural/familial contexts where such demand can be expected to emerge but also, going beyond this, to promote (even create) such demand where it may be weak or even nonexistent.

REFERENCES

Berger, B., & Berger, P. L. (1984). *The war over the family*. New York: Anchor Press.

Bond, M. H. (1986). *The psychology of the Chinese people*. New York: Oxford University Press.

Bronfenbrenner, U., & Weiss, H. B. (1983). Beyond policies without people: An ecological perspective on child and family policy. In E. F. Zigler, S. L. Kagan, and E. Klugman (Eds.), *Children, families and government: Perspectives on*

American social policy (pp. 393–414). New York: Cambridge University Press.

Cohler, B., & Geyer, S. (1982). Psychological autonomy and interdependence within the family. In F. Walsin (Ed.), *Normal family processes* (pp. 196–227). New York: Guilford Press.

Cohler, B., & Grunebaum, H. (1981). *Mothers, grandmothers, and daughters: Personality and child care in three-generation families.* New York: Wiley.

Drinkwater, B. A. (1985). Family size and influence in Italy and Australia. *Australian Journal of Sex, Marriage, and Family, 6*(3), 163–167.

Duben, A. (1982). The significance of family and kinship in urban Turkey. In Ç. Kağitçibaşi (Ed.), *Sex roles, family, and community in Turkey* (pp. 73–99). Bloomington, IN: Indiana University Press.

Engle, P. L. (1986). *The intersecting needs of working mothers and their young children: 1980 to 1985* (Mimeo). New York: The Consultative Group on Early Childhood Care and Development, c/o UNICEF.

Fu, V. R., Hinkle, D. E., & Hanna, M. A. (1986). A three-generational study of the development of individual dependence and family interdependence. *Genetic, Social and General Psychology Monographs, 112*(2), 153–171.

Hiller, D. V. (1984). Power dependence and division of family work. *Sex Roles, 10*(11–12), 1,003–1,019.

Hoffman, L. W. (1975). The employment of women, education, and fertility. In M. T. S. Medrick, S. S. Tangri, and L. W. Hoffman (Eds.), *Women and achievement* (pp. 104–122). Washington, DC: Hemisphere Publishing Co.

Iwasaki-Mass, A. (1984). *"Amae" in Japanese-Americans.* Unpublished doctoral dissertation, UCLA, School of Social Welfare, Los Angeles.

Kağitçibaşi, Ç. (1982). Old-age security value of children and development. *Journal of Cross-Cultural Psychology, 13,* 29–42.

Kağitçibaşi, Ç. (1985). A model of family change through development: The Turkish family in comparative perspective. In R. Lagunes and V. H. Poortinga (Eds.), *From a different perspective: Studies of behavior across cultures* (pp. 120–135). Lisse, the Netherlands: Swets and Zeitlinger B. V.

Kağitçibaşi, Ç. (1990). Family and socialization in cross-cultural perspective: A model of change. In J. Berman (Ed.), *Nebraska Symposium on Motivation 1989: Vol. 37* (pp. 135–200). Lincoln, NE: University of Nebraska Press.

Keniston, K. (1985). "The myth of family independence." In J. M. Henslin (Ed.), *Marriage and family in a changing society* (2nd ed., pp. 27–32). New York: Free Press.

Mirande, A. (1985). Chicano families. In J. M. Henslin (Ed.), *Marriage and family in changing society* (2nd ed., pp. 133–136). New York: Free Press.

Mueller, E. (1982). The allocation of women's time and its relation to fertility. In R. Anker, M. Buvinic, and N. H. Youssef (Eds.), *Women's roles and population trends in the Third World* (pp. 55–86). London: Croom Helm.

Myers, R. G. (1992). *The twelve who survive.* London: Routledge.

Myers, R., & Indriso, C. (1987). *Women's work and child care.* Paper presented at a workshop sponsored by the Consultative Group on Early Childhood Care and Development, for the Rockefeller Foundation, on Issues Related to Gender, Technology, and Development, New York.

Olmsted, P. P., & Weikart, D. P. (1989). *How nations serve young children: Profiles of child care and education in 14 countries.* Ypsilanti, MI: High/Scope Press.

Oppong, C. (1982). Family structure and women's reproductive and productive roles: Some conceptual and methodological issues. In R. Anker, M. Buvinic, and N. H. Youssef (Eds.), *Women's roles and population trends in the Third World* (pp. 133-150). London: Croom Helm.

Rosenberg, T. J. (1984). Employment and family formation among working-class women in Bogota, Colombia. *Journal of Comparative Family Studies, 14*(3), 413–418.

Sinha, D. (1981). *Socialization of the Indian Child.* New Delhi: Concept.

Sinha, D. (1988). The family scenario in a developing country and its implications for mental health: The case of India. In P. R. Dasen, J. W. Berry, and N. Sartorius (Eds.), *Health and cross-cultural psychology: Toward applications* (pp. 48–70). Beverly Hills, CA: Sage India.

Sinha, D., & Kao, H. S. R. (1988). *Social values and development: Asian perspectives.* New Delhi: Sage India.

Storer. D. (Ed.). (1985). *Ethnic family values in Australia.* Sydney: Prentice-Hall.

Suzuki, B. H. (1985). Asian-American families. In J. M. Henslin (Ed.), *Marriage and family in a changing society* (2nd ed., pp. 104–118). New York: Free Press.

Yang, C. (1988). Familism and development: An examination of the role of family in contemporary China, Mainland, Hong Kong, and Taiwan. In D. Sinha and S. R. Kao (Eds.), *Social values and development: Asian perspectives* (pp. 93–124). New Delhi: Sage India.

Ybarra, L. (1982). When wives work: The impact on the Chicano family. *Journal of Marriage and the Family, 44*(1), 169–178.

COMMENTARY ON THE RESULTS OF THE PHASE 1 IEA PREPRIMARY STUDY

Lilian G. Katz. *Professor of Early Childhood Education*
Director of ERIC Clearinghouse on
Elementary and Early Childhood Education
University of Illinois, Urbana

As suggested in the title of this book, one of the unique features of the IEA Preprimary Study is that it includes an examination of the parents' perspectives on the care and education provisions available to their young children. The fact that the majority of parents in all participating countries — with the exception of Hong Kong — express general satisfaction with these provisions is one of the most surprising findings to come out of this examination.

This finding is especially surprising, considering that the specialists in the field of early childhood care and education within each country, and around the world, are greatly concerned about what they believe to be the generally poor quality of early childhood provisions. Indeed, the title of this book's first chapter suggests that the new knowledge obtained by the IEA Preprimary Project is expected to provide much-needed information that will assist in improving the quality of children's early experiences. While not all such experiences are likely to be in organized settings, the trend toward families using out-of-home care and education implies concern with the quality of out-of-home as well as home settings.

The fact that parents and specialists seem to hold contrasting opinions on the quality of early childhood care and education settings raises questions about (1) how this finding about the parents' positive perspective should be interpreted and (2) what it implies for policy and practice.

THE PERSPECTIVES OF PARENTS AND SPECIALISTS

The most plausible interpretation of general parental satisfaction with the quality of preprimary provisions may have to do with the *expectations* of parents. A large proportion of the parents might believe that young children obtain their most important experiences at home. Such being the case, parents expect the settings available to their children to be merely safe and reasonably pleasant and are generally satisfied that present settings adequately meet these minimal criteria.

In the exceptional case of Hong Kong, where parental satisfaction is somewhat lower, parents' expectation that the preprimary setting will give their children an early start on the highly competitive educational ladder may result in their having a keener awareness (compared with parents in other countries) of alternative early childhood programs. Parents who are aware of a range of alternative programs and who have clear but unrealized goals for their children's preprimary experiences are likely to express dissatisfaction. Also, parents who want their children to have early instruction and school readiness activities may be satisfied with programs that are *highly academic*.

But why do the perspectives of parents and specialists apparently differ? The answer again lies in expectations. Early childhood specialists, as their name implies, are more keenly aware of the full range of possible program features than parents are. Also, as might be expected, the specialists are more familiar than most parents are with what high-quality early childhood programs can accomplish. They are thus likely to judge more critically the quality of present early childhood settings — whether they be highly academic or merely safe and pleasant. They may see today's settings as missed opportunities to significantly enhance young children's physical, social and intellectual growth in a developmentally appropriate way.

IMPLICATIONS OF DISCREPANT PERSPECTIVES

The assumption that early experiences significantly determine later development is rarely questioned today, even among lay persons. Kağitçibaşi, a specialist with extensive experience working in many countries, points out in her commentary (p.356) that "in every country much work is needed to educate parents, to raise their expectations concerning services for children, to encourage them to demand better services, and in general, to create public awareness of the importance of early childhood care and education." Most specialists agree that high-quality experiences during the first 5 or 6 years of growth and development lay an essential foundation for the rest of children's lives, and they are usually adamant about this: Provision of high-quality experiences requires personnel with special knowledge and skills that can only be acquired through professional preparation and/or inservice training.

The majority of parents, on the other hand, may not sense the importance of personnel qualifications and skills. They often believe that those working with young children, especially in child care settings, are just using skills that come naturally to any parent, particularly to any mother. Large numbers of parents may believe that child care staff are doing what mothers do all the time, that child care is second nature to women around the world and is based on cultural patterns learned throughout one's own childhood, without special training.

When we specialists assert that good-quality care and education of young children requires knowledge and skills that can be acquired only through specialized training, what does this imply about the competence of most parents? If we imply that parents — especially mothers — *also* need to acquire knowledge and skills through training, what criteria for "good parenting" are we using? Where do the criteria come from? Who is to determine what constitutes adequate, to say nothing of good, parenting? Psychologists? Developmentalists? Pedagogues? Governments?

When official bodies such as government agencies and schools attempt to "train" parents or to change parenting behavior by other means, are they not tampering with the family's own culture? After all, parenting is not merely *related* to culture — it *is* culture! It might be interesting to pursue the hypothesis that the level of dissatisfaction with available early childhood provisions increases with the diversity of a country's population. For educators in most countries, increasing and long-overdue sensitivity to cultural diversity (Treppte, 1993) raises difficult issues of practice in both parent education and early childhood education.

Suppose we reject the view that parenting requires special knowledge and skills and accept the common-sense view that parenting comes naturally — that it is instinctive, or intuitive. Then on what basis can we assert that teachers of young children require specialized training to acquire the knowledge and skills essential for good-quality services? Several possible answers to this question come to mind, and these answers are likely to be directly addressed by the data reported from the next phases of the study.

For the present, however, we might note three major differences between teaching and rearing young children. First, teachers are responsible for *larger groups of children* than parents typically are; second, teachers are *compensated* for the time spent with the children; and third, teachers work with *other people's children*. Let us look briefly at these features and what they imply for parents' versus specialists' perspectives on quality.

Providing care and education for large groups of children, as caregivers and teachers often do, no doubt requires special skills over and above those required by parenting. That teachers and caregivers are compensated for their work — though typically not very well — suggests that in a sense, they must justify their compensation by implementing a program of activities designed to achieve prespecified goals; this also implies a need for special skills. Both kinds of specialized skills — group skills and programmatic skills — are subject to being perceived differently by parents and specialists. Specialists responsible for the training and education of early childhood personnel are likely to judge the quality of practitioners' efforts according to ideal and theoretical standards of program implementation that are unknown to most parents.

The fact that teachers and caregivers work with other people's children raises questions about how they can meet children's needs for close and warm relationships with those who care for them. The interactions and responses of parents — especially of mothers — to their children are based on a knowledge of each of their children that is derived from intimacy, proximity, and constancy of contact with them. Lacking such an advantage, teachers and caregivers suffer something of a vacuum that must be filled by knowledge and skills learned through specialized training and education. The knowledge and skills so acquired can help them to make reliable judgments about children they cannot know as intimately as a parent does.

Can we have it both ways? Can we assert that mothers do what comes naturally but that teachers of young children must have extended, specialized training? How do we avoid implying that children at home, with mothers who have no specialized training, are deprived of opportunities that would enhance their development — and that this deprivation would not occur if they were with well-educated teachers? If we show convincingly that teacher/caregiver expertise is required and makes a substantial contribution to children's development, are we also saying that children without preschool programs are disadvantaged in perceptible and demonstrable ways? Reports of the findings of the next phases of the IEA Preprimary Project will help clarify the answers to these questions.

REFERENCES

Treppte, C. (1993). Multicultural approaches in education: A German approach. In V. R. Fu., A. J. Stremmel., & C. Treppte (Eds.), *Multiculturalism in Early Childhood Programs* (pp. 1–38). Urbana, IL: University of Illinois, ERIC Clearinghouse on Elementary and Early Childhood Education. (ERIC Document Reproduction Service No. ED 360 103)

COMMENTARY ON *Families Speak*

Robert Myers, *Co-director*
The Consultative Group on Early Childhood Care and Development
United Nations

This is an extraordinary project, even in its first phase. It is unusual not only because of its extension to 11 countries, which by itself is an accomplishment. Taken together, several basic decisions made in the course of designing the project help to make this study different — the use of a sample survey method for collecting data; the attention to multiple caregivers and to multiple settings in which care occurs; the focus on *care* within a project that, in its origins, is an *education* project; the emphasis on variation rather than on commonality; and the focus on children between the ages of 3½ and 4½. The study qualifies as one of a kind when it is projected beyond its descriptive first stage into its second and third stages, which examine the quality of child care and early education settings and follow children from these different settings into primary school.

In my comments, I will focus on some conceptual and measurement issues and on child care and early education in so-called Third World, or Southern, countries rather than in the industrialized, Northern, countries, which are so overrepresented in the study. There are very few Southern, less industrialized, countries in Phase 1 of the project, and it will be clear immediately to readers that no generalization should be made from this project about the ways in which care and education are handled in these countries. Indeed, it could be argued that each of the Southern countries (China, Nigeria, and Thailand, and perhaps Hong Kong and Portugal) could be seen as a "special case." Nevertheless, their inclusion in Phase 1 provides an important starting point for reflections about the needs for child care and education in the South and about differences between the way these needs are met at present in various countries of both the North and the South.

A Household Sample Survey Approach

Most studies of early childhood care/education focus on a particular model or program, or they seek to describe child care arrangements in terms of a set of easily identifiable, formally structured programs for which statistics are available. Both approaches miss a great deal of very important informal caregiving and leave out the home as a primary and legitimate educational environment. Rarely do studies seek a broad, epidemiological description of child care, as this one does. A sample survey approach, beginning with families and children rather than with programs, allows that broad overview. It does not limit the research to programs for which statistics are available. That is especially important in most countries of the South, where informal care is more prominent than in the North.

Although the expertise and the sampling frames needed to carry out sample surveys are already in place in many countries in the South, until now, that institutional capacity had not been called upon to look closely at child care and early education. That may be because the relationship is not as clear as it should be between early childhood care/education and such standard sample survey themes as labor force participation, educational attainment, and the health and nutritional status of children or of the general population. If governments were to recognize these relationships and to appreciate fully the potential economic, social, and even political benefits of improving care and education in the early years, they might be induced to make the modest investment necessary to incorporate the topic regularly in the economic and social survey studies now being carried out. The present project shows that is feasible to do so.

Description of Multiple Settings

Even in a survey design, a decision might have been made to restrict the description and analysis of care to the one care setting in which the child spends the most time. We know, however, that organizing care for children is not that simple — that children, particularly by age 4, are likely to spend time during the day in several child care settings. The study dramatically confirms that point. Wisely, the project designers chose to describe the multiple settings in which the needs for daily care are being met for each child and family. From the description, the myriad patterns of caregiving are allowed to emerge in all their complexity. By describing how children are actually cared for, the study reveals the rich variation in responses to child care needs, providing us with a range of possible strategies and models to consider when formulating policies and program plans.

As one looks across countries, the patterning among multiple settings is sometimes surprising and not necessarily what would have been predicted. Nor are differences restricted to North-South differences. Variations in the ways of responding to child care needs are marked across Finland, Belgium, and the United States, for instance. Important differences also exist in the way in which Thailand, China, Hong Kong, and Portugal meet these needs.

CARE AND EDUCATION

One wise decision made at the outset of the project was to gather information about child *care* arrangements even though the original concern of the study, given its sponsorship by the IEA and its proposed follow-up of school-aged children, is with the *education* of the young child. It is unfortunate, but understandable, that the concept of care and the concept of education have taken on such different coloration as they are translated into programs.

In a broad sense, all care involves learning and education, regardless of whether the education is imparted consciously or not, for good or for ill, and regardless of whether the care is at home or in a child care center. That education may involve learning crucial cultural forms of address and greeting and respect but not include learning ABCs. It may involve learning to keep still rather than learning to explore.

All settings that are explicitly labeled as educational settings also provide care in a broad sense, and most such settings do attend to some noneducational needs of children. In these settings, what is forgotten are more often the care needs that originate with the parent than the care needs that originate with the child (programs often include rest time, food, health checkups). There is an increasing tendency to assign the education function to specific "educational" settings and to people formally qualified as "teachers"; this is instead of recognizing care settings (including the home) as learning environments and seeking to strengthen their educational component. This trend is, I believe, counterproductive in a number of ways. It favors the inappropriate practice of extending formal primary school downward into the early years. It makes more difficult the simultaneous response to the needs of parents and the needs of young children.

The results of the various national surveys conducted for Phase 1 make clear that there are wide differences in the degree to which various child care settings are labeled as educational. This is only partly due to the tendency to create bureaucratic divisions — one for child care and one for early education. It seems to be equally a result of the specific needs, beliefs, and expectations of parents. The IEA study seems to show that many parents who use some kind of child care outside the home are relatively satisfied with the care, even when it contains no educational emphasis. Again, this is understandable if we look at care from the parent's point of view.

Within a family the need to provide care for young children may conflict with the need to carry out other roles necessary for the survival of the family and of the individuals who constitute it. A "parent" is also often a breadwinner, housekeeper, and spouse. Each of these roles requires time, energy, and motivation. When the child care role conflicts with other roles, particularly with the work role, seeking extraparental care may have little to do, directly, with the needs of the child; instead, it may reflect the needs of the parents. Yet many so-called child care programs and most education programs are not adjusted to parental work schedules and thus require other arrangements to be made for care.

There is a tendency to think that with industrialization and with the growing movement of women into the paid labor force, the need for extraparental care has greatly increased. Sometimes missing in the contemporary discussions of women's work and child care, however, is an appreciation of the fact that women have *always* worked at more than being mothers and that there have always been role conflicts to resolve. The myth of the mother as sole caregiver is a product of recent history and is largely Western, or Northern, in origin (Myers & Indriso, 1989). Gradually, however, the realization is growing that women are responsible for the greater share of agricultural production in most countries of the South (Leslie & Paolisso, 1989). And even more gradually, the realization is growing among national and international planners that the caregiving role has and will continue to be shared in one way or another. Mothers must be helped.

To demonstrate the seemingly obvious but often overlooked point that extraparental caregiving needs are not simply a result of industrialization, it is instructive to examine the study data reporting on the time that mothers spend away from their children (Table 4.5). One might hypothesize that compared with mothers in industrialized countries, mothers in more agrarian, less industrialized societies would average less time away from their children. However, if we examine the data from China and Thailand and compare that with the data from the United States and Germany, for instance, we see that mothers' time spent away from children is greater in the less industrialized countries. This is so despite differing levels of service availability in the different countries. Indeed, it may be that increased standards of living allow more women the option of spending more time with their children, even though they also have more access to services.

Although there have always been multiple demands on the limited time of women and there has always been a need for extraparental care, societies have developed many ways of coping. What is unfortunate from a contemporary and humane perspective is that one of the ways of coping with the need for extraparental care has been to deny that need and to require mothers themselves to fill the need by working a "double day." This can have detrimental effects on women's health as well as on their ability to work and earn effectively.[1] But, along with the double day, we find a series of informal, extraparental social solutions. Care by members of an extended family, particularly by grandparents, is still important in many countries, as evidenced by the data from China, Thailand, and Portugal. A tradition of communal responsibility for children is strong in rural Africa and Latin America and may account for the "left alone" alternative in the Chinese study. The Nigerian system of "fostering" (i.e., sending children to live with relatives or friends in another location) often provides the host families with young baby sitters or nursemaids, if the children sent to them are of school age (Myers, 1992). In Nepal informal care is provided by mothers who form part of a credit cooperative, and so play groups or neighborhood home day care arrangements are increasingly common, (Landers, 1992). These examples lie, for the most part, outside the formal, institutional, sector.

Although the basic need for extraparental care may not have changed very much, the available ways to meet the need have changed. As industrialization, cash cropping, migration to cities, and women's participation in a paid labor force increase, there is less compatibility between the roles of work, housework, and child care. And slowly, the willingness of women to work a double day is decreasing as well. But more important, the informal coping mechanisms women previously used are disappearing. With the downward extension of schooling, education (instead of childminding) becomes a child's work, so the conflict of roles extends to the older children as well. With migration and urbanization, natural social groupings break down. Parents are often separated from grandparents and other family members. These changes bring the need for new solutions, only some of which have been mentioned here.

In the process of looking for new solutions, there is a tendency to turn to formal child care centers. However, it behooves us not to discard out-of-hand the older, less formal responses to the need for extraparental care but to look instead at ways in which these can be reinforced. That might be done through such an indirect alternative as introducing a system of piped water, thereby increasing time available for child care. It behooves us also to consider new forms of old solutions. For instance, we might substitute "the elderly" for "grandparents" and seek ways in which elderly members of a community can participate more actively in child care, to their own benefit as well as that of the child. We can work through programs such as the Child-to-Child program (Myers, 1992), which is directed toward improving the care that siblings provide to their younger brothers and sisters. Or, we might find ways to improve on, and even help to institutionalize, naturally occurring home day care by neighbors, like that in Finland. This type of care also occurs in many countries of the South, particularly in Latin America (Terán de Ruesta, Rodriguez de Gonzalo, & Tovar de Zarikian, 1993).

This discussion has focused on "care" as seen from the side of the parent, or caregiver, with little reference to the content of care or to its effects on the other party involved in care — the child. That is because to a great extent we need to make explicit that most programs labeled "care" originate with the needs of parents, not with the needs of children. When parents in the study were asked why they chose the kind of care they chose, answers given by parents in the South were predominantly related to the needs of parents rather than to the needs of children. This was not as true for the Northern countries, with the exception of Finland, but the history in Northern countries is also one in which programs labeled "child care" originated to meet the needs of parents rather than the needs of children. The current debates in the United States about child care alternatives center more on the relation of care to women's work than on children's needs.

It should not be surprising, then, that when we think of care in relation to the needs of children, care continues to be used in a narrow custodial sense. *Providing care*, for most people, means providing a place in which a child can be attended to in a way that protects him or her from exposure and injury and disease. But the needs of a child are obviously broader. If care is viewed from the side of the child, it should include meeting psychological, social, and educational — as well as physical —

needs. Note that here we see *education* entering almost as an afterthought.

In brief, the project's inclusion of both care and education is salutary because it allows us to bridge the falsely created differences between these two kinds of programs. It helps us to recognize the important educational and developmental roles played by all child care settings, including the home and other informal settings. It forces the consideration of ways in which care and education do or do not come together, as the case may be. Indeed, the need for planners and programmers to look at the intersection of care and education, viewed from the standpoint of both the needs of the child and the needs of parents is one of the major issues uncovered in this book.

FILLING A GAP IN STATISTICS AND IN THINKING

By providing us with a broad description, for each of several countries, of the various kinds of child care and early education settings being used for children at age 4, this study calls to our attention a huge gap in national and international statistics. That statistical gap, in turn, reflects a major blindspot in the thinking of policymakers and planners about programs for young children, and a major weakness in our systems of measurement. Although there is *some* attention to the nutritional and immunizational status of preschool-aged children, the statistics give little evidence of concern about their mental and social development or about the influence that their multiple environments have on their growth and development.

Consider, for instance, the annual publication of UNICEF (United Nations International Children's Emergency Fund), a report called *The State of the World's Children* (Grant, 1992). Indicators of the status of children are concentrated on nutrition and health during the preschool period, and most statistics are for children under age 2, rather than between ages 2 and 4. Although the UNICEF publication includes information about access to health services and to education, it does not include information about child care services or about education services below the primary school level. This is the case even though children's care and education in their preschool years is known to have an important effect on their futures, including their immediate progress and performance in primary school.

The recently published *World Education Report* (UNESCO, 1991) includes information about the preprimary level in its statistical appendixes and discusses this level briefly in the text. However, the statistics cover only enrollments in *formal* preprimary systems. For instance, the almost 12 million children in the preschool Anganwadi Centers of the Integrated Child Development Services in India are not included, even though the Anganwadi Centers have the specific goal of preparing children for schooling, follow a curriculum, and are run by women who receive some training for the early education task (Myers, 1992). Perhaps of necessity, preschool education is treated in the *World Education Report* as something totally separate from child care (even though programs of child care may have an educational component). Unfortunately, what this misses is the idea that the child who arrives at the school constitutes a very (perhaps the most) important *input*, as well as *output*, of the educational system.

LOOKING AHEAD

As the IEA Preprimary Project completes Phase 2, its findings will make an additional contribution to filling the gap in thinking and in statistics. Phase 2 will look at the quality of the settings in relation to the development of the child, going part of the way toward creating a profile of the status of children prior to their entry into primary school. Creating and re-creating such a national profile, taking a holistic view of a child's development, is sorely needed. Phase 2 findings will allow countries to monitor the changing status of children at a crucial point in their lives, help to identify groups of children (not individuals) most in need of support, and provide measures of early-intervention program effects as well as baseline data about children as they enter schools. Included in this profile might be measures of language development, of preliteracy and prenumeracy skills, and of social and emotional development. Periodic collection of such information could be carried out using a sample survey approach.

Finally, looking even further ahead, Phase 3 of the project promises to add significantly to our knowledge about the relationship between participation by children in different learning environments prior to entering school and their progress and performance in school. This part of the study is especially needed in the South, where very few such studies have been carried out. The studies that do exist (Myers, 1992) follow up children in a particular program and do not allow the kinds of comparisons across programs and across "natural settings" that Phase 3 of the IEA study will allow. For this reason, I look forward to results of the third phase with considerable anticipation and with some hope that more countries from the South can be included in subsequent phases of the study.

ENDNOTES

1. Although the jobs that Third World mothers take may allow a mother to bring her child along (to the field, or to the place where she positions her vendor's cart, or in the home as she takes in washing or tends the family plot), these no-pay or low-pay jobs are often taken precisely because the mother must take care of her child. Moreover, by the time a child is 4 years old (as in this study), bringing the child along is not as easy as it was during the child's earlier years.

REFERENCES

Grant, J. (1992). *The state of the world's children.* New York: UNICEF (United Nations International Children's Emergency Fund).

Landers, C. (1992, July). *Creating linkages: Women, work, and child care.* The Coordinators' Notebook, No. 11 (pp. 1–17). (available from The Consultative Group, CG Secretariat, UNICEF House, Three United Nations Plaza, New York, NY 10017).

Leslie, J., & Paolisso, M. (Eds.) (1989). *Women, work, and child welfare in the third world.* Boulder, CO: Westview Press.

Myers, R. (1992). *The twelve who survive.* London: Routledge.

Myers, R., & Indriso, C. (1989). *Women's work and childcare.* Paper presented at a workshop sponsored by the Consultative Group on Early Childhood Care and Development, for the Rockefeller Foundation, on Issues Related to Gender, Technology, and Development, New York.

Terán de Ruesta, M. C., Rodriguez de Gonzalo, M. R., & Tovar de Zarikian, A. (1993, September). *Programa Hogares de Cuidado Diario: Plan de Extensión Masiva in Venezuela: A Case Study* (Document prepared for the Education for All Forum 1993, New Delhi). Caracas: Ministerio de la Familia, Fundación del Niño.

United Nations Educational, Scientific, and Cultural Organization (UNESCO). *World education report.* 1991. Paris: Author.

Education or Care? A Parent's Dilemma — Education and Care! A Parent's Choice

Sylvia Opper, *Senior Lecturer*
Department of Education
University of Hong Kong

The chapters of this book contain a wealth of information on the availability, use, and characteristics of extrafamilial provisions for 4-year-olds in the 11 countries participating in Phase 1 of this IEA Preprimary Project. Some of the findings come as no surprise. They provide empirical confirmation of what professionals in the field have already known or believed for some time. Examples of this are the findings about the diversity of settings available for young children both within and across countries and about the time that children average each week in these settings (which ranges from only 17 hours in Hong Kong to approximately 55 hours in China and Thailand). It is also not surprising to find that in every participating country, some proportion of the children are in organized facilities, or that in most countries, organized facilities provide both educational programs and care programs.

Other Phase 1 findings are less widely known. For instance, the present study gives information on the proportions of preschool-aged children who attend organized facilities in each country, and it describes the relative distribution of these children between *education* and *care* programs. In Thailand only 33 percent of the sample attend organized facilities, whereas in Belgium and Italy the figures are 95 percent and 100 percent, respectively. Interestingly, in almost every country, among children attending organized facilities, there is a higher proportion in education-oriented than in care-oriented programs.

Are there differences between programs labeled *care* and *education*? Why do parents who send their children to organized settings seem to prefer education-oriented programs? And are parents satisfied with the setting of their choice?

A relatively widespread perception is that there are indeed differences between education and care (Galinsky, 1990); education is not caring, nor is child care education. This perception is based on differences in the origins and historical development of these two types of settings, in their regulatory bodies, in the training of adults working in these settings, and frequently, in their philosophical approaches to the curriculum (Kagan, 1988). While there are undoubtedly variations within and between countries, these two types of settings often have the following broad characteristics.

On the one hand, child care settings, which generally consist of whole-day programs, originated in most countries in response to the needs of working parents for alternative arrangements for their children during the time they were at work. As such, the settings were conceived of as a home away from home for young children. Child care programs are often regulated by bodies with a social welfare perspective, and regulations stress children's safety, health, and physical needs — food, shelter, sleep, daily routine, play (Phillips, Lande, & Goldberg, 1990). Staff training generally focuses on aspects of appropriate care for young children. As a result, staff do not systematically plan for learning. Although in every country there are exceptions, programs in care settings often fail to provide enough intellectual stimulation or challenge. While children's safety, health, and physical needs are important because parents who leave their children in the hands of others need to feel reassured that these needs have been adequately covered, there are other aspects of child development that must also be addressed in settings where young children spend the greater part of their waking lives.

Early education settings, on the other hand, which may offer either half- or whole-day programs, arose out of what parents perceived to be the needs of young children, and this included the need for school readiness. These settings are often regulated by the same bodies that regulate later schooling. Staff training emphasizes appropriate early education of young children, although there is not always a consensus on what is appropriate. The content of early educational programs varies a great deal. In some countries — such as the United States — the initial emphasis was on promoting the social and emotional readiness of children to participate in the group structures of elementary school. In other countries — particularly those of Asia and Africa, where competition for limited educational resources is a fact of life — preparation for formal schooling is often the major brief for preprimary educational settings. In many countries a recent trend has emerged that stresses the need for preschool children to think and act like older elementary children (Elkind, 1981) — to learn to read, write, and do number work. Programs that were originally conceived of as opportunities for social play and interaction have become downward extensions of the school and often use the same teaching methods and content found in the early stages of formal schooling. Such programs are not necessarily suited to younger children.

Though there would thus appear to be differences between preprimary programs offered in educational settings and those offered in care settings, little research has been done on the issue. These differences undoubtedly determine the observed parental preference for educational programs. Families choose a care setting when a single parent or both parents must work and need care for the child during working hours. In some instances the options for families who need such care are limited. Although parents may prefer to send their child to an educational setting, such a program may not fit in with their working hours. In other instances, particularly in many countries of the developing world, the major reason for selecting an educational setting is to prepare the child for elementary school. Whether professionals agree or not, many parents see early childhood education as the first rung in the education ladder. Moreover, they often equate preprimary education with an academically oriented, subject-centered curriculum (Sava, 1987) and do not want to have their child engage in what they view as purposeless play all day long. They feel that if their child can already master the basic skills of literacy and numeracy before going to school, he or she will have a head start in the formal education system. It is sometimes difficult to convince parents who would like to see their child do well in school and succeed in later life that learning to read and write is best left until elementary school. What are needed are programs that meet the care requirements of working parents (Gotts, 1988) but at the same time allow them to feel that their child is being prepared for school; these programs should not violate existing knowledge about early childhood development and learning during the preschool years.

How do parents feel about their choice of setting? The present study provides some interesting and somewhat unexpected findings on this question. In all the participating countries, parents express their overwhelming satisfaction with the child's care/education setting. Against this background of strong satisfaction, however, we find one relatively obscure and surprising statistic. In Hong Kong, where all sample parents express a high level of satisfaction, 20 percent of them also have problems with the philosophy of the setting, compared with at most only 10 percent of parents in the other countries. What is the meaning of this finding? National data indicate that there are two aspects to the problem. Some of the dissatisfied parents (mostly ones with children in education settings) find the programs too academic, whereas others (mostly ones with children in care settings) find the programs not academic enough.

While the situation in Hong Kong may be extreme, it is certainly not unique. The concern of Hong Kong parents is echoed by professionals in the field. On the one hand, authorities such as Smith (1990), Elkind (1987), Mitchell and Modligiani (1989), Hatch and Freeman (1988), and Walsh (1989) all deplore the current trend toward the introduction of the three R's in early education settings; they feel that programs for young children have become too structured, teacher-directed, and narrowly skill-centered. On the other hand, program evaluations using the Early Childhood Environment Rating Scale (ECERS), an instrument designed to measure the global quality of early childhood environments (Harms & Clifford, 1980), have found that one major thing lacking in many child care centers is planned inclusion of materials, equipment, and experiences for educational purposes (Benham, Miller, & Kontos, 1988).

Both types of dissatisfaction, which are really two sides of the same coin, reflect a general malaise about the programs offered. Parents and professionals feel that young children are not being exposed to appropriate learning environments during their time in organized extrafamilial settings. The overly academic, predominantly teacher-directed and teacher-taught program of many educational settings, with its focus on learning to read, write, and do sums, is not suitable for the learning style of preschool children. The same can be said about the curriculum, found in many care settings, that is primarily accidental rather than planned. Programs in both types of settings need to be replaced by programs whose content and methods of implementation are appropriate to the abilities, learning styles, and needs of children of this age-range.

The knowledge base for such programs already exists (Spodek, 1986; Peck, McCaig, & Sapp, 1988). We know that an appropriate education for young children combines challenging content with suitable teaching methods. An extensive literature on specific content in early childhood curriculum is available as a source for stimulating activities in the areas of language, number, physical and social sciences, music, and art. Examples are Cazden (1981), Machado (1985), Kamii (1982), Seefeldt (1989), McDonald (1979), Lasky and Mukerji (1980), and Holt (1977). Work in language development and curriculum has also shown that preschoolers are ready for academic content, provided it is presented in developmentally appropriate ways (Schickedanz et. al., 1990). To help practitioners, the National Association for the Education of Young Children (NAEYC, 1991) provides guidelines for preparing an academically challenging curriculum for young children that is based on existing theory, research, and practice on how children develop and learn.

Suitable teaching methods for young children are those that take into account what we know about early cognitive development and learning. From a general perspective, Piaget's work on cognitive development shows that during the preschool years, children move from a sensorimotor and practical understanding of language, number, and the physical environment to the more formal and abstract understanding of literacy and numeracy found in elementary school. This evolution of their thinking processes should determine the selection of curriculum content and methods that provide them with suitable foundations for the next level of development. We also know that children acquire three types of knowledge — physical, logical-mathematical, and social-conventional — in rather different ways (Forman & Kuschner, 1977; Goffin, 1989). Physical and logical-mathematical knowledge is constructed through active interaction, exploration, and play with objects and persons. For this, children need an environment containing a variety of materials to interact with. They also need opportunities to raise questions and come up with their own solutions. Social-conventional knowledge, by contrast, is transmitted directly to children by adults and therefore requires different types of experiences. There is also available a NAEYC position paper on what constitutes developmentally appropriate practice for children from birth to 8 years (Bredekamp, 1987). Such developmentally appropriate practices are not intended exclusively for education programs but are a basic necessity for all children in all settings.

Recent research into child care has also highlighted some of the features of high-quality care programs (Phillips, 1987). Although many of these are related to structural aspects of settings, such as group size, adult-child ratio, and staff training, one dynamic measure of high-quality care is the amount of constructive interaction between caregivers and children. In addition, the infant and child development literature shows that one of the most important ingredients of learning during the early years is a warm, caring adult-child relationship. These various dimensions of quality for programs are equally applicable to education programs.

The extensive knowledge available on appropriate content and practices for education programs and on quality of care for young children needs to be incorporated into all early childhood settings. All programs need to include education, since that is what many parents are seeking for their child, but this should be education that covers the development of various facets of the child's behavior and personality, implemented in ways that facilitate and promote learning in young children. All programs should also provide an element of care in the form of a warm, concerned teacher who acts as a facilitator of learning. In brief, programs in organized facilities should neither do away with academics nor do away with care. Rather, the content of all programs should be viewed in a developmental way and provided through practices that are suited to the young child's learning style and abilities. The aim should be for all programs to provide for a suitable blend of education and care, of stimulation and nurturing, of work and play (Caldwell, 1989).

While many high-quality preprimary programs already combine these two aspects — care and appropriate early education — precise information on how extensively this is done is lacking, and further research is needed. The second phase of the IEA Preprimary Project, which looks more specifically at the program and social interactions of settings and at developmental outcomes of 4-year-old children, should provide more-accurate details on what actually occurs in different types of programs. These findings should allow for a greater understanding of the differential effect of different types of settings on the development of the children, another question on which little research has as yet been conducted. We therefore look forward to these future findings, which should make a valuable contribution to the cross-cultural literature on programs of early education and care in various countries in the world.

REFERENCES

Benham. N., Miller, T., & Kontos, S. (1988). Pinpointing staff training needs in child care centers. *Young Children, 43*(4), 9–16.

Bredekamp, S. (Ed.), (1987). *Developmentally appropriate practice in early childhood programs serving children from birth through age 8.* Washington, DC: National Association for the Education of Young Children.

Caldwell, B. M. (1989). All-day kindergarten: Assumptions, precautions, and overgeneralizations. *Early Childhood Research Quarterly, 4*, 261–266.

Cazden, C. B. (Ed.). (1981). *Language in early childhood education.* Washington, DC: National Association for the Education of Young Children.

Elkind, D. (1981). *The hurried child: Growing up too fast, too soon.* Reading, MA: Addison-Wesley.

Elkind, D. (1987). Superbaby syndrome can lead to elementary school burnout. *Young Children, 42*(3), 14.

Forman, G. E., & Kuschner, D. E. (1977). *The child's construction of knowledge: Piaget for teaching children.* Monterey, CA: Brooks/Cole.

Galinsky, E. (1990). I have seen the beginnings of a transformation in attitudes. *Young Children, 46*(6), 2.

Goffin, S. G. (1989). Developing a research agenda for early childhood education: What can be learned from the research on teaching. *Early Childhood Research Quarterly, 4*, 187–204.

Gotts, E. E. (1988). The right to quality child care. *Childhood Education*, June, 268–275.

Harms, T., & Clifford, R. M. (1980). *Early Childhood Environment Rating Scale.* New York: Teachers College Press, Columbia University.

Hatch. J. A., & Freeman, E. B. (1988). Kindergarten philosophies and practices. Perspectives of teachers, principals and supervisors. *Early Childhood Research Quarterly, 3*, 151–166.

Holt, B. G. (1977). *Science with young children.* Washington, DC: National Association for the Education of Young Children.

Kagan, S. L. (1988). Current reforms in early childhood education: Are we addressing the issues? *Young Children, 43*(2), 27–32.

Kamii, C. (1982). *Number in preschool and kindergarten: Educational implication of Piaget's theory.* Washington, DC: National Association for the Education of Young Children.

Lasky, L., & Mukerji, R. (1980). *Art: Basic for young children.* Washington, DC: National Association for the Education of Young Children.

Machado, J. M. (1985). *Early childhood experiences in language arts* (3rd ed.). New York: Delmar.

McDonald, D. T. (1979). *Music in our lives. The early years.* Washington, DC: National Association for the Education of Young Children.

Mitchell, A., & Modigliani, K. (1989). Young children in public schools? The "only ifs" reconsidered. *Young Children, 44*(6), 56–61.

National Association for the Education of Young Children, (1991). Guidelines for appropriate curriculum content and assessment in programs serving children ages 3 through 8. *Young Children, 46*(3), 21–38.

Peck, J. J., McCaig, G., & Sapp, M. E. (1988). *Kindergarten policies: What is best for children.* Washington, DC: National Association for the Education of Young Children.

Phillips, D. A. (Ed.). (1987). *Quality in child care: What does research tell us?* Washington, DC: National Association for the Education of Young Children.

Phillips, D., Lande, J., & Goldberg, M. (1990). The state of child care regulation: A comparative analysis. *Early Childhood Research Quarterly, 5,* 151–171.

Sava, S. G. (1987). Development not academics. *Young Children, 42*(3), 15.

Schickedanz, J. A., Chay, S. Y., Gopin, P., Sheng, L. L., Song, S. M., & Wild, N. (1990). Preschoolers and academics: Some thoughts. *Young Children, 46*(1), 4–13.

Seefeldt, C. (Ed.) (1989). *Social studies for the preschool-primary child* (3rd ed.). Columbus, OH: Merrill.

Smith, K. E. (1990). Developmentally appropriate education or the Hunter Teacher Assessment Model: Mutually incompatible alternatives. *Young Children, 45*(2), 12–13.

Spodek, B. (Ed.). (1986). *Today's kindergarten. Exploring the knowledge base, expanding the curriculum.* New York: Teachers College Press.

Walsh, D. L. (1989). Changes in kindergarten. Why here? Why now? *Early Childhood Research Quarterly, 4,* 377–391.